Ex Libris: r '02

Qx,
Thanks for the intro.
your friend,
Q

A Citizen-Soldier's Civil War

Lydia Allyn Vooris

A Citizen-Soldier's
Civil War

THE LETTERS OF

BREVET MAJOR GENERAL

ALVIN C. VORIS

Edited by Jerome Mushkat

NORTHERN ILLINOIS UNIVERSITY PRESS • DEKALB

© 2002 by Northern Illinois University Press

Published by the Northern Illinois University Press, DeKalb, Illinois   60115

Manufactured in the United States using acid-free paper

All Rights Reserved

Design by Julia Fauci

Maps by Mapcraft, Woodstock, Illinois 60098

Library of Congress Cataloging-in-Publication Data

Voris, Alvin C.

A citizen-soldier's Civil War: the letters of Brevet Major General Alvin C. Voris /
edited by Jermome Mushkat.

   p.   cm.

Includes bibliographical references and index.

ISBN 0-87580-298-2 (alk. paper)

1. Voris, Alvin C.—Correspondence. 2. United States. Army. Ohio Infantry Regiment,
67th (1861–1865) 3. Ohio—History—Civil War, 1861–1865—Personal narratives.
4. United States—History—Civil War, 1861–1865—Personal narratives. 5. United States—
History—Civil War, 1861–1865—Campaigns. 6. United States—History—Civil War,
1861–1865—African Americans. 7. Generals—United States—Correspondence.
I. Mushkat, Jerome. II. Title.

E525.5 67th.V67 2002

973.7'471—dc21

2002067766

Contents

List of Maps

Alvin Coe Voris, an attorney, state legislator, judge, abolitionist, women's rights advocate, husband, and father from Akron, Ohio, typified the best qualities of Civil War citizen-soldiers. In September 1861, the thirty-four-year-old Voris volunteered for service in the Union army as a private, confident in the righteousness of the federal Union and sparked by his devotion to the destruction of slavery and to the Republican Party and its free-soil principles. Four years later, he came home, a brevet major general of volunteers, a rank that confirmed his efficiency, combat bravery, commitment to duty, and leadership ability.

Despite his record, Voris's fame was largely confined to Akron. He might have remained virtually unknown and historically obscure except for the 423 letters he wrote to his wife, Lydia Allyn Voris. Their correspondence began with the Ohio legislature's 1861 session and continued throughout the war and into the first stage of reconstruction in Virginia ending in December 1865. Taken as a whole, the letters have a continuity and breadth that makes them a valuable primary source for both military and social history.

A prolific correspondent, Voris usually wrote Lydia every third day and again whenever he found something he thought would interest her. He composed these letters at any possible time and under the most adverse circumstances, frequently writing bits and pieces during the day, sometimes carrying over to the following day. As a result, many of the letters describe events as they happened in a stream of consciousness that allows the reader to become a vicarious participant in the episodes Voris described.

Within the confines of Victorian propriety, his letters were also love letters, full of longing and homesickness. Yet Voris's uxoriousness went deeper than the normal intimacy that developed between husbands and wives. His need for Lydia's love and understanding helped ease his psychological transformation from a citizen to a citizen-soldier. Treating her as his partner and confidante, he sought to prove that the war had not destroyed his innate sensibility to suffering, that the sacrifices he forced her and their children to make were necessary for national reunification, and that his military experiences could not erode his civilized conduct.

Voris's letters tell a history of the Civil War and its consequences as seen through the eyes of a hardheaded, religious, intelligent person with a literary gift. Although Lydia's replies are not extant, the reader can infer many of her wartime experiences through Voris's responses. In their correspondence one sees the war's effect on the lives and the marriage of two ordinary Americans.

Foremost a soldier, Voris filled his letters with rich details of military matters, with all their daily routines, surprises, and frustrations, and the preparation, nature, and aftermath of combat. This concentration did not blind Voris to the war's human costs or to the ethical conflict between his religious scruples and duties as a soldier. Voris had other interests beyond the battlefield. He commented on the strength of Confederate resolve, possible foreign intervention, ties between the war front and the home front, the link between partisanship and war, the novel physical environments he encountered, and the political maneuvering among officers seeking promotions. Voris was often disillusioned with military and civilian leadership that left him aching for peace, but his stubborn will and determination to see the war through prevailed—illustrating one element that made Union victory possible.

Voris also recorded his impressions of African Americans and the institution of slavery. A product of the religious and reformist ferment that gripped prewar Ohio, Voris found little evidence during his service in the Confederate states of Virginia, North Carolina, and South Carolina to contradict his belief that slavery was an uncivilized evil, corruptive of both races. Combat gave him an opportunity to test his beliefs. Initially distrusting the courage of African American soldiers, his doubts disappeared after commanding an African American brigade in battle. He now paid tribute to their fighting valor and indicated his willingness to lead them again, and this respect, combined with his commitment to freedom and equality through the Republican Party's free-labor system, continued through Reconstruction and until his death. Voris reserved his greatest contempt for slaveowners. Often using irony or sarcasm to convey the exact opposite meaning of his words, he assailed them as a pretentious regional ruling class, economic exploiters of both slaves and poor whites, and sexual predators toward African American women.

Voris had a keen sense of history and was proud of his role in the stirring times in which he participated. Whether he wished to save the letters as a record for descendants or intended to publish them is unclear. He did write two postwar memoirs based on this material, and he later appended some explanatory details to a few events he had hastily noted in the letters to his wife. For whatever reason, though, his correspondence remained in manuscript form. Eventually, some of Voris's heirs hired a typist to transcribe the letters and distribute them among family members. Today, the originals are in the possession of Alan Johnson of Akron, Ohio, Voris's great-grandson.

I first assessed the letters in transcribed form and concluded that this eyewitness account of the most momentous period in American history deserved publication. I have relied on Voris's actual letters, because I found the transcripts were inaccurate. Although a reader might consider his postbellum addendums hindsight, I have included some, which appear in italics in the letters. They do not detract from the letter's immediacy, and they add details he thought important.

In editing this work, I have allowed Voris to speak for himself with a minimum of editorial interpolations and have avoided imposing modern usages that might compromise the historic value of his letters. For the sake of clarity, I have made some alterations. When he misspelled proper names as Fort Wagoner (for Fort Wagner), I have retained that form in its initial spelling but corrected subsequent references. I have not modified his idiosyncratic spelling of certain words (verry for very) or abbreviations (Regt for Regiment). When meanings were unclear or misleading, I have filled in missing words by placing them within brackets; italics denote the sections Voris appended. Similarly, I have placed periods instead of dashes at the end of some sentences, converted long paragraphs into shorter ones as topics changed, and added apostrophes for contractions or to show possessives. I have also deleted redundant letters, repetitious material, such as salutations and complimentary closes, passages that repeat his yearning for Lydia and their children, and references to their friends and family. Nonetheless, I have included other duplicate material concerning Lydia and their children to indicate shifts in family and gender relationships.

To give readers a sense of the man and his world, a biographic sketch of Voris precedes his letters, which are arranged here into twelve topical and chronological chapters and introduced to establish context. Since Voris's letters cover a wide variety of subjects, I have annotated and documented the letters, not to correct him, but to identify, clarify, and explain various topics and to provide references to pertinent primary and secondary sources.

. . .

I have accumulated a number of scholarly debts in the course of preparing this manuscript. Alan Johnson generously granted me permission to publish this collection. I am indebted to three of my colleagues, Professors Keith L. Bryant, Jr., Lesley J. Gordon, and George W. Knepper, for their thoughtful criticism. Whatever errors that remain are my responsibility. I dedicate this book to the memory of my friends, Lou and Louis.

A Citizen-Soldier's Civil War

Introduction

"I CANNOT BEAR TO THINK

OF A DISMEMBERED COUNTRY"

Jerome Mushkat

Acting Lt. Col. Alvin Coe Voris, the commanding officer of the 67th Ohio Volunteer Infantry Regiment, sat in a makeshift tent during the late evening of June 22, 1862, writing a letter to his wife in Akron, Ohio, on a wooden board supported by two small stools. During the last three months, Voris fretted, his regiment had zigzagged through Virginia's Shenandoah Valley in physically tormenting marches and countermarches, vainly attempting to trap Confederate Maj. Gen. Thomas J. Jackson and his troops. With his men footsore and dispirited, Voris wondered for what purposes had they made such sacrifices. Plumbing his own motivation, Voris confessed to his wife that he had many reasons to avoid active service. "We have a comfortable home, a promising future, many good friends and I a share of public influence that I can advantageously use if I continue to merit confidence."[1]

Why Voris chose to fight lay in part in the combination of his English-Dutch heritage and his time and place in Ohio. Both sides of Voris's family had deep roots in colonial America. Peter Coe left England in 1634 and settled in Connecticut. Fourteen years later, Coert Alberts Van Voor Hees arrived in Long Island from the Netherlands. Over the next eight generations, some of their descendants moved westward. Peter Voris, Alvin's restless father, followed this trek. Going from Pennsylvania to Ohio, he made his home in the northern part of Stark County, which became Summit County in 1840, and shortened his surname to Voris. He held a number of occupations, some successful, some not, as a farmer, land speculator, lawyer, judge, and Whig officeholder. Alvin's mother, Julia Coe, met Peter Voris while visiting relatives in the Western Reserve. They married sometime in the spring of 1826. Peter was twenty-seven; Julia, nineteen. Their first son, Alvin Coe Voris, was born April 27, 1827. Nine brothers and four sisters came later.[2]

Voris resembled his parents in a number of ways. As he told a biographer, Voris and his mother shared the same New England traits of independence, self-reliance, and industriousness. Equally vital, their devout Christianity gave him a firm moral base and became a source of his inner strength. In describing his father, Voris unconsciously revealed many of his own qualities. Both were caustic, impatient, opinionated, hardworking, sardonic, self-righteous, introspective, and honest, almost to the point of insensitive bluntness.[3]

As a child, Voris attended rural common schools northwest of Akron. When he turned eighteen, he enrolled for one year in the Twinsburg Institute, which prepared young men for higher education. The following year, Voris matriculated at Oberlin College. Unwilling to become a financial burden to his family and unsure of a career, he spent only two years at Oberlin, paying his way as a shoemaker and schoolteacher. Even so, Voris's experience at Oberlin influenced the rest of his life. The Second Great Awakening's religious and reformist ideals at the college reflected his mother's piety, reinforced his own beliefs, and convinced him that the politics of morality could reform human society. Along the same lines, he gained an appreciation for women's rights and antislavery through his friendship with Frances Dana Gage, "Aunt Fanny" to her admirers, an Oberlin abolitionist and feminist.[4]

Leaving Oberlin forced Voris to choose a livelihood. He selected the law, perhaps to model himself after his father or possibly because it seemed to promise wealth, security, and prominence. In 1850, Gen. Lucius V. Bierce, the five-time mayor of Akron and one of its leading citizens and lawyers, accepted Voris as a student. While reading the law, Voris gained practical experience. Through Bierce's influence, Voris served as deputy clerk in the Court of Common Pleas and then in the county recorder's office. A more important post came his way in February 1852 when Ohio's revised state constitution went into operation. Newly elected probate judge Charles G. Ladd, Bierce's former partner and a one-time mayor of Akron, named Voris as deputy clerk, and Ladd soon fell ill. When he died the next August, Voris assumed his place, filling the court's duties as de facto judge. On June 24, 1853, Voris received his license and formed a partnership with Bierce that lasted until 1857.[5]

The thriving community of Akron, a product of the construction of the Ohio and Erie Canal, was barely more than a quarter century old and had a heterogeneous population of less than four thousand when the fledgling Voris hung out his shingle. He was an immediate success in this environment. His first years at the bar, Voris admitted, were "full of wearying labors" and little income. Yet in a short time he "succeeded beyond my expectation." Highly satisfied with his profession, Voris considered the law the most "honorable" career a "high minded" person could follow.[6]

Sometime during this period Voris met and courted Lydia C. Allyn, the daughter of Lucy G. and Israel Allyn, natives of New London, Connecticut, who had moved to Ohio in 1818. On September 25, 1853, the young couple married in the First Methodist Episcopal Church of Akron. Marriage stabilized Voris's personal and professional life. A well-educated and loving wife, Lydia gave him absolute support and became a good, if indulgent, mother to their two children, Edwin F. Voris, born July 21, 1855, and Lucy A. Voris, born June 27, 1859.[7]

Happy in marriage and with his career so promising, Voris, as other aspiring attorneys, turned toward politics and public service. Little was predictable, because partisan flux dominated Ohio in the early 1850s. Voris drifted from his father's Whig Party to the Know-Nothings, before settling in a new political home in 1856. Joining the newly formed Republican Party, he remained a staunch Republican for the remainder of his life.

Voris found the Republican Party congenial for a number of reasons, starting with its linking of religion and reform. In particular, he supported the Republican ideals of Protestant cultural hegemony, moral purification of society through programs such as temperance, and the ability of people to achieve a qualitatively better life through individual regeneration. While not an abolitionist crusader who sought the immediate elimination of slavery, Voris also backed the party's commitment to the eventual end of enslavement through the containment policy. "God forgive our Nation," he remarked, "for its hypocrisies to the world, its cruelties to the African." Voris made good on these sentiments in opposing laws contrary to his convictions, such as the 1850 Fugitive Slave Law. In an act of conscience in 1854, he harbored a runaway African American in his home and "clandestinely" helped the fugitive reach freedom in Canada.[8]

Voris's work ethic, with all its stress on upward mobility, cemented his commitment to the Republicans. Comparing "retrograde" slavery with his party's free-labor value system, Voris stressed that slavery degraded the southern "white population," exhausted the soil, and "debased" the slave. By contrast, "the stimulant of free labor and free institutions" in the North energized "all the elements that give strength, wealth & influence to a people." This free-labor society created an economy that benefited labor and capital and ensured the nation's material prosperity.[9]

In 1859, the idealistic thirty-two-year-old Voris had an opportunity to test these convictions when Summit County voters elected him a representative to the Ohio General Assembly. During his two years in Columbus, Voris rose rapidly in party ranks, becoming one of its most promising newcomers. As a legislator, Voris proved his reformist credentials. He sponsored or voted for bills to make prisons more humanitarian, increase spending for education, expand legal rights of married women, boost funds for mental institutions, and limit sales of intoxicating liquors.[10]

Voris's outspoken dedication to racial equality was evident as well. He made this clear when John Mercer Langston, an Oberlin classmate and Ohio's leading African American abolitionist, lobbied reluctant Republican legislators to revise the state constitution to grant black suffrage. Voris backed Langston, risking his political career by defying most of his party's establishment who abhorred slavery but did not treat free blacks on equal terms. Even more startling, Voris invited Langston to sit with him on the legislative floor, the first time any African American had enjoyed that "privilege." Recalling this incident years later, an African American editor wrote that "this is but one example the colored people have had of the loyalty of General Voris to the rights of their race."[11]

During these legislative duties, Voris began his habit of writing letters to Lydia, usually three times a week. Uncomfortable at being away from her and their children, he confessed that he felt lonely and adrift, unable to become "reconciled to my place," and disillusioned by "impertinent" lobbyists. Amid this litany of complaints, Voris added a prophetic note: "We are deeply impressed with the imminence of civil war."[12]

By February 1861, secession had passed from a constitutional abstraction to reality with the formation of the Confederate States of America. As war loomed, Voris condemned secession, urged President James Buchanan and Congress to stand firm, and refused to back any compromise that allowed for the expansion of slavery. Voris's patriotism peaked when news reached Columbus that Confederates had attacked and captured Fort Sumter. Immediately, he voted for all prowar bills that defended the Union and Ohio "against armed rebellion."[13]

At the same time, Voris's letters to Lydia bore a new tone with a subliminal message. Telling her of the "exciting" preparations for war, he praised the "fires of military spirit" that burned in the state and noted "the army in times of war" offered "great" opportunities for distinction, both for himself and his family. Should he, then, "take a post in the army?" As if arguing with himself, Voris wrote "were I a *single* man I should seek glory in the tented field." He could serve another way, he admitted, by getting a "civil appointment" that would "yield me some $2,500 for you." Yet he assured Lydia that "my obligation to you and our little ones" precluded a premature enlistment. The "course I shall take shall be entirely directed by you."[14]

What passed between them when he returned to Akron in May remains unrecorded. Voris's determination to be a soldier, however, may be reconstructed through his subsequent correspondence. Honor, pride, a desire to test his bravery and manliness in battle, and ambition to achieve "glory" were evident in his decision. As a partisan Republican, he further believed that only his party's free-labor principles could protect ordinary citizens from "want" and provide them with "security & happiness." Then there was abolition. He thought that as the war progressed, slavery would erode to such an extent that Americans "will wonder why they ever were so unwise and so unjust to curse the colored man and damn his friends." Above all, the eight generations of Americans on both sides of his family made him a nationalist determined to defend flag, country, and Constitution. "I cannot bear to think of a dismembered country."[15]

Events came into focus by September 1861. Over the summer Voris had halfheartedly resumed his legal practice but had spent much of his time seeking volunteers for a proposed regiment from Summit and surrounding counties. In September, he succumbed to his own urging, enlisting as a private in Akron's 29th Ohio Volunteer Infantry Regiment, commanded by Col. Lewis P. Buckley, a former West Point cadet. But Ohio Governor

William Dennison, Jr., thought Voris's political stature made him more valuable as a recruiter. On October 2, 1861, Voris mustered into service as a second lieutenant. Within a week, his rank jumped to lieutenant colonel, charged with raising troops in Summit County and northern Ohio for the 45th Ohio Volunteer Infantry Regiment.[16]

Voris faced a chaotic situation. Nearly a dozen regiments competed for troops in the same area. This struggle often led to questionable conduct by rival recruiters that dampened the "ardor" of potential volunteers. Worse, the patriotic passion that burst after Fort Sumter dissipated following the Union's defeat at the First Battle of Bull Run. Even when men enlisted, the state lacked sufficient uniforms and equipment. Against these odds, Voris did manage to raise one company, but those men, he wrote state Adjutant General Catharinus P. Buckingham, preferred serving in the 29th Ohio.[17]

By November 29, the 45th Ohio was far short of the 1,000 men necessary to form a regiment. "Recruitment goes on slowly," Voris confessed to Dennison. Other potential regiments faced similar problems. One in particular also fell below the minimum, the 67th Ohio Volunteer Infantry Regiment, numbering 637 men, mainly from Toledo and western Ohio. In mid-December, the state began to consolidate unfilled regiments, including the 45th and 67th Ohio. Under this plan, the 67th Ohio absorbed the 45th, which had managed to enroll less than 250. The combined unit now had 938 officers and men. Voris's duties clarified on December 18. He transferred into the 67th Ohio at the rank of lieutenant colonel, second in command to Col. Otto Burstenbinder.[18]

While awaiting further orders, Voris assessed Burstenbinder, who had cited extensive European military service to win his commission. Initially, his martial "bearing" impressed unsophisticated observers, including Voris. But gradually they surmised that Burstenbinder had lied about his background, hid a heavy drinking habit, and lacked ability, often leaving Voris as the 67th Ohio's "actual Colonel." By early 1862, Burstenbinder's incompetence had become so blatant that a number of troops in the 67th Ohio and their friends in Toledo clamored for his court-martial and replacement.[19]

Voris let matters rest for the moment. He had much to learn. As the 67th Ohio formed and moved to Camp Chase, the Columbus marshaling area for troops in federal service, Voris poured his energies into studying tactics, training and equipping the men, instilling unit pride and group identity among callow troops, and preparing them for battle. Having only limited prewar experience as judge advocate of "The Akron Rifles," a "showy" militia unit formed in 1857, he also learned the elements of command, literally one step ahead of his men.[20]

Physically, Voris was ready for the challenge. At thirty-four, he was in the prime of life. He had "sallow" skin, a firm muscular body of medium height, and weighed about 175 pounds. His hair was dark brown, worn clipped on the sides and short along his neck. He had a firm chin, straight nose, tight lips, and affected a military moustache that dipped along his sunken cheeks. A wartime photograph testified to his face's most arresting quality, deep-set eyes with a haunted expression.[21]

In common with other Civil War citizen-soldiers, Voris expected a short, glorious war, full of pomp and parades, in which death was painless, noble, and always occurred to someone else, where righteousness meant victory, ending with a triumphant return to Lydia's waiting arms. Voris's first lesson in the reality of combat sobered his romantic illusion. On January 19, 1862, the 67th Ohio, along with other untested Ohio regiments, streamed into western Virginia to secure control of the Shenandoah Valley from "Stonewall" Jackson's forces.

Voris quickly passed his first test of leadership. With Burstenbinder physically and mentally unfit to command, Voris called on his oratorical skills to convince six unpaid companies, which had refused orders to cross into Virginia, to march with the rest of the regiment. Equally important, he directed the 67th Ohio in its inaugural trial at the First Battle of Kernstown on March 23, 1862. Showing personal mettle that bordered on foolhardiness, and ignoring a painful wound in his left thigh, Voris exulted in the excitement of combat. He led his troops into the field and was instrumental in Jackson's only defeat.[22]

Remorse coursed through Voris once his adrenaline slowed and lust for blood cooled in the battle's aftermath. His religious scruples against murder, even for flag and nation, made him question the human suffering of combat. Eventually, he recognized that these qualms weakened his soldierly resolve. Rationalizing that he had not personally killed any Confederate, Voris made peace with himself.

After Kernstown, the regiment spent nearly three months in a series of unproductive marches, covering more than two hundred miles, to trap Jackson. By late June, the War Department ordered some units operating in the valley, the weary 67th Ohio among them, to head east and link with the Army of the Potomac.

This movement gave Voris another opportunity to prove his mettle when the regiment crossed Chesapeake Bay on an unseaworthy barge that floundered. Setting an example of personal bravery, he prevented panic and saved a number of his men from drowning. By July 4, the regiment reached the Army of the Potomac but arrived too late for the Seven Days' battles that had ended on July 1. Instead, his troops made their way to the secure base Maj. Gen. George B. McClellan had established at Harrison's Landing south of Richmond. There the 67th Ohio remained through August.

Voris's thoughts now turned to army political infighting. By late July 1862, a court-martial had found against Burstenbinder. A special order dismissed him from service, and Voris replaced him on an interim basis. The result left Voris dissatisfied. Believing that he had earned permanent command based on his conduct at Kernstown, Voris feared that Governor David Tod might instead name Brig. Gen. Charles W. Hill of Toledo, a politically connected Republican. To retain the position and gain a promotion to colonel, Voris sought the aid of prominent state politicians, enhanced his credentials by publicizing the regiment's actions in open letters to editors of local newspapers, and encouraged Lydia to write Tod. Voris also received his first leave, ostensibly to raise troops but actually to confront the governor. On July 29, Voris reached his goal. He assumed command of the 67th Ohio at the rank of full colonel.

In September, the 67th Ohio relocated to Suffolk, Virginia, some seventeen miles southeast of the Union naval base at Norfolk, an area that blocked Confederate access to supplies from southeastern Virginia and eastern North Carolina. For the remainder of the year, Voris directed the regiment in building a strong defensive perimeter, interrupted by an occasional firefight with Confederates. On December 31, the 67th Ohio left Suffolk. After a short January 1863 tour at New Bern, North Carolina, the regiment headed farther south to join in the siege of Charleston.

Over the next seven months, the 67th Ohio lived on the small islands and camps surrounding the southern approaches to Charleston: Hilton Head, Port Royal, St. Helena, Cole's Island, Folly Island, Parris Island, and Morris Island. The novelty of traveling on the Atlantic and the permutations of a strange environment captivated Voris, who had rarely gone outside Ohio before the war. Moreover, Voris's duties provided him with the opportunity to continue the assessment, which he had begun in Virginia, of Union loyalists and Confederates, and to gauge them as individuals, not as objects of regional biases. Among these people, Voris found that women were often most responsible for sustaining the war but were also its victims. No longer expecting quick victory, he grew to admire the tenacity of Confederate soldiers, the inner strengths of the society that nurtured them, and worried that their ability to capitalize on Union failures would lead to foreign recognition.

Voris's dislike of slavery also hardened as he met increasing numbers of formerly enslaved African Americans. While his dealings with them confirmed his belief that slavery was a crime against humanity and had fostered a backward economic system, Voris treated them with patronization and condescension. He reasoned that the "peculiar institution" had degraded slaves, and its legacy made first-generation freed African Americans incapable of reaching true independence and equality with whites. Even so, he backed efforts of firm abolitionists, such as Frances Gage, who had established self-help and education agencies on the Sea Islands to ease the transition from slavery to freedom. At the same time, Voris acknowledged rampant racism among Union troops. Many of them, he noted, despised African American males but were sexually attracted to African American women.

A day Voris never forgot arrived in the early evening of July 18, 1863, when the 67th Ohio participated in the bloody assault against Fort Wagner. His undermanned regiment, mustering an effective strength of only 210 officers and men, suffered 5 killed, 76 wounded, and 43 missing, a casualty rate of 59 percent. Voris was among the wounded, shot in his lower abdomen about 150 yards from the fort. Nursed by Clara Barton, whom he had earlier met through Gage, Voris began his recovery at a military hospital in Beaufort, South Carolina, where physicians removed what they believed was the entire bullet fragment from his groin. Unknown to them, the bullet had split into two parts when it hit Voris's sword belt, leaving the larger section still "lodged on the crown of his bladder." Under these conditions on July 26, Voris received a forty-day medical leave of absence. For the remainder of his service, he experienced intermittent pain that became agonizing after demanding physical exercise.[23]

Voris resumed command at Morris Island on September 12, 1863. His body seemed healed, even if he appeared often wobbly and weak. But the military and physical environments on the islands hindered his complete rehabilitation. Confederate bombardments, inactivity, boredom, and sand fleas tormented him. Internal regimental politics made his life just as trying. A clique of Toledo officers and men were not reconciled to his promotion. They sought but failed to court-martial Voris on grounds that an official investigation termed spurious at best.

Despite his vindication, Voris was still vulnerable. In December 1863, the Lincoln administration faced a mounting problem implicit in relying upon civilian-soldiers such as Voris. The army needed to retain veteran soldiers whose terms of enlistment would expire in 1864 and to find more recruits. To accomplish this goal, the War Department offered a number of enticements to veterans, including retention of rank, bounties, furloughs, and the opportunity to bring the regiment to full strength by attracting additional men. If three-quarters of eligible veterans reenlisted and did add sufficient new men, the regiment avoided consolidation with other units and received a fresh designation as a veteran volunteer regiment, and its officers kept their ranks and commands.

Acting under this directive, Voris arrived back in Akron on January 26, 1864, to raise new troops for the 67th Ohio. Maj. Lewis Butler, who had led the regiment after Voris's wounding, stayed at Folly Island to reenlist eligible veterans. After spending a few days with Lydia, Voris set a hectic schedule, stumping for volunteers, addressing public gatherings, and meeting with local politicians and newspaper editors. By March 31, he succeeded. Voris kept his rank and command, and the newly designated 67th Ohio Veteran Volunteer Regiment now numbered 841 men and officers. With that, the War Department reassigned the regiment from the siege of Charleston to Maj. Gen. Benjamin F. Butler's Army of the James.

Over the next twelve months, Voris and his troops were involved in the continuous, rolling battles that ultimately ended with Confederate surrender at Appomattox Court House. His first taste of what awaited the 67th Ohio in this brutal campaign began at Chester Station, Virginia, on May 9 and 10, 1864. Even though still a colonel, Voris took command of his brigade, acting as a de facto brigadier general. In the ensuing battle, outnumbered four to one, he positioned his thin forces, held his lines until reinforcements arrived, and prevented a serious setback to the Army of the James. On the basis of this action, Brig. Gen. Alfred H. Terry, Voris's division commander, recommended his promotion to brevet brigadier general of volunteers.

Ten days later the 67th Ohio again saw combat when Confederates attacked Union lines near Ware Bottom Church. Although Voris distinguished himself and the regiment captured Brig. Gen. William S. Walker, the victorious Confederates had now essentially bottled the Army of the James at Bermuda Hundred, preventing Butler from achieving his goals. As the main front swung to Petersburg, some twenty miles below Richmond, the 67th Ohio held their position, spending nearly the next month completing their defenses, strengthening picket lines, and occasionally probing enemy positions.

By the end of June, Voris seemed mired in a stagnant area with little opportunity to achieve his personal ambition for further distinction or to contribute to the war's outcome. He hungered to rejoin his family, and mounting Union losses left him despondent and longing for peace. He began to consider returning home when his three-year enlistment ended in October.

The situation did not last. Beginning on August 13, Voris again exhibited the best qualities of a citizen-soldier during the heavy engagements lasting through November in the northeastern James River sector. Lt. Gen. Ulysses S. Grant began an offensive by ordering an attack at Deep Bottom to break the siege of Petersburg in the mistaken belief that Confederate defenses there were weak. Voris, whose regiment was part of the First Brigade, Tenth Army Corps, directed four companies of the 67th Ohio across a pontoon bridge on the James and reached Deep Bottom early in the morning of August 14. He led a charge on Confederate picket lines and once more took a group of prisoners. By August 20, when the offensive ended with little accomplished, Voris's troops had fought in three engagements over five days, with fewer casualties than others in the brigade. During these hectic days, he gained a further duty, serving as temporary brigade commander when heat stroke incapacitated Col. Joshua Howell, head of the First Brigade.

Voris's reward for bravery and leadership came within days. Following Howell's death, Terry overrode the seniority of other regimental colonels. On September 12, he appointed Voris brigade commander. In this capacity, Voris led the First Brigade in several armed reconnaissances near the "Crater," some 150 yards from the enemy, until he received new orders and greater responsibilities in October. Maj. Gen. David B. Birney, the Tenth Corps's new chief, named Voris temporary head of the First Brigade, Third Division, an African American unit made up of the 7th United States Colored Troops (USCT), 9th USCT, and 126th USCT. Birney also endorsed Terry's recommendation to promote Voris. This duty, despite lasting barely two weeks, confirmed Voris's condemnation of slavery. Although he conceded that few white troops accepted the concept of racial equality, Voris noted that they treated African American soldiers as comrades in arms and respected their fighting ability. Voris especially praised the courage he witnessed when he led the brigade in an attack on enemy entrenchments on

Darbytowm Road. Honored to be their commander, Voris welcomed another chance to lead them.

Voris returned to his home brigade on October 26, just in time for another action near Darbytown Road. Seeking to outflank the Confederates, Grant had ordered the Army of the James to attack along its entire front. Lt. Gen. James Longstreet halted Butler's advance, and in a short time the Confederates stopped the entire thrust. Voris led three regiments in this action, attacking the enemy on its right, and suffered light casualties. At this point, he received one more accolade. With Brevet Brig. Gen. Adelbert Ames detailed on an assignment that lasted two weeks, Voris replaced him as the acting commander of the First Division, Tenth Corps.

Voris took great pride in these achievements. During his three years of military service, he had risen from a private to a proposed brevet brigadier general and proved his worth on the regimental, brigade, and division levels. Only two factors limited his feats. Quality of service could not guarantee his promotion. Bureaucratic bumbling had snarled Butler's letter of recommendation. Voris still remained a colonel, a fact that grated him so much so that he once again contemplated leaving the army. Furthermore, his wound often throbbed with prolonged pain, sometimes disabling him. Needing further recuperation, Voris received a thirty-day leave on December 13, 1864. Col. Thomas O. Osborn, 39th Illinois Volunteer Infantry Regiment, replaced him.

By mid-January 1865, Voris's convalescence was far from complete. But he refused to seek an extension of his leave, and he rejoined his regiment, stationed in winter quarters, along with the rest of the First Brigade, First Division, Twenty-fourth Corps. Voris spent the next two months training new recruits, drilling, parading, and observing the coming and going of the peace commissioners at the abortive Hampton Roads Peace Conference.

Voris received notice of his promotion to brevet brigadier general on March 11, 1865. To atone for the delay, the official order backdated the rank to December 8, 1864. While pleased with this recognition of his merits as a citizen-soldier, Voris considered his star as a largely empty gesture. His new rank did not mean that he would lead the brigade. Thomas Osborn's advancement to brevet brigadier general preceded his, and Osborn had performed admirably during Voris's leave. Voris also lacked the physical stamina necessary for directing a brigade, the probable reason that Terry left Osborn in charge.

Voris did not acknowledge how these developments affected him, but the war had changed his personality in ways he did not perceive. Once avid for personal recognition, quick to respond to every slight, real or imagined, and impatient with human frailties, he was now a more introspective and humbled man than the eager volunteer of 1861. Too, Voris underwent a spiritual rebirth, drawing strength from the belief that a personal Providence would protect him and his family. One point had not changed. Voris remained steadfast in why he fought. He never questioned the need to preserve the nation, his loyalty to the Republican Party, or his opposition to slavery and support of free labor.

As the weather improved, the 67th Ohio received marching orders. On March 27, it moved southward, crossing the James at Deep Bottom and then the Appomattox at Broadway Landing. For the next two weeks, the regiment was in constant motion. After participating in a clash at Hatcher's Run, Voris played a significant role in the capture of Fort Gregg, an earthwork surrounded by a deep, partially water-filled ditch, manned by some 250 Confederates, a critical spot in Lee's line of escape. Joining some 80,000 troops in pursuit of retreating Confederates, the 67th Ohio then fought at Rice's Station and near Farmville, where Lee planned to cross the Appomattox, and arrived at Appomattox Court House early on the morning of April 9. Hearing sounds of heaving skirmishing, Osborn ordered the brigade forward at double quick, just as the Union cavalry fell back in confusion. Osborn sent three regiments into battle, with the 67th Ohio in reserve. When that effort faltered, the 67th reinforced Osborn, helped hold the position until reinforcements arrived, and prevented Confederates from escaping along the Lynchburg Road, their only line of retreat. After the brigade reassembled and prepared for another attack, Voris received orders to halt. The Army of Northern Virginia had surrendered.

Voris remained in service as a peacetime citizen-soldier until his term ended, December 15, 1865. In this capacity, he made one further contribution to his nation. After President Lincoln's assassination, the War Department named Voris as commander of a military subdistrict in south-central Virginia, headquartered at Louisa Court House. During this first stage of Reconstruction, he juggled the delicate tasks of guaranteeing equal justice and fair wages for freed African Americans, establishing a free-labor system, conciliating former Confederates, and healing the nation's wounds.

Yet with each passing day Voris became more the citizen than the citizen-soldier. Although flattered by his promotion to brevet major general of volunteers for distinguished service in the field and by Alfred Terry's encouragement to become a career soldier, Voris left the army with no regrets. As he later explained, "Our soldiers are self-made, and voluntarily unmade."[24]

With his service over, Voris's correspondence with Lydia also ended. As a result, no documentation exists about their relationship or his psychological reconversion from citizen-soldier to citizen. Certain clues exist, however, about their lives together. Neither was physically healthy. Lydia suffered from chronic body pain. Voris's uncured wound sapped his vitality. Even so, the couple had a third child, Bessie, born April 17, 1867. By November 1873, Voris could no longer endure his distress. Physicians recommended exploratory surgery and were astounded when they found and extracted "three-quarters of an Enfield rifle shot, weighing an ounce and one-eight." Afterward, he enjoyed vigorous exercise for the first time in nine years. Lydia was not so fortunate. She fought a valiant battle against her deteriorating body, but cancer spread and she died, at the age of forty-four, on March 16, 1876.[25]

Lydia's death forced Voris to reorganize his life. First came his family. With three young children to raise, he needed a steady income. Fortunately, clients sought out his services, and he steadily rebuilt his professional business. In 1879, Voris further strengthened his practice when he formed a partnership with his son Edwin, a recent law school graduate. Their firm ensured the financial security he wished. With this income, Voris then invested in Akron real estate and built a commodious home in a fashionable part of the city. On February 21, 1882, he finished mending his life. Voris married Elizabeth Ladd Keller, a widow and daughter of Judge Charles Ladd, his old mentor.[26]

During these years, Voris did not forget his reformist roots. Using his legal talents, he acted pro bono for indigents, many of them unemployed veterans and African Americans, who could not ordinarily afford his skills. Motivated by the same spirit, Voris helped form the Akron Bar Association in 1875, and over the next two decades he chaired several of its key committees, chiefly ethics and judicial conduct. In turn, the bar valued his professionalism, speaking skills, altruism, links to the city's early leaders, and stature as a war hero. As a sign of this regard, his colleagues twice named him bar president.[27]

On November 3, 1890, Voris reached the pinnacle of his legal career. With minimal Democratic opposition, "the gallant general" won election as a common pleas judge. By the time his term ended with the May session in 1896, Voris left a record, the Republican *Akron Beacon Journal* commented, "of which he feels proud, and justly, too."[28]

Busy as he was, Voris lent his talents to a host of civic groups dedicated to Akron's betterment, especially the board of trade, the Soldiers' Relief Commission, and the Rural Cemetery Association. Equally important, Voris considered education the "key" to "social progress." For that reason, he served on the city's board of education and as its president. Voris made just as significant a contribution to higher learning. He held a seat twenty-five years as a trustee for Akron's Buchtel College, formed by the Ohio Universalist Church in 1870.[29]

Voris should have felt proud of these accomplishments, but he found little personal fulfillment in them compared to his time in the army. The war, he recalled, gave individuals the unique chance to achieve personal excellence and united troops in a "common brotherhood" impossible in peacetime. Basking in these memoirs, Voris cultivated and enjoyed his renown as a notable heroic figure and Summit County's highest-ranking citizen-soldier. But in rereading his wartime letters and elaborating on events he thought important, Voris could not ignore his own words about the human tragedy the conflict created. Too much the realist to romanticize the military, he concluded, "The bitter fruits of war fill the land with sorrow and our grave yards with victims."[30]

Even by this unattractive standard, Voris's army service profoundly affected his postbellum behavior. Once more invoking the ethos of reform, he used his sterling war record to seek public and private relief for veterans and their dependents. Moreover, he lobbied politicians to give patronage "preferences" to "disabled soldiers," and he pressed Congress to pass a liberal pension bill.[31]

Voris considered fraternal groups and their political arms vital to achieve these ends. In 1866, he joined the Military Order of the Loyal Legion of the United States and took an active part in its charitable, partisan, and literary efforts. The following year, Voris became a founding member of Akron's Buckley Post, Number 12, Grand Army of the Republic, and made it an integral part of his life, including terms as local and Ohio commander. So that future generations would not forget their sacrifices, Voris additionally headed the fund drive for Akron's Civil War Memorial Chapel, assisted in finding its architect, and gave the keynote speech at the dedication.[32]

Throughout these years, Voris's reputation made him a speaker much in demand on a lecture circuit that spanned Ohio and adjoining states. Starting in 1867, he addressed numerous Decoration Day and Independence Day celebrations, reunions of the 67th Ohio, dedications of public monuments, and memorial services for fallen comrades. These speeches gave Voris an opportunity to remember and perhaps recast his wartime experiences into a new and contrived public memory. Many Americans by the 1870s and 1880s had begun to refashion the history of the recent past. Gone from their memory were the divisive issues that had divided the nation, expansionism, containment, slavery, free soil, secession, civil war, African American freedom, treason, and reconstruction. In their place, Americans adopted sectional reconciliation, the "Lost Cause," and a willful myopia about African Americans' contributions to Union victory.[33]

Voris refused to succumb to these imperatives. Speaking to veterans from the 67th Ohio, he happily reminisced about "the proudest associations of my life." Yet he was determined to give those experiences a deeper meaning by exploring why those men gave "the best years" of their lives to save the nation and what they had achieved. This effort, he acknowledged, was difficult. A general tendency among veterans to be selective about the savagery of combat, a reluctance to convey those emotions to nonveterans, "exaggeration," and the haze produced by years of "prolonged recollection" distorted the past. Despite these pitfalls, Voris began with one premise: the Lost Cause, "the idol of the Southern heart," contained nothing but "pretensions and delusive hopes." Instead, Union soldiers had fought to end slavery, "the cause of the war," to defend "free institutions," and to preserve "national unity." They sought no vengeance, no reparations, no "humiliating terms" of surrender. The right of all people and sections to live on equal terms with each other was all that the victors required. Yet "sectional, geographical, and race aspirations" still inflamed the nation. As his solution, Voris recommended national reconciliation, based on interlocking

regional political, business, and social values. Reaching out to former enemies, he urged the "magnanimous" North to restore "all the States and people to the Union." Unlike other reconciliationists, however, Voris had no
intention of using African Americans as pawns for reunion. Recollecting his
traumatic wounding at Fort Wagner, he lauded the "manly" African American 54th Massachusetts for taking "the lead" in the attack. Such courage
had contributed to emancipation and Union triumph, and they deserved
"equal manhood with us."[34]

Voris did not appreciate that his version of public memory was out of
step with postbellum America, both in the former Confederacy and in
Ohio. At heart, Voris was a partisan Republican, one of the state's leading
radicals, "as black as they make them," he wrote with pride. As such, Voris
urged adoption of the Fourteenth Amendment and full "suffrage" for "the
colored man." By 1867, he found a majority of white Ohioans thought otherwise. They rejected an effort to amend the state constitution to allow
African American voting. Furthermore, his effort to ban derogatory racial
terms in the state's "public documents and public school books" gained little backing. By the 1870s, Voris faced more disappointments as former
Confederate states restored white rule and subjugated African Americans. In
response, he sought military intervention in "unredeemed" southern states,
state-supported public education within integrated schools, federal suppres-
sion of the Ku Klux Klan, and national supervision of state elections. Long
after other Republicans tired of Reconstruction, he persisted in pressing for
African American "rights" against white "intransigence."[35]

Voris's belief in equality extended to women as well. His military service
had intensified this prewar commitment, perhaps in tribute to Lydia's support, sacrifices, and ability to function as an independent person during his
long absence. As a delegate at the 1873 state constitutional convention,
Voris, one commentator observed, sustained his credentials as the "cham-
pion of the rights of females" in Ohio. Asserting that women "possessed
the same natural rights as men," Voris pointed out that every objection to
female advancement repeated arguments earlier "said in behalf of the
American institution of slavery." With that in mind, Voris used a variety of
parliamentary maneuvers to introduce a women's suffrage section in the
new constitution, and he led the ensuing debate. His efforts failed. Unable
to secure the requisite number of votes, he could not incorporate the revi-
sion in the document's final version. Even so, Voris's program stretched beyond suffrage. He maintained that women deserved equal protection under
the law, increased job opportunities, similar pay as men for similar work,
and access to higher education, including "learned professions."[36]

One more disappointment existed. As a wounded war hero with an impeccable reputation, Voris expected an easy climb up the political ladder.
Such did not happen. Summit and surrounding counties were rich in
equally "qualified" Republicans. Moreover, his busy practice left him little
time to cultivate grassroots activists. Nor did he have a cordial personality

that voters found attractive. The result forced him to rely on veterans, such as one who argued in 1880 that Voris's most compelling partisan asset was the memory that he "carried rebel lead in his body longer than any of his competitors carried Union muskets." As war memories receded with each passing year, a new generation of Ohioans voted for issues more germane to their current interests. Voris now appeared an anachronism, a relic "of the John Brown persuasion." Given these beliefs, the party valued Voris as a dependable partisan in every national election from Grant's first campaign in 1868 through William McKinley's winning effort in 1896. But political office continued to elude Voris's grasp.[37]

By century's end, Voris slowly slid from public view. Hindered by dropsy, he abandoned his many public activities. He did keep in touch with a few wartime friends, such as Clara Barton, but rarely went to his law office. His health grew worse during the oppressive, hot month of July 1904. The weather caused Voris breathing problems and strained his body. Death, officially listed as heart failure, came on July 28, 1904. Akron staged an impressive military-style funeral, attended by "large crowds," with burial in the family plot next to Lydia.[38]

Amid an outpouring of eulogies, three well assessed the lasting meaning of Voris's life. The *Beacon,* speaking for the community he had helped mold and that shaped his destiny, praised his "moving spirit" in the many reforms that had garnered "good for this city." The Loyal Legion of Labor, an African American self-help organization, lauded Voris's record on racial equality, and noted that in his passing "the negro lost a staunch and consistent friend." The *Leader* spoke for the generation that had saved the Union. Voris "was a true patriot, and his death means a loss to his native state."[39]

Nearly one hundred years after these assessments, Voris has faded from memory, recalled only by his descendants, a street, elementary school, and a chapter of the Sons of Union Veterans of the Civil War in Akron named in his honor, and a few Civil War historians and reenactors, his exploits and sacrifices overshadowed by other soldiers in other wars. Yet Voris should not so easily slip away from public consciousness. Even among the multitudinous Civil War soldiers' diaries, memoirs, and letter collections, his correspondence has lasting historical importance. On January 28, 1863, he wrote Lydia, as if anticipating a distorted public memory in the future when facts became jumbled and meaning turned unrealistic: "The history of the war will be written in glowing terms of the valor of troops, the glory of generals, and after the sorrow stricken thousands are forgotten, nothing will be left but the bright spots of the war. It will write no practical lesson to warn those who follow us of the horrors of war. The cruelties, hardships & woes of the soldier and his fated family will be entirely forgotten. They are never written only in the hearts that feel them & the grave soon obliterates them."

Voris underestimated himself. His letters recall to readers a record of life in the most critical period in this nation's history, on that the passage of time and memory cannot erase.

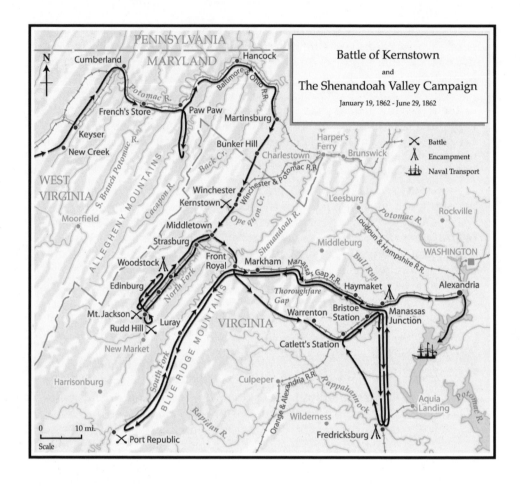

Battle of Kernstown
and
The Shenandoah Valley Campaign
January 19, 1862 - June 29, 1862

"Soldiering Is Romantic Indeed"

ILLUSION AND THE FIRST BATTLE OF KERNSTOWN

DECEMBER 27, 1861 – MARCH 28, 1862

[After the Union's loss at the First Battle of Bull Run on July 21, 1861, Maj. Gen. George B. McClellan reorganized the Army of the Potomac and planned a spring 1862 offensive to capture Richmond. Although Union forces had earlier secured the western counties of Virginia, the Shenandoah Valley remained a vital source for Confederate supplies. On January 3, 1862, Confederate Maj. Gen. Thomas J. "Stonewall" Jackson began pushing toward Romney in western Virginia. His objectives were to reassert control of the valley and to destroy the Baltimore and Ohio Railroad line, a vital communications link between Union troops in the western and eastern theaters. Jackson's thrust forced Brig. Gen. Frederick W. Lander to evacuate Romney on January 10. In this emergency, the ill-prepared 67th Ohio, numbering 820 officers and men, joined other raw regiments streaming into the Shenandoah Valley as reinforcements. The subsequent campaign culminated in Jackson's only defeat, at the First Battle of Kernstown, March 23, 1862.]

CAMP TOD—*Dec 27, 1861*

I arrived at Cleveland safely, a sad journey it was for me, but you know unpleasant things must be done sometimes. My men make me so much trouble. Many of them live so near Cleveland that they get home readily, and all have friends, family, or somebody else that they want to see. Fathers, mothers, brothers and sisters have been after their dear ones all day. The parting goes hard with many a one here as well as at home. You are not the only wife who has great interest in the service.

I hope you will bear up courageously. The war will not last always, and when it is over we shall reap the rewards for the privations, toil [and] pain we may have suffered & bourn. I am so rugged and healthy that you need have no fears for me on that score. I hope you will be cheerful and remember that you, in common with a great many others who are making equally great sacrifices, are doing a duty that every patriot wife & mother owes to the law that gives them protection.[1]

CAMP CHASE—*Dec 30, 1861*

. . . I propose to chat a few minutes with you and cheer your widowhood with a few reflections from a citizen soldier. Soldiering is romantic indeed. A day's history of camp life presents the following glorious realization. 1st, beat of drum to arouse the camp to arise & attend to roll call. 2nd, get your own breakfast. 3rd, to eat with the tin plate, knife, fork & tin coffee cup. Table a single board. The earth furnishes a chair big enough for all the armies ever martialed. Next, General Mounting, then drill, after which comes dinner with the same table furniture, bread, beans, meat & perhaps potatoes. For variety the order is reversed. After dinner drill till dress parade. Then supper like breakfast, only not quite so much so as breakfast. The evenings to the boys must be a good deal of a blank, 16 to 20 of whom are huddled into a little pen about the size of our kitchen apartment. Bunk like canal boat bunks, built up in one end, are the sleeping troughs. Then the felicities of sleeping on a <u>soft</u> pine board with a single blanket under & one above you can only be appreciated after a fair trial of a cold night. . . .

We are comfortably off here, better than when we go into the field. When that will be I do not know. We have a pleasant Col and an Jehu for a Lt Col. . . .[2]

CAMP CHASE—*Jany 4, 1862*

I have not heard a word from you since I left you at the depot. I have not seen Gen Bierce yet but am informed that he is in the city. . . .[3]

On the day fixed for the inauguration. . . we are to have a grand military review. . . . I am going to the city in a short time. I have just learned that a letter & bundle are awaiting me by Gen Bierce. I am quite well and enjoy soldiering quite well indeed. . . .[4]

CAMP CHASE—*Jany 5, 1862*

I got your kind note of Jany 1 last evening with package brought by Gen Bierce. You will receive my thanks for both. We are much more comfortable here than I had supposed we should be [in] this cold weather. My quarters are open, airy & light, say about as good as the generality of horse stables in the country, but then I have an abundance of fuel and a little coal stove about as large as our smallest stove. I have an abundance of bed clothing, but I must say that it is rather cold sleeping. . . .

I am much pleased with the gentlemen who compose the officer force of the Regiment, and on the whole we have a fine Regiment. We are to appear in the city on inauguration day to assist in the ceremonies of the day "fully armed & equipped as the law directs" for review. 2 or 3 other Regiments will join us.

I was at the Capitol yesterday and found nearly a Regiment of office seekers, all of whom thought themselves the best men in the State to fill the few offices necessary to the organization of the Legislature. . . .

A friend of mine sent for a brace of holster pistols for me (to be a present). Now when I get a good sword I shall be fully armed and equipped. What I most fear is that I shall never make my steel pay for itself. I certainly ought to make one secesher feel the momentum of northern lead or the weight of my "Toledo."[5]

My love to our dear children. Tell them papa will come home and see them as often as he can. I must stay a while to make up for lost time. My pay commenced on the 18th day of Dec 1861 for a certainty. I however expect to get full pay some day [for recruitment duties]. . . .

CAMP CHASE—*Jany 12, 1862*

. . . Camp Chase . . . has been mud & rain & rain & mud . . . with the exception of a single day. Well it is muddy, muddy, muddy, over shoe, over boot, over everything, but then I do not have to go out unless I please when it is so bad. Of course I don't please a great deal. It has rained all day, but it is freezing now & will be quite hard in the morning. We expect a grand military display at the Capitol tomorrow, grand as was the last inauguration only a great deal more so. Late Adjt Gen Carrington[6] of Ohio, now Col of the 18th Infantry, U.S.A, is to command the armies and navies to be reviewed by the outgoing and incoming governors.[7]

I can do no justice to the expected occasion. . . . Blood & thunder! With marching & counter marching, music and prancing, brass buttons bright flashing, blue cloth & volunteer civilians etc will [characterize] the day for which all other days in the history of the State of Ohio were ever made. Then me & Fanny, caparisoned, booted, spurred & gloved in the grand march, going to glory as fast as Carrington can command us. O! aren't you glad your dear beloved but humble husband is a soldier. Won't we shout "God and Victory" after we have been marched up and down & in column by the flank & by the rank & in column by the flank & the rank from six in the morning till 3 P.M. . . .

We were thrown into great excitement yesterday morning by the announcement that the 29th Regt (Col Buckley) was to move by 9 A.M. that day the 67th at 9 A.M. tomorrow to go to Romney, Va.[8] The 29th got under way & half way were ordered back. The orders being countermanded, so we stay at Camp Chase a few more days. When we may go no one knows. We may go any day on less than a day's notice & we may stay here for weeks. . . . I took command of the Regt in battalion drill yesterday & made myself hoarse as if I had been pettifogging a big case.

CAMP CHASE—*Jany 17, 1862*

This is probably the last letter you will receive from me at this point. We were quite surprised this morning to learn that we were under orders to go to Romney, Va at once. We leave here Sunday next for the field.

Our Regiment is in no condition to move. It has had little or no instruction. For a week I have been instructing the Regt in battalion exercises. I learned my lessons the night before each day's exercise & then manly go out and put the men through in gallant style. The boys think I am quite a military man but I know better. Still I think they had rather go under me than go as they are. This may be inflated vanity but still I think so.[9] Camp life agrees with me quite well. Cold, wet mud and other disabilities don't hurt me, but I do not expect camp life in Eastern Va will be as comfortable as it is in Camp Chase. . . .

We expect to be paid off in a verry few days. I had hoped it would be before we left here, but it will not be now. I have finally arranged so as to get $105 per month from the 2nd of Oct to the 18th of Dec. 1861, when I will get the pay of a Lt Col. I should have been able to send you some $300 if I had got my pay up to the last of Dec, as I ought to have done if the Government had done its duty. . . .[10]

CAMP AT NEW CREEK, VA.—*Jany 24, 1862*

This is the first opportunity I have had to write you since we left Columbus. I have been either constantly busy or on the way. I took command of six companies from Columbus to the Ohio River where we were detained three days. The River rose to overflowing its banks & caused us to move in the night, the command of which devolved on me.

The Col was gone as well as the Q.M. (By the way I shall have my hands full of business or I shall be entirely cut off from business). The Col is as jealous as his little body can be at my efforts & will do all he can to hinder me. Yet he is so utterly devoid of thorough business capacity that he cannot get along without good help. He possesses a sort of cunning but it is of such a sort that he leaves no confidence on the mind either of his ability or integrity. The first impressions of the man are agreeable, but bring him to the standard of the man who should command a Regiment [and] he so utterly fails that you are led to wonder how an unfledged foreigner of his ability could get such a place, and that too over American citizen soldiers.[11]

On being ordered to leave [men in the six unpaid companies] *refused to go. With all the Col could do, he could neither persuade or force the men to take the train that was waiting to take them. He verry foolishly told the men he would telegraph Gen Lander*[12] *that his men were mutinous and would not go. He scolded away for some time with a weakness that convinced the men they were masters of the situation. . . .*

I told him if he would go away from the camp and leave me in command, I would have the men on the train in half an hour. After long hesitation, and more fruitless efforts to get the Regiment into motion, he left the camp with the pettish order I might do as I liked. . . . I formed the men in a hollow square, got off a few good jokes, and had the boys sing "The Star Spangled Banner." I then made a short speech, told them our comrades over the mountains were after the rebels and wanted help to bag them, that a glorious opportunity was now offered to give the secesh what they deserved with a few variations of blood and thunder that made the whole vicinity ring. . . . [By] 10 o'clock they were wildly cheering the train as it carried them up the hills from the beautiful Ohio. You may be assured this set me up wonderfully in the affections of Col B.[13]

This for the present will suffice for the man who has command of the 67th Regt. If he remains its Col I shall resign. I am not going to trifle through a military campaign. I can do nothing at home as well as here. Don't understand me as being sick of the service. It is not so. I like soldiering. There is a fascination about it that strikes me in a complacent spot.

We are 22 miles west of Cumberland in the mountains & in the enemies country. A dozen miles away Gen Jackson with 17,000 men is waiting to bag us.[14] Whether he will is to be determined by the dawning arbitrament of battle. We might fight. We may not, but we are waiting to hear the pickets give the alarm at any moment, perhaps this night. I will telegraph you after it is over if we should have a battle. . . .[15]

CAMP AT NEW CREEK, VA. — *Jany 26, 1862*

. . . You appear to be lonely from the tenor of your last letter. You ought not to be so for you should recollect that I am well able to take care of myself, am engaged in a most honorable work, and have all the comforts that are usually had in camp. Remember that you are at home comfortably fixed by your little ones whose innocence confidence, affection & plans ought to make up for the loss of a headstrong man <u>who will have his way</u> in spite of an equally obstinate woman.

I am interrupted in this by a visit from several gentlemen from Millersburgh, now in the Va Cavalry Regiment stationed here.[16] These men appear quite cheerful and take soldier's life verry well. It has been a delightful day. Clear, could see the tops of the mountains for many miles around. I did expect to reconnoiter about here today, but the Col who was to accompany me could not go.

I have a nice tent, plank floor, small stove and old rail fence for fuel stolen from the secesh. Can keep warm. By the way a tent makes a verry fine house. The only trouble is that it is too small for all my traps, two trunks, saddle, oats, my boy's bed, then my own, & stove & etc take up most of my quarters. I make my bed on the floor when I wish to lie down, and make it up in a box when I get rested. If I had a stand I should be made up, but as for that I put my portfolio on my knee, and write away as if I had the best desk in the world.[17]

The probabilities are all against our having any fighting for the present. Yet we may be awakened by the long roll tonight calling us to fight by star light. Our boys, innocent creatures, are anxious to have a hand in a fight, yet half of them cannot yet make any practical use of a gun. . . . If I am not deceived we will stay here some days, perhaps weeks, but this war is a capricious chess board. We do not know when or where we shall move next. . . .

FRENCHES STORE, BELOW CUMBERLAND—*Feby 1, 1862*

The fate of a soldier has acted on us within the last 24 hours with a vengeance. At once we were ordered to march in a few hours. We were underway for Dixie. Where we are going I do not know. I will write you at every opportunity, but the grim realities of the war are upon us. We may lay out in the storm tonight. I slept on my trunk last night in a freight car. I bought a horse yesterday, a good strong bully fellow to carry me through mud & secession. I have received no intelligence from you since the middle of Jany. I do not feel as anxious about you as you do about me. But if anything should occur that you must get word to me, telegraph or write to the Adjt Gen of Ohio who will keep advised my whereabouts and will send us messages of importance.

I am cheerful, have good friends in the Regiment. I hope to send you some pay before long but I have not seen any yet. . . . I do not want you to feel solicitous about me. I do not expect to get hurt verry soon. Kiss our children for me. Tell them I shall see them by and by. . . .

CAMP LANDER—*Feby 2, 1862*

How rapidly time flies. It was but a day or two since I left you at Akron depot, Dec 26 last. Now it is the 2nd day of Feby 1862. I wrote you last Sunday, and the week has passed so swiftly away that I cannot realize that it is Sunday again. It is a delightful morning. The sky is clear & the mountain tops distinctly show their pointed ranges for a great many miles. We are on the southern bank of the Potomack on the line between Va and Md.

I am going to Maryland today in company of a few Officers to try the virtue of my twelve apostles. By the way I must explain. I had quite a surprise last evening. Lt Girty[18] with some 20 of the line Officers came to my quarters, made themselves agreeable for a time when Lt Girty got up and made a short speech complimenting me at an extravagant rate, gave me a short lecture, a benediction, and stuck at me a brace of Colts Improved Navy Revolvers, 12 shots & cost the economical sum of $65. I like a poor girl receiving the all important declaration bit my nails, hung my head in awful modesty, awkwardly took a stand up, & nervously grasping the two shooting irons and most feelingly thanked the young benefactor for his munificent expression of his personal regards, and said something about letting daylight through the traitor that dared come within range of their piercing inquisitiveness, & collapsed without any serious loss of breath.

I have broken the thread of my narrative by taking a ride over the bridge into Maryland, crossed the Potomac on a narrow railroad bridge, the ties being covered with plank so that a single horse could be taken across. I led Fanny.

She goes confidently wherever I tell her to go. She is getting fat and sleek & gay as a peacock. I shall be compelled to get me another horse before long. I mean to get a strong go ahead one that can take me through thick and thin at all times. I shall keep Fanny unless I can get a great deal better than she.

The mountain ranges presented to the eye from this neighborhood are exceedingly beautiful. They are not generally so abrupt but that they cannot be passed over by footmen. They do not appear so high as they did when I first saw them.

I have quite comfortable quarters. My tent gives me fully ten feet square. I have constructed a verry comfortable bed stead of boards my boy got some someway. Have my straw tick filled, have a large double overcoat blanket, two comforters as large and thick was one I took from home, & two large quilts, a pillow and slips so that for sleeping arrangements I can do about as well as when at home. . . . There is nothing like knowing how. I am principal housekeeper which adds greatly to one's ability to be satisfied with the domestic affairs of the household. I washed my handkerchiefs, socks, towels & etc. I shall wash my shirts and drawers if I cannot get someone to do it that I can trust. I washed my pillow case yesterday and ironed it in my hands so as to make it quite presentable. If men will take care of themselves the army is not a bad place for them. If Eddie was a dozzen years old I should have him with me.[19]

The boys generally like soldiering. So do I. But we are cursed by an imbecile imposter and knave for a Col, but I am satisfied that he will not stay with us but a few days. Charges are preferred against him. He will be tried by a Court Martial and disgraced. If he were to remain as Col I should get out of the Regt as soon as possible, but the indications are favorable. If he is removed I shall with great pleasure stay in the Regt. The rebels are within 15 miles of us with, but little likelyhood of their advancing on us, or we on them for the present.

I have just tried one of my pistols. It shoots like a six-pounder. Just think of it. Your dear husband of a bright Sunday morning shooting off a six shooter to learn how to use it upon his fellow men. . . . Well I hope I shall use them honorably & preserve them as relics of the war.

Saturday morning, Feby 8. We are still here. Have pitched our tents on the flats of the Potomac. I have been out some 5 miles in the mountains. A romantic ride it was. I saw several Akron folks this morning.[20] The boys are in the mountains in huts made of straw and rails. This soldiering is pretty hard sometimes but I have not yet felt it so hard as to think I can not bear it cheerfully. We may see fight, and again we may not. Our Col does not possess business capacity & gives indications of cowardice so unmistakably that all of us distrust him. I am sick of such Cols.

PAW PAW RIDGE, VA. — *Feby 10, 1862*

Just as I got your verry acceptable letter day before yesterday, 2 P.M. & before I had time to open it, I was ordered into my saddle to go to Brigade head quarters and ascertain about certain details for a march. Like a good soldier I took my sword & pistols, and was off in just two minutes & remained in saddle till 8 P.M. when we arrived at this place, leaving our tents, trunks & everything excepting our arms & rations for three days & a blanket each since which time we have been camping outdoors. It is clear but cold. Our boys put up rail huts, covered with pine boughs, and are making themselves quite comfortable considering.

Within two days from 10 to 12 thousand troops have concentrated here. Some forty canon are stationed at different points near us. So you see that we have the men & materiel for a big fight. Whether we will ever get into fight or not I do not know. But I am satisfied with one thing, that our Col is a great coward and a mean dishonest pretender, who will lead us into disgrace or keep us out of harm's way if he <u>can.</u>

We were ordered to report to Col Tyler[21] of the 7th Ohio, but the Col [Burstenbinder] contrived to make his order miscarry, having learned in some way that I knew Col Tyler and fearing I might have influence with him.[22] It is a disgrace to the service and an outrage to the self sacrificing men who compose our Regt to have it commanded by the foreign unscrupulous adventurer who even insults the good sense of those under his command.

Enough of this. I write you as I feel that you would like to know how I am associated in the service. The Major is a frank generous, honorable and courageous man & has the confidence of the Regt.[23] The company Officers, with a verry few exceptions, are honorable & capable men whom I much respect, and I think they are without exception my friends.

We shall have a new Col soon. Who he will be, I do not know. I would be Col if promotion be the rule, but I do not feel competent to take the command of the Regt & I have no desire to fill a Col place till I am thoroughly qualified to do it.

By looking at our large map you can see where I am. It is almost over the mountains. The Blue Ridge are the only mountains of note that separates us from the Chesapeake. The inhabitants this way are nearly all secech & not of the first order of society by any means. I have not taken much pains to cultivate their acquaintance. So far as their women are concerned you may be assured that they are not so fascinating that I shall stay & "take my stand to live and die in Dixie," & leave my wife & chicks among the Buckeye Husiers to take care of themselves.

You appear to think that I do not sleep well being near the enemy. Why you should think so is a wonder to me. I supposed you knew me better than that. I have never slept better in my life with a hard cold that I have had since I left Camp Chase. My boy, *I mean my African Gentleman,* awoke the other night in great fright & told me that the pickets were being driven in. I told him to lay down & keep quiet. Bang went another shooting iron! "Don't you hear it."? "Yes, said I, & you will catch it if you do not lay down & keep quiet till the long rolls beat." The boy went to sleep & so did I till morning, when we learned that the Regt had been in great excitement expecting every moment to be attacked till after daylight in the morning. I do not mean to let those secesh devils cheat me out of my needed sleep. . . . Not sleep! Do you think your husband a coward? Do you think me no soldier? God forbid that I should not sleep soundly & well with dreams of victory soothing my nerves.

Yesterday was a beautiful Sunday, but it did not appear like Sunday to me. Nothing to do, and nothing to do it with. My trunk & carpet sack were eight miles away. We have no newspapers—dull! dull! vacant day. . . . I saw a Beacon a day or two since of the 23rd of Jany & once & awhile I get a Herald[24] but we are now beyond the post office. . . . 50 miles is some way to go for a letter, but so it is with us.

Wednesday morning. A beautiful day. We just got our tents this morning & are making arrangements to have shelter again. . . . I met with Gen Lander yesterday & am much prepossessed in his favor. He appears to be frank, ingenuous & urbane. He says "by God" in an emphatic way once & awhile, but it is not one of those cus damn swears that startles a Yankee. . . .

CAMP CHASE, NEAR PAW PAW TUNNEL, VA.

—Saturday, Feby 15, 1862

. . . I have been off on a fighting expedition. Our Brigade with some 500 cavalry went out toward Winchester some 20 miles night before last to take on a few thousand secesh. The 13th Ind & 67th Ohio took one road, the 8th Ohio and the 14th Ind another. It was a delightful night, but muddy underneath.[25]

We marched from 4 P.M. till 2 A.M., & halted till near daylight. I rolled up in my blanket and took as good a snooze for 3 hours as I ever did in my life. I was awfully tired. Had the camp diarhea so as to make me feel verry disagreeable and made the ride excessively hard for me. I had just fever enough on me to make it fine sleeping out of doors with nothing but a blanket for my bed. My boy shivered and grunted as if he would freeze.

I just heard the rattle of a couple of boxes as they are being taken from the wagon, containing the bodies of 2 cavalry men who were killed in the fight of yesterday. I did not see the fun. It was confined to the cavalry on our side. They took 65 prisoners, one Col, one [assistant] Adgt Gen, 6 or 7 Officers and 55 privates.[26]

Marching up and down these mountains with gun & blanket with 2 or 3 days rations is verry hard work. We marched 10 hours last Thursday night and six last night, and had the not fun of fording a small river, the north fork of the Big Cacapon River. By looking at the map you can find where we were. It was right in the fork of the Big Cacapon & its north branch. Soldiering is excessively hard at times & again it is verry easy to bear. The 29th Regt are near us, so that I can see old acquaintances quite often. . . .

CAMP CHASE, NEAR PAW PAW TUNNEL, VA.*—Feby 19, 1862.*

I presume I shall write you more like a baby or woman than a soldier, as I have been sick for several days and not feel at all like myself. But that you may have no ill apprehension for me, I will say that I am much better now & hope to be entirely well in a day or two. Have had the camp disentery and an awful cold more severe than any you ever knew me to have. I have recovered from my disentery, and see a verry decided improvement in my cold. My cold has been on my lungs. You know my colds usually affect my throat and has almost laid me out. It has unfitted me for duty, but like a true soldier I have tried to keep up. We have perhaps a hundred men in the Regiment who are as bad off as I have been. Such coughing I never heard before. I have heard the whole camp painfully expectorating like the croaking of the bull frogs at Summit Lake [in Akron] and thereabouts. The snow, rain, cold, & thawing and laying out at of nights is not conducive to the health of raw recruits.

Then our Col has no idea of the wants, capacities or feelings of the men. Of a selfish, ignorant, supercilious mould, he treats his men meanly & fawns at the feet of his superiors. As illustrative of his disposition, I will give you the particulars of an instance that occurred at New Creek. The assistant surgeon had some half dozzen sick men he was desirous to take to Cumberland to the hospital.[27] Our camp was some 80 rods from the depot.[28] There was no fixed time for the train to go to Cumberland, except the passenger train in the night, but special trains went frequently. The surgeon went to the depot with his sick & the train was not there ready to start. It was also a snowy, wet day, & a bad one for sick men to be out. The Col had a large ground floor room at the county tavern there with abundance of room, and comfortable too for sick men. The surgeon thought it right to take the men into this room, & by the way it was the only one that could be had when the Col blustered up & savagely told the surgeon that his room was not the place for a hospital & told him to take the poor sick men out. The surgeon remonstrated but to no avail. The sick men were crowded into a cold wet little bar room with whiskey suckers for three hours by the barbarity of the creature who has the fortune to command nearly a thousand patriotic Americans. Several of these patients were sick with the measles, which the Col knew & he had no fears of them himself, having had this disorder in his childhood.

With such a guardian you may be assured that the health of the Regt will be conserved. My God! is it not this enough for you to know of the man who is to lead us to crush out treason against the Government? By the time treason is crushed out by such means, volunteer soldiers will be crushed out of existence. The finale of this tale is that one of those sick men was men was taken to Cumberland, and died from the effect of that exposure.

It has been a rainy day. I had to go out to Col Tyler's camp some 3 miles up the mountains this afternoon, being Division Officer of the day, and must see matters there & had to visit the outposts and must undertake the trip of visiting the outposts of our camp again just after midnight. But it has stopped raining so that it will not be so bad after all. These rain storms pinch up the men terribly, but if they are shifty and industrious they can make their tents quite comfortable. Ditching will make the ground dry, and stone or turf fire places can be made so as to make their tents quite warm.

I have a sheet iron stove which contributes to make my tent quite house like. Yesterday I had to ditch my parlor, bed room, sitting room, or whatever my army house may be called to keep me from drowning. When I feel well these little inconveniences appear rather romantic to me, but for the last week I have felt as if they were not luxuries that a man would go a great way to enjoy. But still I say hurrah for the luxuries.

We have had no more marches since we went up the Cacapon. That was quite a sharp fight. Some 30 killed & 65 prisoners taken, but we did not get near enough to see any of the work. It is verry doubtful whether we ever do smell gun powder from <u>secesh</u> shooting irons.

I have just returned from my visit to the pickets & got up the mountain. Bang! Went off a musket. By thunder! Is that a bush whacker? Captain Mason who was with me took his pistol in his hand.[29] I looked to my belt, and on we cautiously crept among the undergrowth of pines till we got to this post, when, lo, the sentry had fired his piece, having heard a noise that alarmed him. This is no adventure & I fear I shall have none to relate. I saw the Summit Co boys of the 29 Reg today. . . .

CAMP CHASE, NEAR PAW PAW TUNNEL—*Feby 23, 1862*

I am admonished by the heading of this letter that it has been almost two months since we last met. This makes the longest separation we have had since you & I became acquainted.

The late war news is of that cheering kind that leads one to begin to think the war may have a speedy end, and we poor soldiers permitted to return to the <u>embrace</u> of our wives, sweethearts, babies etc. If the onward movement should be ingeniously prosecuted & as successful as it has been during the month of February, I should not be all surprised if you found me at home to enjoy the 4th of July. You never heard heartier shouts than the boys sent up from our camps when they learned of the taking of Fort Donaldson. It was a glorious victory. A few more such will close up the war, but will cost us hard labor & many valuable lives.[30]

But then the number of lives lost by battle compared to the whole number engaged is so small that individual danger is almost lost sight of. The hospital does vastly more execution than the battle field. Soldiers are the most improvident of all human kind, careless, reckless & thoughtless as to their persons and health. . . .

I was darning my stockings last Sunday as the Provost Marshal called at my quarters on business. I verry kindly offered to let him have part of my stock of yarn and a darning needle. By the way I am reminded of my old college days in many respects. I have my own room and fixens, do many of my own chores, mind my clothing, make my virtuous bed and do my own swearing with no one to molest or make afraid. Talking about swearing reminds me that you may think that wicked. Well that would be under ordinary circumstances. But under this d——d Dutch Col it is a kind of virtue that every true Christian must indulge in occasionally or he would be looked on as being too grossly stupid to be an accountable being. . . .

I am quite well today. Have a full haversack (I mean stomach), have had no bad luck nor been disappointed in the least, and am in the fullest possession of all my faculties as this letter will prove. On the whole I have enjoyed this fine warm sunny Sunday hugely. Was busy till 1 o'clock P.M. Then took a ride with Maj Bond up the mountain to see the country.[31] Had a splendid ride, and neither saw nor heard any secesh.

By the way I took my "twelve apostles" with me ready to preach to any poor devil who should cross my peaceful path. Glorious fun, indeed, for your dear husband to go always with a pair of heavy revolvers lashed to his body whenever he went beyond the limits of his Regimental camp, loaded for offense and defense against his fellow creatures & his own country men at that. . . .

I today saw Capt James Fitz-Green of Gen Landers's staff, who was badly wounded in the Bloomery Gap affair where we went a week ago, Friday last. The poor man is quite sick and nervous over his wound. Confound those ugly bullet holes. I should awfully hate to have one of them put through my tender skin any where near my gizzard. Now this is no joking matter about this. I tell you upon the honor of a soldier—I should hate it.

This blood letting is all nice enough talk if somebody else is to be the subject, but when you bring the thing home you feel as if you had but mightily little claret to spare. Fully impressed with this idea I am bent on keeping rebel bush whackers at fair pistol shot distance from me unless they catch me napping. . . .

As soon as the roads get hard enough to move artillery, we should expect to march toward the enemy. I want to be in one fight before the war closes, a real big _savage_ feller that will be worth talking about after giving up my spurs, sword & shooting irons, never to be taken down in hostile array again, unless by my posterity.

We had a flag presented to the Regiment on the 22nd.[32] Speech by Gen Lander who is a verry fine speaker. He possesses in a high degree many of the qualities of an orator. He is a chivalrous officer. He says he would ask no one to go where he would not lead & ask no one to make a sacrifice he is not willing to share. He has the power of electrifying those he commands with his own courageous spirit. The boys say he is a bully man. I suppose you have seen in the papers before this the verry flattering commendation of the President to the Gen for his Bloomery Gap affair. . . .

CAMP CHASE, VA, AT PAW PAW TUNNEL—_Feby 27, 1862_

. . . I had a great ride yesterday and last night. I was Officer of the Day for this Division, and kept my saddle for the whole 24 hours except to take care of my nags. I went up the mountains to Col Tyler's Brigade after 10 o'clock at night, and visited all the outposts and pickets after night. It was awful dark. I got lost in the pine woods twice, & between rocks, ruts, and ravines and dark woods, I had sharp work to get along at all.

I rode into the furtherest outpost clear in the top of the mountain near the Great Cacapon River, and found the guard all asleep. Their horses and arms were stationed about them, but they were so soundly sleeping that I rode into their midst & halted my horse directly over them. After waiting some time I roared <u>charge</u> in their ears at the top of my voice. The sleepers sprang to their feet thinking they were taken by secesh. I gave them some <u>Hail Columbia</u> and some other hail, and went out for another post.

I got back to camp at 5 o' clock A.M. It snowed part of the time, rained a little & became clear before morning. Such roads & such forrests, and the realization that you are in the enemies country & that they possess a full knowledge of the geography of the same, makes me have a verry kind regard for my pistols. The rebel cavalry were near my path last night, as they destroyed Patterson's Creek R. R. bridge 11 miles from here last night, and had to take direction in retreat near my line of travel. To peace loving folks at home and among women and children this visiting the outposts in the night might appear rather ticklish business, but we get accustomed to it, and see & feel nothing verry bad about it. The men look upon it as being so safe that they go to sleep in their posts, as I have just told you. . . .

The roads are verry bad so as to make it almost impossible to move artillery. As soon as it can be done we shall join the onward movement. . . .

CAMP CHASE, NEAR PAW PAW, VA.—*Mch 2, 1862*

I have but a few moments this morning to write you. Our Division is ordered on for Winchester, and has been constantly moving since 4 P.M. yesterday. We expect to start with our Regt in a short time. Artillery, cavalry, miles of infantry & wagon trains almost interminable have been winding through defile & over mountain all night. I was out till midnight in the direction of the march to post pickets. By the way I am getting to be quite a mountain ranger.

Winchester is going to be a second Donelson, only <u>a good deal more so.</u> The enemy are strongly fortified, have abundance of artillery and about 30,000 men.[33] This will be the great battle for our Division. In less than two days I expect to smell gun powder in good earnest. We may be disappointed, and have no fight. We may have an easy victory. It may be terribly won victory, or it may be a dangerous defeat. God only knows what. But you may be assured of one thing. I shall not come home to disgrace the name and fame of my children with the stigma of cowardice in the field. We will have a march of about 38 miles to Winchester. Some miserable thief stole one of my pistols last night while I was posting pickets. . . .

PAW PAW, VA.—*March 4, 1862*

. . . We are still at Camp Chase near Paw Paw, Va. I wrote you yesterday morning that we were to start at once for Winchester. We had everything in readiness, rations for three days in our haversacks, & had been momentarily expecting to get orders to move for the 24 hours previous. We waited till noon, when it was announced that Gen Lander was dead or dying, and that the troops that had already marched were ordered back.[34]

Our boys were much disappointed as they wanted a brush with the <u>secesh.</u> We have since learned that the enemy evacuated Winchester & fallen back on Strasburg some 30 miles south of Winchester, where it is said they will make a stand.

We expect to move tomorrow to Martinsburg and from thence on to Strasburg. Gen Shields is to take command of the Division, & at Martinsburg will join forces under Gen Banks. With Shields & Banks between ourselves and the enemy we ought to feel well fortified. I almost fear that the rebels will not make a stand till they are driven to Richmond. If so we stand a poor chance to get into a fight with them.

If we were better instructed I would rejoice to go into a battle with the 67th. We have first rate fighting material in the Regiment, and properly handled would give a hard blow in an encounter with the enemy. I found my pistol today with the 8th Ohio Infantry, so I feel pretty well armed again. If I get an opportunity I mean that my twelve Apostles shall render a good account of themselves. It has been a verry unpleasant day. Rained most of last night and most all day at times quite hard. It is raining now, 9 1/2 P.M., but in our tents we are quite comfortable. The troops got in last night from their march towards Winchester before it had rained much. Had it not been it would have been a hard march for them.

We are all supplied with rubber blankets, so that two men can now lie together & have a water proof blanket under and another over them & make themselves comparatively comfortable if it does not rain. But marching in the rain is verry hard even under water proof blankets. . . .

If I was a secesh as I am a Union Officer, and as well acquainted with the country about here as many of their Officers are, I would take some of the field Officers while they are making the rounds prisoners or give them a chase that would set them thinking that visiting the pickets after night was no child's play. It would be an easy job to take us, who are entirely strangers to the country, with a force of half a dozen good men while we are out on this duty. We are allowed an escort of a sergeant and two privates, making a body of 4 men, not a verry large force to move about nights beyond the camp in the enemies country.

Gen Lander's funeral was conducted with military honors, but funeral honors are poor hollow honors indeed. I had rather die at my own home & be buried in a secluded grave by a few friends without pomp, show or trouble to any, than have Brigades for my funeral cortege. The day was bad, raining part of the time we were out, cold, snow & wet underneath. The poor soldiers had to stand out about 5 hours. Then a delay of two hours occurred at the farm house when Gen L. died. The coffin was too small & finally a larger box was used. I was on foot over half the time, but ordered out Fanny & was made quite comfortable. I acted as one of the pall bearers to carry the remains to the railroad, which we did by passing down the lines of the three Brigades out on this duty. It made the largest display of military I ever saw, say 9 or 10 Regts of infantry, one of cavalry and several batteries of artillery. In Gen L. a brave, magnanimous, heroic man has died. He was of reckless daring, of rough manners, but a kind & generous heart, perhaps not a great General but was a noble soldier. It is feared that intemperance had much to do in taking him thus untimely from the field.

I am well, first rate. Able to march this morning (I am finishing this on the morning of the 5th). It is a bleak cold day, wintry enough. A savage wind and floating snow makes it a mean morning in which to move. . . .

MARTINSBURG, VA.—*Mch 8, 1862*

My first duty is to write to you after I can get facilities & time for the purpose when resting from a new enterprise. My last letter announced to you the fact that we were waiting for orders to move on to Winchester. On the morning of the 5th in a March snow storm we struck our tents and got everything ready for a move. At 3 P.M. we were on the cars for this place. We kept on the railroad till we reached Back Creek, some 4 or 5 miles from Hancock where a splendid stone arched bridge had been blown up by the secessionists. We got there in the night, and stayed on the cars till 4 A.M. of the 6th. Disembarked in an open wood and prepared a breakfast. A temporary suspension bridge was thrown across the chasm made by the destruction of the bridge, rather a frail affair but the men one after the other could pass over one at a time. It was a pokerish job to walk over that bridge for light headed persons, as the turbulent stream dashed among the rocks some sixty feet below the narrow thread of this bridge, which swayed to & fro & sprung up & down as it felt every foot step. I passed over three times to give courage & confidence to the men. 5 Regiments having crossed over the creek, the march on foot was commenced to this place, a distance of about 12 miles. I stayed back to get our horses & followed the Regt in the night, & kept to railroad track which was torn up for 4 or 5 miles from Back Creek. Every bridge and culvert was burned or broken down, and hundreds of broken cars were strewed in fragments on the line.

You have no adequate conception of the perfect destruction the rebels have caused to this part of the Baltimore & Ohio road. At Martinsburg depot 41 locomotives were burned & broken down so as to entirely disable them. The work of destruction was so complete that only parts of the locomotives can ever be used again, and about three hundred other cars were completely destroyed, both passenger and freight. It is also said that some 14,000 tons of coal was burned, an article of great utility to the inhabitants of the place. $3.50 per ton was the usual price before the war. $17 has been paid since the burning. A splendid iron bridge supported by 18 stone columns about the size & height as those in the front of our State Capitol was completely demolished. The pillars still stand, but many of them are rendered useless by the injury done them. The most permanent, perfect & useful works on the road have been wantonly and without cause utterly destroyed. The most foolish vandalism & wicked stupidity appears to have controlled the rebel authorities in this, their work of destruction.

It does not appear as if they intended to make a direct & overwhelming attack upon these works of permanent art, beauty & great public utility just for the sake of destruction. The excuse for this was to close up the road so the Federal Gov could not transport troops & supplies over the road. This could have been as effectually accomplished by doing but little or no injury to the permanent & magnificent works of which they have seen fit to destroy.

In their mad fury they made an attack on the civilization and wealth of the people, as much as upon the Government they are fighting, and what is the strangest of all the injury is done to themselves. It is a retrograde move which irresistibly carries them toward barbarism as well as despotism. As railroads are looked upon as a sort of public institution, and their property as quasi public, you may think that private property interests and rights may be conserved. This is not true. The leading idea developed in the destruction of the railroad is manifested toward every interest in community. If the injured party be strongly secesh he is remunerated by Confederate scrip. If not secesh he is paid by kicks & curses because he is not the unfortunate owner of more subject for plunder.

What hope can be reposed in a government inaugurated under and by such means, motives and ignorance as this? I have taken pains to inquire of intelligent persons of both parties here what the popular idea was as to the vigor, ability, policy & future prospect of the Confederate Administration. This would be a verry appropriate question to address an Ohio man, and would be promptly & intelligently answered, but I cannot get a satisfactory response here. The popular mind is not educated here as with us. The people do not read & think on these subjects for themselves. A few men of wealth & influence do that for the masses. These men give their individual impressions, but say that the people are not well informed & again the avenues for information have been closed.

Newspapers are rarely seen from the South. In fact paper has become almost obsolete here. I could not get or buy it here to write a letter till the sutler opened his stall. I saw a Winchester bond or bill yesterday printed on the blank side of a shop bill. When the currency of a State runs as low as to fasten itself to the filthy back of a worn out advertisement, a Yankee would naturally begin to think of bankruptcy or migration.

Martinsburg is a place of about the population & with some of the characteristics of Canton, Ohio, with fewer good dwellings.[35] However it is said to have been a verry active business place before the war, but nothing now is being done. A great many dwellings are abandoned and stores, shops & factories are closed up. A perfect business desolation has ruled the town for months. The people here are heartily sick of the fruits of the war, and appear not displeased at our occupancy of the place.

The statesmen of Va have not manifest their usual sagacity in taking part with secession. They have voluntarily brought upon the State a terrible financial, social and political scourge. A person who has not seen the effects of the war cannot appreciate the extent of the injury. At every place where a camp has been made for any length of time the hand of destruction has fallen, leaving nothing but buildings & the native soil. Fences, hay, grain, crops in the ground, lumber, chickens & pigs have disappeared till the country surrounding the camp presents the appearance of waste. The dwellings & farm buildings are about the only indications left of civilization.

This is true whether the occupying army is friendly or hostile. It is a necessity in part—fences disappear for fuel, hay & straw for bedding. Other articles are appropriated by mischief. And nowhere have these evils so concentrated as in Va. From 200,000 to 300,000 men have over run her sacred soil for months. It is fortunate for Ohio that the stroke of war has only fallen on her sons in the field and far outside her borders. The general evils of war are magnified by being seen & felt. The inconveniences, fatigues and privations of the soldier are not magnified if they are seen from afar.

I am quite well but see no prospect of having a fight. We are in the midst of rebels. Only 25 miles from here there are said to be 30,000 of them, but these cannot be expected to hold what is called the valley of Va, & Winchester is their strong hold in the valley.

You may think this rather an odd letter, but the material parts of it were written for the Herald, and having the matter on hand, I thought it would be of interest to you. . . .[36]

It is Saturday now. The Baltimore & Ohio Railroad will soon be open to this place so that we shall have mails regularly. D——n this war! D——n the men that caused it! I am for fighting them with perfect fury till we have licked them like thunder.

Sunday morning. It is a beautiful morning, but you must be aware that we have no Sunday in the army & time flies so rapidly that I hardly realize that it is possible for Sunday to be here again. Since I closed my letter last night we have the news that Winchester has been evacuated by the rebels & that Gen Banks[37] has taken possession of the place without opposition. The enemy has fallen back to Strausburgh. I can give you no idea what we will do next, nor when we will do or not do it. At home you are as well posted as to the army operations as we are here. . . .

If things go on as they have done since I came into the army I fear I shall have no adventure worthy of being mentioned, unless it be that in going up the mountain. Fanny fell with me, and in getting up held by foot in the stirrup, bringing my heels up and my head down. I caught the bit in my hand, and righted myself without bruise or hurt. . . .

WINCHESTER, [VIRGINIA]—*Mch 13, 1862*

You see by the heading of this letter that we really occupy Winchester. We have heard fabulous stories about the strength and forces at Winchester. Till we got here we labored under the impression that there must be at least

30,000 men here and 60 pieces of artillery. Their force had been frequently reported to us as high as 60,000 with a hundred pieces of canon. Of course a large army was arrayed for taking this place.

Gen Williams[38] of Gen Banks's Division led the advance of the column on the road from Martinsburg to Winchester with 6,000 men. Col Kimball led the Gen Lander Division (now commanded by Gen Shields) composed of three Brigades of infantry of about 10,000 men, and four batteries of artillery, and some 18 or 20 companies of cavalry. Part of the last Division has not yet arrived here, but are in supporting distance.

Gen Banks is on the road from Charleston to this place with a large army. We left Martinsburg Tuesday morning & marched out to Bunker Hill ten miles, and rested till nine o'clock P.M. when we marched till within 4 miles of Winchester and bivouacked in a wood till 3 P.M. of yesterday. We arrived at the wood at 3 A.M., & slept under the trees & our blankets soundly for some two hours, expecting to have a brush with the secesh. Boys will sleep right in the face of the enemy in the full expectation of a battle within a few hours.

As soon as we had taken our breakfast of hard bread and coffee we were marched to the front of the woods towards Winchester, & formed in column by companies, artillery in front, & expected to be attacked before the close of day. But they did not attack us. We expected to storm the lines of the enemy, but we were sadly disappointed in not measuring lances with the rebels. They fled, breaking up their camps at 4 A.M., leaving the town & their carefully prepared defenses to the mercy of the cowardly Yankees.[39]

They were awfully alarmed. They got the idea that we were coming with an army 100,000 strong. I think our boys would have gone into battle confidently, as I saw no flinching among them. I mixed freely with them early in the morning, telling them to be ready, that before night some of them would go to H——l. The boys said that they would give H——l to the secesh, that they had come for that purpose.[40]

In many respects I wish the enemy had seen fit to make their stand here. I then could have the experience of being under fire and the honor of being a fighting soldier. My impression indicated to you in my last letter that we would not get a fight out of these creatures verry soon is being realized all along the upper Potomac Army. It was announced to us at Bunker Hill that Manassas had been evacuated by the enemy.[41] If that be so we will again be compelled to take up the old cry, "On to Richmond." Romney, Charleston, Martinsburg, Leesburgh & Winchester have been abandoned by the enemy in a few days, leaving all this part of Va in the hands of our troops & without any serious fighting.

The folks here are getting sick of the war. The house on the farm we are now occupying had a son killed at the Bloomery Gap skirmish (where we were on the 14th of Feby). Several of our Officers stayed with them last night. I saw the grave of two brothers at Martinsburg who fell at the Manassas battle, both killed at the same moment, and almost in each others arms. A fine brown marble slab lies over their graves with proper inscription if the rebel cause be just, but was entirely too complimentary if our cause be right. . . .

We are in what is called the valley of Va, being a stretch of most beautiful country lying between the Blue Ridge & the Allegheny Mountains, extending from the Potomac River to the southwest part of the state. I know that you would be pleased to visit this part of the country. The Blue Ridge is east of this, some 15 miles & stretches southwesterly as far as the eye can reach, & presents at many places a magnificent sight. I have been among the mountains so long that I am getting to look upon them as familiar objects. Yet there is a grandeur about them that makes me like to look upon them. O! such beautiful mountain streams, water as clear as crystal and frequently flowing from a single spring. . . .

We are luxuriating on secesh chicken now. I got one for 2/c yesterday. It was a chicken indeed, an old he hen of almost a centuries growth, & after boiling it long enough to tan sole leather it made a chicken soup for five persons for supper and breakfast. With a little bread & pilot bread it makes as the boys say a bully good dish for us. I have a plump rooster hanging over my stove & a few potatoes in the canvass & expect to live like a prince for a few days. . . .

12 P.M. 14th. What a creature of uncertainty is the soldier? A battle is raging only 3 miles from here. We hear the artillery & occasionally a volley of musketry. We do now know the <u>force</u> of the enemy. The boys are eager for a fight. We are awaiting orders to pitch in. I am ready to do my part, but the 67th is not in verry good order on account of its unfortunate commander.

Mch 15. 8 A.M. We were not called out yesterday. A skirmish did take place. 2 killed of rebels & 17 taken prisoners. We shall have little or no fighting here.

Winchester is a beautiful town of say 16,000 inhabitants. I passed over the enemies works yesterday evening & got one of the most magnificent views of the country I ever saw. The evening was not clear or I am not sure but I could have seen clear to the Gulf.

You need not fret about me. I am well enough for all soldier purposes. . . . If we should stay here long enough I will send for some things, but we are uncertain creatures. May move today—may be whipped before night—go to glory perhaps.

CAMP NEAR WINCHESTER—*Monday, Mch 17, 9 P.M. 1862*

I recd a verry kind letter from you today dated March 9th I think, for which I am sincerely thankful. We are under orders to move with three day's cooked rations, & expect to be off in three hours. Where we will go, what our errand is, when we will come back, or whether we go at all are matters of entire conjecture with us. But thank God, for one thing, we do not go under the command of Col B. He is under arrest, and will be tried for his impositions by a court martial & if justice is done he will be cashiered. A Regiment of good men with a list of gentlemen for Officers will have cause to rejoice if he is forever deprived of his command. He tried to provoke a disturbance with me on parade last Friday. He was insolent, abusive & outrageously insulting. I at once complained of him to Gen Kimball, who ordered me to make out charges and specifications against him, which I did do, & thereupon he was put under arrest.

This is the 3rd time he has been insulting to me, but the former times he had sense enough not to make the matter public & I felt as if I had too much good sense to be bruiting about a private difficulty. But when he thought he had the power to do it publicly with impunity and exercised it I thought it best to check his tyranny. I shall go in command of the Regt with many feelings of regret that I am so illy prepared to lead & direct the men, but then there has been so little chance for getting at these secesh fellows that I do not feel as if the Regt hazarded much by going under me, as I can march them as far & as long as they can bear it, perhaps longer.[42]

Friday, March 21st. Well we started in the morning [Tuesday] for Strasburg, had a beautiful day for the march, & halted 4 miles north of the village & encamped for the night in the open fields. On our ways we heard canonading to our front some 3 miles, at which the boys sent up cheer after cheer to be able to mix in a few miles march. But the enemy soon ceased firing after they had burned a bridge across a branch of the Shenandoah.[43]

Bright & early we were on the way to Strasburg. Just before we got to the town we halted to let the artillery pass. In a few moments heard a canon boom. Again and again the boys cheered as if the music struck the right spot. I rode to an eminence & saw the bursting of their shells in the air. "Nobody hurt." After a good deal of maneuvering we got under way, & passed through the village to the vicinity of the enemies guns. Our artillery was placed to the front and right of our brigade on the crest of a hill to the west of the village. Two other brigades were formed directly back of the artillery.

I formed our Regiment the first time it ever formed in line of battle before the enemy, a fact that appeared to please the boys verry much. I put my old horse over a rail fence in gallant style to get ahead of the 8th Ohio which had filled the road up so that I could not pass my men, whom I meant should lead the charge if possible.[44]

Such a chase from the 4 Regts, each pushing through on a run to get to the fight first. I feel proud of our fellows. As we were running we could hear the conical shells whiz & ring over our heads from both sides. It was animating music for the boys. Oh! how I wish they have got near enough to the rebels to discharge their guns in their faces.

After marching & counter marching till night we encamped in a meadow near Strasburg, making pens & camp fires of the fencing in the vicinity. It commenced to rain at dark & continued till this morning, (Saturday) with little intermission. We roofed our pens with our rubber blankets, & stole enough hay & straw to make our beds with a strong desire to embrace old Morpheus for a few hours. You would be surprised at the shifty & comfortable manner the boys fix themselves under such circumstances. I grant it is not quite as good as your own bed with a good wife by your side, but it does well in the absence of anything better.

Wednesday morning. We had a hard time marching back to camp. It rained and was verry muddy. We made the 22 miles without stopping but a few minutes, but the men kept up gloriously. The 14th Ind, 1st Regt in our Brigade (ours the second), having ridiculed the raw troops about their inability to march with them, our boys determined to give them a trial. This time our boys had no Dutch Col to annoy or abuse them. The 14th led off & we lugged them close the whole way. When they stopped for rest our boys would make the air ring with on you lazy 14th, & so the chase went on the whole 22 miles. The boys felt quite well last night, and walked to parade with quite a soldier like bearing. We are ready for another march.

How long we shall stay here I do not know. We may go any day, may stay some time if not longer, may see the rebels, may not, may fight them, may not. We have been having such a series of victories of late that we may begin to think the war almost over. I sincerely hope so. I expect to be compelled to send all my things home. I am verry well. I send you a paper with one of the boys, extravagances <u>concerning me</u> showing how boys will write sometimes.[45] I have been so hurried for several days that I could not write much of a letter.

TELEGRAPH MESSAGE—*March 27, 1862*

Bloody fight. Boys fought heavily till night. Slightly wounded.[46]

CAMP NEAR STRASBURG, VA.—*Mch 27th, 1862*

I telegraphed you this evening to make you feel at ease about me, as I supposed that you would get the news of the battle at Winchester before I could write you, & as singular reports have been circulating about my fate you might get them and be sadly alarmed about me.

This last four days have been more full of stirring and terrible events than have ever occurred in my modest life. But I have had the good fortune to pass through the trying realities of the same without dishonor to my fame or serious accident to my person. (I did get a little shot though that has made me quite lame, but was entirely fitted for duty).

I know that you will feel proud of me when you learn the incidents of my short command of the Regiment. I took command of the 67th Regt on Sunday the 16th Inst. On Tuesday following I moved the Regt from Winchester with Gen Shields's Division to make an attack on the rebels under Jackson south of Strasburg, had an artillery fight with the enemy, and returned to W on Thursday. Rested our men Friday & Saturday till 4 P.M. when I was ordered out with my Regt to do picket duty at once. In a few minutes we heard artillery south of Winchester. Our camp was 2 miles north of W. I was ordered to advance my force and be under motion in 10 minutes. Well you can tell whether I flew around or not.

In one hour I was in the field 4 miles from camp & under the fire of the enemy artillery. We were the first Regiment in the fight & felt their fire first, except our pickets. The whizzing & explosion of shells, the report of the guns, struck my men with perfect amazement, but in a few moments we were under full head way & *pushing toward them*. Our artillery soon opened on them, & we were relieved from further fire.

We advanced till dark & lay on our arms all night, *covering our force from surprise*. In the morning (Sunday) we got breakfast (hard bread & coffee) & kept a sharp look out for the secesh, being the farthest *advanced* Regt in front of the enemy. About 10 o'clock I was ordered to deploy my men as skirmishers to the extreme right. After passing 1/2 a mile up & round a hill to the edge of a wood, I soon heard a report of a rifle and the keen buzzing of a bullet directly over my head as I was leading my column *forward*. In a few minutes, bang & whiz, again awfully close to my ears. The boys told me I was in the way of that fellow. Crack & whiz again so close to my head that I did dodge a little (well I do not like to be the target for a sharp shooter). *I cleared the woods of these sneaking sharp shooters*. I was then ordered to support a battery of artillery, again to hold myself in reserve & then to support artillery again. There was a grand artillery fight *all the while going on*. We enjoyed the fun of dodging shot and shell till after four o'clock P.M. when the infantry fight commenced in terrible earnest.

I was ordered to go at once into the fight, & had to pass 1/2 mile over a level piece of ground in range of the enemies artillery & *towards them*. Solid shot, shell and grape showered over us in a perfect storm *as we made this passage*. I had their shells explode over my head which threw fragments over & about me, but did no harm. We then passed in a wood & came into the engagement. O! what a terrible conflict. The most incessant fire of infantry was as incessant as the roar of a long & rapid line of trains.

We were in the thickest & hardest of the fight for two hours & stood our ground firmly from the start to the honor of my Regt, & I say that it was the only one never faulting & gave back from its first position. Capt Ford was shot dead at my side. Young Lantz was soon shot through the arm. Boys were falling under a storm of bullets.[47]

The Regts on each side of me fell back to a low place. I recd a shot in my thigh to tear the flesh, & made a bad bruise & cut the skin & made two holes in my leg as if punctured by buck shot. It brought me down, but in a few minutes I was up and at them with my pistols. Seeing a good chance to make a dash I seized the colors & urged the boys to rally round their standard and push for the enemy. A shout went up from our boys, & the secesh broke a run like ruin. What a run. The rout on that part of the field was complete. We went round their left flank & got too far & had our battle not been successful, I with about 50 of my men would have been compelled to go to Richmond or Hell. Thousands of shot were fired at us but we fell under a low ledge of rock & hugged the ground mighty close for some 15 minutes when the whole force was driven from the field. We then followed the fellows giving them fits till it got so dark I could not see.[48]

I was quite lame from my shot and was compelled to go to my blanket bed. Was not in much pain, and slept well. My leg is considerably swollen and quite dark with blood. I kept to my saddle the next day & have done the duties of my command without serious difficulty. I shall be quite well in a few days, but I now have a receipt that always will show of my active service that can never be lost. You may rest assured I was not dangerously hurt, have only three bullet holes in my overcoat, which I will preserve (the holes I mean). I would like more fully to describe the battle. The magnificent display of men. "Arma virum que cano" says Virgil. So do I. I wish you could feel the exhilaration of a desperately fought battle. Who would not be a soldier?

Wednesday morning. I had a splendid rest last night under a rail pen. I sat by a little stove fire and got my leg well warmed, & went to a comfortable bed & got up almost as well as ever. I am not hurt so as to be disabled or disfigure me. I feel proud of the mark. The contusion has made my leg on the inside "black and blue" from some three inches below my thigh joint to two inches below my knee . . . .

Now you need not feel in the least troubled about me, as we will have no more fighting for a few days, & I shall rest. I would have done so before but we were after the enemy, & I did not want to have the boys think that a slight little wound was a sufficient excuse to lay by in such an emergency. I want my boys to be soldiers & heroes & how can I make them so better than to set them the example. I told them when I took command that I would exact of no one what I would not cheerfully do myself. Those that win in the fight with me are noble fellows. I feel proud of them. I love them & one great cause of pride is that my Officers and men reciprocate my regard for them. It was a terrible battle, the bloodiest this side of the Mississippi River in this war, & my men were under fire during the whole battle and in the hottest part of the infantry fight. I had the satisfaction of making my pistols pay for themselves.[49]

James Bruce (a former clerk of P. D. Hall who says he used to wait on you at the store) shot a secesh major & broke his leg.[50] I saw a sgt single handed take two prisoners alone. I saw terrible sights. I saw the panic of battle. The secesh ran as we did at Bull Run. Our Regt got high praise for its valor. Now I hope the war will soon close. I have had the honor of leading a Regt in a desperate battle & come out it with honor. My ambition is satisfied.[51]

I have seen misery enough.I do hope treason will be satisfied with the woe it has already created & make it unnecessary for us to pursue them with further punishments any further. But if we must fight further I am as zealous a soldier as ever. Explain to our children that I am safe & will come home all right before many months. I must close this as the teams are going to Winchester, the nearest post office.[52]

CAMP NEAR STRASBURG, VA.—*Mch 28, 1862*

I need not stop to tell you now that the soldier is the creature of the most capricious fortunes. My personal history for the last five months has doubtlessly verry unpleasantly convinced you of that. The transactions passed to us are vivid realities but so singular frequently that they appear to be the acts of other persons rather than ourselves.

We know the past, but the future is covered by such equivocal uncertainties that we almost doubt our physical existence. That I have been through a most terrible battle, that I commanded a Regt into the verry jaws of destruction and led the way myself, that I cheered my brave boys to do all the terrible work of slaughtering my fellow creatures, that I did all I could myself to do the same work, that we lay out all night on the bare ground without blankets, went hungry, marched like fury, that I got a contused gun shot wound, are all true. Yet the whole, with the glorious victory achieved, and myself as one of the actors, appears to me as the transactions of a third person. (My itchy thigh appears to be really my own). My identity appears to have been transferred to some other A. C. Voris.

When I last wrote you I had no idea of soon acting in such a desperate battle. Saturday night when I was ordered out with the Regt I had no idea of only a little skirmish. Sunday morning when we were resting further advanced toward the enemy, I had no idea of a general battle, but about noon when I saw the long line of the two thousands of armed rebels in the distance, I told my boys that we had our hands full, that the fight would be desperate, that every man must be a hero, that bullets were cast for cowards, that glory encircled the brow of the brave only, that if they did not achieve victory that we had no place to flee, that we were far in enemy country, that defeat would send us to Hell or Richmond, neither of which places were verry desirable.

Now what will be our next move, where and when, are just as inscrutable to me as to you, but you may be assured of one thing, that I shall try to well sustain what little honor I gained in the Winchester fight. The grandest human effort I ever witnessed, or ever expect to witness, is a great battle. The most welcome sight I ever realized was the flight of the enemy. I cheered my men forward in the charge. I shot my pistols in their *fleeing* squads with perfect delight, and limped after them at a run with my <u>lame</u> leg at a 2-40 rate, urging my men to them Hail Columbia & to take them prisoners. But when it was all over I did really pity the poor deluded creatures who were driven before us. In my deliberate moments I prayed God I may never be compelled to see such sight again. After the battle I soon found the hospitality of a large white oak which furnished me a pillow & leaves for a bed where I soon slept till morning, expecting to be out by 3 A.M. and at the rebels again. . .

I am well and have got nearly over my <u>bruise.</u> I would not have you feel in the least uneasy about me on account of my hurt, as I shall be entirely over it in a week or more. I recovered my overcoat, & would send it home to you if I had a good opportunity. We have received no pay yet, have got so that we do not care anything about money. Uncle Samuel furnished us food & clothing in part, the ballance we can do without or steal from the enemy. . . .[53]

"The 67th Has Not Been Stationary"

THE SHENANDOAH VALLEY CAMPAIGN

APRIL 2, 1862 – JUNE 19, 1862

[Kernstown, while theoretically a Union triumph, was inconclusive. Jackson remained a formidable foe, a master of strategy and deployment who demanded and received the utmost from his troops. Over the next three months, Jackson conducted a series of brilliant movements. He outmaneuvered Union forces, forced them to march and countermarch over hundreds of miles in fruitless pursuit, prevented reinforcement of McClellan, and routed the armies of Maj. Gen. Nathaniel P. Banks, Maj. Gen. John C. Frémont, and Brig. Gen. James Shields. After ending this phase of the valley campaign with a victory on June 9, 1862, at Port Republic, Jackson slipped away to join Gen. Robert E. Lee's newly christened Army of Northern Virginia, leaving his foes, including Voris and the weary 67th Ohio, fuming in humiliation.]

HEAD QUARTERS 67TH O. V. NEAR WOODSTOCK
IN THE FIELD—*Apl 2, 1862*

You see that we are getting "away down in Dixie." Every move takes us further from home, but nearer a speedy return. We have been after the enemy again, but they won't stand. We had a sharp skirmish with them in the forenoon across the branch of the Shenandoah running through this valley.[1] We lost 3 men. Had pretty sharp artillery firing at intervals during most of the day, but actual artillery fighting does not appear half so dangerous to me as it did before I stood under it. It is a magnificent way of fighting so far as pyrotechnics are concerned, but the real heroic way is to take the rifle in hand and pitch into fellows at such range that the shooting tells by the men that must fall before its storm. . . .

I have entirely recovered from my wound. Can walk almost as well as ever, and ride as well as ever. I had a fine rest from Tuesday night on the 25th till the morning of the 1st of Apl. It was what I needed & could my then condition not do without, but I have recuperated in the time & feel quite fierce for the onward movement.

Nothing of interest has occurred in that interval. We heard everyday more or less artillery firing in the distance, an event that for the most first few times was received by the boys with the wildest cheers, but now has become so much a matter of course that a shell must drop near us to attract special attention. The first firing the boys heard was in the last half of Mch, & in a few days [they grew] accustomed to the music of canon & balls.

We are in the woods tonight, the 14th Ind on our right, the 4th Ohio at our rear, the 8th Ohio on their right, Tyler's Brigade to our left & on the railroad. The 29th Ohio is in that Brigade. I have the nicest quarters in the world, which I use for dormitory, parlor, dining room & Regimental head quarters. . . .

Our camp presents a beautiful view at night. Camp fires in every direction in apparently innumerable numbers *illuminate a whole pine forrest.* The hilarity of the boys, an occasional air from the band, love for adventure and novelty make a camp without tents in the wood a place of lively interest. I wish you could see us in our camp as it appears this moment.

Officers in our Regiment who observe men & things say that I am a natural soldier, that I can adapt myself to the little inconveniences of camp life & bear its labors & dangers of the same so well that I ought always to be a soldier. Would you like to have me go into the regular service?

Thursday morning, Apl 3. This is a beautiful April morning. I am sitting in my den with my boots off & no fire writing on a fragment of a barrel head, & squat on my blanket like a tailor on his board on my blanket. I just heard the report of artillery to our front, but presume it does not mean much.

Would you not like to see me perched on a big horse and dodging this shot & shell of some secesh field piece? You folks at home think this horrible work, but it does not appear so bad to us. The boys like it so well that six of my boys ran away over the river yesterday morning to get into a fight with the rebels. They came for a fight, and feel disappointed unless they can mix in every skirmish. The fighting is inspiring work. I think men like the excitement of the conflict, but the battle field after the work is over is a horrible place.

I was not able to see much of it at Winchester, but what I did see of it made my heart sick at the terrible work of battle. Man after man was shot down at my side, some killed, others wounded, & while the fight raged neither could be well removed. Most of our wounded were cared for soon, but many of the enemies lay out all that cold night with bleeding wounds & broken bones, unable to help themselves, and no earthly hand to ease their pain or sooth their wretched nerves. One poor fellow was found dead with a broken leg who had struggled with fate till the ground was besmeared with his blood & scratched up for yards around in his desperate effort to get away. Another had both eyes shot out & the base of his nose shot off. Another lost an under jaw, & still lives with the prospect of a miserable life before him.[2]

My God! what won't wicked men bring upon their fellow man. When I think of the horrors of the war I wish it was over. When I look at the glories of a victory I want to pitch in. Then you and my dear children arise in my vision like the ghost of Banco, pleading with me to be careful, to avoid danger. If this was a war for glory alone I would not stay another day. But duty to you, to my children, to my Government and to myself demands this terrible sacrifice. . . .

HEAD QUARTERS 67TH REGT O. V. IN THE FIELD
NEAR EDINBURGH, VA.—*Apl 6, 1862*

. . . I see the deep traces of war depicted in the brow of many mothers, wives and sisters as I pass through the villages of this valley. Most of the able bodied men from 18 to 45 are in the service. One of the Regiments in the rebel battle was raised in Winchester, a town about the same population as Akron,[3] the men of which fought, bled and died in sight of their own homes. The fate & fatality of the battle was a terrible blow to the city of Winchester and the surrounding towns. The flower of her chivalry was thrown and fell or fled before our irresistible charges. It pains me to pass through their towns. I feel as if I was looked upon as being one who was helping spread this pall of woe upon their once happy homes.

I am not fit for a soldier. Soldiers should be made of iron, with hearts as fierce as fire, and of a purpose as cool and relentless as fate. When I have to fight I can do it with a will, but when it is over I am much distressed at the terrible consequences I help produce. I do not know that I killed anyone in the battle. I am glad of it, but while the battle raged I did all in my power to do so. I used my pistols with a steady and determined hand & perhaps too sure an aim. Yet I console myself that my shots went in with the aggregate. According to this rule I am not chargeable with the death of a mortal in battle. I did throw six good shots which would be equivalent to a slight wound. So you may set me down as having slightly wounded some poor secesh to offset the shot I got in my leg. . . .

Monday Apl 7th. I do not want our place rented, for we may be home anytime. The war may be over in a few months, and then you know that I told you I would spend the winter of 62 & 63 with you at our home. If a Kind Providence spares my life I shall do so. If I give one year to the service, I shall have done my whole duty to "Uncle Samuel."

Tuesday, 8. This is the most disagreeable day we have experienced for a long time. It has rained, snowed & sleeted alternately since yesterday noon. On getting up this morning we found the ground covered with snow, the trees with ice. It is now 3 P.M., and as bad as ever. I have a sheet iron stove that makes my tent quite comfortable. My floor is rather wet to be sure, but I have managed to keep my bed of oak leaves quite dry. You may imagine me with a pen made of rails for the head foot and sides of my bed & staked to the ground to keep them in their place, my overcoat for a pillow. . . .

My furniture is not verry extravagant, nor does it consist of a great variety of articles. I have two camp stools, one trunk, iron sheet stove, water bucket, one camp kettle, two tin cups, 2 tin plates, 3 knives & forks, 3 spoons, a candle stick, two coffee pots, one broken up, one hatchet, saddle & bridle, curry comb & brush. I almost forgot my sword and pistols. . . . Since I came here one week ago today I have had two chickens, three loaves of soft bread, boiled beans & rice, pilot bread, salt bacon, salt beef, fresh pig, fresh mutton for dinner. Coffee, tea and sugar as much as I desire, minus milk of course, but won't I lick the cream when I get home. Dried peaches (the last I brought from home), fried potatoes (desiccated). Now don't this present quite a formidable list. . . .

Soldiering is getting dull again. It would really be a relief to the boys to hear that a fight was to take place and they to take part in it. I have seen all the forms of fighting I wish to see except a cavalry charge upon troops prepared to receive them, and a bayonet charge from our boys. Cold steel is the heroic way of fighting. On the whole it is not more destructive to life than bullet fighting.

The boys are amusing themselves vastly today, knocking the trees to see the ice fall in torrents from the tops of the trees. It would please Eddie verry much to see the sport. You can see that spring is coming, however bad this day by the violet I send you.

HEAD QUARTERS 67TH REG. O. V. IN THE FIELD—*April 13, 1862*

Sunday has again arrived, a pleasant day but indicating rain. We moved our camp yesterday, selecting a beautiful location near a mountain creek and wood. It is in many respects the most agreeable camp we have had since we came into the service. The last week has been the most unpleasant taking all things into account we have had since the Regt went into service. Rain, snow, sleet, a muddy camp & an unpleasant location made us bad enough off. Indeed one of those stormy nights with 3 or 4 inches snow and slush, my whole Regt had to stand picket guard all night. I was on my feet watching for secesh all night except a while I rolled myself up in a rubber blanket and lay down in the snow, a d——d bad bed for a Christian man. . . .

Since I have had the command of the Regiment I make everything appear as easy and cheerful as possible. I do not like to hear my boys grumble, therefore I go at everything cheerfully. I am becoming so much a soldier that little privations & labors do not trouble me. I am as fat as I ever was, enjoying uniformly the best of health and never get the blues. If I were a single man I would be the happiest man in the whole army. Then I am getting a little proud. I have been receiving such flattering congratulations from home and abroad that I could live in the army some time on hard bread etc for the sake of pampering my pride. . . .[4]

Indications are that the war will not last verry long, and why not enjoy my soldiering to the fullest while I am a soldier. . . . 60 days will substantially end the fighting. It may be some time before the army is mustered out, but I do think the time I have given will close up the fighting. Just think of Island No. 10 & Pittsburgh Landing for one week's work.[5]

If Gen McClellan is successful at Yorktown where he is now fighting, Va will be cleaned out in a verry short time. I am afraid I shall be compelled to go home with the honors of only the Winchester fight. Of course I do not know what a day may bring forth, but it does appear to me that this part of Va is not disposed to do any more serious fighting. I have been a verry poor prophet about these war matters, as you are aware but I cannot help indulging in a little guessing. . . .[6]

The truth of what I wrote you about the uncertainties of a soldiers's lot is today illustrated by my being unable to close the last sentence by an order coming from head quarters commanding me to be ready with three day's cooked ration to march at a moment's notice. I left the letter, and went to work preparing for a move. Now 8 o'clock P.M. Have recd notice that the project is abandoned, and we are to stay in this place & camp till which will be God only knows when. . . .

Well if I am to be Col of the 67th, I suppose I am ready to be offered up. Yes, up as high as they are a mind to send me. Who ever heard of a man's refusing to be elevated, but mark I am no applicant for the office. If I get it is in the free offering of the Gov without the least solicitation on my part. I shall try to my utmost to do my duty well.

You seem to think I move too fast. Why bless you, that is spoken of by military men as being one of my peculiar virtues. They praise my promptness and the celerity with which I move my men, & if you read the papers you will find that I lost nothing by being a moving man. The highest honor a half dozzen Regts have claimed for themselves was the honor of making the charge the 67th made at the battle of Winchester. Again one place is about as dangerous as another in battle. Those fellows shoot so careless that no place is perfectly safe. You need not worry about me. I will be careful.

HEAD QUARTERS 67TH O. V. IN THE FIELD—*Apl 20, 1862*

Sunday has again come to the poor relief of our camp. Our boys are tired from the last three days march with a dreary, rainy day to rest upon. Wednesday night at 11 P.M. we were ordered to be ready to march with three day's cooked rations, 40 rounds ammunition and blankets slung. At that time precisely we were ready (you know I am precise to the minute). I on my horse the boys on theirs & at the command were under motion for still further down in Dixie. It was a beautiful clear moonlight night, not verry light however. Slowly and cautiously we moved without noise. About 2 miles from camp we loaded our arms & sent out skirmishers to feel the way for us. Another mile, bang, whiz, went a few rifles with their not verry welcome contents. To us this night fighting was rather an unpleasant novelty; where these ugly things came from, the number or kind of forces we could not see or know. Conjecture under such circumstances does not carry with it the most refreshing associations. We could not tell our rifles from one skirmish piece from the other, but we could tell that their pieces were directed against us by the sharp sound of their bullets as they passed over our heads.

You cannot verry well dodge a rifle ball in the daytime, yet it is more comfortable to me to stand fire in the daytime than in the dark. After a sharp volley or two off scampered the secesh, and nothing was seen of them till day light. As day was dawning I moved 3 of my companies & 2 of the 8th Ohio to the front and extreme right to skirmish with the enemy if they appeared. After moving about a mile & passing through a wood, also the just abandoned camp ground of the enemy, we got a few shells from a battery 1/3 to 1/2 a mile off. The way the shell hailed among the trees was a caution. Being unsupported by artillery or infantry I was ordered to withdraw my men, which I did to the distance of 100 rods. I had one boy, a fine fellow, wounded in the wrist by a canister shot from one of their shells.

We soon advanced but found the scamps had made tracks. We followed them up closely to Mt Jackson when they burned the bridge across the north branch of the Shenandoah. We forded & followed on till we came to an extended elevation a mile or more beyond the town, beyond which was one of the most beautiful open plains I ever saw with a ridge of hills some 60 to a 100 feet in height some 2 miles beyond. This is the famous prospective battle field the secesh have boasted so much about for Gen Jackson where he was to make his final stand & where he was to crush out the Northern invaders. Well I have seen no place where he could have more successfully made a stand than this place. Its natural defenses are as good as the valley furnishes, & then the beautiful plain between the hills to the rear and this ridge is a glorious place for armies to maneuver when they desire an open fight.

When I saw that [Jackson] had abandoned this stronghold, I came to the conclusion that he did not mean to fight in this valley. His rapid flight is also confirmatory of his intentions not to fight us here. We marched over this plain in battle array & spread out some 15 or 20 infantry Regts, making a grand military display. A military display does not make the same impression on me now that it did a few months ago. Here I saw the major part of Gen Banks Corps de Arms with the three arms of the service all in one view, Infantry, Cavalry and Artillery. The cavalry is the most dashing, the artillery the most imposing, but the infantry is still the strong arm of the service, the relied upon & the most capable of sustaining & giving shock.

We pushed on till dark & rested at a place called New Market, lay on the open field with a blanket covering & bundle of wheat for bed. Stayed one day & another night. Yesterday marched back to our old camp at Edinburg. For present our Regt is to be stationed at Woodstock which is made a depot for garrison & Q. M. stores & etc. I hope this is not to be permanent, for I have no desire to stay as the Governor of a country town when I could be making a noise on a tented field. The enemy are no nearer to us as than Staunton & Gordonsville, unless in verry small force. I wish the matter to be hurried up. A great battle is to be fought at Yorktown. . . .[7]

Monday afternoon, Apl 21. It still rains and hard too. 3 days constant rain is rather unusual, but we have been having it nearly all the while for three days, dark, dreary days. April has punished us with really more unpleasant wrath than any other month since I have been in the service, and to tell the honest truth I hate it. I feel mean, look mean & fear I act mean, for how can one act so contrary to his feelings and surroundings as to act well when he don't feel well.

We are much better off than most of the soldiers of our Division as we have tents & their tents are not up to them. I look out of my quarters and almost pity the poor soldiers myself. If I did not think the war was coming to a speedy close I should feel as if soldiering was hard business. I expect easier work for my Regt as my Regt is detached for duty at the post of Woodstock, of which post I am to be the commander. How long I shall stay will be I can only conjecture. I had rather be in for a fight once and awhile than to be forever garrisoned in a country town in Virginia. . . .

Wednesday, Apl 23. We are going away down Dixie day after day, and where we will land we do not know. . . . I saw Capt Wright this evening.[8] He appears to feel bad about the little notice taken of the 29th Ohio. Well that is too bad. And what was worse than all he had seen a Beacon of last week that said "the Beacon was proud of the 67th & A. C. Voris," that two or three letters were in it. I do not know <u>what</u> he means as I have not seen the Beacon. . . .[9]

I got a Toledo paper last night announcing the surprising fact that Lt Col Voris of the 67th was in the city Saturday, the 13th. Some not verry far seeing editor caught a verry small item out of which to make a sensation.[10] The thing is ridiculous for more reasons than one. The papers now have great events to cover daily, and have no need to fish for such minnows as Lt Col of the 67th. Then how foolish I would appear if I should be off to Toledo to catch a few laurels. . . .[11]

If Jack Wright knew how newspaper articles were made, and how exceedingly unreliable they were he would not feel so bad. I see by the Cincinnati Commercial that I got 14 bullet holes in my overcoat cape. Well who ever told that whopper must have thought I had an awful big cape, or that it had lots of bullet holes in it. <u>14</u> bullet holes, enough to make a strainer of it. . . .

POST AT WOODSTOCK, VA.—*Apl 28, 1862*

. . . I am now quartered in the town of Woodstock, but still keep my tent. Being commander of the post here with about 30 miles of public road to guard, I have my hands full. I might take lodgings with the citizens here in some good house if I desired, but the women look so infernally cross that I do not want to get in their way. . . .

No one knows how comfortable a tent is till they have tried it for a season. I ought to be totally well acquainted with it by this time, for since the 1st of Nov last I have been in a tent or barracks the while. I should not feel contented to stay at home now if the war should continue as I shall want a hand in. With all the terrible realities that is included to a state of war, there still is a fascination about it that makes the enterprising man want to be in. Were it not for home and its obligations I would always like to be a soldier.

It has been over four months since I was at home, & over six since I have lived away from home, yet I think I can stand it till the 1st of July next when I expect to be home on a visit at least. There is a contingency however that may bring me home at any time. We are unable to get our Col to trial though he has been under arrest since the 16th of Mch. The Lord only knows when he will be disposed of. The command is verry embarrassing, as I am only recognized as a temporary commander.[12]

If the Col should be acquitted, I would resign at once. Again Gen Hill[13] of Toledo is expecting to be the Col in case of vacancy. Indeed he says it was offered to him as far back as the first of Feby last. But circumstances have so changed since that time that all military usage would point to me as the Col, if a vacancy should occur & I should be wanting in self-respect if I do not resign. Gen H wrote me a long letter assuming that he was to be the Col dated 13th Inst., requesting of me a frank reply. I did reply frankly by saying that if he "should be appointed over me I should ask to be relieved from a service that did not regard present service and a strong smell of gun powder." I also wrote to the Gov giving a copy of Gen Hill's letter, & my own in reply to it to show him how I felt about it. I have never uttered a syllable or written a word to the Gov or to anyone else to see him about the colonelcy in case of vacancy, as I have meant to have the office conferred on me by the unsolicited judgment and favor of the Executive & mean so still.

Yet I am not unwilling that the Gov should know how soldiers feel who have endured the fatigues, struggles & dangers of a campaign. Toledo can bring to bear a strong influence that may move me out of the line of honorable promotion, but I have brought to bear on them a verry annoying battery in the short letter I wrote to Gen Hill. I will be myself, a man though I should lose the chance to place an eagle on my shoulder (an eagle is the designation of a Col's rank). What ever may now eventuate I have the consciousness that I have done all that duty requires of me. . . .[14]

I have this day sent the children two secesh children's books. . . . I am verry well. Weigh 171 1/2 lbs and constantly getting heavier. If it keeps on I will weigh a ton or more.

POST AT WOODSTOCK—*May 1, 1862*

You see by the heading of my letter that we have not moved far since the 1st of April. We are not far from the camp we then occupied. We have however been as far as New Market & back to this place. Our Regt has been doing garrison duty at this place, Edinburg, Strasburg and Mt Jackson, I having 4 companies here. Maj Bond 4 at Strasburg & one company at Edinburg & one at Mt Jackson.

If I were not in an enemies country I should be quite happy with my duties, and could make things about me quite to my liking. I might have good society, but as it is I am cut off from anything like social intercourse. The tenor of society here is hostile to us. I cannot go into the social circle of a Virginia family and not feel unwelcome. I took dinner yesterday with a rebel Captain at Edinburg. He had abandoned the service. I became acquainted with him by causing his arrest, and sending him to Gen Banks, who by the way did not think it best to send him North, an opinion I had previously entertained in his case. On this return from head quarters I called on him, & being about dinner time he prevailed on me to stay. Aside from the associations our hostile positions created, I had a verry pleasant visit with the Doctor (he is also a physician) and his wife. When I was introduced to her I said to her that she must have felt rather unamiable towards me on the day I sent her husband off to New Market. She confessed that she felt verry badly at his leaving, for she had hoped that he might be sent to stay at home during the further continuance of the war, but his arrest had awakened in her the apprehension that he might be compelled to go to Columbus or some other Northern prison for rebel soldiers.[15] But after a general talk with her she became quite inclined to talk, & when I left the Doctor followed me to the gate to bid me good bye & verry cordially invited me to call as often as convenient. But all the while I felt as if it was an affected exhibition of politeness common among well bred people in Va & in fact when even gentlemen & ladies exhibit themselves. I try to make all I come in contact with feel as if we were not conquerors, that we did not feel exultant, that all we wanted was a sincere recognition of the obligations to obey & support our own Government, that we had no disposition to play the tyrant when discharging a high political duty, and are disposed to do it in a manner that would be of least offensive to their sensibilities. . . .

If I was a Virginian as I am an Ohioan by the Eternal I would do differently than do the FFV in this fight.[16] I would strike here, there & everywhere when a foe presents. I would not run unless to strike at a better point, & when I did strike I would make it till the enemies of my state fell in battle rather than by the fleetness with which I fled from the approach of the <u>"cowardly Yankees."</u>

They call all northern troops Yankees, the Virginia loyal Regts as well as the New England Regts. The broad headed, square bottomed Dutchman from Pa they call Yankees. The sharp visaged lank Hoosier from southern suckerdom they called Yankees, in fact all the loyal soldiers are called Yankees. Before the war Yankee was a term of reproach. Now it is the accompanyment of fear. They do quail before the steady fire, persevering industry and unyielding courage of the northern soldiers.

Thursday morning. . . . Enclosed you will find a paper on which is written "Lt Col A. C. Voris, Comd. 67th Regt O. V. Infty, from his friends in Toledo." This accompanied a beautiful field glass of the Opera style. It has the power of magnifying 16 times, and makes me an excellent instrument indeed. I shall always feel proud of it, as it is a token of esteem of disinterested friends who have never known me personally, but only as an officer and that through their friends I am commanding in the field. . . .

We will probably be on the Blue Ridge soon. I understand we are ordered to Warrington and may go at any time. Our boys are anxious to join the Brigade as soon as possible. They do not like to be doing police duty about town.

The boys are beginning to look forward to the time when this accursed war will be brought to a close. Events look verry discouraging to the rebels. New Orleans, the whole Mississippi, the seaboard forts, Yorktown and all the later battles must be exceedingly unconsoling to them. . . .[17]

I do hope the war will soon end. I shall yield up my place with great pleasure if an honorable peace can be speedily secured. I am ambitious, would like to be a General & might have been one if I had gone into the fight at an early day. I made a great mistake. I see it now, but I would not like to see the war prolonged to give me a chance to secure promotion. I love peace, and have no personal ambition that I could not cheerfully sacrifice to secure it honorably. If we could get rid of the infamous Burstenbinder I would have no obstacle in the way of my being Col of the 67th, but the Lord only knows whether he will ever be tried. However that may be, I am de facto Colonel. I have the command. All that is wanting is the possession of the rank. . . .

POST AT WOODSTOCK, VA.—*May 4, 1862*

. . . A Sunday like quiet reigns in the towns of the valley. All business is suspended. The men are mostly in the rebel army, the women, felicitous creatures, are crabbed and blame the Yankees for all this trouble. Well, I don't blame them so much. Our occupation of this valley section is unpleasant to them. Their fathers, husbands, brothers & lovers have been driven off by our army. They cannot even get out or into town without a pass from the Provost Marshal. They snap and snarl a right smart bit while answering questions put by the Provost. The war was well enough for them while our army was on the Potomac, but since it has been brought to their own door they are dissatisfied enough. The women are bitter secesh & spit it out with venom. The men are mostly so, but are more discreet and keep their sentiments to themselves. . . .

Spring is not much earlier here at this date than it usually is with us. Peach & cherry trees are now in full bloom. Forrest trees are just beginning to show the leaf, but little plowing has been done. Corn is not planted. In fact most everything here is about as it is in Northern Ohio about the 12th of May. The war has much retarded farmer's work here. The horses have been taken by the secesh away for cavalry & for army purposes till but a few are left.

Woodstock is a town as large as Cuyahoga Falls, but is built on the style of the villages in Stark County, but fewer good buildings.[18] Otherwise it is quite a pleasant place. The ladies deep in the fashions of the times speak English after [Noah] Webster and hate the Yankees as they do the d——l.

The court house is an old stone building with pointed steeples in the middle, & bears the marks [of] having a Yankee shell directly through it. The court house is abandoned, the offices vacated. The lawyers have abandoned their offices in haste leaving their books & private correspondence, one young attorney leaving all his correspondence for years with his sweet heart. . . .[19]

FRONT ROYAL, VA.—*May 14, 1862*

. . . It has been a miserable night, and a verry unpleasant day having rained for nearly 24 hours constantly & hard at times. I have been hard at work ever since Saturday noon when I broke up camp at Woodstock and marched to Mt Jackson, then again back to Woodstock & then back to Strasburg, then to Middletown & thence to his place. For the first time since I have commanded the 67th has the whole Regt moved *together* and that alone. I moved from Strasburg to Front Royal to clear the way for the wagon trains of our Division. Had no incidents worthy of notice, except we made the ford of the Shenandoah just above the junction of the two branches of the North & South forks. We had a rickety old scow to ferry over the men & wagons. We did the work of crossing the two rivers in about 12 hours. Nobody hurt.

It is night now and raining so as to make it verry disagreeable. You would say it is awful for the poor soldiers. We have in effect abandoned our tents not keeping more than 20 to the whole Regt. I of course kept mine [for headquarters]. . . . I can go to a good house & bed, but then the boys would be compelled to stay in camp where they are. To make them feel as if all was right I am going to set them an example of fortitude. Example is worth a great deal to them. . . .

Thursday noon. . . . I permitted my boys to occupy barn sheds & houses hereabout during the rain as much as possible, but being some ways from towns not many could be provided that way. . . . The darkies are sliding off rapidly here. Our army has a bad effect on this kind of property.

We are on our way to Richmond or somewhere else, but things look but little like fighting here. The rebels may rally at some point & give us trouble, but it does look as if they were abandoning Va without the intention of making a decisive stand. I wish they would fight it out here and now, and let this be the end of the matter. The war is the prolific source of so much misery I do wish it could end. . . .

HEAD QUARTERS 67TH REG O. V. IN THE FIELD
NEAR WARRENTON JUNCTION, VA.—*May 19, 1862*

I wrote you last night from Front Royal, but by the heading of my letter you l see that we are advancing. We are now in Eastern Virginia or "Old Virginia," a beautiful country it is but I should say not remarkably fertile. This is certainly true for the parts we have passed through since leaving the heights of the Blue Ridge. I never saw more picturesque scenery than during the last three days. Mountain, hill, valley, bottom and plain land interspersed with forrest & grove, farms and villages stretching out as far as the eye can reach.

It presents a peculiarity that you would not anticipate. That is the population is sparse, a few fine residences, [and] more squalid ones *indicates* the accompanyment to the farm residences of negro quarters. As a general thing these quarters are of the quality of our better class of building for stock. I said better, in style they are no better, but are made warmer, otherwise have no more of the comforts or conveniences of home than my horse barn with none of its arrangements.

The negroes appear pleased to see us. The whites act sullen. This side of the mountains the slaves are not as well clad as in the valley. They appear to be raised for the market rather than labor. The women are prolific if the little woolly heads hanging on the fences are any indication. I know they must be the offsprings of colored mothers by the wool, while there is a great variety of color in the same family. . . .

Enough for the country and its population. No, I must say a word about Warrenton. It is the prettiest town I have seen in Va. It presents an air of aristocracy & refinement rarely found in a town of 2,000 to 3,000 inhabitants. We passed through the town on Sunday when we could see the elite in their best bibs and tuckers. The women were pretty enough but looked awful sour. A verry pretty young girl made a nasty face at me as I rode at the head of my column through town. . . . The girls feel chagrined at the fact that their fellows have been compelled to make tracks before the cowardly Yankees. Our advent wounds their pride as well as their affections. Their hate is as much the hate of wounded pride as of anger.

We are now on our way to Richmond. The cry of "On to Richmond" is becoming a reality to us. We will be in Fredericksburg in a few days where we expect to join Gen McDowell's Army.[20] The enemy act now as if they intend to fight at Richmond. I hope they will. If we can gain a signal success at Richmond it will send a shot through a vitals of the Confederacy. I do want to see a few home thrusts made that will kill the monster. I do want to see an artery cut. A lost foot [or] hand, even an arm or leg, disables but does not kill. . . .

As soon as our Richmond campaign is settled I mean to make a visit home. I am not satisfied with the way our matters are left. I am in command of the Regt. Col B is at Winchester under arrest (not yet tried & God only knows if he ever will). I do think we are not well used. I shall make a vigorous effort as soon as I can to get to Columbus to have matters corrected.

FREDERICKSBURG, VA.—*May 22, 1862*

You see dear wife that we are still moving. . . . Every move we make we go further down Dixie. We are now where the rebels have been verry strong, and only a verry few miles from the "All quiet on the Potomac,"[21] but I will venture it will not be all quiet when we go. We have a fighting Division, we are in a fighting Brigade and my Regiment is one the fighting Regts in the Brigade.

The country immediately about here is beautiful & fertile, but the section we have passed through the last few days is barren & poor in the extreme. The people are poor, the niggers are ragged & ill looking. To a casual observer they appear to be the staple production. . . .

If the rebels should make a vigorous stand at Richmond we will be verry apt to go there. The weather is getting quite hot, making it unpleasant marching in the middle of the day, but I stand it like a soldier, am tanned as brown as an Indian, can roll up in my blanket and sleep as well as anywhere in the world.

Only one thing troubles me, that is anxiety about my men. I find I must be brains and propelling power for them. I must be their father, see to their wants, comfort, health and order. The company officers are careless, their men more so. They would go hungry & ragged if I did not see to their conditions myself. I am up first in the morning, give orders then see to it myself that they are executed. I do get exceedingly tired & scold at them like fury making everything hum, but withal my men are obedient, kind, obliging and think I am a first rate good, kind, affectionate officer, which I try to be. I am trying to fill up the Regt so as to make it one of the largest in the Brigade & hope I shall succeed. I feel proud & want the best Regt if I can have it. I shall command the Regt while it remains in the service or there will be one Lt Col less in the service.

Did you get those pictures for me? I should like to see how you and our dear children look again. . . . The band is now playing. We have fine music daily. It helps a march verry much.

IN THE FIELD NEAR RECTORSVILLE, VA.—*May 29, 1862*

You will see by looking at the map that the 67th has not been stationary for the last two weeks. We left Woodstock Saturday night May 10th, since which time we have marched over two hundred miles in the hot sun over hard dusty roads.

I must confess that I have seen more of the hardships and trials of the soldier in the last 20 days than I ever saw before. I do really pity the poor soldiers at times. It is not always so bad with us, but somehow or other the Department has an idea that our Division can fight and march and endure hardships as if we were made of iron, while the Eastern troops are distributed over the country in fine camps with nice tents, and all the comforts near proximity to the seaboard or cities can afford. Our boys call these troops Band Box soldiers, and next to thrashing Jackson would like to see these bandbox fellows <u>licked</u> by the secesh.[22]

Now look at the map and see where I have been with my boys since the 10th Inst. Woodstock to Mt Jackson 12 miles, back to Strasburg 24, to

Middletown 5 miles, Front Royal 13 miles, to Warrington 38 miles, Catlett's Station 10, Fredericksburg 34 miles, back to Catlett's 34 miles, to Manassas Junction 12, this place 30 miles, besides getting off roads & back for camping grounds.

I would make a valuable soldier, but do not make a good officer. I cannot drive up the poor foot sore, lame and frequently sick soldier who falls back from necessity. I can scold, storm & drive a lazy fellow who will not do, but I have no heart to put the goad to good men who feel & act the man as long as they have the heart to do so. The battle field is not the only place where the heroic qualities of the soldier manifest themselves. The man who will day after day endure pain, fatigue & privations cheerfully, and encourage his fellows to do likewise by a happy example, is as much a hero as he who can face the enemy without fear on the battle field. This requires the constant exercise of perseverance and fortitude; the other is rather an impulse of the moment to be sure springing from a heroic nature, but does not require that patient constancy that the long weary march does.[23]

I bear up well under my labors, but get exceedingly tired. I rest horse & myself by walking and riding alternately, going half the time on foot. So far as physical labor is concerned I of course get change enough to rest me more than they do, but the care and anxiety I must give to matters is as much as I can well bear. Most of the time since the march commenced I have been the only field officer with the Regt. Maj Bond is absent sick. Capt Commager is acting as major in the absence of the Major. I am up first in the morning, see to matters all day & go to sleep at night with an anxious eye to what I must attend in the morning, liable to be called to attend to orders at any & every hour in the night.[24]

I have made up my mind that I am not going to manage the Regt much longer if the authorities do not speedily do justice to the 67th. We have been cursed and Dutch damned from the start till the 16th of March, and since that time the uncertainty that has attended our organization till now has embarrassed us greatly. For 2 1/2 months I have night and day, week day & Sunday without one hour's relief been charged with the responsibility of the command of this Regt. During this time the Regt has marched about four hundred miles, fought one savage battle, been in three skirmishes, and guarded 35 miles turnpike & telegraph lines, and garrisoned four towns, stood Regimentally on picket every fourth night for three times in succession in the face of the enemy, without shelter in the most inclement season of the year, laid out in the open night air night after night in storms of rain and snow with only our clothing & blankets, liable to attack & other dangers attending the occupation of the enemies country, and not the least been compelled to go ragged & march without good shoes.

Now if this is not enough to secure to the Regt permanent organization, and to me the place I am asked to fill I do not know what is. The authorities may soon fill it by a man ambitious more than myself. Col B is a scoundrel & is doing all in his malicious power to damage the Regt he cannot command. Just as soon as I can safely leave my Regt, I mean to see Gov Tod & say to him plainly this is injustice to the Regt and to myself. If the country needs the life & ease & comfort of good men it must know how to treat them. I ask nothing that is not strongly my due. Other Lt Cols who fought with me at Winchester have their commissions as Cols from other states. I mean that Ohio shall do her duty.[25]

We are going toward the Shenandoah Valley again. Where I do not know. We may fight soon but I do not think we will. You need not fear for me. I will be careful.

FRONT ROYAL, VA.—*May 31, 1862.*

We are again back to this place, having been on the march for two weeks and traveled some two hundred weary miles. I am verry well, but much worn out. I am really tired, not so much from the march . . . as the care and anxiety I have for my command. The march has been a terrible one. I really do pity some of the poor men especially, lame, foot sore, sick and wearied out. I have been compelled to yes drive them along with the column. No act of my life has been that as painful to me as the necessary exercise of force that I have been compelled to use to keep my men in their places. The man who goes into the army whether officer or soldier makes sacrifices that are not well appreciated till one has tried them.

The Division to which I am attached has been perhaps the most industrious and active as any in the service. Since the 5th of Feby we have marched about 500 miles, and done much other hard work. Many have fallen victims to this accursed rebellion, say 15 in battle, twice as many by disease and many partially disabled by wounds, in two or three cases entirely so in important members. Lantz you know lost his right arm at the shoulder. Young Beecher is failing in health & is not with us.[26] Left him at the hospital at Strasburg to take care of the sick where he and Lantz have gone since Gen Banks was compelled to evacuate Strasburg. The whole valley of the Shenandoah was taken by Jackson as soon as we left it, but we are back again & will make Old Stonewall see the difference between Yankee & Western soldiers. . . .

I had rather lead my men into battle than to undertake such a march as we have endured the last two weeks. I shall see you just as soon as I can. I mean now to lie down and sleep a while. I have no letters from you later than three weeks ago.[27]

HEAD QUARTERS OF THE 67TH OHIO VOLS IN THE FIELD
NEAR LURAY, VA.—*June 3, 1862*

. . . We have been marching, marching, marching till motion appears to be almost our normal state.[28] Since I wrote you last I have twice taken my men out for a fight & both times had the good fortune to lead the column. You know mine was the first infantry Regt on the field in the Winchester battle. I do like to be on hand when called on. I can start quicker with my men than the best of them.

We came here last night through a verry severe thunderstorm, and made our camp in a cedar woods, with abundance of mud underneath and water over head. I got my tent pitched and made my bed in the mud, having the benefit of a current of water through the tent & under my rubber blanket for the night. It rained hard in the night. I washed up in the mud, almost shoe deep. By the way the <u>mud</u> makes a softer bed than I have slept in sometimes, but tonight I have a better bed made than I have had for nearly a month. I dug a ditch round my tent, cut cedar boughs for a carpet and a sort of piling to keep my bed out the mud, then a layer of green wheat straw, & on top of the whole a bundle of dry straw, then my blanket. A glorious bed it makes. A good bed of straw is a great luxury to a soldier on the march. . . .

It is getting quite hot here. My flannel shirts & drawers are set pretty snug to the skin. I begin to want a change, as I sent my winter clothing home by Capt Spiegel. These long hot days on the march would make a linnen shirt feel comfortable <u>I reckon.</u> We are living rather plain just now. Hard bread, a little bacon, fresh beef, coffee and sugar. No butter, no milk, no saucer, no eggs. . . .

We have had rain, rain, rain for the last six days. We have marched in the night, in the hot sun and in the rains. Night before last we lay in the woods 4 or 5 hours with rain rattening down on the tired boys, not one but day out as to awaken if they slept at all wet to the skin. It is bad, but the boys are getting used to it. . . .

Just think of laying down on the wet ground with wet clothing on & wet blankets to lie in a rubber blanket, perhaps to hang up for a tent perhaps nothing but the boughs of a tree. Then do this for day after day after marching all day & you have an idea of the ineffable glories of the last few days soldiering. I do not feel like complaining at all on my own account for I can do better than most of them. I always carry my tent & carry clothing to keep me dry if it rains. I do not feel many of the inconveniences the soldier but I do pity them at times. . . .

I think this will not last long. This extraordinary marching must soon be over. The authorities are verry anxious to trap Gen Jackson. After driving Gen Banks across the Potomac he in turn has been whipped and driven back up the Shenandoah by Gen Banks. For two days we have heard brisk canonading a few miles from us, but have been so far from the work as to not to be able to get in. Jackson is in a bad box, and most likely will be taken by some of the army organizations now after him.

Not having seen the news lately we do not know what McClellan & Halleck[29] are doing, but think matters must be right. I see no prospect of a fight for us. The secesh cut stick as fast as we come anywhere near them. . . .

Thursday noon. We are still here in the midst of a terrible rain storm. Rained hard all last night, making our camp almost a river, most of the boys being compelled to take the water for it. They bear it was well, however, much better than I supposed. They sing as they wade about, saying "who would not be a soldier." Well, we have got so used to hard usages that trifles do not disturb us much. I wish you could see our camp just as now is. You would say it is horrible. . . .

We expect to go to Stanardsville from here, but there is no certainty the movements of soldiers. We may take the back track, but I hope not. As soon as this rain storm is over I hope for better weather.

HEAD QUARTERS 67TH REGIMENT O. V. IN THE FIELD
NEAR COLUMBIA BRIDGE—*June 7, 1862*

Time wears away rapidly, and along with its current we drift quickly into the uncertain events of the future. I sometimes almost wish I was granted with prescience, but when I reflect what desperate efforts I would make to avert what offered misfortune, disappointment and pain and what intolerable impatience I would feel to precipitate what promised pleasure, profit and success, I think it is well that we look into the future only by conjecture, that hope sufficiently lifts the veil that darkens the future for our present happiness. The future is an unexplored Ocean whose waters are best navigated by the hand of patient fortitude *by those who are* satisfied with doing what they can well do; and not disappointed at what cannot [be] known or accomplished.

I at time think I am a verry foolish man to let ambition to take part in public controll my actions. If I only would say so, I could content myself to return from the cares, vexations and disappointments of public affairs, and retire to a strictly domestic life and contently let the world slide. I know if I would only curb my restless disposition I might become a happy, contented unaspiring man, "passing rich with forty pounds a year," but then I won't, or I don't want to, so awfully bad that I won't. I grant it is all folly, but who don't at times deliberately make fools of themselves? Still this is a matter of taste rather than duty, and no one under Heaven has a right to question the full exercise of choice in the individual, which every path he may choose, whether it be of domesticity or restless energy to mix in the public affairs of the world. Having chosen his course, the man is unwise who is dissatisfied and unhappy at the natural and ordinary sequence of his choice.

Therefore if I should at my age in life come to the deliberate conclusion that I could be happier with my little family and insensible to the fierce conflict of the world for place, power, wealth and influence, I should contentedly ever after through life stick with my decision that I knew would not suit you, would not suit my children as they become older, and I now feel would not suit my precious self. As I now feel I do not think there is much danger of tyeing myself to such narrow limits. I do not like making a complete summersault with my aspirations. Therefore I am prepared to take things as I find them in my chosen pathway with fortitude, patience and all possible happiness.

I have never been the favorite of fortune, and whatever of success I gain must be acquired by dint of labor, pains, will and brains. This military life in many respects suits me finely. I think I would make a fair soldier if I had a fair opportunity. I have tried to do my duty well & hope when the war is over that I shall be able to review my brief military course with the satisfaction that I have no positive wrong, but on the contrary been of some substantial good to the service. I know that you and ours will ever take satisfaction in knowing that I have acted a manly part in this great struggle. Now wife have I not philosophised sufficiently to make you wish a change of subject. . . .

I am getting shoes for my barefooted men, have enough food for them for several days. The boys have been helping themselves. Beef, mutton, ham, bacon, bread, honey, onions, chickens, ducks, geese, turkeys, eggs, butter, bread, milk, sausages & etc & etc, have loyally contributed to their wants, without the formality of drawing rations. Our Western boys are shifty animals and well adapted to looking out for number one. I rather think the poor deluded secesh through the parts of the country where we have been will always remember the advent of the "Yankee soldiers" among them as the Egyptians do the flight of the Locust, or the prairie farmer do the army worm.

Trick, traffic, artifice and force already have cleared the whole country of food for both men and beasts. All the available horses are pressed into the service on one side or another. Farms are desolate. I turn my horses loose in a good meadow with 60 or 70 other horses for the night, and find them in the morning as sleek as silk. The fences are torn down to make shelter and fuel for the army. My own victuals and tent have consumed many rods of Old Virginia fence since I first set my foot on sacred soil. These Virginia chivalry are much tamer than our Buckeyes would be under like circumstances. . . .

HEAD QUARTERS, 67TH O. V. IN THE FIELD
NEAR LURAY, VA.—*June 12, 1862*

I am again permitted to write you after four days of excitement, excessive labors and alarms. Since I wrote you Gen Shields Division has been fearfully mangled. The 3 & 4th Brigades,[30] (I am in the 2nd) were on Monday last terribly cut to pieces. Col Buckley lost 2/3 of his Regt, Lt Col Clark among the number. Maj Clemmer was shot in the knee, quite a serious wound.[31] Several of our Akron boys were wounded, and many others taken prisoners.[32] Of course I am glad my Regiment was not in the fight for I look upon the sacrifice of the good men who fell in this battle as being butchered by the stupidity or wickedness of those authorities that conducted this movement.[33]

We have felt for weeks that we were being led into ruin. We have seriously doubted the sincerity of the Commander of the Division, and how terribly has this been realized.[34] I saw but little of the misery of the battle of

Winchester, being so hurt myself that I could not get about readily & never saw many of the killed and wounded. But here though not in the fight I *saw* enough of the unfortunate ones to make me feel heartily sick of war. Still I believe I could fight if called on with as much zeal as ever.

We were drawn up in a line of battle for several hours, expecting an overwhelming force of the enemy to fall on us. They flushed with victory; we dispirited by the sight of the panic stricken refugees from the ill fated battle field [of Port Republic]. I made a short speech to my boys, telling them we were in an awfully tight place, that we must face the music to the bitter end, the moment we turned our backs to the enemy that moment we were fated to destruction, that a bold determined unyielding front would successfully withstand any force that "Old Stone wall" Jackson could bring against us, that we had licked him once and could do it again. With us it is death or victory. You must win or go to total destruction. Will you stand by me till victory is ours? Those who are not prepared to do this may go back to camp. Those who have made their minds up to whip anyone stand by me and victory is ours. I could read in their eyes a flash of holy fighting fire that told me I could trust the boys. But no enemy came & we retired.[35]

We are now some 25 miles back from the place of battle. I tried to make the boys think that they could do anything, that I had the greatest confidence in them, that they could stand a terrific fight, but to tell the truth I did feel all the while as if we were in a rather bad scrape. Pride and a sense of duty would make me as cool and unmoved as a stone in the verry jaws of danger, even were I was disposed to feel timid.

In eight days three times I have taken my Regt out to fight. I talked as cheerfully and encouragingly to the boys as if I leading them out on a holliday excursion. The pain and anxiety I felt for them was covered up under a smiling face so that they could <u>neither see nor feel</u> anything of the thoughts *within* me. I dread a battle from its terrible consequences to my men, for whom I to a certain extent feel responsible. I do not think much of personal danger. I may get wounded. I may get killed, but the chances are so many in my favor that I do not feel much concern for myself. So far as my individual self is concerned, I feel about as little trouble as if I was following my profession at home.

We are so cut off from news that I do not know what is going on. I have not had a letter from you since May 11th; have seen only two newspapers later than May 24. We hear idle rumors about victories and defeats & etc, etc, but have no reliable information. I take it for granted you are all right at home. If not you would get word to me by telegraph or some other way. . . .

IN CAMP AT LURAY, VA. —*June 15, 1862*

A delightful summer day is this quiet Sunday, the sixth in succession my Regt has had to march. We have not yet taken upon the line of march for the day, this Regt being left behind for rear guard. The boys are now preparing dinner, so as to be able to work on the road with vigor. We have had three days rest, welcome indeed how these days of rest have been for us. My men have been almost tired out with the incessant march, nights, days & Sundays ever since the 2d Saturday in May. We have been in no actual fights, but have been called on four times for fighting, but have not had the fortune to get into action. We are going towards Front Royal, 25 miles from here, from thence probably to Warrenton Junction, Fredericksburg, or some other place in that vicinity.

I am desirous of recruiting for the Regt, want 275 men more to give me a complete maximum organization. I think I shall be able to make arrangements by which the men can be secured. If I am to have the command of the Regt I am ambitious of making it a first rate one, and to secure that I must have the men. I do not see much doubt as to my being keeping the command of the Regt as three months ago today. I took command of it and have continuously held the same during that length of time & every day I stay in command strengthens my claim to the rank as well as powers of a Col of a Regt.

I am sure my case is an anomaly in the history of the war. I have commanded a Regt through one of the fiercest battles with success and honorable mention by the commanding General, been through many skirmishes, have been ordered out several times for a fight always with promptness and address, led my Regt through one of the most toilsome and long continued marches of this war with success, sharing all the toils & privations of the same seeking to encourage my men by an example, met all the dangers incident to the enemies country with a murmur. Yet I have been permitted to struggle in this with the opposition and influence of an unscrupulous and irresponsible Col meeting me at every point by all the power a Col under arrest could wield to my disadvantage and to the disparagement of the Regt [through] falsehood & intrigue. The untiring influence of his friends in & out of the Regt, as well as the influence of the press they have imposed upon to gain their ends, all of which have been against me. Yet the authorities of my native State have stood by, and given me no sort of aid. I mean to have this matter settled at the earliest possible day. I shall assert my right, and firmly insist upon having it done to me. I have the promise of time to see to this matter as soon as we get to a place of rest.

During half of this time I have been the only field officer with the Regt, and for a whole month in fact ever since this painful march was commenced I have been the only field officer present in the Regt night, day and every day, and all times of the day have I been compelled to be on duty. Now I am not as deserving of consideration as some political aspirant with important friends to log roll for them who never smelt gun powder & never intended to? I shall submit to neglect with impatience, and till I am convinced [otherwise] I shall feel as I now do. If matters do not take a change during the ensuing month the Governor may reorganize the [command] of the 67th Regt as soon as he pleases, and with just such material as he pleases. But I know one thing. I shall not be among the favored ones of his patronage. I <u>have</u> done all that <u>duty</u> demands of me. I <u>have</u> at least contributed my full prorata share to my country. Since Sept 1st last year till now, I have done all I could. Now unless I can secure what is a matter of right to me, I shall come home.

Gen Hill has become Adjt Gen of Ohio, and as such will have his weight with Gov Tod in his military appointments.[36] He does not feel any of the most amiable to me. My letter to him was rather sharp to suit him. I may have to encounter his opposition which may be much in my way, but I shall make an effort that will indicate that I know my rights and how to vindicate them. If I do not have an opportunity to get home soon I shall write to my friends at Akron who I think will cheerfully do for me anything that is expedient to be done in the premises. Our great trouble, however, will be this trouble: They know so little about the machinery of military matters that they may not be as effective as if I could superintend the matter myself. . . .

Front Royal, June 18th. We came here yesterday morning, and are waiting to get supplies, such as boots, shoes, clothing & mean to be paid before we leave here. I shall send you say $350 which is all I can spare you of March & April's pay which we draw at this time. On the last day of this month the Government will owe me $396 more, $350 of which I can send you if I do not get home as I expect. With these sums you will be able to get along for the present. . . .

You say that friends call on you frequently inquiring kindly of me. You can say to them I appreciate their kindness, & hope they will continue to remember you and ours kindly for my sake, for if they knew the trials of a soldier in this enemies country cut off from all association and almost communication of home & friends, with danger to increase the solicitude, I know they would take pleasure in looking to the wants of their families at home & try to give them the good cheer of attention.

I pray God that this wicked war may soon close. I see by every issue of the local papers that the people everywhere are feeling the terrible consequences of the war. Disease, death and permanent disability are reaching many & many families. . . .

IN THE FIELD NEAR FRONT ROYAL—*June 19, 1862*

I feel quite relieved at realizing that I am not quite beyond the pale of civilization for since we left Fredericksburg a month ago we have been shut out from mail facilities, from news and newspapers till we got to this place day before yesterday. Here we get the daily papers the day they are printed, and occasional get mail. We knew nothing of the enlisting furor in the North till we came here this week, and to us it was not a little surprising as we cannot see the real utility in procuring three months men on account of our reverses in the Shenandoah Valley.

Without any pretension to more than ordinary forethought, I expected that the rebels would make substantial such demonstrations as they have made during the last month. The way from the South through Richmond & Lynchburgh has all the while been open to them. They have had tolerably accurate information of the Federal forces in Virginia and their movements, and with an eye on the vital importance of holding their Capitol how could they permit a junction of our forces without knowing that it must be fatal to them? Feeling this they thrown in a few thousand of their best troops under a verry able General into the valley to make a diversion from Richmond, and to make this effectual have attacked our forces in detail not with the view of taking and holding any given locality, but to harass, cripple and divert the troops designed for the work of taking their Capitol. In this way twenty thousand rebel troops have kept in check say sixty thousand Union men, the verry object sought. If our attentions were confined to the valley alone, I should say it was a disastrous move for the Confederates, but when viewed in relation to the great results of the war we are compelled to admit that they have well secured their object, delay.

Jackson has been driven back to his starting point, but in the [meantime] has won as many battles as he has lost, has taken say three thousand prisoners and destroyed millions of dollars worth of military stores for us, and made us march hundreds of miles, and protracted the siege upon Richmond to *an indefinite* period at least long enough to permit large reinforcements to come from the South to come to their aid, and cheered the South by a show of success & given them new hope, and as you know alarmed the North exceedingly. Yet in all this I can see no permanent results promising success to their wicked cause. When their efforts are viewed in the light of their various surroundings, they appear more like the spasmodic efforts of desperation than the well matured plans of a campaign intended to win and hold the fruits of the undertaking.

Were I a rebel commander under the same circumstances, I probably should have done as Jackson has done only a <u>good deal more so.</u> I told my fellow officers a <u>hundred</u> times that I would fight as Jackson is fighting if I were a rebel, not because I thought I would be doing a great deal, but because I could thereby probably prevent a vastly larger hostile army from accomplishing its designs and thereby gain time.

Our army is made up of as fine soldiers as the world ever saw, but I fear many of its commanders lack that sincere unselfish ability that ought to command the self sacrificing citizen soldier who has gone into this work inflamed by no higher ambition than duty and love of country & her preeminently liberal & benign institutions. The scramble for place in the army is fraught with as much unscrupulousness as it is in the field of politics, and frequently with vastly more terrible consequences. A reckless and ambitious man will risk everything to gain promotion, and in the hazard will throw the lives of thousands of his fellow citizens. Their health, comfort and personal safety are hardly thought of by him, and if thought of are too little consequence to interfere with his own advancement. The people at home know but little of the irresponsibility of many of those who command & hold the lives of their friends in their hands. If they knew more many an officer who has a fair share of fame would sink so low in public estimation as never to be heard of only as an object unworthy the place and responsibilities he holds.

I am interrupted right here to attend Deep Parade. That over I must visit the pay master & get my hard earned wages, only $398 for two months, but what must I think of the poor soldier who gets only $26 net for the same time? Many of their cases are hard, and daily am I compelled to do in regard to them contrary to my feelings. A poor corporal came to me tonight and wanted leave to go home to see a sick wife. He expects she will die. I had to say to him no, having positive orders to permit none to go home unless to save life or prevent his permanent disability. One came to me and says his wife is about to go under the trial of maternity, that he had a promise from the recruiting officer that at the time he could go home, his wife in almost extreme fear begs him by letter, with tears down his check he comes to me, begs to be permitted to go but a few days, & shows me his letter. This is repeated over & over again, but the service will not permit even in small cases the absence of the soldier & I must say no. You may judge whether it is not painful for me to do so. Yet duty to my place and frankness to my men compels me to say, no. War is a terrible calamity, and terribly will its authors be damned for its cruel results.

I see its effects are being felt in every neighborhood throughout the country. I do not take up a local paper but I read accounts of its ravages either by disease or battle. I have less than six hundred men with me of the 820 who left Ohio Jany 19th last. Fifty of these were wounded or killed in battle. Many have died from diseases contracted in the service, the ballance are home or in hospitals recuperating their healths. . . .

I only refer to these evils not in despondency, but because I expect reverses, and aggravated evils in the service, and a great deal of suffering and neglect, for I see in the main that our army is doing a great work. The Mississippi is open. Missouri, Kentucky, Tennessee and 1/2 of Va and N Carolina are controlled by us. Their armies have been compelled to fall back from place to place till they must be verry despondent.

Still I have changed my opinion as to the duration of the war. When it will end no one knows. If we gain a signal victory at Richmond it may be substantially through, but if they are permitted to withdraw as at Manassas, Yorktown & Corinth we will have plenty of fighting before the rebellion is crushed out so that we can say the Government is restored.

June 20. Nine years ago today I was admitted to the bar, a stroke I thought at the time, but after nine year's trial you may think I was no more fortunate that if I had taken some other business for a calling. I doubt not however but that you think it a much better profession for yourself and little ones than my present one. But if I come out of the war honorably and safely I certainly shall not loose [lose] anything by it. Soldering is becoming so much a matter of course that I take all its trials and vicissitudes <u>with my wanted patience.</u> . . .

This war has greatly interrupted my line of business, but I shall always feel that what I may have lost that way will have been made up by the sense of having discharged a great duty to my country, and will have a little satisfied pride to boot to throw in the scale, provided duty weights too lightly in the scale of benefits. I might not feel quite so well compensated if Uncle Samuel should take an arm or leg or make a bullet hole right plumb through my precious head or gizzard, but I am not now contracting for bullet holes. Still I may get one big enough to let daylight through me as big as a comet. . . .

EDWIN. I GOT YOUR LETTER. I WAS GLAD TO GET IT. YOU OUGHT TO GO TO SCHOOL. YOU WILL NEVER HAVE A BETTER TIME THAN NOW. I WILL COME HOME AS SOON AS I CAN GET AWAY. BE A GOOD BOY AND OBEY YOUR MAMA. I WANT YOU TO WRITE TO ME OFTEN.

"Terrible Realities of a Protracted & Savage War"

THE PENINSULA CAMPAIGN

JUNE 22, 1862 – DECEMBER 31, 1862

[On June 26, 1862, the 67th Ohio, along with three other regiments from the Second Brigade, First Division, Department of the Rappahannock, moved eastward from the Shenandoah Valley to link with the Army of the Potomac. The regiment arrived July 2, too late for the Seven Days' battles that had raged from June 25 to July 1, 1862. By then, McClellan had begun a withdrawal across the peninsula bounded by the York and James Rivers to a secure base at Harrison's Landing, about twenty miles south of Richmond.

During July and August, the 67th Ohio camped along the James River and at Yorktown even as the War Department recalled most of the Army of the Potomac, demoted McClellan, and transferred many of his troops to Maj. Gen. John Pope's Army of Virginia. In September, the regiment moved again, this time to Suffolk, Virginia. For the remainder of the year, the 67th spent hard, monotonous hours, interrupted by sporadic clashes with the enemy, constructing a strong defensive position. On December 31, the regiment received new orders to head farther south and toward a bloody fate that awaited them in the Sea Islands off Charleston and in the attack on Fort Wagner.]

IN CAMP NEAR WHITE PLAINS, VA. — *June 22, 1862*

. . . Today I have been marching through the dust over hill, in the valley & among the rocky passes of the Blue Ridge, away down Dixie, at the head of a loyal Regiment of volunteer soldiers, making way to the celebrated field at Manassas, which place I expect to see tomorrow. Beyond that I know nothing. I might say properly that I <u>know nothing military wise</u> only as it is practically developed. . . .[1]

We are in a beautiful section of the country, fertile, well cultivated, finely watered by mountain streams. The farms are larger with aristocratic mansions and tenements. The few own the country and almost the ballance of the population, but how they do hate the Yankees. Well they might. The boys trick, steal and destroy almost their entire personal estate. I may be home next week. I made application with some show of success.

Tuesday morning, June 24. Instead of reaching Manassas last night as expected, we are on Broad Run toward Catlett's Station. We are here because we cannot get over Broad Run. We had one of the hardest thunder storms yesterday afternoon I ever experienced. The boys had the benefit of so thorough a soaking as if they had been tumbled into the water all over. This Broad Run is near to Bull Run where the celebrated Bull Run fight was precipitated on Gen McDowell & his forces.[2]

If I wanted to fight a great battle I would never reject the plains of Manassas, the claimed inability to flank it not withstanding. We hear a great deal of humbug from the army, and from verry high authority too. The American people love to be humbugged, and this war has contributed more to this appetite than anything else ever presented our nation. We are good soldiers, but have rather crude ideas of military science which makes us the easy subjects of imposition, through a vicious and ignorant press full of the great idea of creating a sensation who find the war a rich vein in which to exercise their talent.[3]

We are within 6 or 8 miles of Manassas, and at every step see the devastating hand of war, large farms entirely turned to common, buildings destroyed, the people driven from their homes & everything indicating desolation. Little did the South think they were invoking such destruction when they precipitated war upon the country. Little do our people of the North know of the manifold ways the war is cursing the South. Poor Va. No state has been destroyed as she has. Army after army has passed over thousands of miles of her fair territory, blasting for the year everything in their reach. Banks, Shields & Fremont on our side, & Jackson on the rebels, have cleaned out the Va valley. All along the Potomac and Chesapeake the same has been done by other armies. Our boys are bent on making the war felt. The deprivations they endure make them unfeeling. They are becoming real soldiers & are making a real campaign, making war a reality.[4]

The campaign is becoming some what monotonous as we are passing over the same ground in some instances three & four times. Where we are going is uncertain, as the fate of war which is extremely uncertain with us as we have so many Generals who are not military men in any sense of the term, & who are of such doubtful loyalty that we must look for defeated plans. I am well.

IN CAMP NEAR MANASSAS JUNCTION—*June 26, 1862*

I sent out a letter to you this morning which was commenced as far back as Sunday last, since which time I have recd three letters from you, large fat ones. In one you say that you have recd forty letters from me since I left home. Well that certainly does not look as if I had forgotten you. I am glad they appear valuable enough to you to make you desire to preserve them. I of course have forgotten most of what I have written, but I presume they will give a totally full history of the operations of Gen Shields' Division in the Shenandoah valley.

We are now on the celebrated plains of Manassas & a short distance from the celebrated battle field where our troops so ingloriously fled from the rebels last July. My Adjt[5] rode over the field yesterday, & reports to me that it is an open country well adapted to military operations, that Bull Run is a little brook easily crossed, that the fortifications about the Junction could be easily flanked if desired. The press have endeavored to make the nature of the country aid the rebels here, but their lying has done vastly more *harm* than the condition of the country had on our grand Army on the Potomac.

I got a Beacon only one week old today, the first time I have had the news as early from home for a long time. I see the patriotic citizens of Summit Co intend to celebrate the 4th of July in a manner becoming the day. Well let them honor the good old day, have processions, speeches, fourth of July military displays, fire works for evening & all sorts of good displays to honor the day. But remember the more patriotic soldier who is celebrating the day really in arms & in earnest fighting for the liberties we celebrate on that day.[6]

I did hope to be at home on that day, but it is verry uncertain now. I have sent in an application for leave of absence on purely military reasons, but the liberty to go home has been so much abused that I may be disappointed. I do want to arrange some Regimental matters and <u>will</u> do it or <u>resign.</u> I am becoming rather independent & mean to be treated as others are or I shall modestly retire from the stage of military actors.

I presume we shall go to Richmond but of course do not know. We will move to Alexandria on the 28th. How long we shall stay there I do not know. We are to take the cars, the first lift for the men have had in all their toilsome marches since the 5th of March last. I do think, however, that the war is coming to an end. If we are successful at Richmond it will be the death blow to the rebellion, and we will assuredly succeed there.

June 27th. Captain Spiegel came here today bringing your pictures, a letter and the articles of clothing you sent with cigars & a suit of clothing from <u>Goldsmith,</u> with the exception of the boots you forgot to send me.[7] Matters are all right. . . .

Capt S is a warm friend of mine & a first rate man. He tells me that our home looks beautiful. . . . This is my pet's birthday. I have her before me. I would like to send her a present but I must forgo the pleasure. Why do you not get her a book and call it from her <u>papa.</u> . . .

I have been verry much out of patience today, done some tall swearing, but it bodes no good but still there is satisfaction in blowing the froth off when it will come up. Col Buckley has resigned. I saw him today.[8] Soldiers are not well treated in this Division. We still need clothing. I have men who are barefooted.[9]

STEAMER HERALD — *June 30, 1862*

I had all my plans laid for getting home yesterday. Was only four miles below Washington City and had leave to go over the river to see the Secy of War, but as I was going to the dock to take the boat I was ordered to embark my men at once on board of vessels for Fortress Monroe.[10]

I must go with the men you know. The bad whiskey of Alexandria had a terrible effect on them. What a task it is to command men liable to gross intoxication, especially so when they have been deprived of this beverage for months. My Regt was not as bad as many others, but was bad enough in all conscience.

Now I must give you some idea of the trials of the command of a Regt by me for the last two days. At Alexandria we were thrown into camp at 11 P.M. Saturday night. The cars had stopped at different points to give the men an opportunity to get whiskey. By daylight in the morning the suckers had their canteens filled and ready for a joyful day. To keep them in camp was impossible. About 4 P.M. I commenced moving my men to the boats, & some so drunk and ugly that I had to bind them hand & foot, gag their filthy mouths & by force load to get them quietly to places of embarkation. One old soaker swore he would not go. I rode up to him go and ordered him aboard. He drew his musket to knock me off my horse. I turned my horse to one side when he threatened to shoot me. I opened my holsters, and presented one of my apostles. I could not shoot the poor creature, as I certainly would have done had he been sober and as I would have been be justified in doing. The guard took his gun from him & loaded him in one of the baggage wagons. One poor Devil would not march. I tied him to the tail end of a wagon. He sprawled out on the ground & permitted himself to be dragged lengthwise on the ground for rods.

Then to get them on board safely required hours of hard labor. I stowed away six companies in a large barge made larger enough for the accommodation of 200 men.[11] Up came rain and pattered on those on deck where 2/3 of the men were placed & where they had to stay till morning, but by good fortune I lost no men in getting aboard. The 4th Ohio lost 3 men. . . .

Well I bear all this with my usual patience. I am a good deal better man to knock these fellows through than any subordinate I have in my Regt. If things do not move I take hold, and such a hold that the fellows know means something. I pulled a fellow up in rather an unceremonious heap last night with my own hands & repeated the dose on another this morning. I mean to see order preserved if I have to conquer for it, but these scenes rarely occur. I pass among my men as one of them enjoying their fun and jokes, endure their labors and hardships, build temporary bridges across little streams to keep their feet dry & save them all the labor I can.

They know this and appreciate it. When my men are sober I can do anything I desire with them. As an equivalent for this division of labor, they divide a chicken, pig, lamb or ham with me. If they purchase honey I get some, and on the whole I live as sort of young patriarch among them.

When my boys are not tired out and half starved I enjoy myself with them finely. I do not mean that they shall suffer from hunger in a land of plenty, & as a consequence have shut my eyes to many things resorted to by them to procure food that would be hardly justified in a law abiding community. . . .

Monday. We are out on the Potomac steaming down a beautiful river. Now opposite Ft Washington & in sight of Mt Vernon. Do not of course go near enough to the land to see as much of Washington's old home as I should like, but with the help of my field glasses can see the mansion & some of the negro quarters. One of the outside doors is open, so that I can say that I have seen in Washington's home. No Washington is there. Old Va has no Washington now. She has a glorious history, but is fast blotting out all its glories. The homes of the old patriots are now ruled by traitors.

Tuesday. After making a pleasant trip down the Potomac for I don't know how many miles, we came into the broad Chesapeake Bay shortly before night. The boys acted finely having abundance of room, [and] fortunately finding a steam boat which with our barge gave us abundance of room. Our sleeping places were the decks of the steamer & barge. About two hundred stayed on the barge when I went to sleep.

I had a poor short sleep. The bay became rough about midnight. I lay awake a long time & finally I got up to lighten the upper deck, fearing the barge might capsize. By some unaccountable accident, the rope broke that towed it. The rudder was crushed to atoms, and we were tossed over the angry waves at the mercy of the wind. Hardly had my men begun to come from the upper deck before the timber supporting it began to creak & give way. The steamer was still away to the front, many thinking it had left us. A few plunges, and the deck gave way pitching to the right and front. Such a scene as followed, screaming, praying & scrambling to get from the broken deck. I crawled out through a hole I made in the side of the deck. I tried to calm the fears of the boys, took a lantern and signaled for the steamer. Guns, equipment, baggage, and horses & I fear some men were precipitated into the bay. (Fanny has gone to revel with <u>old sea horse</u> & act as palfrey for the mermaids). She was a fine animal, kind, gay and an excellent saddle horse, was the finest in the Regt. Well may she have a fine time in the princely stables of Old Neptune. Say nothing to Eddie about it, as I will get him another horse when I get home to stay.

Away we foundered for 1 1/2 hours before we could make fast to the steamer. To many it was a terrible time. Death threatened us with verry strongly, and many in anguish shuddered at the thought of sinking into the deep ocean. I had too much real responsibility on my hands to be much troubled about myself. I gave commands with as much firmness as ever, scolded some, encouraged others, shamed a few & threatened to throw one poor devil over board who constantly kept interrupting me by bellowing in my ears in such fear that my commands could not be heard. I told them I was Col, and no poor rotten tub like this one should cheat me out of my office.

Several ineffectual efforts were made before the line from the steamer could be fastened. At one time we drifted off & quite a ways. The timid ones began to howl again, cursing the captain for abandoning them. It was so dark that I could not ascertain the extent of our injury nor the real danger we were in, still I knew it was bad enough. Fortunately we became attached to the steamer, & such a scramble to get on board I never saw. One poor man jumped overboard in his anxiety to get off the barge before the steamer got near enough to reach by a jump. It was really dangerous work to get off as the barge plunged terribly. I stood on the highest part of the broken deck, and gave orders encouraging the men to be steady, careful & calm as they tumbled into the steamer, & to give them to understand that I feared no danger. I did not move till all were safely landed. I then broke for the steamer, just in time to make her. I got quite a bruise on my thigh in the operation.

My lantern went out while we were trying to fasten to the steamer which made matters worse. As soon as all were off we let the old tub drift, I saving my pants, vest, shirt, shoes & the contents of my pocket all told. After landing my men we went for the barge, where I found two men & my trunk, bedding, saddle, glass and side arms, only losing my army legs, but I can go on foot a few days till I can capture a horse. . . .[12]

Wednesday. It is raining today. We are up the James some ways. July 5th. Am near Richmond. Had a skirmish before daylight yesterday morning, had 8 men killed & wounded. Am well. Will keep you advised as well as I can. Do not worry about me. I am bound to win. I would write more but have no papers nor envelops.

HEAD QUARTERS 67TH REG O. V. IN THE FIELD
BELOW CITY POINT, VA.—*July 7, 1862*

. . . The trip and its stirring events you already have. I discover however that the papers are verry cautious not to say anything about the reckless cruelty of Uncle Samuel in putting his faithful soldiers on board of rotten unseaworthy tubs, in which merchant men would not risk their pork for a voyage down the bay. If I was where I could make this thing public I would make such acts of official barbarity ring in the ears of the Department till an indignant public sentiment would correct the evils or crush out of power such faithless servants.

I see so much of incompetency & recklessness in the administration of army affairs that I begin to despair of any good growing out of the war. If individuals managed their private affairs as the public is doing, bankruptcy & ruin would inevitably and speedily follow. There appears to be an utter want of system, leaving matters to the capricious developments of time, making luck instead to engineer to conduct the war to a speedy and successful close. The army is entirely too large, is so unwieldy that it is managed with immense loss of force, & great suffering must necessarily exist because of the present inability to remedy the evil. We have not learned to manage the affairs of an army of such great proportions. No one knows what will be done when the 300,000 additional troops are put into the field now called for by the President.[13] This wicked war will be full enough of woes and horrors before it ends to convince this generation that they had better pursue the paths of peace.

The management of the army is verry much like the chaotic management of our early railroad enterprises, only the army has vastly more of uncertainty & irresponsibility in it & but little of that searching supervision over subordinates exercised in private undertakings. The papers give a verry imperfect idea of the war. Much of the published matter is utterly untruthful, more near fiction, being the visionary dreams of paid letter writers, and with the semi official telegraphic war news is the fulsome praise of retained Boswells who only write high falutin panegyrics for the hand that fosters them. An inevitable defeat is made a masterly strategic movement. A scandalous rout is reported as a change of position & in good order to accomplish some preconcerted plan of the Gen commanding. Victories are highly puffed. Defeats are so rarely sustained that little romance is wasted on them. If you only knew of the immense amount of ingenuity exerted to make victories on paper you would almost forget the poor efforts of the soldier who suffers & labors to accomplish substantial good to his country. . . .

By this time you have learned about our position as well as I can tell you. We will not have a fight here. Our gun boats are a perfect terror to the secesh, & our flanks & rear are protected by them. Since we came here last Wednesday night and lay down in the wet & muddy woods we have been constantly on duty day & night, and only a verry short distance from the enemy, so close that we can hear their drums beat and bugle calls through the thick pine woods. Lt Girty with his [company] shot three rebel calvary men Friday last as they were on picket.[14] The secesh came so close to our camp at night that our boys could frequently see them almost within gun shot range.

We have been on the extreme left & furthest advanced towards the enemy, have kept our guns stacked in line and the men just behind them all the while, & have had the bad fortune to be called to arms every night till last night since we came here. This constant watchfulness at night and hard labor during the day is verry wearing.

On the morning of the 4th we were attacked just before day by a squad of the enemy. Our men sprang to arms in an instant, and fired at random in the dark & woods. We had 2 men killed & 6 wounded. That makes a loss of 15 men during the week of the 4th by march & battle. I expect such disasters as matters are arranged, but either never ought to occur. The wreck was a crime chargeable to the Q. M. The night attack the result of criminal negligence. I was sent to the advance after night & told when to & what to do, & had every reason to suppose picketing had been properly done. <u>Was so told.</u> On riding to the picket post in the morning, [I] found our front entirely exposed to the enemy, a Brigade having been withdrawn just at dark & taking with them their pickets. You may begin to think I am not well pleased with this way of doing business. I am well & prospects look more like having a little rest than for the last two months. I will answer Eddie in my next. I have not purchased a new horse yet, but have an old mare to ride. I may not get another now.

IN THE FIELD NEAR HARRISON'S LANDING, VA.—*July 13, 1862*

We are rather pleasantly encamped on the N. E. bank of the James River some twenty five miles below Richmond. The camp has been verry strongly fortified since we came here making it almost impregnable. As long as we stay here we have but little to fear from the rebels. During the last week we have had no molestation from them. They have probably gone back to Richmond, not wishing to risk a fight with us in our present position. They have a mortal fear dread of our gun boats, which in large numbers guard the river and command most points of approach to our camp.[15]

This is the first quiet Sunday we have had for two whole months. It is really gratifying to have a quiet day in which to rest, and feel free from care, labor and dangers. We have done an immense amount of hard labor during the last two months, and terribly has it left its mark on the men of my command. On the 12th of May I left Strasburg with 601 men, 18 of whom were reported sick, one half of whom could march with the Regt relieved of their arms & accoutrements. Today I have only 504 men with the Regt, of whom 95 are sick, that is as sick as the 18 were at Strasburg. The march, change of water, sparseness of wholesome food, want of shoes and dangers, connected together with the excitement caused by alarms have made this extraordinary infirmity list. Where we now are. . . we can rest. Our men will mostly recover soon.

I do not expect an immediate forward movement, and when we do move it will be by gradual approaches. Our defeat before Richmond is a disastrous defeat. The world will look upon the fact that we were compelled to raise the siege before Richmond, and our hasty retreat under the cover of our gun boats to this point, however vigorously our army fought, as evidence of a bad defeat.[16]

I have felt despondent ever since Gen Halleck permitted Gen Beauregard's army to slip from his power.[17] The reactionary movement in the Shenandoah gave me no comfort. The distribution of our Virginia forces and the concentration of the rebel forces at Richmond have resulted in just what ought to have been reasonably expected out of the usual course of human events. A vigorous and skillful management of Gen Halleck's forces at Corinth, and at the same time a like effort by Gen McClellan with the combined forces that should have been concentrated about Richmond would have seen the war substantially ended by this time, our united national existence assured and our military fame commanding the admiration of the world. But instead of this, the chances & terrible realities of a protracted & savage war are thickening around us. Doubts serious and mostly of grave considerations will be raised by European governments whether the rebels have not the resources & qualities requisite to maintain a separate national existence. Their recognition is now highly probable.[18]

I think that time will give Richmond to our arms, but it takes a long time to make up for such terrible losses as our army has sustained here, and to recover from the moral effect of permitting a great & all important advantage pass without securing any of its results to us. Were it not for our navy, we could have verry little to boast of over the rebels in this war.

I am writing in sight of the place where William Harrison was born.[19] Am really in Old Virginia. The soil is rich, but much more sparsely populated than I had heretofore supposed. The estates are large, some of the largest plantation in Va are on this river and in this part of the state. The Harrison estate is still owned by some of the family, all of whom are intensely secesh & on the advent of our army fled for Richmond.

We encamped for a few hours in a newly harvested wheat field directly in front of the mansion home of the Harrisons. The boys made beds of the bundles, cattle & horse ate the grain and in a few hours a splendid grain field had gone to destruction. This is the fate of every place occupied by an army, even if only for a short time. Our men are becoming regardless of anything belonging to the enemy. We are in effect adopting the doctrine that the secesh have no right that white men are bound to respect. This goes so far as rebel property is concerned. I fear for the moral and social degradation of the army. View it as we may, the service has the tendency to make men reckless, hardened, unrefined. . . .

You may think me away from the world, but it is not so. We are nearer civilization than when in the valley. We get our mail from Ohio in 3 & 4 days, get the papers from N. Y., Phila, Baltimore & Washington the day after they are printed. Being on the river it makes it verry easy to get in and out of camp, provided you have the right. Officers and men are however for the present not permitted to go away for anything save to preserve life or permanent disability, so you see that I am not in a verry flattering situation to expect a leave of absence for a trip to Ohio. I must write a short letter to Eddie, perhaps a verry little in for my pet. . . .

IN THE FIELD NEAR HARRISON'S LANDING, VA.—*July 20, 1862*

. . . This hot weather and the great change of climate has made me rather thin in flesh, but otherwise I am as blooming as ever. I was verry much used up after I had been here four or five days. Had quite a diarrhea, but I am quite well now. . . . For two weeks we have been trying to rest, and are reaping benefit from it. My sick list is large, entirely too large. Yesterday's report showed 10 Officers and 126 enlisted men on the sick list. Verry few of them will die, but still it makes a great deal of suffering in the aggregate.

This being sick out of doors is not half as bad as many suppose. . . . What once appeared verry hard to be bourn now appears trifling. Still I would not underrate the trials and sufferings of the soldiers. When I left Woodstock May 10th I had 625 men & officers. Now I have 563. Only 16 of them have been among the killed or wounded. All the others have failed in health or ability to stand the hardships of our tedious marches.[20]

Were I the Secretary of War I would have concentrated my forces at a few points and at once fought the enemy. I would have crushed them wherever I found them in arms, but would have occupied but verry little territory. I would do the work up as speedily as possible. I don't think I would let a whole army be wasted away by disease, consequent upon prolonged exposure and long continued & fruitless labor. I would organize a fighting army and move it according to the ideas of the age. I would not forget that this is an age of iron and steam. The old antediluvian way of plodding along won't do. Nor will the policy of distributing the army all over the country do. I would concentrated on the enemy, and drive him back and punish him whenever opportunity offered.[21]

I cannot say when I shall get home. I would not think of it now were it not to arrange matters for my Regiment, but I am determined to get these matters settled or get out of the service as soon as I can do so honorably. I had a pleasant visit with Judge Key, late of the Ohio Senate, this morning. He is now Judge advocate general on Gen McClellan's Staff & ranks as Col. You must recollect him. He is one of Ohio's able, honest and good men. Ever since I first met him I have liked the man. He is a Democrat, but what of that. He does as he pleases & thinks for himself. . . .[22]

HARRISON'S LANDING, VA.—*July 23, 1862*

I have a few minutes before going out to visit the picket lines to give instructions to the new Officer of the Day. . . . I see you have addressed a note to <u>Gov. Tod</u>.[23] Your letter was well written but more amiable than I should have written, were I a poor soldier's widow with two babies to care for, and a neglected husband off to the wars bearing all the dangers of the camp and the horrors of transit from different points. After all I tell fellow officers that I am quite as patriotic as any of them, that for over a third of a year have I commanded a Regt as Lt Col while the incumbent has been drawing the pay of my place & one he was never fitted to fill, & had the ease of hotel life.[24]

The air is pleasant, being quite cool for this time of the year. I have just returned from the outposts, and would have had a pleasant ride if I felt real well, but riding all day yesterday fatigued me a great deal, as I am not as well as I should be from diarrhea, a disease that has quite pervaded the whole Regiment. It has killed no one and probably will not, but has disabled for the time being a great many of my men.[25]

The country is really beautiful along this river, and fine farms are made of it, but the owners are not making much out their estates this year in the vicinity of the army. I saw large grain fields of hundreds of acres in extent partially harvested left in that state to go to waste, houses abandoned by their owners, not even leaving their negroes to look after affairs. Speculating in the colored population has become a verry poor business in this region. Poor Virginia has suffered terribly from the war. It will take years of prosperity to put Virginia in anything like her former position. The war on her part was so careless that her sensible inhabitants must bitterly repent their folly.

It is a foolish war for us as well as them. How we are suffering from its terrible consequences. Our armies are being consumed, an enormous national debt created and daily augmenting. Society is becoming poisoned by the influence of war instead of developing the elements of national strength by the production of such results as strengthen society, make men happy and promote the elements of an enlightened civilization. All our resources are directed to the production of engines of destruction. Men are taught to exercise their fierce and barbarous qualities, to ignore the charms of home & society, and glory in the dissolute charms of camp life.

When I think that we are taxing all the scientific preeminence of this age to its utmost to injure & destroy the lives and resources of our fellow creatures, & of my participancy in this hellish work, I really shudder. What may man not be led to do? I hate war. I abhor its terrible cruelties. I commiserate with the fate of the poor soldier who is compelled to wear out his physical frame and crush out his manly nature to become the cruel machine in the hands of his commander. Still there is a fascination about the army that drowns all these considerations, that apologizes for murder, wholesale & remorseless, and justifies wrongs and cruelties that shock the human heart.

I have written this by piece meal. It is now the 24th in the afternoon. I have just closed a verry long letter to Gov. Tod which will make him think some if he does not act much. We are again regaled by the refreshing intelligence that Col B is coming back to the Regt to take command, but this is so often repeated that I begin to think it all bosh. I feel quite well today.

BELLAIRE, OHIO—*July 27, 1862*

You may expect me home sometime this week. I am staying here tonight. Will leave in the morning for Columbus. Will get home as soon as I get my business accomplished [with the governor], and will stay for a few days say till 10th or 12th of Aug.

I may go to Toledo before I get round. I am quite well <u>considering,</u> and much better than I was ten days ago. Had a sort of camp disentery that prevailed with us as an epidemic. I may be at home as early as Wednesday night & may not till Friday or Saturday. It will depend on business. I am bound to have my Regt fixed up before I go back.[26]

IN THE FIELD JAMES RIVER—*Aug 14, 1862*

I arrived safely at camp after a fatiguing and almost constant ride to this place on Monday evening. I found matters all <u>well</u> at Columbus, but could not get rank back at of the time of Col B's dismissal, the 29th of July. I was in hope we might rank from the 23rd of Mch last. Gov. Tod said we were equitably entitled to it from that date, but as no vacancy occurred till the 29th of July *he could not make two Cols for the same Regiment both holding rank at the same time.*

I found matters [here] as favorably as I could expect. Capt Spiegel had been in command of the Regt from the time I left till my return, Maj Bond and Capt Commager both being sick. Camp was broken up & my men except the sick were out on picket some four miles beyond our camp. No accident has happened to them since I left, yet most of the time they have been out to the front expecting at all times to have a brush with the secesh, but this is not verry likely to happen here. . . .

I am verry well now, but find soldiers fare not so palatable as I thought before I have been at home. I begin to think <u>civilized</u> life quite as good as this hard soldier's fare. I hope you will not feel troubled about me now. . . .[27]

IN CAMP NEAR YORKTOWN, VA.—*Aug 23, 1862*

. . . You write of my visit as being a dream. Well it was, but who would not dream of friends and their sweet communion? Who would not relish the bliss of such dreaming? I am free to admit that my visit was not as pleasant to me as I should have liked. My time was so taken up with business that I did not get rested, and had hardly time to realize that I was really at home. I did not intend it for a pleasure trip. My errand was <u>business</u> and I had the satisfaction of accomplishing what I went to Ohio for.[28] Col B's friends were much disappointed when they learned that he had been dismissed from the service. . . .[29]

Where we shall go I do not know, but I think my declaration to you that we were to go to the Potomac will be true before long. I am not apprized of the plan of operations, but I do hope it will be much more vigorous than the movements of this Department. The war should have been closed before this, but as matters now indicate we will have another bloody year. I am not in a writing mood today. You will please excuse this poor effort, and write me a good long letter in return for this.

IN CAMP NEAR FORTRESS MONROE—*August 29, 1862*

We are under orders to move to Suffolk, but may not get off till tomorrow. We have been pleasantly located here. Had but little to do, and secured for ourselves a fine rest. All of us are feeling quite well. Suffolk is said to be a fine place, and will afford us many advantages we have been unable to have while on the march.[30]

Since we left Harrison's Landing we *passed through* Williamsburgh where McClellan had a hard battle in May last, and through Yorktown, a place of historic celebrity. The battle at Yorktown between Cornwallace & Washington was decisive of vast results, though the troops engaged in point of numbers would be utterly insignificant if compared with the army that we now have in the field. We had about as many troops on our side at the battle of Winchester as both sides in the revolutionary battle at Yorktown.[31]

I have been over the bay to Hampton. . . . The town of Hampton was before the war as large as Cuyahoga Falls & quite an aristocratic place. Had three churches, contained the summer home of ex President John Tyler, but now all lays in ruins. The rebels *under Magruder* burned the entire town, the churches included at the approach of the Union Army.[32]

Fortress Monroe is 2 miles from this place and is a delightful summer retreat. The sea breezes modify the heat of summer & cold of winter. The fig, orange & pomegranate grow here. Here are the great "Union and Lincoln guns," each weighing 25 tons or 50,000 lbs, and carry a ball weighing five hundred lbs.

Just here the mail came in and I had the good fortune to get two precious letters from my dear wife. Nothing pleases me more than to get those tokens of your affection and remembrance. These kind remembrances of friends at home, and especially when the tie of family exists does more to cheer the soldier than all the glory and promotion in rank can possibly do. . . .

I have felt more homesick since I got back to my Regiment than I ever felt before. It has a bad effect on a solider to bask under his own vine and fig for a few days and then be send back to the field again. . . .

IN CAMP NEAR SUFFOLK, VA.—*Sept 1, 1862*

. . . When I think of the enlisting furor at home and the terrible realizations of the draft I am glad I am in the service with my status fixed.[33] I know that you will much console yourself with the reflection that if your husband must be in the service, it is much better for him to have a highly honorable and responsible position where he can discharge his duty to his country in a way creditable to himself & honorable to his family, than to stand the chances of the public demands at home. As I go further and further from the time of our separation, I become more and more satisfied with my lot and am again becoming quite reconciled at being in the field. . . .

Tuesday Evening, Sept 2, 1862. Since I commenced this letter terrible news has come from the army about Washington. Disasters, victories, defeats & advantages have been so weighed with the fortunes of both parties that we are tortured with the uncertainties of the momentous events already developed in that locality.[34]

I almost wish I was away from this quiet place with my command and taking a part in that terrible struggle. As much as I hate the awful scenes of the battle field I cannot read the accounts of those conflicts without wishing I was with those honored with the distinction & dangers of fighting that desperate & mighty army arrayed against our capitol. I see the names of quite a number of acquaintances who have been sufferers in the last days fighting. Gen Schenck

(Bob Schenck) lost an arm.[35] What gives the matter more interest to me is the fact that I have been over most of the ground twice in arms . . . & most of the places mentioned in the accounts of the various maneuvers of the respective armies. You of course look at the affair in quite a different light than I do, as you rejoice to think I was spared the pains & hazards of the Potomac Army. Women are affectionate, men ambitious. Wives are timid for their husbands. Husbands are heroic for the honor they would confer on their wives. . . .

If we are successful at Washington the place we now occupy will hardly be the place of much account, but should we be defeated there we may have the felicity of taking the back track. I can now see where we lost many an opportunity that might have closed the war ere this, but may now be to us the fatal blunders that will give us final defeat instead of merited and then attainable success. . . .

SUFFOLK STATION, VA. — *Sept 13, 1862*

I had the good fortune to get your letter mailed last Wednesday. I might have written before this but I thought I must wait and answer your next, which I now proceed to do.

First I will write an item of business. I purchased a horse of Lt Col John D. M. McGregor 4th N.Y. Vol, and drew on [the bank] for one hundred and fifty dollars, thirty days from date (8 Sept). . . . I wish you to deposit [that amount] before the 8th of Oct to pay the draft. . . . I have $550 due me from the Government besides my present month's pay. That includes the value of Fanny, $150, which I hope to get. . . .

Gen Ferry, one of his aides & myself took a long ride to the outposts this forenoon, & coming in he proposed to me if I wanted to test the speed of the nags.[36] This was not displeasing to me, as I wanted to try the mettle of mine. So off we dashed for a half mile, side by side for a few rods, then I cut out for the lead which I soon took & shortly was away a head gaining rods in the race. . . He will make a fine family horse, gay, hardy, strong, gentle, and intelligent. I call him "Rob Roy" (McGregor).

I almost got an order that would send me home for a few days to look after the draft, but my services here were considered so valuable that it was finally thought best to keep me here. Well I do not feel at all disappointed as a flying visit to Ohio would do me nor you any good. I have not got over my trip yet. Had the jaundice till I was as yellow as saffron. By the way jaundice appears to be a prevailing disease here. You know we are near the Dismal Swamp, 1 1/2 miles off only. . . .

SUFFOLK, VA. — *Sept 20, 1862*

. . . During the last week I have been on the alert all the time. Gen Ferry was led to think in the early part of the week that the enemy intended to attack this place in force, say with a Brigade of cavalry, 8 Regts of infantry & 4 Batteries of artillery. We had an inadequate force to successfully resist so large an advance.

We made the best disposition we could make for the time being till reinforcement could be brought to our aid. We had ten field guns, a Brigade & one additional Regt brought up since the alarm was made, and now having sufficient force to feel secure we learn that the enemy existed rather in imagination than in reality. Gen Ferry is extremely cautious, does not wish to risk [battle] unless he sees his way clear, [and] many of his field officers are [away] from duty. I was senior officer next to the Gen until day before yesterday, and in case of the disability of Gen F would have been compelled to have assumed command here. For a while I did not relish the idea of making a fight with the rebels with our force & I at their head, but by the eternal I should have fought them with a determination & vigor that would make them earn all they gained by the <u>hardest.</u>

As matters now are we will have no fighting here. I am sorry we were not on the Potomac. The rebels have been getting awfully punished there lately. It has cost us many valuable life, but if it is followed up with vigor it will do a great deal to bring the war to a close.[37]

The invasion of the North is a suicidal policy for the South. If time was of any object to them, Richmond was the place to gain it. It would have been a long time before our armies could have invested it, but they have precipitated matters, and in all probability have by this time lost all they gained during the last three months, and have lost a larger amount of their supplies and military store before they get back to a place of comparative safety. Their army is daily becoming weaker, ours is constantly becoming stronger. The time of year is at hand when we can't work with comfort. The failure of the rebels to make a successful invasion of the North, their utter inability to cross with any force into a free state, will be a disastrous disappointment to the hopes of their soldiery. They have been encouraged with the idea of gain & plunder from the rich Northern cities. Their cupidity has given them a great stimulus of extraordinary action. This impulse being taken away they will be thrown back upon the simple desire to whip the Yankees, and much of their confidence in their ability to do that job will be dissipated by the time they are driven back to Richmond by the cowardly Yankees. Gen Mansfield who had command of this post when we came here is reported killed.[38]

The Ohio Regts had some hard fighting to do, but as we do not get Western papers I cannot tell much about the part they took in the battle. The 87th O. V. was taken at Harper's Ferry.[39] They were 3 month's men, & their time was nearly out. It is not much a matter now to be taken prisoner, as they are paroled speedily. Still I have no wish for that sort of adventure. . . .

We are comfortably situated here, but that signifies nothing so long as we are apparently doing nothing to bring the war to a close. We are in the Dismal Swamp country. I have been into the swamp as it is called several times. It breeds a dismal influence over white folks, niggers, mules, horses and other people. I frequently see a poor dilapidated mule hitched by a harness that never cost over 20 cents to a more dilapidated cart with two or three women coming to town. It is not at all unusual to see one ox harnessed in the same way to a cart with a dilapidated wench for driver. Poor cows are put to the same despicable work. Poor white folks, niggers, horned cattle & worn out horses occupy the same glorious level. They must be happy, as they have nothing to lose but their poor lives, and they are worthless as they have nothing to live for. Southern society does verry well for the aristocracy, but nobody else.[40] It is raining. I am well.

SUFFOLK, VA.—*Sept 28, 1862*

I am weary from long and hard exertions. I think of home and its comforts & them of this abominable way of living, and really wish this damnable war with its long train of immeasurable woes was over. I do wish I could sit by your side this quiet Sabbath evening with our children about us at our home, safe from dangers and free from the cares & trials of a military command. . . .

I have kept two horses busy for the last ten days, and kept from 400 to 1,000 men at work slashing timber, digging trenches and laying in wait for the enemy. I have no sort of idea that the enemy intend to attack us here. Our situation is becoming one of great strength, which means the enemy would not have permitted us to fortify had they the intention or means of driving us out.

. . . I have been writing this since Sunday. It is Tuesday morning now before breakfast. I had thought I would not write till I answered your letter, but none has come for the last 10 or 12 days. . . . My boys look for the coming of the mail with vastly more interest than they do the advent into camp of the secesh. If they do not get frequent letters from home & friends, they feel neglected, and to some extent they justly feel so. The mail is the only sure way of transmitting little evidences of kind recollection from friends at home to those whose hard lives in the field have separated them so widely from almost every thing that makes society and home the center of so many attachments.

Wednesday morning. It is as hot as summer here. I can see no appreciable difference between this month than of August, unless it be that the nights are a little cooler. The band are just going by my window. Have been out for an hour. We get up at 5 1/2 A.M., and stand in arms half an hour, then get our breakfast, then go out to our trenches and work the rest of the day. The cavalry have been out for their 1/2 hour, and are just going back to their camp which is just in the rear of mine. This is the only *cornet* band we have at this post.

We have been working so hard that I got my boys a few gills of whiskey Sunday & have been giving it out to them by 1/2 Gill doses when they get verry tired. It makes them feel <u>mighty good.</u> Of course they do not get enough to make any one tight. I wish I could get it for them oftener. . . .

I am tolerably well. Have been having a diarrhea for several days. The water here is abominable. Poor whiskey does not spoil it a bit. My commission as Lt Col is of the date of one year ago tomorrow, so that I have been in the service one year when this day is gone. In that time I have seen a good deal of soldiering. I shall send this & not wait to answer your letter, but I shall not promise to do so again.[41]

SUFFOLK, VA.—*Oct 7, 1862*

I recd letters from you Sunday evening and tonight which makes me indebted to you one letter. The mails were delayed at some intermediate point for a fortnight. When they did come we had a great bag full. As I tossed the same up to the sight of the boys as they were forming lines for Deep Parade, their hearty cheers went up at the appearance that their friends at home had not entirely forgotten them. . . .

SUFFOLK, VA.—*Oct 12, 1862*

. . . We are having a verry disagreeable fall storm. Has rained hard for the last 31 hours, cold as the equinoctial in your latitude. I almost dread the cold & storms of winter. Last winter while I was out and taking the rough of camp life I was not in much trouble about the weather, but the cold storms are commencing. I dislike to think what it may bear. I am occupying a large building erected for a country fair building about the same class of our agricultural buildings. It is no where as good as my barn. I have an upper story with a veranda in front and rear, a first rate place for summer quarters, but rather hard for winter quarters even in this latitude. You may consider me stabled out for the present. I have my usual allowance of straw and coarse blanket. . . .

My boys all pray for the war to end. I am well satisfied that could the soldiers vote there would verry soon be an end to the war. Had the people known of the horrors of war before the war began I am wont to think we would now be living in peace, but this generation had grown up in profound peace. They had not the remotest idea of the terrible realities of war, and they almost thought it was an entertaining experiment that would give our country character and enterprise without much cost, but how has the history of the last 18 months demonstrated the error. The North then thought 75,000 men for 3 months could put down the rebellion, & since that time more than a 1/2 million of men have been in arms & have had their hands full to hold their own. Matters look more encouragingly now, but still McClellan's grand army that was going to wipe out the rebels is still waiting for something to turn up. God only knows what. The ground where our little army whipped Jackson on the 23rd of Mch last is now occupied by him so strongly that we do not attack him now. If we had a Western army in Va, I believe matters would be better. Western men fight better than Eastern men. When they fight they mean something. . . .

Oct 13. This letter was commenced Oct 12 in a most disagreeable rain storm, and will be closed in the same intensified. For two days we have had a terrible storm for outdoor men. . . .[42]

SUFFOLK, VA.—*Oct 20, 1862*

. . . When I shall get any more money the Lord only knows. Uncle Samuel will owe me over $800 at the end of this month for salary, if I am not <u>taxed</u> to death, besides $150 for Fanny. I hope the pay master will be here soon, but I may not see any more money for months to come. I expect to get pay for Fanny, but I find as many crooks & turns and technicalities *in the Department* as in the labyrinth of the law. By the way the Government can never compensate for the many pecuniary losses sustained by the people, to say nothing of the shattered constitutions, wounds & maimed unfortunates. And then think of the woes and horrors of the field and the sorrows of the friends at home. What a horrible cause is war. . . .

We have been at this place longer than at any other time since the Regiment came into service. Our long line of tents begin to appear quite like home. Speaking of home reminds me that several officers have their wives here, Gen Ferry among the number. This would do well enough if we were quartered here for the winter, but as matters now are we may move any time. The place is strongly fortified and is not likely to be attacked by the enemy verry soon.[43]

If you would like to come here after matters get settled for the winter you can do so. Still I am not sure that I could advise you to take such a course. If I were at Fortress Monroe where there are facilities for living I would do so most cheerfully, but at this time of year you would not thrive verry well in a cold tent or an open barn like place like by present head quarters. You know I must stay in camp. The town is so secesh that I could find little society for you. . . .[44]

SUFFOLK, VA.—*Oct 26, 1862*

I have just awakened from a short nap, having for the last 48 hours been on the way to & from the Blackwater on a reconnaissance in force to ascertain the force and location of the rebels in this direction. In this time we have marched fifty miles, half the way during the night over strange roads. This night marching is verry wearing on the men. The exhaustion of the labor in marching is augmented by that of the loss of sleep.

Saturday morning at 3 1/2 o'clock we lay down to sleep on an open field where we slept for 2 1/2 hours, as strongly as if we were in the best beds & most comfortably situated. My big overcoat and blanket kept me as warm as could be desired. This is the first march we have made since we came to this place. My boys were all much pleased when I announced to them they must hurry up, and be ready to start for the Blackwater with three day's cooked rations, overcoats & blankets and be ready to start by 4 1/2 P.M. (in 3 hours). I had over a <u>hundred new men</u> to arm & equip. . . .

I hurried up matters in my usual style when I mean that things <u>shall</u> move. I pitched in myself. Drove all loungers out of my stone house, set some thirty men to work at opening boxes, assorting belts, shoulder straps, slings, cartridge bags, cap boxes, bayonet-scabbards, rifles and bayonets. All these had to be combined to make out the arms and accoutrements for a single man. Then ammunition had to be distributed to each. This you can imagine made a great deal of work to be done in so short a time. You may be assured that I set no one at work or even left him in sight who could not hurry and <u>bear hurrying.</u> The boys have learned that when I say <u>move,</u> I mean motion & they pitch in. By the required time I had my Regiment under motion with as many men as any other Regt in the Brigade.

We had no fight. The enemy were in small force, but made but little resistance, wounding a verry few slightly. Cider whiskey called "Apple Jack" did more work than the enemy. The 13th Ind had one man killed by a comrade, had his head broken by a blow from a gun. The assailant broke the stock of his musket on his head, he struck so hard. A captain of the 62th Ohio was shot through the body by Apple Jack. Will probably die. He is another of the unfortunate class of the 4th of July morning at Harrison's Landing who was shot through the breast & just escaped with his life. On the whole my boys did finely. Only one case of intoxication that made any disturbance & he was not ugly.[45] We passed through a desolation during almost the entire march. Old cultivated farms entirely abandoned & miles upon miles of once cultivated land overgrown by young pines.

Monday morning. We had the benefit of a drenching rain just before we got to camp. This has kept up during the night. The wind is high. On the whole it is a very disagreeable storm, and fortunate were we in getting back to camp as we did. Last night would have been an awful night to lay out with nothing but overcoats & blankets for covering. . . .

The major part of the country I have seen in this part of Va has almost entirely changed in appearance during the last 40 or 50 years. Much of the country that *was cultivated* so long ago is *now* entirely overgrown by an almost impenetrable growth of pine. This is so distributed as to make a beautiful appearance in many places, being of every stage of growth from 3 or 4 feet high to full grown forrest trees, which from a few feet to 50 or 60 as they stretch off in fields of regular graduation *form scenery of great beauty.* The growth is luxuriant, and perhaps no forrest is richer in foliage than the long leafed young pines of this section. . . .

SUFFOLK, VA.—*Oct 27, 1862*

. . . I am doing a large work for a little Regiment. I am just completing 880 yards of breast work, all done by my men. This is only part of the line I am to defend in case of attack from the enemy. My line of defense is 1,000 yards long, in front of which I have a slashing nearly a half mile in width directly in front that will trouble the secesh awfully to get through. Then my sharp shooters will make that trouble more difficult.[46]

I see in the papers talk of rebel proposition of peace. They are all delusive. Neither party are yet prepared for peace. The scale of success between the contending parties is too evenly ballanced to make either side yield much. Those having the administration of both governments personally have not felt the pressure of the war. They have no appreciation of the thousand pangs that penetrate the hearts of the people who make up the mighty army & do the ugly work. To carry a gun & knapsack for $13 per month is one thing. To Officers it is quite another. To administer the civil authority another. If the mothers, wives & sisters of the land could say, the war would be ended instantly. But the pride, ambition and passion of the authors of this war will not be broken till they feel the terrible weight of the war.

SUFFOLK, VA.—*Nov 1, 1862*

. . . My camp has verry much changed in the last few days. The boys have been building log huts. From my front window I can see almost a city of log houses of every size and conceivable style. The whole country has been scoured for bricks and windows. The smallest huts are large enough for two men. The larger ones accommodate say twenty. The smaller ones would make decent dog kennels for the back woods. . . .

SUFFOLK, VA.—*Nov 3, 1862*

. . . The expenses of this war are becoming so enormous that we will be taxed to death to manage the great national debt. Well I am glad I am out of debt. What little we have got is our own. I hope peace will come before long. The war is not accomplishing what it was intended to, and I much fear that it never will. The North will never submit to the despotic terms of war long enough or fully enough to conquer the South. I am really of the opinion that the Confederacy is a foregone conclusion in the estimation of the World.

SUFFOLK, VA.—*Nov 9, 1862*

. . . The last three days have been bleak, chilly, freezing, rainy and snowy November days of the same unpleasant strips of Northern Ohio fall weather. The ground has been covered with snow, and stayed on for nearly two days. My cotton socks and thin check shirts are not very consoling to my poor body, but thank fortune I have been detached on a general Court Martial which relieves me from the outdoor work of camp. Have a tolerably respectable place in which to hold Court.

My profession has taught me that courts of law should be avoided, and following out the analogy I have also thought that military courts also should be avoided, & as I see behind the curtain I am more of the opinion that all courting is folly. Nonetheless I would like to do some of my old courting over again. . . .

SUFFOLK, VA.—*Nov 17, 1862*

. . . I have been sitting as part of a Court for the last ten days & am now relieved for 4 whole days. This afternoon I have been drilling my Regt. Have shouted off commands till I am about as hoarse as if I had been arguing a long case in court. My boys look well, feel finely and make a fine show when under arms.

We had a Grand Review last week. Gen Dix came up to see how the army stationed here was managing matters.[47] Upon a large field the men paced. The infantry say 15 Regts, 2 of cavalry and three batteries of artillery marched in review past the Gen and his cortege of mounted <u>ossifers.</u> I thrashed about on my sorrel horse at a great rate, and marched my men <u>up</u> and <u>down</u> as gay as a holliday. Well these Grand Reviews will soon crush out the wicked rebellion. I am for reviews. They cost but few lives, and as a consequence one can show off without much danger to his precious <u>"body."</u>

I am seated before my great fire place, writing as snugly as if I were at home, and what is verry consoling I am not much afraid of rebels just now. The great Potomac Army is attracting all the attention of the Virginia Army now, leaving us on the Nansemond [River] secure from danger. To be sure a little skirmish once and awhile does take place out on the Blackwater off some 20 miles, but few are hurt and nobody feels apprehensive of serious harm from that quarter.

If we do not get at it pretty soon we will be compelled to wind up our bobbin for the winter. I suppose the good people of the North are satisfied now that Gen. McClellan is removed.[48] Well, I hope something decisive will now be done. But I fear that the people are becoming sick of the war, & will soon invoke peace without settling the great question of the ability of the North to conquer the South.

If the 1st of January does not see the great rebel army driven from Va, I shall expect to see the Confederacy recognized by the European governments, and will be almost sure that we will concede as much ourselves. If the vast army we are putting in the field does nothing before the close of this year, when will it ever be able to do anything? The elections in the North indicate that the people are doubting the competency of the present Administration to manage the mighty realities pressing on them. I sometimes think it is an indication that the people are becoming sick of the war. I know that some of the meanest disloyal demagogues in the nation have been elected to seats in Congress, for what I do not know unless it be to express a disposition to favor anything rather than the vigorous prosecution of the war.[49]

There is some feeling in the army at the suspension of Gen McClellan but I think it is neither deep seated nor extensive. The army as well as the people at home are generally dissatisfied with the general inaction of the 1/2 million troops in the field. For this I think the President is to a great degree responsible. He has been too <u>conservative.</u> He has been afraid to resort to the strongest measures, measures that were almost a <u>sine qui non</u> in the exigencies of the times. The army was permitted to dwindle down to half of its original number, and he dared not say to the people, you must furnish me men at once to fill my army now organized. The idea of a speedy and effective draft haunted his vision. He saw the necessity, but dared not meet it in a way the times demanded. He thought it best to compromise with fortune, & beseech the people when he should have taken the bull by the horns and said to the people I must have your vigorous cooperation now and in my own way. But anxious office seekers in the army and timid executive officers of the several stations held his judgment in abeyance for four long months till the uncertainties of capricious winter came upon his newly organized army.

Well what the use to think over the mistakes of the Government now. "Old Abe" is honest, loves the United States, cherishes constitutional liberty, hates the appearance of tyranny, has probably looked upon the system of European conscription with horror and with his conviction matured before the war he thought he was doing the verry best he could. I am well. Tell my Pet I got her letter.

SUFFOLK, VA.—*Nov 20, 1862*

Seven days now and you will have Thanksgiving in Ohio. Last year on that Yankee anniversary I think I was at home. . . This year I certainly will not see home. . . . O! this cruel war will never end. . . . National pride is a great thing, but the cost of supporting it now is terrible. But why should I write thus. You at home probably feel the sad effects of the war more acutely than we do in the field. You are constantly tortured with the uncertainty of the fate of those who are absent, whereas they only feel danger while it is presented to them.

You know I have with my Regiment been through a terrible campaign since leaving Ohio last winter, not so much from the enemy as from the suffering from privations, fatigues and climate. . . . We have recovered from all that, that is, those who are with me, but with my 200 new recruits I have only 600 enlisted men now in camp. We left the State with over 800 men, have had over 200 new recruits since that time, & now have only 600 enlisted men & not been out of the State more than ten months. My Regt has not fared worse than many others. There are other Regts here having fewer men than the 67th. I am not worked so hard now. I take more leisure.

And while in this Court Martial which may continue for some time yet, I am doing verry much such business as I did when about my professional business at home.

SUFFOLK, VA.—*Dec 6, 1862*

. . . I think when I last wrote you I stated that I had been sitting on Court Martial for some time. Well that is over and I have been doing the ordinary business of my office for over a week. Confound this courting. I had rather anytime do the old fashioned courting where judge, jury, counsel and witnesses are wanted, but why talk about things one likes when it is utterly impossible to realize what is wished for. . . .

I have several men in my Regt who have been discharged on account of disability who have enlisted as soon as they got well. There is a fascination about a state of war that bewitches men in spite of their brains. . . .

I am afraid that Gen Burnside will have more of an undertaking than he expects if he is going to crush out the rebellion this winter.[50] The roads become impossible in a verry short time at this season of the year. You have no idea of what bad roads are. Then move an army with its heavy artillery, wagons & baggage trains, and no country can furnish a good road for them. The streets of Suffolk are a perfect stream of mud, thin and pasty. At Harrison's Landing in the middle of July & Aug, with almost a tropical sun, the mud was so deep that teams could hardly pass. The long hot dry suns of those months could hardly do anything toward drying up the nasty slough holes our provision teams made.

SUFFOLK, VA.—*Dec 10, 1862*

. . . I find it much more perplexing to manage men while in camp and free from the excessive fatigues and exposures of marches than when we were almost driven to death. Officers become indifferent, men indolent and all sorts of effort required of them seems irksome. We have been here more than three months, and so far as I can judge we are just as likely to stay three months more as to move. The place is becoming strongly fortified, and the weather during this & the next two months must be verry uncertain.[51]

I have had a way [to win] for a long time, a vigorous and effective one, but <u>the President</u> has not nerve enough to adopt one of its stringencies. The country is suffering now on account of his hesitancy and conservatism. There are now 500 old Regiments in the field with less than half an organization. I doubt verry much if of these original 500,000 men there are 250,000 now in the field fit for duty. If these Regts had been filled to their maximum within 30 days after the disasters of June last and kept full by continuing levees, we might have had since the first of Sept last an <u>efficient</u> army of half a million, an army that <u>would bear down</u> all opposition if properly massed & managed. But instead of that we have probably a few more than a half million men in the field, one half of whom are new Regts and certainly not sufficiently disciplined to be reliable in the field. I just read in the papers of an entire Brigade being taken after a loss of not more than sixty men, 3 Regts all new, put into the field. I can't say what I would do under like circumstances, but I should feel disgraced under ordinary circumstances if I should surrender my Regt of 500 men for duty with a less loss. I think I could hold my men till they had sustained a greater loss than sustained by probably four times their number in the Brigade I have just referred to.

Well I am glad I am not President, for who does not feel able to find fault with honest "Old Abe," and who does not feel competent to advise him. Nevertheless I think I would pursue the most vigorous policy, would fill my army up in the least possible time, & without regard to the thousands of aspiring gentlemen who want shoulder straps. I would make the existing army organization complete and keep it so, & if the people would not sustain me in the effort I would plainly tell them that I should settle the question without further fighting if they did not sustain me fully. War is not a town meeting to be ruled by the ayes and nays. War to be successful must be despotic. One great & vigorous head must give it direction, and the will of everybody else must yield to that controlling person. The South yield to it & we must or we will fail.

You will find at the Depot a saber and belt. I sent it by a Mr Cobb to Cleveland with directions to have expressed to you. You will keep it. It is a present from "Ned Buntline," a celebrated novel writer, who is a Lt in the 1st N.Y. Mounted Rifles.[52] It is the first Union saber that crossed the Blackwater since the war broke out. I carry one just like it. It is a <u>cavalry</u> saber. . . .

SUFFOLK, VA.—*Dec 14, 1862*

. . . I came home last night after three days constant labor and watchfulness on a scouting party to the Blackwater. I was on my horse all day and all night of Thursday last & on my feet or in the saddle all of Friday. Camped out the cold frosty night of Friday & came to camp Saturday, and had all the anxiety of an expected fight on my mind during the two last days. Friday night I could sleep, but little as I always want to be ready in case of alarm to meet it with the utmost promptness & I dare not trust too much to the vigilance and fidelity of others. . . .[53]

SUFFOLK, VA.—*Dec 18, 1862*

. . . We have had another terrible battle, and fearfully disastrous to our cause. What its final results may be I cannot divine, but the present effect is to prostrate the hopes of the army, and I fear will beget disaffection at home. When I was at home in the summer, I tried to convince my friends that we had a stupendous undertaking on our hands, that the South had a vastness of resources that they did not appreciate, & an intensity of purpose that would be calamities from which the people of the North would shrink.[54]

When I hear people talk of the poverty of the rebels & the want of supplies for their army I pity their ignorance. Those who thus console themselves with the reflection that starvation and want will bring them to their knees are verry much mistaken. The rebels have enough to make them good soldiers. Napoleon lays down in his maxims that "the first qualification of a soldier is fortitude under fatigue and privation." Courage is only "secondary: <u>hardship,</u> <u>poverty</u> and <u>want</u> are the best school for a soldier." Napoleon knew well enough what was essential to the success of an army. With this view no great amount of consolation can really be drawn from the fact that the Southern Army is destitute of comforts. They have the advantage of mobility and an quantity of courage, and are vastly more self-sacrificing. They are united & common danger cements them. We are unsettled in policy. The Government is timid. Our leaders are jealous of each other's success. The South recognize a leader. <u>We are all leaders,</u> both civil & military, and express verry decided dissatisfaction if our peculiar notions are not followed. You know I have some notions that ought to be carried out to save the country, but thank the Lord I shall not abate one jot or tittle of my ardor because they may not be adopted.

Well wife, one year ago today, the 67th Regt had its organization completed. Nine months of it I have been its commander. Its history during the year has been certainly eventful looking at it with the eye of a peaceful citizen. . . . What a year has it been to the friends of those in the Regt, mother, wife, sister, father and brother. How have their prayers been directed to the God who rules over all to smile propitiously upon the absent in the Regt. I never want to see such a year again. The past year I can cherish in my memory, but earnestly wish I may never realize another such. <u>But what is the future?</u> I fear to lift the veil. The prospect is dark, hope is not buoyant. Ah! cruel fate! Why will men be so wicked?

I sometimes have fancied that I was a good soldier, but my stay in the army has not had the effect to make me like the associations of war. I do wish the further progress of its calamities might be stayed. I of course do not indicate any such feelings to my command. I talk to them hopefully, encourage Officers & men by precept and example to bear with fortitude what sort of hardship or misfortune they in common with the army have to bear. I frequently smile over a sorry heart. I am up early in the morning, take my full share of the labors of the day, do everything with zeal & act as if everything that we had to do was certainly going to accomplish some substantial end. If I did not do this I would be unworthy the command of a Regt. I told Governor Tod when he signed my commission that when I could not guarantee the commission fully I should resign & go home. As a true man I will not hang on to a place I cannot vigorously and cheerfully fill.

This may appear inconsistent with what I have just written, but it is not so. I do my duty though to me it may appear profitless with cheerfulness & zeal for the effect my example may have on others. If I were the only man in the Army, I assure you I would do no differently. I have always tried to discharge my official obligations fully & always shall. When I feel that I cannot, I will resign. . . .

CAMP SUFFOLK, VA.—*Dec 24, 1862*

. . . Looking at the present conditions of affairs I do not see that we are any nearer to the end of the war than one year ago. In the army we have no hollidays. To us all days are alike. Sundays, week days, hollidays, work, drill, march, camp & bivouac are the routine of the days, weeks, months & year. The men have become so accustomed to soldier's life and fare that they take matters as they come along cheerfully.

To be sure they grumble. All grumble in the army from the poorest soldier in the rear rank to the Major General. It is the soldier's privilege. It means nothing. The privates grumble at the Corporals, the Corporals at the Sergeants, the Sergeants at the 2nd Lts, the 2nd Lts at the 1st Lts, the 1st Lts at the Captains, the Captains at the Regimental commanders, the Regimental commanders at the Generals, the Generals at the War Department, and the War Department at the Generals and all subordinate to them, sometimes at the Almighty. So you see there is a complete circuit of complaining. Who has the best right to exercise this privilege is not determined and probably never will be. Saving this little shortcoming, the army is a glorious institution. The soldier wakes up in the morning, and looks out of his tent or quarters with perfect indifference as to whether it is fair or foul, whether anything is to be done or not. He eats his allowance with satisfaction, with the least possible care for the morrow, knowing that Uncle Samuel will provide. . . .

This is not true of the Officers who have commands to look after, if they do their duty. A company commander who truly feels the responsibilities attaching to his place has enough of labor & care to keep him well occupied, & what is true of a captain is doubly true of a Regimental commander. I find the care and vexation of a Regimental commander frequently as much as I can bear. If I wanted an easy place in the army with highly honorable ranks attaching to it and fair pay, I would select that of Lt Col. Perhaps there is no more pleasant or easier place in the whole army. . . .

Christmas in camp. This morning the Cols of our Brigade with their field and staff officers rode through the camps making Christmas calls. A fine cavalcade it made. Your own willful husband was there on a dashing horse full of the spirit of 1862. Our sport was much curtailed by the necessary preparations we were compelled to make in anticipation of a move from this place. Yesterday afternoon we received an order announcing that we must get our commands ready to move at a moment's notice, no explanations being given. I at once got my men together, had blankets rolled, overcoats out, ammunition prepared, two day's rations in haversacks & everything in readiness to move <u>at a moment's notice.</u> I am ready now, but matters look like quieting down again. Whether we shall go from here or not is not yet settled. If we go, where and when are equally uncertain. . . .

NORFOLK, VA.—*Dec 31, 1862*

I am placing my men on board a fine ship for <u>somewhere.</u> I hope you will not feel at all uneasy if you do not hear from me for some days. You need apprehend no danger as we are fixed in the best possible manner for safety. But where we are going the Lord & the Gen only know.[55]

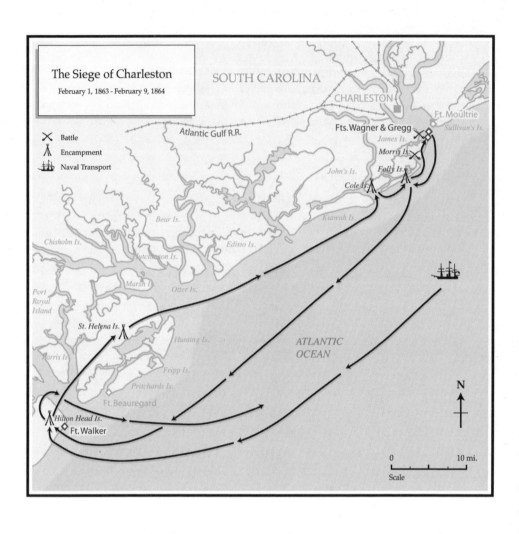

The Siege of Charleston
February 1, 1863 - February 9, 1864

✕ Battle
⌃ Encampment
⛴ Naval Transport

SOUTH CAROLINA

CHARLESTON

Ft. Moultrie

Sullivan's Is.

Fts. Wagner & Gregg

James Is.

Morris Is.

Folly Is.

John's Is.

Cole Is.

Atlantic Gulf R.R.

Kiawah Is.

Bear Is.

Chisholm Is.

Edisto Is.

Hutchinson Is.

Marsh Is.

Otter Is.

Port Royal Island

St. Helena Is.

Hunting Is.

Harris Is.

Fripp Is.

Pritchards Is.

Ft. Beauregard

Hilton Head Is.

Ft. Walker

ATLANTIC OCEAN

N

0   10 mi.

Scale

"Never Ceasing Scramble for This Bauble Glory"

THE CHARLESTON SIEGE AND FORT WAGNER

JANUARY 1, 1863–JULY 20, 1863

[In February 1863, the 67th Ohio, after a short January tour of duty at New Bern, North Carolina, joined troubled Union forces besieging Charleston, South Carolina. Their problem centered on a high command that lacked coordination and differed over tactics. Rear Adm. Samuel F. du Pont, leading the South Atlantic Blockading Squadron headquartered at Port Royal, opposed Secretary of the Navy Gideon Welles's insistence that a naval bombardment, mainly by improved monitors, which were essentially floating artillery batteries, would alone force Charleston's surrender. Instead, du Pont favored a joint naval-army operation to seize the city. In April, du Pont followed Welles's directives—and failed. Maj. Gen. John Quincy Adams Gillmore, an expert engineer and artillerist, commanding the Department of the South, and Rear Adm. John A. B. Dahlgren, the chief of the Bureau of Ordnance and du Pont's replacement, adopted the main elements of his combined plan of operation. Their efforts culminated in the bloody July 18, 1863, assault on Fort Wagner, an earthen redoubt on Morris Island that guided the harbor, about a mile and a half from Fort Sumter.]

ON BOARD SHIP J. MORTON, NEAR FORTRESS MONROE
—Jany 1, 1863

I dropped a very short note to you yesterday at Norfolk, announcing that I was making arrangements for a short voyage on the Atlantic. Well it will be short as our destination is fixed. Still it may be some days before you hear again from me. . . .[1]

ON BOARD SHIP J. MORTON OFF PT. LOOKOUT
—*Jany 2, 1863*

. . . Have had a fine sail with a stiff wind astern that has floated us along at the rate of 8 1/2 miles per hour. I have always fancied a voyage on ship board, wafted along by old fashioned winds, waves and sails. There is something substantial about it. These new fangled steam concerns may do for fast "young Americans," but the Yankee invention is so liable to blow up that there is no trusting it.

My boys have enjoyed the journey hugely with some exceptions. The exceptions are those who become so sea sick that no novelty could please them. The vessel pitched & rocked enough to make all more or less sick. I felt my share of the burden, but sea sickness never kills any one, and no sick one can find friends sympathetic to pity him. Think of 800 men stowed away on a ship of 1,200 tons burden, & all compelled to stay between decks huddled as close as three in a bed and knocked about by the waves for two or three days with a board bed & one blanket for bed and seat, with bunks set up 3 stories high & less than 3 feet apart, and you will have some idea of our conveniences & pleasures on this voyage.

Sunday Morning, Jany 4, 1863. We have had a glorious ride, are now just going into Beaufort, N.C. From hence expect to go to New Berne. We have had sufficient variety in our voyage to always remember it with pleasure. . . .

The first night was rough enough for fun. The chairs danced a cotillion on the cabin floor all night. Once & awhile they would waltz from side to side with a venom that would have been dangerous to shins. My trunk, lazy and fat on its leathery sides, got ambitious of taking a seat with the cabin furniture, and out it slid from under my berth & across the floor it went in gallant style in the giddy maze. The music was not of that soul cheering kind that you would invoke if you felt out of sorts. But still the party could keep time to the creaking of the timbers, the slamming of doors and the whistle of the rigging. We are so far south that I saw swallows skimming over the water as gaily as in mid summer in Ohio. . . .

When I next take a sea trip I hope to be encumbered with fewer responsibilities. 800 men are no pleasant associates to place on one ship of 1,200 tons burdens & under the care of a land <u>lubber</u> like myself. A pilot has just come on board, & a tug is coming to tow us into port. We might have made the journey much shorter, but a ship of 15 3/12 draft could not pass over Hatteras Inlet. As a consequence we had to go into Beaufort. We have been for the last 40 hours in sight of the light house, but so becalmed that we could not get into harbor. . . .

The Capt of [the] vessel has taken great pains to make us feel pleasant on the trip. I shall always remember him with pleasure. . . . I am on foot again. I was compelled to leave my horse at Norfolk. I expect him by steamer, but the Lord only knows whether I will soon see him or no. He is a noble horse. I would not lose him for less than $200. I hope you & children are well. I have been remarkably well for the last three months. It will soon begin to be spring again in this latitude. I hate the idea of winter.[2]

IN CAMP NEAR NEW BERN, N. C.—*Jany 7, 1863*

Well wife here I am in an old cornfield in a tent again. It seems rather odd to take a tent after four months residence in a house. . . . Night before last, the 5th Jany, we lay out doors in a pine woods. I slept as well as if I had been in doors. Think of laying out all night in mid winter in Ohio, but the climate is so much milder than in our State. It was quite chilly this morning, but did not freeze. This is the poorest God forsaken country I ever saw. The whole way from New Bern to Beaufort as far I could see on either side of the trail road is not worth my last year's labor in the army. . . .

I have my horse again. Came with the 62d Ohio this morning. Santa Clause did not come by Suffolk, so I had nothing in my stockings. I get no money yet & the Lord only knows when I shall get any. . . .

IN CAMP NEAR NEW BERN, N. C.—*Jany 12, 1863*

. . . It will soon be spring again, but will the balmy influences of spring bring any assurances of peace? At one time since I came into the army I indulged the idea that by this time the fighting would have been over & we of the army at home enjoying the good results of a successful war against the rebellion, but I have no such hope now for any subsequent period. We are still no nearer that end than we were this day 1862. As far as I can learn the army in the Southwest has been successful, but the success had been so terribly brought that we cannot stand many such victories.[3]

And what signified a victory to either of the contending armies? Both are as elastic as gas and tenacious as Devils. Such victories as have been lost & won in this war would have decided the fate of empires on the European Continent. But with us New World people instead of settling the difficulty they only protract the struggle. We are not like any other people. We frequently hear of an army being cut to pieces, utterly routed; its baggage trains taken, its artillery & small arms captured, and tens of thousands of prisoners being taken, forts and cities stormed, and the verry next thing we hear of the defeated army is that they have arisen in a new quarter, more numerous and powerful than ever before. Some of this is mere bombast in the journals, but still there is much real truth in these reports.

As astonishing as this may appear compared with what other nations would do, it is natural enough when you look at the characteristic of our people. We are indeed a peculiar people. The West turns out a real dashing fighting Army, the East a showy, make believe and magnificent institution like their vast pretensions of holding the commerce of the Western

Continent, but like their commodities a great deal of it is mere show. But with this fatal difference, it wins in peace but sadly fails in the trials of war.

I do not believe that the grand Army of the Potomac will ever accomplish its mission. It commenced wrong. It has been defeated again & again, and never has had the prestige of a decisive victory. It has fought well at times, but entertains the fatal idea that it can be overcome. It has not the assurance of invincibility. It fully indulges the hope that it may succeed but has not that bold confidence that assures success.[4]

I think better of the army in N. Carolina. Operations here have been successful. The soldiers really believe they can thrash the secesh, and will go at them with a will & confidence that *will* be likely to succeed. I have a fine Regt of five hundred able bodied men for duty, lusty fellows who will fight a long time before they will back down. There are three other Regts in the Brigade that will stand up to the work like men. Then we have two Militia Regts (conscripts). What they will do the Lord only knows. They may fight well, again they may not. They are verry uncertain troops to rely on, but we have enough of the old element to give confidence to these new troops.

This is poor God forsaken country, the embodiment of sterility. The people are poor, everything is poor. Since the slaves have been declared free, what little movable wealth there was in the country has disappeared. The town of New Bern must have had 7,000 or more inhabitants before the war broke out and *possessed* considerable wealth, but the same business prostration affects it that is seen in all the towns on the border between the contending armies. With this difference, however, that small merchants & settlers are occupying the old business rooms vending such articles as are used in the army, to wit tobacco, groceries, provisions and notions, being little seven by nine establishments hardly giving the name of business to the aggregate of their operations. Shipping comes up to this place, and with an enterprising population would become a place of considerable importance. Pitch, tar, turpentine, lumber, secesh & niggers are the chief commodities of this poor country.

We are now occupying a farm of a citizen making some pretensions to wealth, but since the 1st of Jany last has lost $14,000 worth of human chattels that slipped out of his grasp, naturally enough. The ungrateful colored population left without as much as saying good bye, or leaving even the house cook to get the next meal for the poor woman of the house who had never got a meal of victuals in her blessed but profitableness life before. She complains piteously of the unkindness of her servants, because they even took off her old miss who had minded her and her children from their infancy. What cruel niggers to thus go away from the blessed institution of slavery and the happy associations of their childhood and servitude. I am verry much afraid these contented & happy slaves are not to be trusted as much of their fidelity to their owners vanishes before the withering touch of the Emancipation Proclamation. . . .[5]

IN CAMP NEAR NEW BERN, N. C.—*Jany 14, 1863*

It is but a day or two since I wrote you a long letter, but you may not get it for a considerable time as an expedition is being fitted out from this place for some unknown locality, & to prevent intelligence regarding it being communicated to the rebels and the greedy newspapers of the North no letters are permitted to go out of the Department for the present. . . .

You have doubtless read much of the Union sentiment in North Carolina, and will expect that where we are now it manifests itself if anywhere. New Bern is the seat of government for the loyal portions of the state. There is so much of this element here that "honest Old Abe" has seen fit to appoint a military governor with general civil jurisdiction to conduct the affairs of the State for the loyal people of the rebel state of N. C.

I have not had good opportunities for ascertaining the sentiment of the people, but to the extent of my opportunity have I sought to find this Union sentiment, and as yet have not found the first North Carolinian that was <u>per se</u> a Union man whether or no loyal. I fancy the Union sentiment is just enough a myth to make a search for it interesting, but it is a fine hobby for newspaper correspondents to ride. I have been verry unfortunate in my inquires for this element. During all the last year in all my journeys through Virginia I never had the honor to meet with a man of intelligence and influence save at Strasburg who was a genuine Union man from principle & affection.

An election for member of Congress has been held in this district, but the thing has proved a mere farce. It may be a fine thing to tell in the North, but it is not one of those substantial exhibitions of political regeneration from which much consolation can be drawn. I would give more for the effect of one thorough victory than for 10,000 such elections. I learn that the rebels voted in many instances, and that there is a strong possibility that the election will be declared void, but I see so little of the papers now that I can't tell much about matters that do not fall directly under my own observation. . . .[6]

IN CAMP NEAR NEW BERN—*Jany 20, 1863*

. . . I am still here. Don't know when we shall leave. Do not get mail here regularly, nor do we have regular facilities for getting our mail away. I am feeling well this evening. Have been having the diarrhea but not so bad as sometimes. . . .

BEAUFORT, N. C.—*Jany 24, 1863*

I suppose you will not be at all surprised to find that transition is the lot of the army & that I am compelled to yield to the usual fate of the soldier. Three weeks tomorrow I came into this port & went by rail from here to New Bern. I am now going on board a propeller on an unknown expedition.

So far as I can learn it is not to be of verry long continuance, and will not go a great way. (Yet I know nothing).

We are now on a new strong boat & will be able to ride the storm with safety. I am more comfortably situated on the boat than on land. Get fair meals, a tolerable bed & room. Last night was the first time I have had my clothing off to go to bed since the 12th of Aug last. . . .

Sunday Afternoon. We are still in port and are likely to be for some time. . . .

BEAUFORT, N. C.—*Jany 26, 1863*

I have an opportunity to send mail, and will embrace the opportunity to write you a few additional lines. The morning is delightful. I wish we had as pleasant winter climate as they have in this latitude. With our productiveness & varied production, with this climate for winter, we would have a perfect paradise in Ohio. But they have serious disadvantages here that entirely over ballances these advantages of climate, a miserable soil, few productions & anything but desirable inhabitants. Sand and pine forests all along the coast for miles into the land make up the country. Lumber, pitch, tar & turpentine are the staples. Oysters & clams, sea gulls and ducks, and a little stunted corn the luxury the soil produces for human food.

The good Lord did not intend this country for any great amount of the human family. I am told however after you get back from the coast 50 or so miles, the country becomes verry fine, but our army will not get permission *to visit* that part of the state for sometime to come. I am not writing, I see, for either your profit or amusement, and will therefore nicely stop.

You may not hear from me for the next two or three weeks, perhaps not for four, as we will unquestionably be beyond mail facilities for some time. I am expecting mail from you before we leave here, but may be disappointed.

I am well situated while on this boat. My men are distributed on two boats. I am on the Geo. C. Collins, Col Commager with 4 companies on the Oriole, both strong propellers.[7] A large fleet is preparing here, but I have become accustomed to seeing a large aggregation of shipping that it is not unusually interesting. I have seen say two hundred vessels at one view & in the course of a day four or five hundred. You of course would be surprised if you should learn that I had turned sailor. Well I shall hardly at this age in life take to the salt water, but I have become somewhat a navigator after all. When I get home and this war is done I will take you to sea some time so that you may see what we now realize by being war ship bound.

ON BOARD PROPELLER GEO. C. COLLINS
—*Beaufort Harbor, N. C. Jany 28, 1863*

The monotony of ship board hangs heavily on my hands. For four days we have been on the water, waiting orders to sail. Reading matter is almost inaccessible, no newspapers, no books save my tactics & the Bible. By the way "Les Miserables" by Victor Hugo has been placed on board by the Sutler with some 25 gentlemen to read it. If it does not get read it will not be the fault of the book. I am learning to do nothing, a hard job for me. For all of the disagreeable misfortunes of my life, the worst is nothing to do. But then I am learning as much as I hate to sit still [to] overcoming that dislike; should I live to be an old man I will become fat, lazy and easy of habits. I am also overcoming much of my nervousness. I never get mad without being angry, nor do I swear without being somewhat profane. With all these virtuous tendencies I am not sure that a long stay in the army will not be without its disadvantages. . . .

How long this voyage will continue I cannot tell, but if we make no more headway than we have made in the last two weeks it will be intolerably long. On the 12th Inst. we got our orders to be ready to embark at twelve hours notice. We embarked on the 23rd, and are still waiting to sail this 28th. Four weeks ago we embarked on board ship J. Morton at Norfolk, since which time we have been waiting for "something to turn up." I presume we in the army are quite as impatient for work to be hurried up as the people at home.

With all my fund of patience I get terribly out of sorts with this playing at war. The worst of all is the little hope I see of a speedy and successful end of hostilities. This feeling is indulged into a verry great extent among all those in the army I have had the opportunity to converse with. I think I am not mistaken when I say there is a verry <u>considerable</u> feeling of despondency in the army. This results from two causes, the want of success in our military operations and the failure of the Government to pay off her troops. Verry many poor families are & have been for months suffering for the necessities of life, because the unfortunate husband & father have been for more than a half a year been deprived of his hard-earned wages & as a consequence the poor wife and children at home have none of the advantages of his wages.

The soldier feels as if the Government neglected him, and as a natural sequence he does not feel an ardor for the cause of a Government that does not (as he thinks) feel for him. To me this matter of pay is a small item, as I know that you can get along comfortably if I do not make remittances, but with the poor soldiers family this is quite different. The <u>by monthly</u> installments the Government has promised to pay are necessary to their comfort.[8]

The domestic misery this war has entailed upon the nation will never be known. Mankind are miserable enough without war, but ambitious, wicked, thoughtless men do not realize it until it comes, and then the ones who are really responsible for the calamity do not see & will not feel the effects of their calamitous conduct. "When the wicked rule, the people mourn."

The history of the war will be written in glowing terms of the valor of the troops, the glory of the Generals, and after the sorrow stricken thousands are forgotten nothing will be left but the bright spots of the war. It will write no practical lesson to warn those who follow us of the horrors of war. The cruelties, hardships & woes of the soldier & his fated family will be entirely forgotten. They are never written only in the hearts that feel them & the grave soon obliterates them.

This day a good soldier came to me & begged for leave to go home & see his dying wife & sick infant. For a whole year has he been from home & well served his country by cheerfully doing his duty, and now when the terrible realities of death are invading his family, he is compelled to stay & fight the enemies of his country & the pangs of lacerated affection as well.

Such cases as this are of daily occurrence in the army. 20 days cannot be given to the patriotic soldier who has left home, comforts & family to return to those he loves & perform the last kind offices humanity requires. I am not sure but I spoil the soldier in me by indulging in these reflections. My becoming accustomed to these scenes does not in the least soften the view. They are just as disagreeable and woeful to me as at the first view.

Jany 29th. It is Thursday afternoon again, and we are still where we were six days ago. High winds have prevented the flotilla from sailing. You ought to see the Old Ocean once in a rage. He makes a <u>considerable</u> splurge. . . .

Am now going further south to hunt secesh, and glory. O! what a word?—glory. What won't mortals do for glory. Work night & day till decrepitude ends the struggle. Tricks, artifice, fraud & force wear out the brain. Honor & dishonor are bartered. Ease, comfort & natural ties are put in the scale. Danger and death in all its horrid forms are braved in the never ceasing scramble for this bauble <u>glory.</u> . . . I really believe the contented, modest, honest man who only is ambitious to meet the responsibilities that are cast upon him by the relations of society & Heaven, and is happy in the enjoyment of his little family, and is satisfied with that his honest efforts secure for them, who is not ambitious to rule, cares not for fame and borrows trouble never, only finds true glory. . . .

HILTON HEAD HARBOR, S. C.—*Feby 1, 1863*

Here I am full fifteen hundred miles from home by the present route of travel.[9] Just came into port. On the whole had a pleasant passage. Yesterday was a delightful day on the water. Ocean was at repose, but the day before it was wild in its fury. Big waves made our steamer plunge about at a great rate. A fierce wind was directly in our teeth for twenty four hours after we got out of Beaufort, say 5 P.M. Thursday, till the same time hour Friday. In the night of Thursday we had a fierce gale that made things rattle. I did not appreciate the extent of the storm as I had that plague of all sea voyages, the sea sickness. I lay in my bunk with an angry belly & dizzy head, not caring to see Old Neptune in his wrath.[10]

Our flotilla made a grand spectacle as it put out of Beaufort harbor for sea. Some fifty vessels, more than half of which were steamers, dashed heroically through the surf that plunges upon the shore. The broad wings of the sail vessels & the majestic movement of the steamers gave a novel view I never expect to see again.

Well, wife, I am not in a descriptive mood this morning. Nevertheless I can hear the winds whistle through the rigging, see the furious waves carrying on their heads (bearing aloft) a fretful crown of white foam (don't you think "bearing aloft" sounds better). Can feel the bounding of the vessel, and every few moments feel that sickish dizziness up my diaphragm. Still with all these vivid realizations, I can't write the things down.

Writing the world "down" makes me think I am away <u>down</u> in Dixie. Just think I am below the rebellious City of Charleston, that infernal hot bed of treason and civil war, at the mouth of the Savannah River, with a strong inclination towards the City of Savannah and the aforesaid rebellious City. Now we are preparing for hot work.

I will write you about business matters so as to apprise you of each item as may be of use to you in case I am unfortunate in our present enterprise. First I only got pay as 2nd Lt from Oct 2d 1861 to Dec 18th 61, whereas I was entitled to pay as Lt Col. I was mustered at 2 Lt Oct 2nd 1861 & immediately thereafter promoted to Lt Colonelcy, promotion bearing same date. The differences should be paid. I shall do what I might to collect if I live. If I do not you should have it. My wages are in arrears from the 3rd of June last to the 29th of July following. I rate as Lt Col with allowance for two servants and my allowance for forage, excepting one horse for which I drew forage in kind since 29th last as Colonel. The Field & Staff muster rolls will show my musters till the 31st of Dec 1862. There are to yesterday seven months wages & allowance due me. I have one horse & equipment here with worth at least $200, out of which you ought to realize $175. This I shall make arrangements to have sold here. This is all I have out of which any money can be realized, or that I desire to have converted into money.

My trunk & clothing I shall have ordered to you. My best uniform you may preserve if you like. My shoulder straps (bullion ones) are <u>fine</u> & worth preserving. My field glasses, pistols, saber and watch will be sent home. This personal property I hardly know how to divide among you & the children. I will indicate what I think will be fair, reserving the right to select what you please from the above articles for yourself. The watch being a plain silver hunter case will only be suitable for a gentleman, therefore give it to Eddie. The pistols also are only suitable for men. He may have them. My field glasses which I prize verry highly will suit my little Pet, which she may have. The saber you may dispose of as you please. The best shoulder straps you may keep if you desire, with the uniform to which they belong. You may also keep the traveling trunk to offset against Eddie's watch. When my Pet gets large enough to know how to use one you may purchase for her a nice ladies watch worth at least $50. This you can afford to do if you are not unfortunate with what you may get. I almost forgot to say that I had $150 in money & due bills against my Officers for money loaned that you should have. (I will give you proper directions about this). You will also be entitled during widowhood to $30 per month or in case of death or marriage my children will be entitled to the same sum during minority from the Government.

All this is made to meet a contingency that I may be unfortunate. But I would not have you lose either sleep or appetite over the reflection that I might get killed, for I "indulge in no such hope." You know that I expect to come home all safe and sound, "not even the smell of fire on my garments."

I am going to do my duty like a man conscious of dangers, but hopeful for the future. I want to live for you & my children, but if I should die in battle teach them to respect the memory of a father who did strive to leave them a firm & beneficial Government without which they could not expect to live in security & happiness. I have the satisfaction of having tried to the extent of my ability discharge my duties as an Officer with fidelity and earnestness of purpose. I hope my children will grow up intelligent, virtuous and industrious. Do all in your power to make them what they ought to be. . . .

HILTON HEAD HARBOR—*Feby 6, 1863*

I have not had any intelligence from home for more than a month. Your last letter was dated Jany 4th. Since we left Suffolk we have been shut out from light from the civilized world. Newspapers, the light and luxury of modern times, I might say almost a necessity to our existence, have been cut off from the 30th of Dec last to 30th Jany following. . . . Since history is recorded in the daily papers, and one loses the connection unless he gets the papers substantially as they are issued, this meager arrival of papers does not satisfy those who are anxious to keep informed of the important events that succeed each other in such rapid succession. Western papers rarely reaches us here now. In fact I have not seen a Western paper since the commencement of the present year. I am not so cosmopolitan as not to have a partiality for the news from my own beloved State, Ohio. Why Ohio is worth all the sea coast from New Jersey south to the Rio Grande. . . .

The coast is of singular formation all along the Atlantic from Del to the Floridas. Shoals and high sand banks that are shifted by every gale make a changing and bleak border that almost forbids habitation. The harbors are of difficult access by reason of the frequent changes made in the channels by heavy winds. When we reached Beaufort harbor we found one of the monitors aground. The pilot thinking he could follow the old channel used a few months before, ran his craft into a sand bar that nearly cost the destruction of the iron clad. Of course I need not describe to you an iron clad of the Monitor model, as the illustrations in the pictorial papers give a verry correct idea of these terrible engines of war.

At one glance of the eye, I can see ancient and modern naval architecture and gunnery displayed. The majestic old ships of the line, then the steam frigates, still later the gun boat and now these impregnable monitors. The first with her five or six hundred men, three decks and almost a hundred guns looks almost a fortress. Her spars, arms, rigging & sails especially when filled with wind almost makes us wish that steam & Jonathan had not interfered with those wonders of the past.[11]

Next the steam frigates are a beauty among this naval armament, less bulky, not so big, more trimly built & rakishly rigged with fewer guns and great speed. In their time they were the pride, the idol of all those who looked to the navy for protection. They with their grand sires the old ships of the line gave complete protection to our commerce wherever our restless enterprise has sent a vessel or adventure bid a challenge. These were our front competitors for the equality if not the mastery of the seas for fifty years, and only ceased to do this on the advent of the iron age that looks upon modern walls & stone ramparts with perfect contempt.

Gun boats were improvised to meet our immediate want and for our shallow bays, harbors and rivers. These are of every conceivable model from a corn crib to a first class steam frigate. These iron clads are of diverse model. The old but ill fated Monitor when afloat looked on the water like a mammoth Indian snow shoe, with an enormous half bushel measure resting on her deck.[12] The Galena is an iron clad gun boat, verry much after the style of many of the low deck propellers used in commerce. The new Iron Sides at a little distance does not differ much in appearance from the steam frigates of modern date except it is much stouter built.[13] Well what is the use of spending time to describe to you what you know already, about as well as if you had seen the same.

On the 10th of Sept 1860 with 80,000 other eyes I feasted with admiration on the reproduction of the Battle of Lake Erie, so gallantly fought & won 48 years before. The flotilla then impressed [and] filled our minds with the majesty of naval armament, but how has my mind been enlarged with the idea of the vastness of our naval resources since that time by seeing how our armies are moved and supplied on the Atlantic coast.[14]

The Army of the Potomac had over five hundred vessels attending it while at Harrison's Landing. In this harbor one hundred vessels can be seen from this craft, comprising vessels of classes from the ship of the line & the Ocean steamer to the schooner & harbor steam tug. Perhaps no sight made by human hands is more grand & imposing than the simultaneous movement of a great armed fleet. Fifty vessels left Beaufort harbor at the same time with the three divisions of the 18th Army Corps. The sea was quite rough, the harbor being surf bound with the exception of a narrow channel made the passage into the broad Ocean an additionally interesting undertaking, for hardly had we made the blue water before the ordinary digestion was so interfered with that the appetite excused the commissariat department from the further issue of rations for the next forty eight hours. Twenty two sail vessels with their wide spreading sails dashing through the surf after each other in as quick succession as safety would permit with their spars oscillating like a pendulum with this difference, the pendulum should be on water.

This is part of a letter I have written in intervals during the last two weeks. I have been on & in their terrible monitors & through the finest frigate on the Ocean, the Wabash. I have heard the darkies sing and learned a <u>heap.</u> . . . It is the 10th & we are still here doing nothing, & when we will do something I do not know. . . .[15]

ST HELENA ISLAND, S. C.—*Feby 10, 1863*

I am on <u>terra firma</u> again, and in my own canvass tent. I have a hard-board box fitted on three pegs for a writing desk, and a pine board for bed, sofa and table. . . .[16]

Today has been delightfully warm & has also furnished my men with a fine opportunity to stroll about the island. It is made up of several large cotton plantations & of the same low flat sandy character of the lands around New Bern & Suffolk, pine timber predominating, but live oak is found in considerable abundance as our evergreen. In fact most the timber growth is evergreen & with the warm weather dissipates the idea that we are in mid winter.

It is evening now. I have not been the sea side, but have been over to Hilton Head & had a pleasant visit with several Cleveland gentlemen who are connected with Government service in both military and civil capacities. I learned also that "Aunt Fanny" (Gage) is within four miles of our camp, having charge of a colony of contrabands. I mean to see her at my earliest convenience. Of course I am much pleased to find acquaintances so far from home.[17]

There is an Oberlin lady & gent about 8 miles from here having charge of another colony of colored <u>pussons.</u> This individual is quite an institution in these parts, but rather distasteful to the newly arrived soldiers. Last night the 9th N.J. & a Conn Regt burned out a colony of say 150, with a will that indicated that they had but little sympathy for the slave. Still with all this repugnance to the race there is mingled with it an affinity for the female portions. Most of the Negro rows arise from abuses to the female portions by amorous Negro haters.[18]

. . . It will be St Valentine's day tomorrow but I hardly expect anything from the merry Saint. Uncle Samuel is not verry attentive in his effort to furnish mail matters. The Regt has had no letters for nearly a month. You are probably aware that it is some what dangerous navigating the Atlantic coast from New York to this place unless a convoy of armed vessels accompanies. We came here on the 1st of Feby, now the 13th, and only one boat has been here from N.Y. since that time, the Arago, a splendid Ocean steamer. When I go home I mean to ride on such a craft.[19]

We have been expecting the Augusta Dinsmore, U.S.N. Propeller for several days.[20] By her we expect to get a mail. The boys take almost as much interest in the mail as they do in the arrival of the Pay Master. . . .

It seems a long time to us because we feel spring upon us at this time of the year and anticipate the time in your latitude by some six or seven weeks. The birds are chirping & singing in the early morning as merrily as in May in Northern Ohio. If this was a fertile country I should like to live here during the cooler months, but the sand, intolerable sand, indicates sterility & in the summer it must be verry unpleasant. I have no desire to stay here during the summer & will be much disappointed if compelled to do so for the ensuing one.

When I last wrote to you I expected before this time to have accomplished the end for which we came to these inhospitable savannahs. But time drags along with seeing anything of practical utility being developed. The Generals cannot agree. Harmonious cooperation is out of the question. Personal ambition is of too much consequence to give another a chance to distinguish himself unless it can be done by the resources within himself. Well I won't detail the unpleasant rumors I hear connected to our present status, in which there is some truth. But I know one thing, matters do not go on smoothly. The expedition is for the present postponed, for what reasons I cannot say, nor can I tell who is to blame but there is a mighty responsibility resting upon someone.[21]

I cannot but feel disheartened. The army feels so. Its enthusiasm has departed. If the people at home feel as the army does, our cause is in a precarious condition. It is not good to be borrowing evil. Nevertheless we must open our eyes to the trouble. I do not expect success, nor do I expect all men in power to be honest, but I do think there should be more integrity and fidelity to the obligations of places entrusted them than I too often see. There are those who are anxious to prolong the war holding high places in this army who are doing all they can to make themselves the end of the war rather than the good of the country. . . .[22]

ST HELENA ISLAND, S. C.—*Feby 23, 1863*

. . . I wrote yesterday a long letter to you of lots of nonsense with the intention of having it published in the Beacon, but upon reviewing it I thought it would not be in good taste to make you the innocent means of procuring its publication, so I scratched out "My dear wife" and put "Friend Lane" in [its] place and sent it off. It is over the signature of "Mary Ann," and may contribute a good laugh for those who are pleased with nonsense.[23] I wrote a letter for the Cleveland Herald which will be produced about the 1st of March, perhaps a little later, which I wish you get and preserve among my papers. . . .[24]

I made a visit to see "Aunt Fanny" Gage Saturday afternoon. Had a pleasant visit. Took tea with her. She is the sole white woman on Paris Island, her son, George, the only white man. She has three hundred and fifty contrabands under her controll, & is expecting three hundred and fifty more. I sent you some rose seeds from her garden & a full blown rose that matured out of doors, also a few holly seeds.[25]

Aunt Fanny thinks I have grown fleshy & better looking. Did not find hollow cheeks & sallow skin as she fancied I looked when at Columbus.

Well, I am improved somewhat in personal appearance. My cheeks are filled out. My countenance is fresh for a brown man. I am really heavier than I have ever been before. I weigh plum up 174 lbs. . . .

This war goes on so slowly that I fear that the end is verry far off, if it does not close till the rebels are subdued. They are desperately inclined & will fight as long as they can hold their own as well as they have been doing for the last year. I have no means of knowing much about the feeling of the people in the North. We get the papers so irregularly and at such long intervals that I can get no fair idea of the intensity of the war feelings at home or the disaffection of any considerable portion of the North as many politicians would have us think.

I see Congress is passing a stringent conscription bill, making all persons between the ages of 18 & 35 amenable to a call, & from 35 to 45 after the first class are exhausted. Are you not glad that I am in a situation not to be harassed by these conscriptions? I am in a place voluntarily assumed, & had much rather be there than be forced to take a musket and be told that I was forced to fight for my country. Drafted men get many dry stands in the army. Volunteers don't like them.[26]

Thursday 26th. We have had a Grand Review today. It went off verry pleasantly. Had a fine day. Quite a party from New York were present. Fletcher Harper, the elder of the Harper Bros, Mr. Raymond of the Times & sundry other gentlemen & a few ladies.[27] I had the good fortune to go with same party with Gen Hunter and staff to Beaufort. . . .[28]

I learn that Miss Mary Gage has arrived, much to the gratification of her mother. I shall go over to Parris island in a day or two and make them a call. . . .

ST HELENA ISLAND, S. C.—*Feby 27, 1863*

. . . I do not expect that we will remain here much longer. Say ten days or two weeks at furthest. Still this is all uncertain as we know nothing of the future especially of matters depending upon the will of a General and the fortunes of war. We expect to go back to New Bern after this expedition has accomplished its purpose, but when that will be I cannot tell. The enterprise is entirely different from any I have before participated in, to wit the taking of a strongly fortified city and the means with which it is to be accomplished are also different.

Here the navy with all the overwhelming power of modern science as applied with skill in the naval architecture and gunnery will be the chief instrumentalities used. The infantry as an auxiliary will do the work after the batteries of the enemy are reduced. I have not been a careful enough reader of history to announce with absolute certainty, but I nevertheless hazard the opinion that the expedition now fitting out at this place is the most formidable naval array the world ever saw.[29]

It would not be expedient for me to tell you where the expedition is expected to go, nor all I know about the preparation made, but I can safely describe to you the means and classes of war implements prepared for the siege. I have already said it was chiefly a naval armament. I will now describe the different naval engines to be used without giving their number.

You will not expect me to enumerate among the old ships of the line with her triple decks, wide spreading sails, lofty spars and fortress like walls, as steam and Jonathan have consigned them to the rubbish of the past, but every other class of water craft, from their immediate successors, the steam frigates, to the surf boats will be used, embracing these splendid steam frigates, gun boats, iron clads, and every sort of transports.

I will describe the Wabash, as she is said to be one the finest steam frigates afloat, the flag ship of the squadron, commanded by Captain Rogers.[30] It is a craft of beautiful mode, first class in size, a three mast square rigged steam ship manned by nearly eight hundred men and forty seven guns, forty two nine inch Dahlgrens, one eleven inch Dahlgren, a hundred pound Parrott, the ballance smaller rifled pieces on carriages so that they could be used either on or off the vessel. I had a splendid view of her battery on the 2nd deck, fourteen inch guns on a side. Where were placed all her men I could not see, but her immense room did not give the appearance of being crowded. What most stunned me aside from her heavy armament was the perfect order and neatness of everything on board. The decks were scrubbed till they looked as white as the new fallen snow flake. The men were tidy in dress and person, and behaved themselves with perfect decorum. Ten years ago the Wabash was competent to meet any war vessel on the Ocean. Today the insignificant Monitor Patapsco with her two guns could knock her out of the water in five minutes.[31]

Those Dahlgrens are smooth bores, and are made for battering wooden walls, for which purpose they are much better than rifles. The great velocity of the rifle projectiles causes them to cut their way through wood work, making comparatively a clean hole while the smooth bore with less velocity tears its way, knocking the splinters at a fearful rate.

I will not attempt to describe the appearance of the monitors, as you have seen them verry faithfully portrayed in the pictorials, but will give you an idea of their armament. They are armed with two monster guns, a fifteen inch smooth bore and a two hundred pound rifle. The fifteen inch gun discharges a projectile weighing four hundred and fifty pounds, or a shrapnel charge of seven thousand bullets. These guns are worked within a revolving casement made of solid iron plating eleven inches in thickness, called a turret. In this the captain & his men can work in almost perfect security. Everything is so perfectly adjusted that a light touch of the hand is sufficient to elevate or depress the heavy gun weighing over twenty two tons. A simple movement of a lever causes the turret to revolve around any given point of the compass. This modern leviathan is supplied with ten steam engines, two to propel her, two to pump, two revolve the turret, two for lungs & two to create nothing (a vacuum). When it is prepared for an engagement, it is water tight air except through the turret, and as dark as a pocket below. The deck is a *plain* surface bomb proof with no possible place for a ball to lodge. Then her breathing apparatus is necessary to sustain its crew.

Since I commenced to write this, I have learned that the Montauk has entirely destroyed the rebel steam Nashville. She passed by the batteries of Fort McAllister paying no attention to them, & [they] fired one of her fifteen inch shells into her & shattered the rebel craft to atoms, sinking her at a single shot.[32]

I can hardly describe the gun boats, as they are of every conceivable model. Merchants craft of almost every sort have been converted into these warlike engines. They are usually mounted with 1 heavy gun & seven rifled guns from twelve to hundred pounders. In fact most all Government boats may be called gun boats, as they usually have armed with one or more guns. I have seen old ferry boats converted into gun boats. The vital parts of all the wooden ships are protected by sand bags placed about them in sufficient thickness to stop ordinary canon projectiles.

Next come the mortar boats, schooners of say two hundred tons burden. To outward appearance they do not materially differ from the ordinary schooner. The mortar looks some what like a monstrous elongated cast kettle with a hollow chamber fifteen inches in diameter & some three feet deep weighing twenty five to thirty thousand pounds. The greatest diameter of these arms is say some five feet. A discharge from these short Toms reminds one of an explosion from one of our powder mills. Let these drop a few of their jewels into Fort Sumpter & I will wager that Beauregard will scramble to get out.[33] But shower some of their hail into the streets of Charleston, and it will soon have fewer rebels within its fanatic precincts than at anytime since the advent of the last century. It is Tuesday morning Mch 3d & this is yet unsent, but as the mail closes this morning I must cut this off though not half done.

ST HELENA ISLAND, S. C.—*Mch 8, 1863*

. . . I have two letters from you before me, one of the 8th, the other 18th of Feby last. . . . I have copies of the Beacon of the 12th and 19 Feby, & I expect a big mail in the next mail steamer which is past due. The last Beacons did not afford me much news, still I read them all through. Newspapers are so scarce that I am glad to get anything to read. . . .

I was broken off right here by the advent of Capt Ammen, Commander of the Patapsco,[34] a monitor iron class, whereupon we took a sail on horse back over the island. Rode some 15 or 18 miles through quite an interesting country to us. We passed through deep pine forrest interspersed with live oak, palm, palmetto, cedar and a great variety of evergreen underbrush, many of the trees being literally covered with Spanish Moss, hanging in festoons many yards in length from the limbs, making them look gray with this pendant vegetable hair. This island is almost perfectly level, sandy and dry. The roads are straight and narrow with woods on each side with their branches almost overhang the road way, & festooned on each side by curtain of moss and the yellow jasmine which is now in full bloom. I can hardly conceive of a more picturesque drive. . . .

I have been writing this by little snatches & will continue to do so till time for the mail to close which will be several days. . . . Col Pond & myself went over to Parris Island last week & stayed over night with Aunt Fanny Gage, a splendid visit we had.[35] The good woman shed tears when we left. Mrs. G is a noble woman. She & her son are the only white persons on the whole island. She is braving almost every privation to do good work to the poor liberated slaves. They are indeed a degraded people. The abuses of the "blessed institution" has almost obliterated the last vestiges of humanity in them. If God be just & visits retribution upon the wickedness of man commensurate with the aggravation of this affair, His terrible wrath must be visited upon the authors of the abominable crime of American slavery. Humanity revolts at the cruelties & degradation of the system.[36]

ST HELENA ISLAND, S. C.—*Mch 16, 1863*

One year ago this day I assumed command of the 67th O. V. since which time I have had the labor, care and responsibility of its command. I assure you that however gratifying it may be to one's ambition to be head of Regt in the field, it nevertheless is an undertaking on many accounts not verry desirable. Still I would rather be commanding officer than subordinate if I am to remain in the service. While I get the blame for all that goes wrong, I am somewhat compensated by the praise of what is well done. It is a peculiar privilege of the army to grumble, and all indulge in it from the small boy in the rear rank to the Major General in Chief, a great deal of which means nothing & therefore does no harm unless to the verry thin skinned individual who is always in danger. I have had abundant opportunity to indulge in that Christian virtue you so freely & always accorded me in an eminent degree, patience. But, dear wife, I fear if I stay much longer in the army I shall exhaust all my store of that article, and be left for the rest of my life upon the shoals of impatience. . . .[37]

One year ago I little expected to be in the service at this time and still less did I think I should be below Charleston, S. C. . . . I then fondly hoped the war would soon close with a restored Government & a peaceful & happy people. O! how have my hopes been blasted. Then the people of the loyal states were united, now they are quarreling among themselves about party ascendancy. The army is distracted by divisions and unpatriotic officers, while defeat and disaster has almost annihilated as fine an army as the world ever saw, and the war is raging with more tenacious fury than ever, leaving no substantial prospect of peace for a long time.

I always theoretically knew that war was a terrible calamity. I now know practically that it is a curse immeasurably worse than I ever anticipated. Well said an ancient King, "let us fall into the hands of the Lord for his mercies are great and not let me fall into the hands of man" for he well knew the cruelty of man to man.

But why should we who were so preeminently happy and enlightened, & so nurtured in all the arts of peace so madly rush into this terrible state? I sometimes feel that the present evils of the war are not the most to be dreaded. What is to be the moral, social and political status of this vast army? Will the soldier who has become accustomed to the horrors of the battle field and the demoralization of camp life, who has lived upon the excitement of active campaign & forgotten the restraints of society, ever return to society and be content with the tame pursuits of quiet industry and peace? Will the Officers who have learned to command be satisfied to lay aside the exercise of power, and himself become the patient subject subordinate to civil authority? We are certainly making a fearful experiment. I pray God that wise counsels may overrule us, and work out for us a speedy return of honorable and enduring peace. . . .

Since I last wrote you I have been to the head of the island. . . . Went to a negro meeting, heard them sing, pray & exhort. I talked to them a while about preparation of themselves to live well for this world, though they have been taught enough about living for Heaven. Poor creatures. They have been living for Heaven all their benighted lives, had nothing to live for on this to them inhospitable earth. I have but little hope for the present generation. They are dispirited, suspicious, timid, grossly ignorant and degraded as poor mortals can be. . . .

ST HELENA ISLAND, S. C.—*Mch 24, 1863*

. . . The Arago has made her trip to New York from this place in sixty hours. I wish you had come on her instead of sending letters by mail.[38] This getting letters makes me homesick. Then I would so dearly like to see the children and certainly would not be displeased at seeing their mama. . . .

You write me of your ill health. This information makes me feel verry unpleasantly. I hope you may continue better. But I must say that I have had serious fear on account of your liability to cold and their effect on your lungs. . . .

You should apprise me fully and frankly of your health. Those children of ours must have a parent to care for them. If I am to remain in the field, you should do everything to promote your health and protract your life that they may have the care of a mother if their father should be unfortunate in battle. If you had serious apprehension on your own account, I would come home at once to stay, for I little relish the idea of leaving our tender infants to the cold attention and sympathy of the selfish world. You should deal frankly with me. I shall certainly do what duty to my children demands. . . .

ON SHIP BOARD PORT ROYAL HARBOR, S. C.—*Apl 2, 1863*

I sent you yesterday check for $1,142.23, which you will please acknowledge. I this day send you $40.00. You may make the draft $1,150, that will make $2,000 I have sent you in all. . . . I hope to be paid soon again when I will get four months pay, this is already due. I keep but little by me, as I do not wish to loan much as you and the children can make much better use of it than the rebels. Write me all about your success in getting the check & the letter with contents.

PORT ROYAL HARBOR, S. C. — *Apl 2, 1863*

I am again on ship board. Came here two months ago yesterday. Have had quite a pleasant stay here on the whole. The winter & early spring months are quite pleasant here. I am sure you would like the winters here verry much. The days are getting quite warm, the nights cool enough to need two heavy blankets. You know I always did like a good deal of covering. I almost hated to leave my camp on the island. It was so neatly fixed.

Cole's Island, Apl 5th (Easter Sunday). Since commencing this letter we have changed our location. We are now within ten miles of Charleston. Can see the secesh across a marsh some two miles at all hours of the day. The iron clads passed the harbor this afternoon for the City of C. We expect to hear the big guns in a few hours. I wish I could be near enough to see it, but from present indications I am fearful we will be too far off. I have written a letter to each of the children which you will preserve for them till they are old enough to take care of, and preserve them if I should lose my life in the coming struggle. I expect to go through all right but may not. We are in a D——l of a hurry this morning, (Monday)[39]

HEAD QUARTERS 67TH REGT. O. V., COLE'S ISLAND, S. C.
— *Apl 9, 1863*

. . . I have been exceedingly busy for the last fortnight occasioned by an exchange of our old arms and the removal to this place. Perhaps you would like to know what sort of a place Cole's Island is. Well, it is one of those low coast islands so common on the Atlantic border of the Carolinas & some two or three miles long, quite narrow, bounded on three sides by low marshes which are overflowed by flood tides daily, and about a dozen miles south of Charleston. It is barren enough in all conscience with no inhabitants & nothing but a few old forts of 1812 to relieve the tedium of its sand ridges, which shift considerably by the winds that most constantly blow here. . . .

The poor secesh are evidently afraid of the cowardly Yankees, for they have left many pleasant homes without a single tenant to guard them from the ravages of time or the advent of new occupants, the barbarians of the North. What foolish people. We would not hurt them if they only behaved themselves decently. The original inhabitants along the coast wherever the army has been so far as I have learned have abandoned their homes & fled to places within the enemy lines. In most instances, however, they have not shown that self sacrificing disposition they so much boast of as to burn their towns & homes before leaving. They evidently expect to come back some of these days & again occupy their former homes.

Yesterday was quite an exciting time in camp on account of the opening of the bombardment of the forts about Charleston. For two or three hours verry heavy firing was heard. All hands were on tip toe to see what was going on. I was in the tip top of a tall pine tree with glass in hand looking toward Sumter which is off some 10 or 12 miles. Of course I could see but little, <u>but what I could see I was determined to see.</u>

Fancy me in the verry top of a huge pine swaying to and fro with the branches watching the clouds of smoke as they rolled from the heavy artillery of the forts and gun boats. I could see Ft Sumter but the sky is so smoky that I can see it but verry indistinctly. I occasionally see a butternut on the other side of the marsh lying to our front, but they are careful not to come in range of our sharp shooters. I have an excellent Regt of marksmen. I doubt if it can be excelled by any infantry Regt in the field. . . .[40]

I see that "Mary Ann" is amusing the people considerably about that colored person that waits on her. Several letters of inquiry have been sent to the Regt asking about the personage called "Mary Ann." I long ago heard the cry from the Officer of the Day "Lights Out," so I must obey my own commands & put mine out, too.[41]

COLE'S ISLAND, S. C.—*Apl 12, 1863*

I am not in a verry good nature today and perhaps ought not write. But you want to be posted as to the news of this expedition. This magnificent naval expedition of the iron clads was to have blown Charleston out of the future geographies. The expedition has gone up—gone off—gone to the D——l <u>with flying colors.</u> The iron clads are a failure, and after this terrible lesson "Old Gideon"[42] will wake up (if the war wakes) to the significant reality that the nation has expended millions of money, lost much precious time and many valuable lives to make an experiment that should have been tested long before this when serious disaster could not follow failure. But so the war goes.

For almost three months have we been waiting for the perfecting of this naval armament that was to strike an irresistible blow upon this center of rebeldom. We were led to think that success would necessarily follow in the wake of these terrible sea monsters. Our men were jubilant over the anticipated occupancy of Charleston. Well, where are we? The fleet has gone, the army save one Brigade has gone, victory has gone, the enterprise has hopelessly gone, confidence has gone—all gone—gone—gone. Appearances indicate that we will be going before long. <u>Nolens volens.</u>[43]

Just think of it. One Brigade holding Folly & Cole's Island, my Regt holding Cole's Island alone, with thirty or forty thousand vigilant rebels all around us save to the seaward. If I were a rebel as I am a loyalist, I would gobble up this entire invading force in the next twenty four hours or know the reason why. We have enough boats to take us off at any time, and are supported by the sloop Pawnee and a tolerable gun boat. But either of them could be crushed by an iron clad ram. If the secesh had enterprise enough to pitch into these vessels they might clear this inlet in three hours time and take every mother's son of us into Charleston with our arms and banners inverted. I hardly think they will attempt this. But if they do they will have a snug little job to bag the 67th. . . .

I can't say that I have unbounded confidence in the management of affairs here, because I know little or nothing of plans or the disposition or ability to execute them. I have been so shifted about in the few months I have been in the service that I do not have time to learn the characteristics of those having Command. Gen Lander was a <u>heroic</u> soldier, and would win by his impetuosity. He soon died. Gen Shields was a brave man, but insincere, capricious, unballanced and aimless beyond self. Could do nothing as a subordinate & lacked judgment and honesty so essential to an independent command. Him we forced out of the service. Gen Kimball was cool, brave and popular. His men would fight at anytime, and win, too. He was emphatically a fighting man & thoroughly believed in the philosophy of hard knocks. We won with him. He was only a Brigadier, but is now a Major General. Gen Ferry was cautious, conservative, honest, careful of his men. Had firmness to a fair degree, & would fight if necessary with stubborn energy, but would not fight for the fun of the thing. He acted from a sense of duty & would modestly do all that he felt he was required to do whatever the cost might be in a straight forward way without ever thinking of artifice or intrigue, and after all was over would not mount in a balloon to blow his horn. Gen Peck was a nervous, dyspeptic gentleman who would fret himself to exhaustion for fear that he might be caught napping. Many a night have I when General Officer of the Day laid out with the picket to guard against imaginary surprises. . . . About Gen Foster I know but little, save that he was very zealous in our behalf while he thought we were an integral part of the 18th Army Corps, but neglected us with a vengeance when he found our status was in doubt. Through his instrumentality our payment was deferred some two months. In personal appearance he was head and shoulders above any of the Generals I have lately seen and is much beloved by his officers. Gen Hunter is military in his bearing, systematic in his business affairs & fond of military display, rides a beautiful horse with elegance & admires the strong muscle of the hardy Western soldier, while he takes almost equal pride in the polished trappings of the soldiers of the Eastern Army. Nor does he despise the misfortune of the poor negro. He is sometimes called "Black Dave," because of his efforts to ameliorate the condition of the poor blacks.[44]

This is quite a digression from the object of my letter. To repose confidence in a commander one must know something of his qualities. In the active field we much sooner learn our superior officers than when in camp. In the field we necessarily come in contact with them and they with us, but in camp they are almost as inaccessible as the inmates of a Turkish harem. Of these that I have mentioned Gen Peck was the most inaccessible, Gen Kimball the most accessible. . . . I do think it has a bad effect upon soldiers to transfer them from command to command, as has been the case with my Regt. I must say that I like Gen H better than any I have seen in a long time.[45]

But this damnable failure, it will have a bad effect on the men & a disastrous effect upon public sentiment at home. We need a few decisive victories, can afford but few defeats or our cause is forever gone. Our people are so spasmodic and fickle that little results may bring about great ends. . . .[46]

Wednesday, Apl 15, 1863. I am off Cole's Island with the Brigade on Folly Island, a heavy wooded, wild island bordering on the Atlantic on one side and one of those tidal rivers so common here. I hear the loud roaring of the Ocean at all time as the waves break over the shoals, making a dangerous surf as far as the eye can reach with few intervals.

We are emphatically in the field again. . . . We had a heavy thunder storm last night in which my men lay without shelter. I was visiting the pickets to see that they were perfectly placed when the rain came on as I had never been in the rain before. The marshy border of the line was on one side with many places knee deep. It was intolerably dark. I floundered about my track several times, but finally got to my place of destination when I lay down to rest with two companies of my Regiment. . . . My night rest was not verry refreshing. I had to sleep with one eye open that I might be ready for any time for emergencies. . . .

I am again living on a very simple diet, to wit hard tack, salt pork, coffee. I have a little slice of cheese & a few ounces of butter left. . . . On the sea board we can get good living when one is not a stickler for style by paying for it. . . . There are wild turkeys, geese, deer & cattle on this island, but we dare not shoot, and if we did, the quantity would hardly give a taste to the army men. . . .

I can see Charleston, but what good does that do? Many an army could say, <u>Came—Saw—Skedaddle.</u> Frequently there is only one step between victory and a fizzle. . . .

Thursday morning. There is no danger, no rebels, no prospect of fighting. . . . We are sending our sick to Fortress Monroe now. It is said to be one of the most healthy places on the coast. The sea breezes always so modify the heat of summer that it is always comfortably cool.

FOLLY ISLAND, S. C. —*Apl 19, 1863*

We are still in the woods enjoying the balmy influences of a southern clime, sand flies and mosquitoes. The sea breezes make the middle of the day tolerably comfortable. The mornings are warm and enervating. Hard tack & open air, exercise and rest, give us great zest for the enjoyment of the peculiar privileges we have the felicitous fortune to enjoy. We wash clothing ourselves, and cook out of the same magnificent swamp. The nectar we drink has that beautiful deep hue and odor of the chocolate waters of [a] swamp. . . . The nights are cool, making a thick blanket essential to my comfort, though overshadowed by the thick over spreading branches of a huge pine.

I have been over the island and can find few attractions for myself. It is barren, sandy, uninhabited. Not much different from the general characteristics of the coast islands from Cape Henry to the Floridas. . . . This island is some seven or eight miles long, a half mile wide. . . . The timber is mostly different from ours, being Pine, Palmetto, Live Oak, and a thick jungle of underbrush of scrub Live Oak, Pine and Sweet Gum. . . . I almost forgot to enumerate the Magnolia with its deep green glossy foliage. The leaves are verry much the shape of the Paw Paw, the upper side of the deepest and most glossy green, the down side buff or fawn color. The bark resembles the bark of an old birch.

I am finishing this letter up near the head of the island in sight of Ft Sumter and the City of Charleston. Rebels and rebel canon are bristling all round us save the sea side. Daily we hear the booming of heavy artillery from our naval fleet, and the response from some rebel craft. I am in hope to see the attack on C renewed. [I] hope our folks will not leave the contest until the problem is fairly demonstrated whether or not Charleston can be taken.

I am perfectly willing to bear fatigue, privation and pass through danger, but I want to see some good resulting from it. If a corresponding result cannot be accomplished bordering on an equivalent from the sacrifices we are making, I shall feel dissatisfied, perhaps disappointed. But I am not disappointed as often when I first came into the service. I expect failure, blunders and trickery, and this among officers high in command, & am prepared to bear such events with resignation to a certain extent. But these should not be the rule. The ballance should be largely in our favor.

Apl 21st. . . . After the siege of Charleston shall have been accomplished, I shall most likely make a trip to Ohio either to stay for good or make some arrangements that will place me in another Department. Three Western Regts, 39th Ills, 62nd Ohio & mine, are still held together, but with the tinkering we are continually subjected to as we go into a new Department makes it verry uncertain how long we may remain together. Our boys have no sort of affiliation for the Eastern troops. Gen Ferry has been relieved of his command. What for or where he has gone we do not know. . . .[47]

We can see no good reason why a Western Brigade should not be commanded by one of their sort of men. We are too far from home and cannot get the benefit of home influence. Favoritism and outside influence had a great deal to do in the organization and management of the army, and all this is held by Eastern interests. Eastern papers, Eastern money, Eastern politics and Eastern pride controll this coast army. We may do their fighting, dirty work and save them from destruction. They will call us good fellows & give some Yankee Brigadier all the glory. Well, we are fighting for a country controlled by patriotism, but at the same time do not feel as if we wanted to be deprived of the usual concomitants of valuable and meritorious service. The East ought to take care of the coast.

I see by the papers that the Connecticut troops claim the post of honor in the attack upon Charleston and that Gen Terry (not Ferry) has the command.[48] This announcement has been in all the Western papers. Now there is not one word of truth in the statement. The 100th N.Y. was the first Regt to land; next our Brigade, a <u>Western</u> Brigade. The 100th held the advance for a few days until they made bad work when they were withdrawn and our Brigade was thrown to the front, and has held the position right under the guns of the rebel batteries for two weeks. We have been in the advance all the time, the 100th with us at first but soon that was withdrawn. . . . . This newspaper post of honor is all bosh. . . .[49]

FOLLY ISLAND, S. C. —*Apl 25, 1863*

. . . I have just been to the head of the island (as we call it) next to Charleston. I can see Fort Sumter, Moltin[50] and many river fortifications, as well as lots of grey backs. The rebel pickets are across a narrow tidal river not more than 200 yards from our pickets, so near that they talk back & forth and occasionally send a paper or plug of tobacco for a little coffee. A note came over the other day in a half coconut shell boat. I looked into their sand batteries & behind their breastworks with my glass, with their big guns pointing at me at a range of a half mile. That is about as close as you would like to get to rebel canon mounted on their own forts with study fellows almost beyond harm's way to operate them. . . .

FOLLY ISLAND, S. C. —*Apl 27, 1863*

. . . I have not had my clothing off to go to bed during all this month. I do not get rested. My bones ache. I feel dull and dislike to stir. I have a hard cold which accounts for much of my unpleasant feeling. Again the anxiety and exposure of the last month has worn on me. A thoughtful man cannot command a Regt in the field in the face of a vigilant and powerful army, and not feel the effects of anxiety & care. I will sleep, but the sleeping is not refreshing.

My lot has been particularly one of anxiety since leaving St Helena, as most of my time I have been in the sight of the enemy with heavy batteries, within range of rifle shot in an unknown county, with an enemy having the moral advantage of having repulsed the most formidable naval expedition ever arrayed on the American Continent. . . .

April 28th. . . . Col Osborn of the 39th Ills has spent the last half hour with me, this moment gone. We consoled each other with the reflection that we were a long way from friends, among non homogeneous associates in arms, with rival Eastern officers, that we might have a good deal of the hard work to do, but little credit, less sympathy, & etc & etc. We talked of the prospect of the war, the undecided policy of the Government, the timidity of the Generals, the probable duration of hostilities and the like, and finally came to the verry wise conclusion that we knew absolutely nothing, & that we knew just about as much about the war as any of them and pledged ourselves "to be, to do, and to suffer" and patiently wait the Lord's own good time.[51]

I was down to the end of the island this forenoon to take a peep at the rebel works. They are quite busy throwing up earth forts and fortifying their side of the river. We are quietly sitting down doing nothing while they are as busy as beavers. I was asked what I proposed to do by a Regular Army [offi-cer] about this matter. I told him, "Do, why bless you, sir, I mean to sit down before them and make ugly faces at them till they get everything ready to shell us off the island and then make a mighty splurge and change my base of operations." I told him that was the strategy that was conducting the war.

As ridiculous as they may appear we are doing the verry thing. The rebels are bland, even sociable. They send tobacco and papers over to our boys, who in turn send them coffee. The pickets do not disturb each other. We are deluded by the rebels with the idea that they are friendly, harmless. We are pleased with their inoffensive demeanor while they are profiting by this armed neutrality by making fortifications & mounting guns within almost a stone's throw of our picket lines. O! shame. It makes me sick to see this game of playing at war practiced in my face and with my own men. I am led to despise the service <u>that is so debased</u> by inefficiency & reckless stupidity. What are we coming to? Will the people submit to be trifled with in this way much longer? The spring is wearing away & what has it brought?

FOLLY ISLAND, S. C.—*May 1, 1863*

The dirtiest place in which I was ever placed is my camp on this island, unless I except the threshing machine. The black sand, dust ashes and fine soil constantly kept in motion by the stirring coast winds permeates every-thing, desk papers, trunk clothing, victuals, even our precious bodies. I am nearly as black as my nigger.[52] You never saw anything to compare with it in the most dusty time or place in Ohio. The fine sand is drifted here like the light snow flakes in our Winters.

I washed my own pants, drawers and shirts yesterday, and made them look nice, too, but tomorrow they will be soiled again. To keep myself clean I plunge into the surf once a day. This Ocean bathing is splendid sport. The dashing billows will plunge all over you, pitching you at a great rate. The surf here is never quiet. The white caps are here always visible. One can wade out twenty rods, the beach is so gradual, & get tumbled onto the shore by the waves without much effort. I would like to live on the sea shore if I could have the making of the land and climate. But here I would never live only by compulsion. . . .

FOLLY ISLAND,—*May 5, 1863*

. . . Only two or three nights [ago] a squad of rebels had visited our picket line, challenged the sentinel, & the instant he replied they shot him through the body & seized his comrade. The following night, as you may imagine, all hands were vigilant and nervous, so much so that Capt Rogers of the 62nd Ohio was shot dead by one of his own men taking him for a rebel.[53]

The next night was I floundering around the lines without guide, without knowledge & worst of all in total darkness. Twice I lost my way, but by the aid of an occasional flicker of lightening I succeeded in finally finding my place. On foot, or on the wet ground, I spent the entire night. It rained furiously & I had waded nearly knee deep through mud and water when I had no guide but poor miserable guess work. These are some of the labors and dangers the army is meeting for the good of the country & for posterity.

It is a glorious thing to be a Field Officer some think. I was frequently told while recruiting that it would do for me, that I could talk, that I was an Officer & etc. So I expected to be, but this being [Field] Officer is not always so pleasant after all. There is a romance about being on horseback, but not much poetry about such an undertaking as I have just narrated. Nevertheless being boss of the concern has many advantages too after all, if it does not bring with it dangers and responsibilities. The time was when I would think this a terrible experience, but I have become accustomed to many bad things that I take as a matter of course that once would make me hesitate and verry likely refuse.

I had a little adventure while on Cole's Island that came verry nearly giving me a visit to Charleston. If I had followed the inclination of Capt Chapman, Field Officer of the Day, both of us would have a rare chance to partake of secesh hospitality.[54] In the affair we broke the leg of a poor secesh. This is war. . . .

May 9th. I have slept cold for the last three nights under two blankets. The nights are quite cold. Charleston still stands.

FOLLY ISLAND, S. C.—*May 11, 1863*

. . . I do not at present anticipate trouble here. The policy is not to rush matters. By the help of God we mean to starve the poor rebels out. I have been up to Light House Inlet this afternoon to make ugly faces at the secesh across the inlet. I think I shall be able to dislodge them in a few days. If I don't I shall change my base of operations. I am conducting a war upon the strictest rules of strategy, ie., I don't mean to run any risks. I don't mean anybody shall get hurt. I shall have lots of Grand Reviews, dig trenches, throw up rifle pits, make forts, mount them with Quaker guns & blow in the papers.

We learn that Gen Hooker has had a great battle and has been successful. But the reports are so conflicting that we are left in great suspense as to the results. The rebel pickets told our boys several days since that "crazy Joe Hooker was licked," but a day or two ago they reported that he had the best of it. We have papers as late as the fifth Inst., but the news in them shows nothing decisive. If we are defeated on the Rappahannock, it will be a disastrous check to our cause that may in the end be fatal to us. Should the rebels gain a decisive victory over the Army of the Potomac, I should not be at all surprised to hear of foreign recognition. I hope for a successful campaign. Gen H is a fighting man, and believes in the strategy of hard blows.

Being cut off from the luxury of newspapers except at long intervals makes us feel quite uneasy as to what is going on in the World. . . .[55]

FOLLY ISLAND, S. C.—*May 18, 1863*

I suppose you will be disappointed if I do not appropriate some part of each Sunday as they pass to the limited means I have to communicate with you. . . . But what shall I write? There are no novelties on this island. I have written you already all about it, and a good deal more. We are doing nothing here except dig and drill a little, lounge a great deal & wish for a change. We see nothing, hear nothing & of course have nothing only what we make of whole cloth to write about. . . .

Just here I felt like taking a drink. I have described the highly colored and odoriferous properties of our water before. Well to drink it I have a drinking tube made of rubber with a stone filter arrangement at one end, a mouth piece at the other through which I suck the water. This is a fine arrangement for the waters in this country. It saves one from digesting the thousands of animalcule that inhabited this wholesome beverage, such as lobsters, crabs, alligators, sharks and other quadrupeds.

Monday evening. I find on reviewing this letter that I have succeeded so well in writing a letter out of nothing that I am much encouraged to finish it.

The sand flies have been remarkably persevering this evening in their investigation of the properties of the human blood. They are the real phlebotomist against whose attack there is no escaping. They bite as wickedly as fleas, and are as numerous as the frogs of Egypt. I don't know what the infernal scamps were made for, nor do I care to know if to know is to experience the insinuation of their blood thirsty bills. I suppose they have bills, for they punch like the verry D——l. . . .

On the point next to Fort Sumter they grow much longer. My Adjt went up there a few days since to see the Lt Col who has been there stationed for picket duty. Upon the Adjt shaking hands with the Col one of these infernal flies in a hungry mood thrust his bill clear through both their hands. The Ajdt's hand being on the opposite from the fly & feeling a sharp pricking through his article, looked down & saw the extremity of the bill sticking out of his hand, took it be a mosquito. Striking a quick blow to expunge the creature he clinched the bill, completely fastening his hand to that of the Col, and so strongly too that amputation had to be resorted to, to get Mr fly from his unfortunate bill.

You make think this a big story, but let me remind you that I am not Gen Pope, nor am I an army correspondent of any of the leading papers and fed by army corps commanders.[56] The most remarkable thing I have lately seen was a shark, caught by the boys at the landing. Mrs Shark was the victim of a nautical blunder that caused her to strand in the water too shallow for her to navigate. As a result of her impudence some twenty or thirty boys pitched into the water after her. A venturesome teamster caught her by the tail to skull her to the shore, but Mrs Shark taking umbrage at so free use of her caudal extremity gave him a flap with her sculling apparatus, knocking him under the water, at the same time seizing him by the leg biting it terribly. With guns, axes and clubs the shark was compelled to let him go & was soon killed. It weighed over three hundred lbs & was 8 1/2 feet long. Had the water been deep the man would unquestionably lost his leg. As it was he only [suffered] a severely wounded limb. This letter ought to convince you that I am well and in full possession of my faculties, or as the boys say "sound in my head."

FOLLY ISLAND, S. C.—*May 24, 1863*

. . . I am procuring twenty five furloughs for that number of my men. A dozzen of them have already gone to their friends for the period of thirty days. I hope they will have a good time, but these furloughs will make them dissatisfied for a long time after they get back. I know after I had been home for a long time I was dissatisfied with camp life, but time sets all things even. Those reflections have all worn off. I hardly want to come home for a few days. When I return I want it to be as permanent as you allow.[57]

I think of making application to get my command into Western Virginia. I exceedingly dislike this nothing way of living I am compelled to endure here. I am spoiling to do something. If there I might have a chance to operate in the mountains against those infernal guerrillas. . . .

FOLLY ISLAND, S. C.—*May 30, 1863*

. . . Wood ticks are not friendly to my repose. They play hide & seek over my nervous body, and frequently take a nab at a point where blood may be extracted. . . . I have their ugly marks all over me. They are so voracious that I am frequently wakened by their attacks.

How rapidly time flies. It is now the last of May. Leaves of absence are being granted to my officers. Several officers go on the next steamer to their homes for twenty days. My Lt Col goes. When he returns I expect to let the Major go. Then the Col will take his turn, which will be in August, unless I should get ordered away before that time. The consolidation of Regiments and the organization of the Invalid Corp may reach the 67th.[58]

Consolidation takes affect when a Regt is reduced to 500 men. The consolidation musters out the Col, Maj, one ast surgeon and the supernumerary line Officers. If my Regt is to be consolidated I will be mustered out as if my term had expired. This would certainly be much better than to resign. You know how I would be looked on if I should resign. My pride does not at all favor the ideas of my drawing off from the service unless there is strong reason for the course.

Still if your health should fail you, indicating permanent or fatal disability I certainly would come home, for I can never think of leaving my children motherless and fatherless, too. I will do what is right, I hope. I certainly will if I know what is right. You should borrow no trouble on my account, for I am as safely situated here as at any other point in the field. It is healthy here, and too little prospect of fighting. The fighting season is over in this latitude. . . .[59]

FOLLY ISLAND, S. C.—*June 10, 1863*

. . . I see a great many letters from the army, but in verry few of them is there anything that pays for a reading. . . . What is usually written is fictitious or not worth knowing. I sometimes feel like writing an article on the management of the war, but then I think how little my opinions are worth, and how impolitic it would be to tell the truth that I desist. Nine tenths of what is written for publication of army operations is untrue. I saw it gravely stated in an Eastern paper a few days ago that we had gained a lodgment on Morris Island & had been engaged in skirmishing the enemy, one of the most groundless assertions in the world. We have had only one man on Morris Island. A foolish boy swam over for fun, and has been court martialed for his exploit. As for our skirmishing, the Gen is afraid of nothing more than that we will accidently get into a little brush with the secesh.

All you have seen printed about Charleston is mixed up so much with romance, unreal and foolish, that you know but little about what has been or is intended to be done here. The astonishing accounts in the papers are really surprising to us, who have been on the ground for the last four months.

Admirals and Generals have their trumpeters about them who sound their horns to suit the pride and caprice of those to whom they are attached. Admiral A wishes to win his laurels easily. He must be a hero. He must have fame. He knows it is much easier to write than fight his way to glory. He employs an artist and a special correspondent, talks of mighty undertakings, puts on mysterious airs, looks grave, has mighty secrets, is constrained by the War Department so that his genius cannot act, makes a reconnaissance in force, fails, has been denied supplies and reinforcements by tardy "Old Gideon," was compelled to act under imperative orders against his judgement, but nevertheless was eminently successful in all he undertook, and will accomplish the grand result as soon as <u>sufficient</u> reinforcements are furnished. He is a hero, a genius.

The pictorials represent him a la Neptune, with fifteen inch guns protruding from his breeches pocket, horse pistols in his boot legs, mortars in his cap, with a cutlass forty feet long in his right hand, with eyes as fiery as dragons eyes, and brow as threatening as a thunderstorm, his flag ship shattered & splintered, with mangled cavalry and infantry piled in heaps on deck till the bulwarks are no longer able to hold the array of this carnage. On one flank you may see a fine Ocean steamer, just in the act of being exploded, shattered to atoms, with fragments of marines whizzing through the air, other vessels biting each other to pieces, while the air miles round is full of round shot, chain shot, rifled shot, cold shot, hot shot, spherical case, shrapnel, canister and the terrible English pointed shot, shot seen and unseen, enough to sink all the navies in the world.

Fifty dollars makes "Frank Leslie" believe all this. A snug bottle & the little comforts of living makes the special correspondent know it is true, and by the time the people off a thousand miles get the news, ocular and auriculare, they believe Admiral A is a hero. The point is gained, he is a hero. Immortality stares him in the face. The General employs the same agencies, varying the scenery, and he too goes to glory.[60]

Now dear wife you may think this a queer letter for me to write you, but it would write & you as well as myself must take them as they come. Yet with all this I take consolation in the fact that the rebels are as big fools as we are and manage their matters about as loosely as we do. I know one thing. We cannot beat them by lying, but are a match for their stealing. . . .[61]

FOLLY ISLAND, S. C.—*June 16, 1863*

If I am not mistaken this is the anniversary of your 33rd birthday.[62] I will do better than you did by me my last anniversary by celebrating yours with a letter. This is certainly the best thing I can do for you under the circumstances. . . .

I have a pine apple on my table just taken from a wrecked steamer from the W Indies that attempted to run the blockade a few nights ago, but ran aground a few rods from our picket lines. This vessel has been in the habit of running the blockade for months, going out & coming in near the coast in shallow water where the heavy navy vessels cannot go, always taking the advantage of dark nights, but this time she missed her reckoning and ran aground. I have smoked her cigars and tasted her pine apples. We are getting her cargo as fast as we can under the rebel fire. They set her on fire, but being an iron clad only partially burned. Here are two drops of pine apple. Perhaps you can get a smell.

That ugly steamer has made us a great deal of trouble. The rebs got mad at their misfortune, and have been shelling us every night since. Their mortar practice has not been fatal in a single instance, but has the effect to keep all hands wide awake on the picket lines. I saw a pine tree cut entirely off its stump the other day by a forty pound shot. The projectile was not over four inches in diameter, but it went with such velocity that it cut a tree clean off 15 inches in diameter. Last night a rebel steamer did run the blockade with perfect ease as they are doing at this time of the moon every lunation. The navy is asleep.

FOLLY ISLAND, S. C.—*June 19, 1863*

. . . My Regt is becoming much reduced in numbers, and must ere long be consolidated under an order from the War Department that requires consolidation when a Regiment is reduced to half of its maximum number.

In case of consolidation I will be mustered out as a supernumerary, as there will be no necessity for a Col with a battalion of five companies. As this will undoubtably take place before the time mentioned I can come to you honorably discharged from the service, without even so much as the seeming to desire to get from it. Unless some new order directing it to the contrary be announced by the War Department, you may expect my time of service to end before a great while elapses. I verry much dislike the idea of resigning, still if your health should continue bad I will come home & take care of you and be a father to our little ones.

If I should stay till that time it will make more than two years that I have devoted all my time to the public. I do not feel as if I was doing much good here. My Regt is small (less than 500 men for duty). The Regular Army takes the entire controll of matters here. The civilian is despised. Yet if a volunteer officer should manage matters with no more ability or credit to the service than so far has been exhibited by the Officers having command here, I should send him to that institution in Columbus opposite the blind asylum where they attempt to manufacture brains for those unfortunate ones when nature has failed to supply them.

The cruel want of policy & decision and the trifling policy of the command when any has been adopted on this island makes me sick of the service here. We have been holding Folly Island on one side of Light House inlet, the rebels Morris Island on the other side within rifle range of each other. After we had occupied the island for a few days the rebels became pacific, hobnobbed with our boys. We sent sugar & old newspapers to them, they tobacco & newspapers to us. But all the time they were busy as beavers throwing up rifle pits and earth forts, mounting guns, mortars and making their place strong, and what is most remarkable, their guns were mounted in our teeth threatening our whole position on the inlet as well as covering our camps. This was done while we had the decided advantage in position and means for offensive operations. We could easily have prevented their operations or simultaneously put up works that would silence any demonstration they could make from their stand point. But no. It would aggravate the secesh if we did not let them get everything ready to their liking on their side of the inlet, before we did a thing, and then it would be ungenerous for us to do anything to hurt them in case of any pugnacious demonstration on their part.

The <u>magnanimous</u> did controll. When the rebels got ready they rained down a storm of iron hail upon our men for days and nights, and ours were perfectly powerless to do the least thing for defense. Our boys on their own hook dug <u>rat</u> holes & burrowed like badgers to save themselves from the enemies guns. The authorities have finally awakened to the necessity of the case, and significantly declare "something must be did." Therefore under the cover of the night, under the steady fire of rebel mortars, our men are making embrasures in the sand banks & mounting guns. Well I suppose military science requires that this work should never be commenced till actual demonstrations have been made indicating that they would be needed & that they should be constructed under the fire of the enemy, for the morale of the troops would not be tested if the works were made when the enemy had not perfected his means to knock us out of our position. But what is most remarkable of all is after the rebels had thoroughly shelled the head of the island, & shown us eight & ten inch mortars and splendid six & four inch rifled and other splendid guns, we had two little twelve pounders placed in position & it was gravely intended to fight them with twenty four pounds of metal while they at the same time could throw a thousand pounds as often as we the 24.

This is what we are doing, rather what we are not doing with the resources of the nation, and this Department has not been neglected as far as supplies & munitions of war are concerned. I cannot look at matters as they are now brought before me here without becoming heart sick. I know that matters are verry badly managed. All the military savants of the age could not convince me to the contrary. I cannot think military science & art so different from the laws that controll men, matter and nature as to make this stupid, inefficient and aimless policy even a fair exponent of military skill.

I know we "political" colonels (as we are called by the West Pointers) are despised, but I would remind these gentlemen of the fate of Gen Braddock when advised by a militia Col, derided it and ran into ruin.[63] I hate the manner of many of these army officers, deplore their want of good business sense & pity the soldier that is compelled to abide their time & manner of ending this war. This feeling I presume is mutual, but with it I have the reflection that the responsibility is not resting upon the volunteer officer nor the citizen soldiers. This Department does verry well on a peace establishment, but so far has been fruitless of any practical results as an organization for warlike operations. I have no confidence in the powers that controll matters here, nor any hope unless a different policy be adopted. But enough of this. I suppose my opinions would cost me my place in the army if known, a fate that ought to be measured out to those guilty of the trifling exhibited here.

As I feel now I can be of but little service here. And feeling ever so will, unless the administration is regenerated, I could do little or no good. I shall never feel like filling up my Regt if the good citizens of Ohio are to be used for the aimless purposes that my Regt has been used since it came to this island. They had much better stay at home and raise supplies for the army in some quarter, or go into some other Department. I expect blunders, defeats & disasters and crimes in the prosecution of this war, but I have no patience for the stupidity exhibited on this island. . . .

FOLLY ISLAND, S. C.—*July 3, 1863*

. . . I feel rather sadly this afternoon & have just returned from a visit to the hospital. Stayed half an hour with the sick boys. One poor fellow will probably die in a few hours. He was in a close corner of the tent, & could not get air enough & was quite restless because the attendant would not roll the bottom of the tent up. I ordered a seam to be ripped open near his head, remarking that the Col was good for something yet. "Yes" said he, "I always told them that." He wanted me to sit down & fan him awhile which I did, so much to his satisfaction that he soon fell asleep. O! how I pity the poor soldier who has to die in the field far from home. No kind mother, wife or sister to attend him as his trembling body sinks in the rivers of death. No one at home will ever know how much they owe to the patriotic soldier who thus offers up his life, a sacrifice for his home, his country.

I fear another Harrison's Landing drama will be witness by us. We landed there July 2nd last year. Hard work and exposure soon reduced my men in camp to half their number. I do not now recollect that I had a single case of death from disease at Harrison's Landing, but I do of having much suffering from fatigue and sickness. We are much better provided with shelter now than then, and have better food, yet we are wanting in what is verry essential to our continued health, <u>vegetables.</u>

Everything we get comes from the North, a climate two months later than this. I have some seventy five reported unfit for duty, yet verry few cases are dangerous. Dysentery, diarrhea and low fever not severe are the prevailing camp diseases. I have lost only two men by death since I came on this island out of some 580 men and Officers. We have been working exceedingly hard for the last two weeks. Night and day my men have been on duty, but I hope now to see a little cessation.

O! wife, I do hate to drive tired men. I can order, perhaps like to command. The exercise of authority is pleasing to me when not alloyed with the quality of pain, fatigue & ill temper of those I rule. I believe my Regiment have an affection for me. All treat me kindly and with confidence. Of course both Officers and men get out of patience with the exercise of authority, but as a general thing they in sober moments concede that I only do what I think is necessary. I am quite well myself. In fact I have not been compelled to work very hard myself. My labor has been more the work of direction than execution. . . .

Hear verry discouraging news from Ohio. I fear the anti war party is bent on mischief. I do not like this party rancor that appears to be growing at home. It bodes evil. I shall in all probability be at home before the election long enough to do a little for the county, <u>but will promise you I will not make more than six stump speeches a week.</u> . . .[64]

I suppose by this time you have got over your scare about the invasion. I think it will help the draft. A raid into Ohio will open the eyes of the peace men a little.[65]

FOLLY ISLAND, S. C.—*July 5, 1863*

A quiet Sabbath day has again almost passed. To me it has been almost a lonely day, as my Regt except my staff officers and sick ones are all on picket, some two miles to the front. My camp looks almost deserted. I ought to be with my Regt, but Col Dandy of the 100th N.Y. is in command at the head of the island where my Regt is doing duty, who is my junior, being a Regular Army officer and <u>perhaps</u> has special duty to perform, he cannot be relieved by a volunteer.[66] As a consequence I am ordered to stay in my camp far from the labor and responsibility of my command.

It requires a deal of figuring to keep the <u>"political"</u> colonels out of the way of these Regular Army gentlemen. I grant there is an advantage in favor of the man who has made the art of war his study, but that is only the advantage of theory. And where that theory has never had any better opportunity to develop into practical knowledge than the lazy limited routine furnished by the little standing army of this Republic, I must say that the advantage is not verry great over a thorough, intelligent, practical business man. I will not write you a sermon on the conduct of the war, but I had to inform you of the many burdens and responsibilities I escaped by being a <u>political</u> Colonel.

Everything indicates that an effort is to be made soon to drive the rebels from the islands fronting Charleston. Prudence dictates that I should look unfavorable contingencies in the face and be prepared for them. Yet I would not have you feel apprehensive of anything more than may attend me any day as long as I remain in the service. I do not expect to die in the service. I have a strong & abiding faith that I shall come home to you and the children safe and sound, which certainly will be a happy event to one little family circle. However it may eventuate I hope we shall never be unmindful of the many blessings a Kind Providence has bestowed upon us.

If I should die here, <u>I must be buried here.</u> No provision is made for transporting dead bodies from here in hot weather. It cannot be done. You most likely will learn my place of burial, and at a future time if desirable can secure what remains of my mortal self. But why be troubled about that? If my poor body should die I shall continue to live, I hope. I want no extravagance or show made over me. A plain slab, with a simple inscription will please me much better than a costly monument with pompous inscriptions. You may think from reading this that I am full of gloomy foreboding. But that is not true. I am cheerful, hopeful & full of courage. . . .

My Regt endured a most terrific shelling two weeks ago and came out of it without a scratch. I know if you had observed it you would have wondered how a man escaped but so it is with artillery shelling. There is much more noise than execution.

July 7th. We expect a dash at the rebels before long. You will hear of it, probably before news directly from me. If I should get killed remember that it is in the line of my duty. If I should live it will be another reason for being thankful.[67]

MORRIS ISLAND, S. C.—*July 17, 1863*

You have frequently heard of a drum head court martial. Well this is not a drum head court martial, but it is a <u>drum head epistle.</u>

Since I wrote you I have changed my quarters from Folly to this island. On the 10th Inst. our batteries opened on the rebel works with such a terrific storm of iron that in three hours all their works on the southern front of this island were ours & three fourths of this island occupied by us. We opened with some forty five guns besides those of the three monitors from the Charleston harbor side of the island. The rebels were completely taken by surprise, and what was best of all made but a feeble resistance to our attack. Fort Wagoner and Cumming's Point Battery are all the rebels now hold, and these have been daily bombarded by our gun boats with destructive effect.

What we are doing on land now I cannot write you, only that we are almost ready to not only knock them off the island, but to knock Sumter out of the bay. I have been within a mile & a half of the old fort several times & much nearer Fort Wagner, and for the last six days have night & day been under their fire. The sand hills of this island afford almost perfect protection against the artillery of the enemy. As for infantry it is next to impossible for them to land here, & if they did our field batteries and navy would annihilate them before they could do us much damage. Yesterday morning they made an attack on James Island upon our troops commanded by Gen Terry & were repulsed by our gun boats.[68]

Our losses have been verry light. My Regt has not lost a man. The men have learned to take care of themselves. With a shovel in a few minutes they make pits that are [bomb] proof against their heaviest guns. By the way the rebs are much more afraid of our metal than we are of theirs, and they have occasion to be. They have nothing to compare with our fifteen inch guns. Then our monitors can take these heavy guns up to their fort walls and batter away with little danger.

I see the New Iron Sides with her 16 heavy guns and five monitors not more than 1,500 yds from my tent quietly waiting to be ordered up to give the fated forts on the head of this island and Sumter their final blow. We have done much hard work the last month, but it has made its mark not so much upon the statistic boards for lost in battle as what is has otherwise materially accomplished. The position we now hold with what we must gain in a verry short time will place Charleston at our mercy. Get the forts on this island and Sumter reduced, and our fleet can bombard the City with our iron clads without taking any more of the forts. Yet to do this effectually I think Fort Johnson should be silenced.[69]

I am really roughing it now, as all my personal effects except hammock & clothing I have on my person are at my old camp on Folly Island. I am occupying a rebel tent to the windward of a dry sand bank that shields me from the rebel guns, but snows me all over with sand and fleas. I lay on the ground night before last and had to cover my head entirely over to keep my eyes, ears and nostrils from being the receptacles of this infernal sand. Add to this the almost intolerable heat of this climate & you can imagine whether laying siege to Sumter is fun or not.

We are all rejoiced at the success of Gens Grant & Meade.[70] The boys almost think the war must soon end. Of this I dare not now express an opinion, as I know so little of what has been really accomplished. I just heard a shell explode to the front. Your last letter was dated July 2nd. I have the Beacon of the 5th.

We are having heavy rains, is raining some now. Rained hard last night, wetting most of my boys to the skin in which condition they had to lie all night long. The rain has this advantage; it cools off the air and prevents the sand from drifting.

I am in good health and bear the wear and tear of campaign well here. I hope to be able to write you in a few days of a successful termination of our labors on this island. Kiss the children for me. My love to all our enquiring friends.

BEAUFORT—*July 20, 1863*

The mutations of fortune have verry unexpectedly brought me to this place with a bullet hole in my left side. You need not be startled at all by this announcement, as the wound is not dangerous & will disable me only for a few weeks at most. I certainly feel as if I had great cause to feel grateful to a Kind Providence for tempering the terrible blast my Regiment was compelled to pass through so kindly to me.[71]

My Regt suffered awfully. I have no means of giving the loss, but I know of 13 Officers among the killed & wounded. Col, Lt. Col, Adj't, & Sgt Major of the field & Staff were wounded. One Capt & two Lts killed & most all the ballance more or less battered. I have the names of some sixty men who were wounded with a verry large list unaccounted for.[72]

More than half the men that went into the fight at sundown were lost before 9 o'clock P.M. But why describe the result of this terribly disastrous assault against Fort Wagner. You will get it from the papers, & I am not in writing mood just now.[73] I shall probably see you by the end of the month, as most of us are to be sent North. I would not write this, but I shall stay till the 2nd boat goes, as I am not so bad as to need speedy removal. Now do not fret in the least about me as I feel quite well & am able to help myself, but I am compelled to move verry slowly.

Tuesday afternoon. There are some 40 Officers here with all sorts of wounds, but you would be surprised to see how cheerfully they bear the misfortunes of the field. I know the dear wives, mothers & sisters at home suffer more pain than we do over our misfortunes. We have been visited by ladies frequently since we came here, and truly have they been messengers of good to us.

The Government has been to great expense in providing comforts to the sick & wounded in the army. Clean clothing & bedding, wholesome food & medicines, good surgeons & nurses. In fact no place short of home could do more than the Government is doing here. I am on my back most of time, but can get up if necessary. The laying in bed all through the long hot day is not verry inviting.

Wednesday. I did expect to take the Arago tomorrow, but I understand now we will not take that boat but will soon be off on the Cosmopolitan.[74] I am doing verry well & have no fears as to the final result. Mrs Gen Lander is going to take me in her carriage to see my boys soon.[75] I hope you will get this early enough to allay any fears you may have from the news in the papers. I have not writing facilities here except what are exhibited in this paper.[76]

[Voris's letters to Lydia left no record of his immediate reaction to his wound. But this injury left an indelible physical and psychological mark that he carried for the rest of his life. On March 7, 1888, Voris delivered a paper, "Charleston in the Rebellion," to the Military Order of the Loyal Legion of the United States. He discussed the preparations for the attack, his personal recollections of being hit, and the care he received. The following excerpt about his traumatic wounding comes from that address:]

I was shot with an Enfield cartridge within 150 yards of the fort, and so disabled that I could not go forward. . . . As faintly illustrative of how the soldier feels and suffers under such trying circumstances, I will relate some of my own experiences of the awful struggle. When struck, I fancied a fragment of shell, many pounds in weight, had torn away a large portion of my left side, in the region of the lower ribs. I plunged forward, whole length, on the ground. In a moment, I raised up partially, and began to feel for the extent of my injury. Ascertaining that I was not lacerated as I had supposed, I thought I would push forward with my men. Getting up, I started to step off with my left leg, soldier like. No sooner had I thrown weight on it, than I fell again, finding myself wholly unable to walk. I was in an awful predicament, perfectly exposed to canister from Wagner, and shell from Gregg and Sumter, in front, and the enfilade from James Island. I tried to dig a trench in the sand with my saber, into which I might crawl, but the dry sand would fall back in place about as fast as I could scrape it out with my narrow implement. Failing in this, on all fours, I crawled toward the lee of the beach, which I hoped might shelter me a little, which was but a few yards distant. Reaching it, I found Sumter, Moultrie, and the batteries on Sullivan's Island had a most uncomfortable range on the beach. The whole sky was full of destruction, and the very earth was plowed through and through with the share of death. What could I do, helpless, and these horrors about me? I lay down in the billowy sand to rest and soothe my shocked body and perturbed nerves, strained by the awful tumult ranking around me, anxiously wondering what become of my heroic boys, who were contending against this savage havoc of iron, steel, and gun-powder. A charge of canister, striking all round me, aroused my reverie to thoughts of action. I moved toward the rear at the slowest pace possible and cannot say that I made any progress. I could hardly move, and then those dreadful guns! Charge after charge of canister followed my pathway, until the fort was so completely in our hands that its guns were practically silenced; but the infernal tempest from every point kept up with unabated fury. My movement not being toward the enemy, whenever I heard a shot following in my line of march, I rolled over on my side, not wishing to be shot in that part of the body never suggesting of valor, and where cowardice is said to place its most notable scars without provoking envy. After working this way for a half hour, and making perhaps 200 yards, two boys of the Sixty-second Ohio found me, and carried me to our first parallel, where had been arranged an ex tempore hospital, consisting of a huge earth bank, and a surgeon, who, with the zeal of a reformer and curiosity of a philosopher, undertook to fathom the depths of my wound. With forefinger up to the hilt, he sent his savage finger nail into my lacerated side, and pronounced the bullet beyond his reach, and that I would not need his further attention. Like a baby, I fainted, and, on reviving, laid my poor aching head on a sand bag to recruit a little strength. That blessed chaplain found me, and, good samaritan like, poured oil of gladness into my soul and brandy into my mouth, whereat I praised him as a dear, good man, and cursed that monster of a surgeon, which led the chaplain to think the delirium of death was turning my brain, and he reported me among the dead of Wagner.[77] He was never more mistaken in his life, and I never more truthful or sentient; both the surgeon and the chaplain were truly entitled to all that I gave them. After resting awhile, I was put on the horse of my Lieutenant-Colonel, from which he had been shot that night, and started for the lower end of the island, one and one-half miles off, where better hospital arrangements had been prepared. Oh, what an awful ride that was! A soldier walked along on each side of the horse to hold me from falling off. It did seem as if I would die before getting to the hospital. But I got there at last—by midnight—a decidedly used up man. I had been on duty constantly for forty-two hours, without sleep, under the most trying circumstances, and my soul longed for sleep. . . . Clara Barton was there, an angel of mercy, doing all in mortal power to assuage the miseries of the unfortunate soldiers. . . .[78]

At early daylight the next morning, I was carried on a stretcher to a steam transport, which was crowded full of poor fellows, with every sort of injury, and in every stage of mortal extremity, on which we were taken to Beaufort, S.C. There I got a change of clothing, and had my wounds dressed for the first time, in the afternoon of the second day, forty hours after being shot. The blood that saturated my clothing had hardened with the sand in which I had struggled, till my drawers and woolen shirt were as hard and rough as sandpaper, that tortured the tender, lacerated part of my body at every movement, and I was vastly more favored than any of our men. . . .[79]

"Old Promptly Has Returned"

CHARLESTON UNCONQUERED

SEPTEMBER 9, 1863 – JANUARY 22, 1864

[Voris resumed his command on Morris Island, September 12, 1863. During his convalescence, the Union's siege of Charleston had taken on a life of its own. In August, Union artillery and naval guns targeted Confederate positions with heavy bombardments during the day, including civilians in Charleston, and at night infantry dug saps and parallels under the beach toward Fort Wagner. By September 6, Gen. Pierre G. T. Beauregard, who headed Charleston's defenses, concluded that Fort Wagner and Battery Gregg were not militarily tenable and ordered their evacuations. When Union naval forces could not take Fort Sumter the next day, Confederates resupplied the fort, despite its reduction to rubble. Charleston remained unconquered, leaving Dahlgren, Maj. Gen. Quincy A. Gillmore, and their men, the 67th Ohio included, stymied. Voris faced another difficulty as the new year began. Under a War Department general order, he needed to reenlist sufficient veterans and attract new troops to maintain the 67th's structure or he would face consolidation with other regiments and forfeit his command.]

NEW YORK—*Sept 9, 1863*

I arrived safely here yesterday morning. Stayed with Mr Chamberlin last night and start this morning 11 o'clock for Hilton Head on Steamer Fulton.[1] Have a comfortable place to lodge and find several officers of my acquaintance on board.

I of course will not write you a long letter now telling you how sadly I felt at leaving you and our dear children. I hope I shall be spared a repetition of the trial. Take care of our children, try and make yourself comfortable. . . . I need not say I wish I was at home.

STEAMER FULTON OFF PORT ROYAL—*Sept 12, 1863*

. . . I am indeed unhappy. But what will resolve of this kind do? The times are so rugged that no man can travel smoothly & in the way of his own selection. The war must be prosecuted & men must be had. If they do not voluntarily enter the war conscription will do it, and should the worst come a retired Col might be constrained or compelled to go into the ranks. . . .

Dear wife, I will write more cheerfully now. I am in sight of Port Royal Harbor. Have had a delightful trip so far as externals could make it so. If it were going home to stay instead of going <u>from home</u> into that awful field I should have been in perfect ecstasies. My health is fine, my side is healing over, has almost closed. I have no lameness, only occasionally feel some pain in my side, but nothing that bodes danger. . . .

Sunday Morning. We are just nearing the dock at Hilton Head. 7 1/2 months ago a fine Sunday morning for the first time did I enter this harbor. It was winter then but summer now, but the change is slight. The same verdure then was apparent that now is seen. Since then but once till now have I visited the port from the seaward, then upon a temporary bed ex tempore to comfort a wounded side. The next time I enter it I hope will be preparatory to my journey for home, dear loved home. It is Sunday now, but no quiet Sabbath rules here. How different from the few Sabbaths I lately spent with my dearest ones on earth.

I hope to get to my Regt tonight. I learn of a repulse of Fort Sumter with a loss to the navy of some 130 men. I know no more than that.[2]

Afternoon. . . . Fort Wagner & Battery Gregg are ours. My Regt holds Gregg. I shall not reach them till morning. I learn that we have made verry decided headway against Charleston. It must come down. Fort Moultrie has been much damaged by our artillery. I will write you as soon as I get to the island. . . .

MORRIS ISLAND, S. C.—*Sept 14, 1863*

You see by the heading to this letter that I am again at my Regimental home, which appears as familiar as though I had left it but yesterday. I can hardly realize that I have been absent from the Regt lacking only four days of two months. Yet I did make you a good long visit, staying five weeks to a day. . . .

In the little time I have been absent great changes have taken place here. The southern part of the island is completely covered with tents. New works have been constructed, and shipping almost surrounds the island. Fort Wagner & Battery Gregg are no more throwing their ugly missiles against us. Now our troops occupy the whole island. The shovel & pick caused it to be hastily abandoned without *serious* loss to us. I know that you will rejoice with me that these places are no more in our way, and instead of threatening us with danger are really shielding us from the shafts of the enemy.

Sumter looks a vast pile of ruins, not unlike the views given in the illustrated papers. Yet it may be some time before we occupy the fort. It cannot be of much importance to them as an offensive position, but nevertheless may retard the navy in their operations. I fear the navy are not cooperating with the land forces with that vigor that should characterize the navy of the United States.

I wish you could see the island as it now is, perfectly planted over with tents as close as they can be well packed & could hear the booming of canon that every few minutes are discharged from the Woods battery & Fort Johnson on James Island and from Fort Moultrie & the batteries on Sullivan's Island. The navy nearly demolished Fort Moultrie a few days ago. One of the monitors[3] got aground & the ballance of the iron clads were compelled to go to her assistance to save her from destruction. They gave Fort Moultrie a terrible battering & set Moultrieville on fire. The bombardment is spoken of as presenting a most magnificent sight.[4]

My men appear much pleased to see me. Just as I had blown my light to go to bed the Regt paraded before my quarters and gave three cheers for the Col. It was rather a late reception, but I stepped to the door in my drawers & acknowledged the compliment. When they were bent on a speech I declined, promising them however to do as they requested when I presented the flag. The reason of their late call resulted from the fact that they were on picket duty & were not relieved till after dark. I certainly ought to feel proud of my men, as I do.

I have informed them that a <u>little woman</u> up in Summit County whom I respect & love above all others has heard of their valor, constancy and patriotism, and as a token of her high regard for their virtues has sent them a beautiful strand of colors. . . .

MORRIS ISLAND, S. C.—*Sept 16, 1863*

. . . I presented your flag last evening at Dress Parade. A large concourse of Officers & soldiers from other Regiments were present. I expressed my gratitude to a Kind Providence for my preservation & that of so many of my Regt through the terrible events of the campaign, told them of the anxiety felt for them at home, the pride felt for them in Ohio, that they had truly won great honor for their state & themselves, and as token of this good feelings for them at home I had been commissioned by "a little woman at home" that I delighted to honor to present them with a beautiful strand of colors. . . .

I have given a copy of your letter to several of my Officers and men for publication. They say it is first rate and comes from the heart of a <u>bully woman.</u> If you inquire for a Herald . . . you will find a letter from the 67th Regt containing it. . . .[5]

Now it is not perhaps altogether proper that I should boast of <u>your</u> letter, but as a true husband should feel pride in the praise awarded to his wife <u>I will say to you in all confidence that I am indeed proud.</u> It is a good letter, a first rate letter, one you never should be ashamed of. It is from the heart of a sensible woman. . . .

Neither of us fancied the state of things that have made us so much unhappiness. Yet with all of this, I hope we may reap good from it. I know I shall appreciate home more than I ever did before the army deprived me of it. I know I shall love you better than I should have done had I not experienced the terrible social misery of field life far from the embrace of wife and children. I shall love you for the heroism you have manifested in bearing up so nobly under your trials. Few women have done as well as you. When peace is secured or I am honorably discharged from the service, I hope to be able to make up in part for what you have suffered. I mean to be more patient, not so awfully hurried about everything, shall devote more time to the social wants of my family. I will try and reap some benefit from my ten years' experience as husband and father.

MORRIS ISLAND, S. C. — *Sept 21, 1863*

. . . My Regt is so employed in fatigue and picketing that I am not compelled to be on duty much. I stay in my tent during the heat of the day. By the way it has been quite cool for several days; we almost expected frost last night. Taking all things into account I have been remarkably well, much better than I dared expect when I left home. Had I known as much about operations here before I left home as I do now I should certainly have stayed another week with you. . . .

My position is not one of danger, nor severe labor. I would not engage in severe labor unless in case of an emergency, not feeling that I am called upon to do more than is really necessary. Still I think my presence here is of value to my men. I have been on horseback twice since I returned & can manage to ride as well as ever if I do not sit in the saddle too long.

MORRIS ISLAND, S. C. — *Sept 23, 1863*

. . . I shall be able to tell you before long whether I am to come home or not this fall. How would you like to have my friends get the command of a Brigade for me in case my Regt is consolidated?[6]

Men that have not seen a tithe of the service, never fought a battle or got a shot have been made Brigadier. On the score of meritorious conduct I could lay a strong claim upon "Honest Old Abe." Of the three Colonels commanding our Old Brigade, I am the only one that has ever been in a fight.[7] Gen Ferry who commanded it for eight months never was in a battle. Col Osborn who now commands it never was in a battle, yet I who have been in several and some what scarred up am about to lose my place in the army. I think Judges Wade & Spalding would be pleased to aid me. Gov Dennison and Secy Chase I think would aid me. Now Dear wife I will do just as you say about the matter. If you say try I will do so; if you say no I will relinquish all ambition in the line of the service. It certainly could be nothing less than highly flattering to you and our children to see me wearing a star instead of an eagle. . . .[8]

MORRIS ISLAND, S. C.—*Sept 24, 1863*

. . . The old flag has gone to Toledo to be preserved in memory of the brave men of the glorious 67th who so heroically supported it through many a hard day. Yours is to be returned to you when the Regt is mustered out. If I should die in the field you will remember this. It is to be your property. I am quite well. . . .[9]

MORRIS ISLAND, S. C.—*Sept 27, 1863*

. . . At all hours of the day and night I hear heavy canonading. Sometimes it is quite rapid, again at intervals of fifteen minutes to half an hour. The heavy Columbiads from James Island in the night sounds like heavy thunder. Capt Woodruff of the 39th Illinois was killed by a shell last Wednesday night. I saw his poor carcass. His face was much disfigured by burned powder, indicating that the shell exploded near him. He was shot almost in the same part of the body I was, only his was a little deeper.[10] I am so thankful mine was no worse than it was. I hope I shall never get any more shots. Two scars are enough for my ambition.

My camp is on the same ground occupied by the Regt when I left here in July. The men have their tents and are much more comfortably fixed than I left, and since Wagner & Gregg have come into our possession no more shot or shell are thrown into our camps. The rebs are apparently not well supplied with rifled canon, and are unable to reach us while in camp.

The navy still remains inactive. I am more & more convinced that I was right last spring in saying that an Admiral will never take Charleston. I said then that Charleston would never be taken by an Admiral and a Major General. There is a defect in the management of our army and navy when cooperating. The General commanding the Department should have the command of the whole enterprise. The caprice and hesitancy of one man is bad enough, but of two with the jealousy that must exist when each are independent of the other makes the matter intolerable.

Gen Gillmore has done all he undertook to do. The navy has not. What they might have done nobody will ever know, and what it is capable of doing we will never know while managed by the timid, trifling, unbusiness policy that has characterized it since Charleston has been the object of this campaign. I have not the means of particularizing, but I know I am not mistaken when I say that no adequate efforts have been made to demonstrate what the flotilla here can do, else why is every vessel brought to operate here still kept in a perfect state of conservation, ordinary wear & tear excepted.[11]

We learn from rebel sources that had the iron clads worked a few min-utes longer on Sumter their magazines would have been blown up. Also that an order had been issued by the rebel authorities to evacuate Sullivan's Island, but the navy retired just as they were about to execute the order. I am sick of playing war.

MORRIS ISLAND, S. C.— *Oct 6, 1863*

. . . I am interrupted by Capt Girty who has brought a half dozzen letters from as many young girls in answer to a matrimonial advertisement he had inserted in the Herald. I have enjoyed the felicity of reading them. Matri-mony is suggestive of so much interest that these younglings are embarking on a strange correspondence, some for fun, others in real earnest hoping to catch a fellow in its meshes through such doubtful means. Capt G expects fine fun from the fair correspondents who are writing to Mr "Yates," 67 Reg O. V. I told him it was rather a poor investment, but he thinks it will pay. You must say nothing about it, so that Mrs Girty should learn about it, as she might fret over his flirtation.[12]

I called on Gen Gillmore an afternoon last week & spent an hour verry pleasant with him. He still claims to be an Ohio man and intends to vote our state ticket at the ensuing election, & will vote as every man who re-gards the honor of Ohio should vote. I was well pleased with his manner, finding him possessed of that cordiality that I have so frequently marked as existing among Buckeyes. . . .[13]

MORRIS ISLAND, S. C.— *Oct 7, 1863*

. . . I am making general reforms in my Regiment. Till within a week I did not feel able to do much, but I feel quite well and have been exercising my peculiar talent, scolding at a great rate for a few days. Everything has been exceedingly laxly managed since the 18th July till I took the reins. Gen Terry told me the Regt needed a Col verry much. On my return I found a verry slouchy camp, no regard to taste & but little to comfort or neatness.[14]

I have entirely overhauled the camp, leveled off the streets, taken down the tents, had them pitched again & elevated from the ground, caused the ranks of tents to be placed in line & with uniformity, and on the whole am making a fine camp. Men and Officers are verry much like children. They need constant watching. . . . My Officers think I am exacting, my men that I am strict, but having the machine running loosely for so long a time, they agree that it is much better to have discipline enforced & in-ternal matters looked after. I am making my men keep their persons, clothing and quarters neat and tidy. You ought to see me knock things along. If you could only hear me put some careless Officers through you would forget that I ever scolded at home. I have had great trouble to make my Officers remember that I was given to punctuality. But placing a couple under arrest for tardiness, and blowing up others with a long strong d——m, has made them open their eyes to the fact that "Old Promptly" has indeed returned.[15]

I suppose you do not know what I mean by "Old Promptly." Well, I will tell you. I had a slow captain in my Regt who frequently needed urging to bring him to line. I frequently felt compelled to call out to him to move promptly, "Co K more promptly," the "right Co more promptly" & etc. This nettled Capt L & when he would see me going by he would say to his brother Officers, there goes "Old Promptly." This name then attached to me & I am frequently called Old Promptly. . . .[16]

I had two boys wounded by shell a few days ago while at work at Battery Gregg. I see some poor fellows almost every day carried by to their camp who have been wounded while at work to the front. The rebels keep up a constant firing upon the works we are constructing. . . .

MORRIS ISLAND, S. C.—*Oct 8, 1863*

. . . We have papers of the 3d Inst., which brings us down to last Saturday, but get no news by these dates. Rosecrantz was badly punished in the battles of the Chicamauga, but probably not much worse than the rebels. At least they were not in condition to take advantage of the apparent successes they gained in those battles.[17]

Gen R had a splendid army that felt its strength. I had hoped that it was invincible, but it was overpowered. The public mind I fear is not prepared for such reverses. But from what I can learn we are preparing an effort that will tell against the rebels in the neighborhood of the late battle.

I dislike to hear of the terrible carnage of our battle. I have no taste for the misery they entail. Yet I would force the enemy to fight & that speedily. If we succeed we must fight. The sooner the horrid realities of the war are over the better for us all. I think I could fight as well as ever. At least I am no more afraid of rebel bullets than I was before I got hit. . . .

Matters are progressing moderately so far as I can see. My observation is quite limited however. The navy is doing nothing. In fact they have not fired again till Tuesday night last since I came back, only to salute Gen Gillmore on the receipt of the news of his promotion [to major general of volunteers]. We are not all satisfied with the conduct of Admiral Dahlgren. He is represented as having chronic sea sickness, a chronic dislike to danger & hardship, and above all, a chronic dislike to do anything. A good joke is told of him as originating with the commissary sergeant, who deals out the fresh beef for the Officers of the post. Admiral D ordered five lbs fresh beef & five pounds tripe. The sergeant struck out the tripe and inserted pluck, saying that even that small quantity would be of great advantage to this navy.

I am sick of the trifling policy many of our leading commanding Officers adopt in the discharge of their high functions. I have seen a great deal of it.

I am well satisfied that Charleston would today have been in our possession had the navy done what it was capable of doing. They are so afraid of
losing a vessel that they would rather see a Brigade of infantry go to destruction than lose one of their boats.

The President is too easy with such do nothing Officers. If a subaltern
does not do his duty off goes his head. If an enlisted man commits a blunder or neglects his duty, he is put to work in our forts with a forty lbs ball &
chain to his ankle & at the end of the service dishonorably dismissed without bounty & no pay. But a General or Admiral may defeat the end of an
entire campaign by his blunders & neglect, and perhaps be retained in his
command, at most only relieved of his command with full pay & allowances, and nothing under Heaven to do but eat, sleep & enjoy himself
at the expense of the Country. This is all wrong. I hope the next Congress
will correct these evils. If it does not it certainly will not be doing its duty
to the people. . . .

MORRIS ISLAND, S. C.—*Oct 13, 1863*

. . . We are having election today. No scrambling, no electioneering, no
drinking, no quarreling, everything is as quiet as if it were the Sabbath. I
never knew an election to go off so quietly. Your flag is steaming to the
wind, its silken fold rejoicing with the men that they have the opportunity
to give the Copperheads a rebuke. I announced an order this morning giving my views of the duties of soldiers at this election, a copy of which I
send to the Herald for publication. If it is published you can get a copy of
the paper for preservation.[18]

As I am writing I see the steamer Spalding coming into the channel. I
presume she is in from the North, may have the mail. Certainly will bring
in some Northern papers. We look with great anxiety to the news from the
army, as well we may for our operations are not so separated from that of
the army in general as not to be materially affected by our good or ill success. Of course we do not expect any verry startling news now but we want
to get all that may affect us if it be not of the most important kind. . . .

I made a visit to Folly Island yesterday, calling on the Ohio Regiments
there, of which there are three, 25th, 75th, and 107th. The 107th was organized in the northern part of the state. I found several acquaintances in the
Regts. I passed through my old camp ground on Folly, but found no attractions for me. . . .

I am writing this a good deal by piece meals. I am constantly called on
for law in relation to the voting and other business so that you cannot expect a verry connected letter. Since I last wrote to you I have been all over
the island. Being Gen Officer of the Day I had duty to the front. Was at Battery Gregg, Fort Wagner and along our batteries to the front. I saw the huge
two hundred pounders shooting toward Ft Johnson, and could follow the
projectile with my eye almost across the bay. When behind the artillery

you can see the ball as it rises from the canon, and follow it as it goes through the air until it gets too far to make a sensible impression on the eye. Our men learn to keep out of the way of the rebel shell quite well. They keep watch till they see a puff of smoke when they call "Cover from Johnson, Moultrie, Bull of the Woods" & etc as the case may be, and all hands fall behind sand bank or other cover that may be convenient. I must say that I like to see a shell after night take its linear course through the air & see it explode at the end of its journey, but while my curiosity is being gratified I like to have my precious body kept where there is not danger of spoiling my tender skin.

From either Wagner or Gregg a fine view of the city of Charleston may be had. With my glass I can see the Charlestonians at home. Ft Sumter looks battered enough. A few soldiers are still there, but for offensive operations Sumter can do but little.[19] Nevertheless it can be held against a large force. If I had the fort under my command & I were a rebel I would make an earth battery of it that would make Gen Gillmore or any other man trouble that attempts to throw up batteries on Cumming's Point. The rubbish would make just as good a fort as ever Wagner was, and much more troublesome to take because no parallels could be thrown against it. Sumter, you know, is an artificial island sunk to the front of Charleston harbor by the Government. . . .

The election passed off very pleasantly. I believe all the native born Americans voted the Union ticket. Some Irish, Gov Seymour's friends, voted for Vallandigham.[20] The Irish as railroad hands are well enough, but as citizens they are sure to be on "the rebellion side, by Jazes." The intelligent colored man is much more respectable and safe as a voter than the Irish.[21] If I had taken a big jug of whiskey, I think I could have controlled the votes of the Irish company, who voted 9 for Brough and 17 for Vallandigham, 26 in all. Thank God I had no Officer in my Regt who disgraced himself or the Regt by voting for Val.[22]

MORRIS ISLAND, S. C.—*Oct 14, 1863*

. . . I see something everyday that makes the state of war more & more horrible to me. I had a poor man die today, leaving a poor wife and children to mourn his loss, and what is worst of all is that he leaves nothing for them to live upon. At the time we came onto this island he stayed back in camp at Folly Island in disobedience to orders, he claiming to be sick, for which he was tried by a general court martial, and ten dollars per month of his pay was declared forfeit by the Court as a penalty for the period of six months. A few days ago his poor wife wrote a letter appealing to him for money. It so worried him that he pined away & died. Alas! a victim of the cruelties of this wicked war.

This island has been a terrible place for my Regiment. Since I came [I] have had thirty two men die from disease & casualties of battle, and in all have had one hundred and fifty casualties. This may look large, but the campaign of this summer has not been as destructive to my command as that of last summer. My men are kept constantly at work, but on the whole look quite well. The weather has become so much cooler that we do not suffer from the heat of the climate. . . .

We are being paid off today. Pay day is always embraced with joy by the men. The <u>Green Backs</u> are such nice things to send home. The fond wife is delighted at seeing them coming from her far off husband in the army. She sees in them a token of the remembrance and affection of her dearest friend in the army. He sees in them the means of adding material comfort to his family. My men send most of their money home. I encourage them to do it. They should save their money, for it is earned by the hardest *efforts*. . . .[23]

MORRIS ISLAND, S. C.—*Oct 18, 1863*

. . . My Regiment is fast melting away. I have say 445 men left. Of these 40 are reported for the Invalid Corps. I expect an order in a short time from the War Department transferring them. This being done I shall not have enough men in my Regt to make five maximum companies. . . .

My men are all out to the front today at work on the forts. Matters are hurried up with a vengeance. The men are constantly employed. I have as compared with the other Regts on the island as few sick as any. Some of the Yankee Regts have more than half of their men sick. They do not stand grief as well as the Western men do. There is more show about them, but vastly less mettle. The most showy Regiments on the island, 7th N.H. and Independent [New York] Battalion, have by far the filthiest & ill arranged camp here. In making my report as Gen Officer of the Day I pitched into their filthy habits. Cleanliness is verry essential to the health of a command like ours. . . .

MORRIS ISLAND, S. C.—*Oct 19, 1863*

. . . I see by the Beacon that you and your flag have been the subject for some letters written from my Regiment. . . .[24] We are rejoiced at the election news from Ohio & Pa. We learned as early as Sunday afternoon that the elections were all right. So far as Ohio was concerned I never had any doubt, for never was the great conscience of the people appealed to in any political struggle in my native state, and true to its honor vindicated its intelligence and political virtue.[25]

Poor Vallandigham will hardly march in triumph to the State Capitol with his two hundred thousand supporters to be inaugurated the next Governor of Ohio. My men gave nine hearty cheers when the news was communicated to them. I had them assemble, told them that the home guard had achieved a great victory at home over the traitors there without our help, and that the citizens at home had given us the assurance to the majority of a hundred thousand, that they would take care of the miserable traitors at home & not permit a fire to gut us in the rear while we were fighting rebels in the field. . . .

MORRIS ISLAND, S. C.—*Oct 24, 1863*

. . . From the papers (we have dates to the 19th Inst.) fully confirm the former reports that the loyal men of the North had acquired a decided yea, an overwhelming victory over the Copperheads in the elections of the 13th. This is as it should be. I am pleased at the demonstrations of joy everywhere exhibited at this great moral victory. The political leaders of the Vallandigham party ought not only be vanquished in the elections, but should be punished in our prisons for their filthy acts of treason. Never were men more deserving of severe punishment for infidelity to their Government than the men who threw the democratic party into such a slough of hostility to the great cause of the Government. Political defeat is too good for them. I hope the people will mock these traitors, and forever after shut them out of the control of public matters. I would dearly love to have stayed till after the elections and taken an active part of the stump against them, but the situation of my command before Charleston made me feel that a strong duty called me there. I felt as if the home guard ought to take care of the traitors at home till after the war when we will finish the work by laying them out forever. . . .

I see by the last news that "Old Abe" has called for 300,000 new volunteers to fill up the old Regiments. I shall send home some recruiting Officers to secure volunteers, but have no faith in their efforts. For two months I have two captains & four or six sgts recruiting who have procured just six men, not as many as I have lost in that time by half.

MORRIS ISLAND, S. C.—*Oct 27, 1863*

I have been to the front looking at the big guns play away at Sumter. The ruined and unsightly walls of Sumter are still the object of the serious attention of our batteries and the bugbear of the navy. After Sumter had been reduced by the land forces as to be useless to the rebels for defensive operations, then the navy should have lost no time but at once operated against Charleston, not giving the enemy a moment's time to repair their damaged works, or collect from the shock given them. Taking the demolition of Sumter in connection with the fall of Wagner & Gregg, there was no earthly reason why the fleet did not at once set about to execute the mission for which they were sent here.

Nearly two months have elapsed since Sumter, Wagner & Gregg were silenced, giving the enemy abundance of time to erect new works, strengthen their old ones & repair the injuries done them, as well as to mount new guns, renew their supply of ammunition, and make all needful preparation for a vigorous if not successful resistance. I have no doubt but that Sumter today is armed with mortars, perhaps heavy guns that make it really as formidable as Wagner was before its fall. At any event they have had abundance of time to have made it so, & to presume they have not done so is to presume that they have been sleeping upon their opportunity, which they would hardly do. We have three splendid earth forts at the head of the island. Gregg & Wagner have been made entirely new & mounted with a better class of guns than the rebels ever saw, but while we have been doing this the secesh have been active at work making strong defensive works.

It is cold enough to want a fire & has been so for the last two or three days, verry much such nights as you have in the last of Sept excepting the frost which we do not have near the sea coast. I presume there has been frost out from the Ocean 60 or 70 miles. I am getting to be a great deal of a baby about exposure. I dislike many of the hardships of the field much more than I did the first year I was in the field. . . .

It has got be Friday night. I think it is Friday but have no Almanack. Can't be sure. Time is passing away much more rapidly than it did when I first returned. I have been out all day at work laying out camp and superintending the work for our new home. My camp is assuming shape rapidly now. . . .

FOLLY ISLAND, S. C.—*Oct 29, 1863*

I quit off rather abruptly night before last as the adjutant announced that the Regt must be under arms at 4 A.M. & wanting sleep before the trials of an early rising, I thought it best to pile in. On awakening next morning I got order to be ready to move to Folly Island by 8 1/2 A.M. We moved at 3 P.M., lay out all the ensuing night on Light House Inlet in a chilly beating wind. Today we arrived at our new camping grounds in the woods, in the lea of a high bank & thick wood, which will save us from much of the force of the winds coming from the sea. . . .[26]

I got papers yesterday of the 23d in which I learn that Rosecrans is relieved by Gen Grant. We always esteemed him one of the best Officers in the army & cannot appreciate why he was relieved. It is intimated that he was given unmistakable evidences of insanity.[27]

We have had a grand move, taking everything with us to the barrel staves the boys used for slats for their bunks. It makes an immense amount of luggage, say fifty wagons. Your humble servant had fully a half wagon load of stuff. . . . When we move I do quarter master's work by directing the operations. When we make camp I lay out the ground and see to the manner of doing the work, & everyday have to see that the Officers do as they are ordered. Irresponsibility from beginning to end is a fearful characteristic of the army. All do what they feel compelled to do. Few show cordiality, zeal & efficiency. . . .

Saturday Evening, Oct 31st. I have been at work today & am quite tired. My side aches. In fact I get lame there after any hard exercise. I do not feel as if it was at all dangerous, but I dare not lift or work hard yet, and am careful about exposure. I hope by careful management to be entirely well from my wound in a few months. These bullet holes are not the most easy things to patch up. It takes long months to put them in a condition as good as new. . . .

Sunday Morning. I hear them booming away at Fort Sumter this morning. Yet with what results I don't know, but understand they have leveled the sea face almost to the water's edge. We did suppose an assault would have been made last night, but have heard nothing from Morris Island since yesterday morning. I am expecting to hear of the opening of Charleston harbor to our iron clads verry soon. We have done most of the hard and dangerous work to accomplish that end, & if the navy does its duty we shall soon say to the wicked City surrender or we will lay you in ashes. . . .[28]

FOLLY ISLAND, S. C.—*Nov 2, 1863*

. . . All is quiet tonight. I hear no angry canon belching forth their hideous peals of thunder, no heavy trains of ammunition, nor numerous bodies of fatigue parties which are constantly passing my tent to and from the front. All is quiet save the ceaseless roar of the surf and the chirp of the crickets. . . .

FOLLY ISLAND, S. C.—*Nov 5, 1863*

. . . I read your letters over last night & this morning before I got up. I have eleven in all, the last is date Oct 21. We have dates of Northern newspapers as last as Oct 31, by which we learn that Bragg has been defeated by Gen Hooker. We also have the Charleston Mercury of the 2d Inst. in which is admitted that Bragg has been defeated and has been compelled to fall back. If the Army of the Cumberland does its duty well it will next to closing the Mississippi do the most to bring the war to a close.[29]

I do not know what we are to do here. Our batteries have been playing away at Sumter for the last ten days & have nearly leveled the sea face to the water's edge. I think it will be taken soon. Then the navy must go in. I have never looked upon the capture of Charleston of great significance as a military movement. The moral effect would be good, but what is it worth to us when we have taken it? Its harbor has been blockaded for a long time & verry effectively, too. We are out of danger now, and should the navy do well we may occupy Charleston before long & that too without much sacrifice of life, but to take the City by the land force here I hardly think is contemplated. . . .

I understand Aunt Fanny went North on the Arago at her last trip. You may see her. Her son Geo is on Parris Island & her daughter Martha is employed . . . as a clerk. How would you like a clerkship? It would be so much easier than sewing with a <u>machine.</u> . . .

Thursday, Nov 6. When I left you I expected to have been home by this time, but now I do not see any prospect of my getting home for a long time. The call is for 300,000 men to fill up the old Regiments. Ohio will raise enough men to give me some three or four hundred in addition to those I have now.[30] I do wish the war over. If Grant does what we have reason to expect he will in the next sixty days, the South will begin strongly to think that the state of war and rebellion are not suited to their wants.

I dread the coming Presidential canvass. If the war was over it would be harmless enough, but with the war on our hands will be a bad affair. I hardly think the Copperheads will make such a fight as they made in Ohio in the last election, unless we should be verry unfortunate in our operations. The lesson of this fall's election must be heeded by them, but the peace men are so unscrupulous and presumptuous that they will make the struggle a dangerous one. I wish we did not elect our President so frequently, and that he should forever be ineligible after once holding the office for a time.

I am not afraid of the army. Its fidelity to the country has been too well tried to have any fear on its account. But the filthy demagogues of both parties will do anything to advance their own ends. I now think "Old Abe" will be the next candidate, but the next six months may develop new men & a new state of things so that nothing but the merest conjecture can be given now. Of one thing however I am quite confident; you nor I will not be candidates in the ensuing or any other canvass. I have verry much pitied "Honest Old Abe" at times since his election. He has aimed to do right, but has had the most conflicting and dangerous counsel to follow or avoid of any man ever at the head of the nation. And a purer man never filled the executive than he. Perhaps he is too slow, but moves with great force when he does move. "Large bodies move slowly" is an old adage. The President is a fair illustration of its truth. . . .

I hear the heavy guns occasionally, but we are off too far to hear much of what is going on. It must be all of ten miles from here to Sumter. I am almost sorry that they sent us away from Morris Island so soon, but my men needed rest. . . .

Saturday evening has again come. It is as quiet as it is at home save the roar of the sea surf. I have often told you that the sea shore always vibrates to the roll of the waves whose ceaseless surges are ever making a roaring sound heard for a long way inland. I hear an occasional laugh and a little whistling & the low murmuring of the camp, but so low as to be scarcely audible. . . .[31]

FOLLY ISLAND, S. C.—*Nov 10, 1863*

I wrote you yesterday, putting the letter in the mail only today, but I am sending a detail to Ohio to recruit. Sgt Bruce will probably be in Akron soon & will call & see you & bring with him a piece of the brick of which Sumter was built. It was taken from the ruined walls of Sumter on the night of the 2d Inst. by Private Charles Eurimius, my Regiment.[32] It is part of the first bricks taken from Sumter by a Union man since it fell into the hands of the rebels. . . .[33]

I suppose I might have got away on this recruiting matter if I had dared leave my Regiment, but to tell the truth it needs the <u>old one</u> here. "Old Promptly" is required to keep things straight.

FOLLY ISLAND, S. C.—*Nov 13, 1863*

. . . It has been quite warm today, not at all like a November day in Ohio. It is clear and still outdoors, save the incessant roll of the surf. It sounds loudly now as the tide is at its flood & comes quite near my tent. When it subsides it is off some twenty rods or more further. I have become so accustomed to its tumult that I sleep on its banks as soundly as I would were I at home. Nor do the fiercer surges of armed traitors in sight of us rob me of my dear benefactor, rest. I go to bed at night with the same calm assurance I do at home. I have no fear that thieves will break through & steal, for I have nothing to be stolen, and should the secesh make an effort to get here in the night we could get good and ready before they could do us much harm. Could do just as well as if they attempted to reach us in the day time.

No man is fit to be called a soldier who is continually fretting for fear of danger. Of all the men in the world the soldier should be the most cheerful. We really have too few comforts to indulge in unpleasant reflections. You would be surprised to visit a camp in the field and find so much hilarity & good feeling among the men. They make enjoyment for each other. Their arms, accoutrements and clothing take up a great deal of their time to keep them neat. Their quarters need much care, and with proper encouragement the men find enough to do to fill up all their time quite pleasantly. The soldier is not the most unhappy mortal in the world by any means. He has no care under Heaven, only to eat & wear what Uncle Samuel provides & do what he is instructed to do, but when that is done he is entirely relieved from care. If he works hard he has a corresponding period for rest. If he has to encounter danger, he has the satisfaction of adventure, and if unfortunate he knows that a grateful people & a just Government will protect the objects of his affection and save <u>him</u> from want. . . .

Monday evening, Nov 16. I have been attending to the duties of inspection all day long. Early in the morning the men were blackening their boots and accoutrements, polishing their brass plates & burnishing their guns, scrubbing themselves and dusting their clothing. By two o'clock all were in line with knapsacks on and all their soldier gear snugly packed therein save arms, accoutrements & equipment. A fine looking set of fellows they were, too good for rebel bullets.

With all the appliances of a rich town, the Akron Rifles never looked as well as my men did today.[34] Mine are not band box soldiers by any means, but I try to make them neat and tidy as the circumstances will allow and I succeed fairly. I think I have as neat a camp as there is on the island. I know it is spoken of as being so by strangers. They say it shows taste and attention to adornment, but it requires constant attention. The tendency of the field is to slackness. We form no attachments for place, at least we should not. It is laid down among the maxims of war that the soldier forms no attachments for his place of encampment or barracks but always be on the ready to move; to be so little satisfied with the present place they are pleased to go to a new one even if met with danger and privations.

The men frequently say, "what is the use, we will not stay long to enjoy it." [I reply] if you black your boots, they soon get soiled. I shave my face, but it soon get dirty. Your clothing soon fades and wears out, but who ever heard of one refusing to wear clothing because it wore out. We all our lives are doing what does not pay in dollar & cents, still we may make it pay in personal gratification, which is as good a return for our efforts as money. Money is only the means of procuring what will satisfy our wants or caprices. . . .

We have had no mail since a week ago Sunday last, but I learn that a portion of Lee's army have been engaged with our <u>Potomac</u> Army & got badly punished, that we took some 1,800 prisoners and some dozen pieces of artillery. That will satisfy the Eastern papers for a whole month, and give that army rest for twice as long. All hail to the Potomac Army.[35]

I would really like to know what Gen Halleck's theory is for the management of the war. He must have some definite plan, but events do not develop it so that I am able to tell what it is, but it does look a great deal like trying to worry the rebels into subjection rather than by hard knocks. I want to see the devils <u>licked</u> & believe we have the means of doing it if they were well & vigorously used.

The new call for 300,000 men looks like protracting the war for a year & a half much more than a vigorous prosecution of the work to be done. I admit the conscription a failure, but admit we need the men & should have them. If the President had no authority to enforce a vigorous conscription, let him have called Congress together as soon as that fact was developed, get the authority & then give the rebels thunder. This call is doing what ought to have been done a year and a half ago, to fill up the skeleton regiments, but is entirely too slow in operation.[36]

I know I could beat Old Abe in some respects. I could make matters move faster. I could get armies in the field sooner & make them more efficient than he has. Of all the levies raised last year but little good arose. New Regts of three year men & nine month's conscripts were not worth half as much as if they had been placed with skeleton regiments, & they were so long in being placed in the field that they availed but little in the campaign of last Fall, Winter & Spring. Vigor is an essential condition of successful warfare. . . .

FOLLY ISLAND, S. C.—*Nov 24, 1863*

. . . My darky has just stuck his head in my tent door and asked, "does you want anything Curnel"—I say "no, do you read your book evenings"? He say, yes, where I sent him to his books for the ballance of the evening when he sent himself to bed. Our colored boys live better in the army than they ever did before in their lives, and appear to like it verry well. I have not heard of an instance of one going back to his master after joining his fortunes with our army.

My boy has an idea that I am going North before long, and is on tip toe with the expectation of going himself. I tell him he is a good boy, I will take him where he will not only be safe but where he can be a man & nobody can abuse him. They have high ideas of a free society. In all their actions they exhibit a recognition of their subordination to the white race & frequently yield to outrage from them as a matter of course as if it were a destiny from which they had no power to escape. Our boys treat them much better than they did a few months ago. The hard work the coloreds did on Morris Island was a good thing for them in our estimation.[37]

FOLLY ISLAND, S. C.—*Nov 26, 1863*

Thanksgiving is almost over and I have had neither turkey or pumpkin pie, nor have I been visited by a single soul that sustains to me any other relation than that of friend. At Dress Parade this evening I read the Governor's Proclamation and made a few remarks to my men, reverting to the scenes of danger & trial through which we had passed during the last year, how we had been cared for & protected by a Kind Providence, how the dear ones at home had also been sustained by the same powerful hand, and how much had been bestowed upon us for which we should be thankful, after which the chaplain offered up a prayer and all then separated to their quarters. Not to their cheerful homes would to God it had been so. I shall certainly try to spend the next Thanksgiving with my jewels at my own dear home. I pray God it may be with peace pervading the nation.

None are so anxious for peace as those in the army & their families. Yet how the soldiers vote contrasted with that of the people at home. One was the determined voice of patriotic self sacrificing honor, the other the miserable echo of cowardly cravens who dared not do right, their vote might require effort and sacrifice on their part. I shall always honor the patriotism, bravery and fidelity of the volunteer citizen soldier. . . .

Monday Evening, Nov 30, 1863. . . . We learn from rebel sources that Gen Grant has gained an important victory over Bragg near Chattanooga recently, that the rebels have fallen back to Atlanta, leaving their dead & wounded on the field with some five thousand prisoners.[38]

A national salute (I believe thirteen guns) will be fired at 12 noon tomorrow. I say shute and shout over the victory. A few such in that quarter will do us a great deal of good. It will assure our possession of Tennessee. If Rosecrans had done as he ought to have done we might have had this victory more than two months ago. A battle is such a terrible ordeal. It is hard to tell before hand who is sufficient for its realities. To fight a battle well, all must feel that they had rather die than be beaten. That spirit will almost always win.

The policy of the Government now should be to strengthen Grant. He should have a hundred thousand new men. With these he could clean out the fellows effectually, but he should have them at once. He should be able to march on their important lines of railroads and destroy their connexions & rolling stock. This to them is equivalent to the destruction of their armies. Destroy their mobility and you destroy their efficiency. Prevent them rapid concentration and you can cut them off by detail.

If I was at the head of the Government and planned a southern campaign I would make it strong enough to overwhelm the enemy by keeping the strength of our organization good after a battle, so that we could follow up the advantages of a victory with dispatch and crushing weight. The trouble with most of our victories is that we were too weak after a battle to make any substantial gain out of the enemies defeat, a grievous blunder for which somebody or bodies high in authority will have to answer when they render an account of their stewardship.

We had quite a rejoicing yesterday (Tuesday) over the victory of Gen Grant. I formed my battalion, explained to them the news and while the canon were shouting we were shouting. We sent up three times three for the Western army and their victory.[39]

We get mails now only once in eight days. Occasionally a transient mail gets in but none lately. Unless we by chance get a Charleston paper we do not get the news short of once in 8 days, a long time to wait for intelligence when so much depends on what a day may develop. I hardly dare hope for a speedy close of the war, though I think I see signs of the breaking up of the Confederacy. Take the South as a whole. They bitterly hate the North. They style us abolitionist. What is nearly true of the entire North [is] a term of the highest reproach with them, worse than arson, rape, murder & etc. This feeling must be overcome by the realities of what we can do when we are enemies before they will yield. Nothing but force can ever make them submit to the generous rule of the General Government, which to them has always been liberal in the extreme.[40]

It is Thursday night now. . . . The rebels in Charleston are quite gloomy. No flags have been seen on their forts for several days. Our batteries have occasionally been playing on Charleston with considerable effect. I am told the Charleston papers say that that part of the City toward our batteries must be abandoned if we continue to fire upon the City. This morning about three o' clock our batteries opened on the City with great vigor, some ten or twelve shots per minute were fired. I lay awake an hour listening to the thunder belched forth from our heavy guns. It was not displeasing to me, but I fear the rebel tormentors of the county were not as well pleased with it as I was. On the whole I would not feel as if injustice was done to the City if our army should demolish it. It has been a hot bed of political disturbance for the country for more than thirty years. If it were made what ancient Nineveh was the impartial historian would write justice has overtaken the wicked City. . . .[41]

HILTON HEAD ISLAND, S. C.—*Dec 9, 1863*

Since I wrote you last I have again changed my place of abode, a matter that does not signify much to us in the field especially after we have become accustomed to the mutations of a military command. . . . I do not feel in a writing mood at all tonight. I have been so occupied with moving that I have had no time before today to write. . . . I think my men are quite comfortably fixed here, but not so well as on Folly. Probably never will be again.[42]

Gen Grant's was truly a brilliant victory, but the major part of the enemy got away. . . . Gen Meade has accomplished nothing unless his movements were merely feints to occupy the attention of Gen Lee, which is probably true. But might not a real demonstration have been made with the probability of success? He must be winter bound now to remain so until next March. In the meantime Gen Lee can spare a large force from his Va army to aid Bragg and Longstreet. I did hope when I first learned of the late battles at Chattanooga that Grant would wipe out Bragg before he gave up the pursuit, but I am disappointed. Not badly, however, as I have learned that decisive battles are not of verry frequent occurrence. . . .

HILTON HEAD, S. C.—*Dec 12, 1863*

. . . If my Regiment is not filled up this winter I shall resign. I do not like the idea of commanding a skeleton Regiment. I would like to have a thousand men in my Regt. I could content myself to stay a while with it, but with 360 enlisted men for duty does not all satisfy me. And for the good of the service it would be better to consolidate the companies into maximum companies and muster out the supernumerary Officers, of which class I would be <u>one.</u> . . .

Sunday evening. . . . Many of the old Regiments must go out of business. Ohio has too many Regiments. She cannot keep them full. It is verry bad policy to keep up a lot of skeleton organizations. The State had better keep eighty Regiments in the field with eighty thousand men in them than keep her one hundred forty two or three regiments in existence with only eighty thousand in them. There will be fewer Officers to be sure, but just as many men & certainly a more efficient state of organization. . . .

The State could keep that number of men constantly in the field. I have long deplored the unbusinesslike policy that has kept so many fragmentary regiments in the field with so few men. I had hoped before this some systematic policy would have been adopted to keep that number of Regiments the Government thought to be the best adapted to accomplish the end sought.[43]

I would entirely reorganize the whole army as fast as it could be done, and upon a somewhat more permanent basis and keep that organization intact as long as the exigencies of the service demanded. I would make conscriptions say every three months, end the conscripts to camps of instruction, and distribute them to the various regiments of the states from

whence they were taken as often as the men were needed to fill up any deficiencies on account of losses by diseases or disasters in battle. I would make
it a matter of direct & determined business with no let up. I would not beg
for volunteers. I would demand men, and I would have them, too. If the
states furnished the men by volunteers so much the better. I would have
few armies but they should be armies. When they moved no rebel resistance should be able to long resist them.

I would also retaliate with a vengeance upon the rebel prisoners for the
scandalous manner our prisoners have been treated by the rebels.[44] I
would keep Mr Johnny Reb on the same rations and in the same kind of
quarters they keep our prisoners. I would teach them humanity by making them feel the pangs of their own barbarism. If they excused themselves by saying they were not able to do any better I would say to them,
you have no business to hold prisoners if they cannot treat them as human beings deserve. . . .[45]

HILTON HEAD, S. C.—*Dec 18, 1863*

. . . I have read the President's message, Proclamation & of the organization of Congress. I hope the action of Congress will be wise, dignified and
harmonious. I am pleased with "Old Abe's" message. The style [is] homey.
There is nothing startling in it but shows an honest purpose to do right. I
think he is placing the Government & himself before the world in such a
light that the sympathy of all those whose sympathy is worth cherishing
will be given to us. He certainly is a wise man and pre eminently just in his
intentions. He is my candidate for the next Presidency. He is abolitionist
enough for me, is conservative enough for any honest man and has had
enough experience to make a better President for the ensuing years than
any man I know of in the nation. Next to him I look upon Gov Chas of
Ohio as the man. I look upon Chase as being the stronger man, but not so
unselfish as Lincoln. Honest Old Abe labors for the good of others. Gov
Chase fishes for salmon. Still I think Chase is a pure statesman, an honor to
our State, Ohio.[46]

Monday Evening, 21st. . . . I will wish you a happy new year in this as
you will hardly get another letter till after the 1st of Jany 1864. I also wish
the children a happy new year. Now I will make no rash promises, but I do
really expect to be home at the next return of the hollidays. . . .

The President's annual message put the question in the right shape. It
will command the confidence and sympathy of the good men of the world,
and place the insurgents with the issues based upon the accursed system of
American slavery as its main foundation. Those who now fight for the Confederacy do it to uphold this disgrace of this enlightened age. . . .[47]

Mr Benedict of the Herald will make us a visit before long, as the Governor has appointed him commissioner to look after the interest of the Ohio
troops in this Department. This was done at my insistence. He has a son in

this Dept, and desired to make a visit to see him. Knowing this I wrote Gov Tod requesting him to appoint Mr Benedict to the place. . . .[48]

HILTON HEAD, S. C.—*Dec 23, 1863*

. . . We have been having another Grand Review this afternoon. I had my little Regiment out. Not to exaggerate in the least I may say that the 67th was the neatest Regt on the ground and executed its movements with more precision than any of the ten regiments on review. I think this is saying a good deal when I compare my toil worn and almost used up Regt with the Eastern regiments here, many of which have done hardly a day's service in the field since the war commenced. . . .

Christmas Eve. I was compelled to stop here last night by the call of Col Howell and several others to go to Gen Gillmore's party, to which most of the field Officers of his command had been invited. It was a magnificent affair. A building made of boards framed to hang canvass over was prepared. The interior was draped by some twenty or thirty huge bunting flags & several Regimental colors. Evergreen and moss was used for pendant ornamentation. The pieces of timber were covered with moss or cedar. By candle light the effect was exceedingly fine. All the white ladies in the Department must have been there (over 60 in all) and some 150 Officers. They danced, the music played, the wine flowed and I <u>flowed</u> about eleven o' clock P.M. for my lonely tent. I would have been O! so happy had you been there but there you weren't. I was not very gay for some reason or other.

Christmas Eve. . . . It is two o'clock now, but my boys cannot get still tonight. They are singing and having a merry time. We have our camp nicely fixed up again. It looks like a thick pine grove of some half dozzen years growth. I am setting the Yankee fellows about us a lesson of taste and good order. I can show them that our Western men can appear as well as they can fight.

Sunday evening, Dec 27. . . The climate on the sea coast is so far as I have observed much better than in Ohio. It is not cold in winter and the sea breezes so modify the heat in summer that one feels quite comfortable in the middle of the day. Many Northerners are purchasing of the Government lands forfeited for taxes or confiscated because they belonged to rebels, with the view of locating here. I can't say that I like the country well enough to make it my future home. . . .[49]

HILTON HEAD, S. C. —*Dec 31, 1863*

. . . You see by the date of this that poor 1863 is on its last legs. Three hours more will place it among the things that were. What a year. One year ago this night we started on the campaign that brought us to the Carolinas. For the first time in my life I then went on a mighty ship to try a trip of the broad Ocean. The Ocean, shipping & traveling off land were objects of curiosity to me. Now I have become so used to see shipping, great navies and the surges and scenes of the sea that I look on them in the same common place light I do the affairs of our own little City Akron. . . .[50]

Jany 2, 1864. I came verry near spoiling this form. This is the second time I have tried to write dates in the present year. I am not sure that 64 will look as well as 63. I mean to make it excell, but rather mean to do it by deeds than words or figures.

You ought to be verry good yourself by this time, for you have had a long time to yourself, no tormenting man to estrange you from the paths of goodness. You should be the excellence of womanhood improved by a few years experience with the frailties and follies of the lords of creation. You have had abundance of time to separate the good from the bad, the excellent from the indifferent, and confirm yourself in all the virtue that your constitution will admit of.

As for me I know I am a better man. I am much more decided and self reliant. I can command with the success of the Centurion spoken of in the New Testament. Come, go, & comes & goes is the irresistible result. I have already had so much experience in the command of men that I do not hesitate in saying I can make one woman and two babies do just as I will, Nolens volens.

We expect the Fulton and Arago in tonight or in the morning with lots of mail & holliday remembrances. The arrival of the Fulton and Arago are great events in this Department. Once in eight days unless extraordinary happens we are visited by them with the news supplies from the North and the messages of affection from our friends at home.

It would be a wonder passing strange to our sires a century ago to see how we bridge the Ocean with our steamers. Our steam horses would surprise them. A steamship is a miracle of wonders. What shall I say of the power that flies with a whole village in its wake with the impetuosity of the tempest, safely transporting all its inhabitants, who hardly realize that they are in motion. I wish steam engines were made to do our fighting. The idea is not so impractical as the first blush would indicate, for the success of an army does not so much consist in its destruction of the lives of the enemy as in the demolition of his materiel. What a sight it would be to see the vast machines that we could make go into each other, all the while realizing that no lives were to be sacrificed. Gen McClellan had some such idea. He was going to worry the rebels into submission by his "all quiet on the Potomac" Grand Reviews. O! shame that the rebels would not let him end the war that way.

HILTON HEAD, S. C.—*Jany 6, 1864*

. . . The Regiments from New York & the New England states are being filled up by conscripts, making large Regiments compared with the 67th. But with what I have left I can do as much hard fighting as any of them. My men feel so and would do it if called on. . . .

HILTON HEAD, S. C.—*Jany 10, 1864*

. . . I do not believe you feel any more solicitude about me where I am than many, verry many wives feel about the results of the coming draft. Those who may be hereafter drafted will for a long time be compelled to serve in the ranks while your dear husband has the benefit of a good position in the army, where while he is discharging a duty to the Government he is saved many of the disabilities of the service. And then I am no conscript. When the army is made up so largely of volunteers as is now the case, the conscripts are not appreciated with that cheering cordiality so consoling to social custom like the genus homo. If I had the misfortune to be conscripted I certainly would secure a substitute or volunteer. You ought to rejoice with me that matters are as flattering with me as they are.[51]

HILTON HEAD, S. C.—*Jany 16, 1864*

. . . When I sat down Saturday evening to write you I intended to write you a good, long affectionate letter, but somethings prevented. Yesterday I inspected my Regiment which with my usual duties took all my time till 2 1/2 o'clock P.M. Mr Benedict & friend coming just before supper made me conclude to take a ride to Spanish Hills some 7 or 8 miles southward. So your intended letter had to remain in embryo till further & more propitious time. . . .

Mr B has stayed half the time with me since he came here. These visits from persons of my acquaintance in Ohio call up the associations of home so strongly that I cannot help feeling lonely. . . . Mr B and friends started [on a visit to St. Augustine, Florida] yesterday. Had I not been busy trying to re-enlist my Regiment I should have tried to make the trip too.[52]

Friday 22 Jany. The routine of camp life on Hilton Head has but little variation from the beginnings to the end of the week and this continues till the month is closed. . . .

"Days of Intense Anxiety and Peril"

THE ARMY OF THE JAMES

FEBRUARY 21, 1864 – MAY 13, 1864

[Voris achieved his immediate goal over the winter of 1864. The 67th Ohio ful-
filled the requirements to become a "Veteran Volunteer Infantry Regiment."
That done, the War Department transferred the 67th Ohio from the siege of
Charleston to a staging area outside Washington. Combat awaited. By the first
week of May, Lt. Gen. Ulysses S. Grant, the army's highest ranking officer and
its general-in-chief, launched his long anticipated offensive. Grant planned a
five-pronged, coordinated attack that finally concentrated the Union's advantages in men and materiel. In the east, the Army of the Potomac under Maj.
Gen. George G. Meade targeted Lee's Army of Northern Virginia, and Grant entrusted Maj. Gen. William T. Sherman to capture Atlanta. But Grant had no
respect for the three political major generals, Nathaniel P. Banks, Franz Sigel,
and especially Benjamin F. Butler, who led the other parts of his overall campaign. Realizing that he could not replace them for political reasons, Grant ordered Butler's Army of the James to move from Fortress Monroe up the James
River with some 30,000 men, including the 67th Ohio. Butler established his
command at Bermuda Hundred, a peninsula bound by the James and Appomattox rivers, almost twenty miles south of Richmond. Butler had two interre-
lated objectives: menace and perhaps capture Richmond from the south; and
distract Confederates to prevent reinforcements from reaching the Army of
Northern Virginia.]

CAMP CLEVELAND—*Feby 21, 1864*

I expect to go to Toledo with the men early in the morning. Will not get
home before Wednesday, as I shall ride my horse which will make a long
day's journey. I will send my boy on the cart. Take care of him till I get
home. I have been exceedingly busy today trying to get my men off.[1]

ARLINGTON HEIGHTS, VA.—*Mch 31, 1864*

I am again safely in camp after a most trying trip from Cleveland to this place. But on the whole I think I made as successful a trip as ever was made with the same number of soldiers. I left no men by the way except a poor corporal who was suffering from the delirium tremens and jumped from the cars while they were in motion.

I had no drunkenness all the way from Cleveland to Baltimore & then only two or three cases. The men were kept so closely & quietly on the cars that the people of Pennsylvania thought we had a lot of rebel prisoners. The result is certainly remarkable, but cost me a great deal of pains and trouble. If I was not the most patient man in the world as well as a verry persevering mortal I never could have got through as I did. To convince you this is no joke I inform you that I blacked an ugly d——l's nose for him, because he tried to fight. I rather think his nose was not as hard as the right fist of a hard working man. I overheard one of the men say, "Well I declare that looks as if Old Promptly means something." I never want to get together another furloughed Regiment and start them off for the field with their lax notions of discipline a loose time at home begets.

I am well but somewhat tired. Have not slept in bed yet & lay down only half of last night since I left you & that was on a hard floor with only a blanket to soften the plank. I find the 39th Ill., 25th & 62nd Ohio here from the Dept of the South. I hope to go to Washington in a day or two to see the sights. I got out of there with my men just as soon as possible, for cities are the worst places in the world to keep men. Whiskey & women of loose morals or none at all destroy all ideas of subordination with some men. . . .[2]

CAMP DISTRIBUTION NEAR WASHINGTON, D. C.—*Apl 3, 1864*

. . . I have been so busy with the cares of my command that I have had no time to be tired, lonesome or homesick. . . . I know you are more happy than that timid unpatriotic wife who fears her husband may be drafted as a common soldier. I feel myself much better situated than the poor harassed man at home who is taxing his energies to escape the impending conscription. Above all if I should have the good fortune to come out of the war with a respectable combination of soul and body, won't we always feel proud—proud—proud that we have contributed so much and heroically suffered so much to save so good a Government as ours. . . .

Have had a severe rain storm the last twenty four hours, but my men have had the good fortune to be in comfortable barrack with good food and furnished them in abundance. I am some four miles from Washington & by going a few rods can see the City from Arlington Heights. I passed through a few streets of the City but have had no opportunity of visiting any of the attractions of the Capitol.

The public buildings are truly magnificent. The Government has lavished vast sums of money upon the City. No people under the Sun have greater cause to feel devoted to their Government than the inhabitants of Washington, but I fear they have been foolishly & wickedly ungrateful beyond a parallel in the annals of civilized nations. Ingratitude in them is a monstrous crime.

It is evening now, and having closed up the business of the day I am not so occupied but that I have time to think of the confounded loneliness of my situation. It is quiet all around me. I see & hear nothing but soldiers, not one of whom I can claim for a closer communion than that exists between commanding Officer and subordinates. . . .

I expect to go to the City in the morning & hope to see some of my Ohio acquaintances, of whom there is quite a number. But I have so much to do for the present I shall not have much time for visiting, and if I did prevent my men and Officers from going to the City I must stay in camp myself, for what is precept worth if it if not enforced by consistent example, yes example, that is the thing. You know how well I enforce all my good theories by the most consistent example. For a whole week I have not scolded much nor got out of temper a great deal for me, and having some five hundred persons among whom to distribute these special favors, the quantity got by each individual was so small that there was but little occasion for censuring me. Whatever I did was done in such a mild way that if any one felt dissatisfied he felt inclined to pocket the affront rather than apply to me for change of treatment. I don't like this exercise of arbitrary authority. However much others may think I like to dictate I am free to confess that I am frequently verry unhappy over many things I am compelled to do.

How is your side? How is Eddie's mumps? How is papa's Pet? You are all my pets. How I wish I could be home to pet you. I wish I could get out of the war <u>honorably,</u> but how could I till it is over?

CAMP DISTRIBUTION, VA.—*Apl 5, 1864*

. . . I see but little difference as to climate here compared with northern Ohio. Snow, sleet & rain have attended us ever since we reached Harrisburgh. I have no doubt we encountered just as bad weather two years ago in the Virginia valley, but the novelty of the incidents to a soldier's life helped us to bear it better than now. I must confess to an aversion to those stern realities of the field. . . .

I visited the Capitol yesterday. Saw Judge Spalding, was invited by him to take a seat in the Hall of the House of Representatives, which I was much pleased to do as I saw posted on the entrance none but members, ex-members, the President & his Cabinet, foreign Ministers and the Governors of the States will be permitted on the floor. Well, I looked wise, stood up as straight as an arrow and made as imposing impression as a live Colonel could. I will not attempt to describe the Hall to you, nor the great men who frequent it, for I intend to do better by taking you some day to Washington and let you see all for yourself. I expect the Capitol to stand till I get out of the war, and there is no verry great danger that all the wisdom of the world will die with the termination of the present Congress. Then who knows but I may some day ornament the Speaker's desk with a living bust.

The most striking impression I got from viewing the interior of the Hall was its flashy appearance. Instead of massive & dignified taste it exhibited the tawdry conceit of the parvenu. The rotunda when finished will be truly magnificent. Historic paintings and statuary of life size cover the panels & ornament the niches of the walls. I will write no more describing it & I mean you shall see for yourself.

I called on Judge Wade, whom I found in one of the committee rooms. On meeting me he most cordially took me by the hand and greeted me with grave politeness and Senatorial dignity as follows—"Why Voris I am d——d glad to see you. I am by G_d I am." Now dear wife don't you think I was awe struck with such marks of consideration so elegantly bestowed on my modest self.[3] I also met Mr Edgerton & had a pleasant visit with him. Judge Wade promised to come to camp & see me. If he does I hope he will not have as hurried a ride back to Washington as he did from the first Battle at Bull Run. . . .[4]

HD QRS., 67TH REG, O.V.I.—*Apl 6, 1864*

. . . I went to church this evening and heard from several of the leading lights of the "Christian Commission." The President, a Mr Stuart of Philadelphia, pitched in real old fashioned Methodist style. I made quite a sensation by stopping the preacher and calling the boys to order as they started to go out on the sound of the bugle for the evening roll call. I made a few <u>appropriate remarks</u> that elicited applause in the pit. After [the] meeting was out I was quite a hero among the divine. The chapell will hold over a thousand persons & was nearly crowded. They are holding sort of revival exercises, and had the experience of several of the new converts given by the <u>patients</u> themselves. Their religious experience did not much differ from that you have often heard at Methodist meetings at home.[5]

I am fixing a new camp. If the weather continues at all pleasant I shall go into tents in a day or two. I have been quite busy all day, and of course feel well and contended. I presume I shall remain here for several days, perhaps weeks. . . .

CAMP GRANT NEAR WASHINGTON—*Apl 8, 1864*

. . . It is raining hard & has been since 9 o'clock A.M. I do dislike these gloomy do nothing days. We are again brigaded & Col Pond who has never seen a fight, been off of duty half the time since I have been in the army, and once ordered before an examining board because of his inefficiency & neglect of duty, has been placed in command. I hope it will be temporary. But temporary or permanent it is an outrage to Col Osborn of the 39th Ill and myself. If I was fighting for the sake of personal ambition only I would tell Uncle Samuel to select his Officers and conduct the war as he pleased. . . .

As it is I will try to do my duty for the present. Col Pond is socially agreeable to us, but his official conduct has been of no sort deserving of approval & certainly not of advancement. Brass is worth more than brains, impudence more than sense, luck more than effort in the army frequently. I feel as if this was a grievous case of injustice that must not be long continued.[6]

CAMP GRANT NEAR WASHINGTON, D. C.—*Apl 10, 1864*

. . . I am discontented almost unhappy. I know I could enjoy the pleasure of your company at our own guest home for a few hours if I could only be with you this evening. . . . This may appear odd talk to you when you consider how many Sundays I have spent in my office and how many evenings, yes night till almost morning, I have consumed in the laborious duties of my profession. My stay at home part of last winter will however convince you that I have undergone a considerable change in that respect since I went into the army. My habits are certainly easier than they were before I joined the army. I do not offer what you saw of me in Camp Cleveland for evidence, but that is <u>rather</u> an exception to my general army habits. I would be happier if I had as much to do everyday as I had the few days you were in Cleveland. I read till I get tired, get up and look at business matters as long as I can find anything to do, then read again, but it don't satisfy me. You know how easily I am satisfied. I have been reading Motley's Dutch Republic & find it intensely interesting. I would advise you to read it if you can find time to read anything. Motley has a verry high estimation of the Dutch character, so have I. We may be Dutch men.[7]

The Dutch certainly are of no mean origin. They have developed themselves, originating in the great hive of <u>barbarians</u> that held and overran western Europe two thousand years ago. We are all descendants of barbarians, involving nothing more than <u>a question of time.</u> This war is a manifestation of our barbarian *extraction* and tendencies. . . .

Monday evening, 11th. I am again writing in a tent for the first time since the 22nd of Jany last, almost three months ago. How rapidly times flies. It is nine months ago since we went on Morris Island, that terrible place for us, & in one week more it will be nine months since I was wounded in that terribly disastrous assault on Fort Wagner. I still have the side ache from that wound. While enjoying the ease of home I did not feel it, but not a day has passed since I left Cleveland but I am reminded of that awful night by the twinging of my left side. It is not severely painful but is quite unpleasant, making me feel as you frequently have on walking briskly for some distance. Fatigue, exposure, a cold and the like produce an unpleasant irritation in that locality. You need not make yourself at all uneasy on my account from these indications, for should they annoy me so as to interfere with my ability to discharge my duties in the field, I will take the proper measures to save myself. My general health is good, save I do not feel that healthy vigor I sometimes do. I want to lay in bed in the morning, and do not object to taking my ease in a verry quiet manner. . . .

The President has his last grand party tomorrow evening. I propose to let such of the Officers as can go down. I will stay in camp & take care of matters & let them go and enjoy themselves. . . .

IN CAMP GRANT NEAR WASHINGTON, D. C.—*Apl 12, 1864*

. . . My Officers have gone to the City to the President's levee tonight. I am staying to look after the camp. My entire field staff and most of the line have gone. I confess that I would like to have gone, but they felt so anxious to go that I thought I could forgo the pleasure easier than they could, so I told them to go & that I would stay at home and keep house. Mothers of little children are compelled to do so frequently, but as they love their little ones it is a pleasure to them to do the little folks good, though at their own expense. This is to be the last of his receptions for the season. The notables of this Country & Europe will be there in great splendor, an entertaining sight for vain women and curiously inclined men. . . .

There are a couple of young ladies not more than forty rods from my quarters, fair, intelligent, lady like who have been quite inquisitive as to my domestic relations, with the earnest desire no doubt of furnishing some dashing Officer a chance to convert a little capital in personal stock. . . .

CAMP GRANT NEAR WASHINGTON, D. C.—*Apl 15, 1864*

. . . I have been in camp for most a week with a fair degree of comfort, but this morning brings a rain storm that makes us bad enough off indeed, mud, damp tents and rain overhead, with poor arrangements for eating. We will not stay here verry long I think. When we will go the Lord only knows. . . .

CAMP GRANT—*Apl 17, 1864*

. . . A carriage is coming to the door. Gov Dennison, Judge Swayne of the Supreme Court, Gen Garfield, Professor Peck of Oberlin & Mr Wetmore of Columbus have been here. I got my Officers together, introduced them, had my men fall in and each [made] a speech to the boys. Then visited the 25th & 62nd. It was a happy surprise indeed. I am always glad to see my Ohio friends, especially when they take an interest in my command. . . . I had a verry pleasant visit, only regretted that it could not be longer. Seeing my home friends carries me back to the times when the country was at peace and all were enjoying natural prosperity & happiness. . . .[8]

Monday morning 18 Apl. I expect to be ordered away from here before long. Where to I cannot even suspect. . . . We have a status nowhere and never will as long as I am pelted about to suit the caprice of some ambitious, impudent aspirant who cares not of <u>any other man.</u> I wrote you the other day how I felt about the Brigade [under Pond]. This had intensified my feeling. My judgment, pride & self respect revolt at the indignity, I say indignity, because it is a personal insult, an outrage. . . . My patriotism does not hang on promotion, but it does affect it to be subordinate to one who has neglected his duties continually and imposed intentionally his burdens upon brother Officers.

CAMP GRANT, VA.—*Apl 19, 1864*

. . . It is evening now, have had a Grand Review of our Brigade by Maj Gen Casey. He highly complimented the 67th, and criticized all the other Regiments in the presence of the field Officers commanding them. I felt rather pleased at this, as he is the Gen Casey who published the system of tactics by which we are governed and looks to the details with sharp eyes.[9]

My Regiment was clean, the men soldierly in their bearing and did verry well considering the number of new men in the ranks. They had clean clothing, neat white gloves & well polished brass & blacked leathers and shoes, accomplishments that are pleasing to an Army of the Potomac Officer. He was especially severe on the 62nd Ohio, Col. Pond's Regt.[10]

I am going to the President's levee this evening if I do not break connexion. I wish you were here to go along. . . .

Wednesday morning. I did go to the President's levee. I believe they call it reception in the papers. What a name for such an assemblage. It is a hideous mob of foreign ministers & actresses, Maj Generals and newer boys, state celebrities and flash women, military heroes and grocery keepers, old people & young, gay people but not pretty, & some old maids foreign & natives, of all sizes and grades and character (I kept my hand in my pocket book all the while). False hair, teeth, limbs and hearts were there in their glory. I hardly had breath enough left to keep from suffocating. . . . From the entrance to the yard throughout its front and in every room, the White House was crowded to the utmost packing point. It took an hour to get into the house and make the circuit of the rooms thrown open to the <u>American Aristocracy.</u>

Had I supposed a week ago that our prospect was good to stay here for a few weeks as it now appears, I would have invited you verry strongly to come & stay with me a few days. If you could get here immediately you might get a couple of weeks of camp life with me. I say two weeks. You might not get a day. I might be yet here but I hardly think so. . . .

We were thrown into quite a current of excitement yesterday morning at the announcement that we were to go to the depths of the South immediately. It turned out however that the 25th Ohio is ordered South. The other Regiments remained here for the present. . . .

I must be with my Regiment most of the time. I can make matters go on well when I am present, but the moment I am out of sight there is a disposition to shirk duty and responsibility. Officers do not feel that they are bound to do anything unless it is forced upon them by virtue of an express order. I am full of orders. I make enough of them & then see that they are obeyed, but it is an awful task. You saw something of it at Camp Cleveland. Still I feel proud of my Officers. They are verry much better than the average of volunteer Officers. I make it a part of my daily duty to see that the orders are observed.

GLOUCESTER POINT, VA.—*Apl 27, 1864*

A few days ago I indulged the fond hope of having your company this day, but the fickle fortunes of the war have destroyed all my hope in that behalf. I nevertheless have had the consolation of seeing you and our dear boy but two days ago. I am glad indeed that we had the good fortune to spend the last Sabbath together. If Eddie had not been with you I should have taken you to Yorktown with me, but I could not think of sorrowing the boy by the trials of the field so long. We had a delightful passage down the Potomac & the Bay and up to Yorktown.[11]

I have as good a bed tonight as I had the two nights you stayed with me, but could not verry well provide for a third person. I hope you were pleased with your trip to the army & with your visit in the City & ride home. I know Eddie will always remember it as one of the great events of his life. All I am sorry for is that it continued so little time. How did you get home & did you see the mountains? I am in an awful hurry getting my things in shape.

GLOUCESTER POINT, VA.—*May 1, 1864*

I wrote you a short note on Thursday last but had so little time that I did not write you anything other than I had safely arrived at this place.[12] We have been in such an infernal hurry to get things in shape that I have had no time for anything but business. I just now came off duty as Gen Officer of the Day, started at 2 A.M. this day for my second round. It has been raining since early this morning, making it quite chilly without fire in our quarters. But we must make shift as we can till it gets warmer weather, as we are cut down to the lowest allowance for transportation, being allowed only one wagon to carry the baggage for all the Officers of the Regiment. My line Officers and men are in the shelter tents, each man being required to carry his own part of the tent.

The field and staff are allowed three such tents, as I occupied when you stayed over Sunday with me. Officers are only allowed to carry a small valise or sack for clothing and their blankets. All other property has been sent to Norfolk, Va, or gone home by express. . . . I am taking nothing in the line of clothing excepting what I carry on my little hand trunk. This is the way to soldier, carry nothing. Then you have nothing to lose, nor anything to care for, only yourselves. . . .

We do not expect to stay here long, all ready to go now, are waiting orders. Had a Grand Review yesterday by Gen Butler. I have drilled my new men one day, and attended reviews & inspections twice since I came into the field the last time. The 67th made a good appearance. Gen Terry who commanded the review reported that the 67th was the best appearing Regiment in the review.[13] There were some 20 Regiments on review, among them the flower of the New England states. Pa & New York were there. Bully for 67th.[14] It has been quiet this afternoon. Business has so far subsided that I really believe it to be Sunday afternoon. . . .

Monday morning. A beautiful morning. I am quite well save a slight side ache, occasioned from laying on the ground. Poor Bob is quite lame this morning. I must close this as I have much to do outside. I hope to get a letter from you in a day or two. I have been so much engaged in the administration affairs of my command that I have had no time to feel lonesome. I like to be head & ears in business. Time flies so hurriedly that I skip over the hard spots as if nothing was in the way.

GLOUCESTER POINT, VA.—*May 3, 1864*

I have recd no letters from you since your return, but suppose of course that you arrived safely at home, else I would have heard from you before this time. Everything has been hurry and confusion since you saw me on Sunday the 24th of April last. But I am relieved a little now, as are ready to move at a moment's notice. I have given up my tent for the purposes of the Adjutant.[15] He poor soul is so frustrated by the hurry that he does not really know whether his soul is his own or not. We are as near denuded of all the luxuries of the army as it is possible for us to be, excepting we have the usual army allowance of commissary supplies. In that respect we are better off than we were in April last year, but then we had the advantage of a much milder climate. It is quite cool here yet at times, though corn is up & the trees are beginning to leaf out. We had a terrible rain and hail storm last night. The wind prostrated our tent. The rain wet our men, and on the whole we had one of the hardest storms experiences by us for a long time. I did not get out, however, but had to sleep on the damp ground, but fortunately had a dry covering. . . .

Wednesday afternoon, May 4th. We are all board a fine steamer, "John Tucker" and bound for the Good Lord only knows where.[16] You unquestionably will soon learn of our operations. I will write you as often as I can. . . .

We are now in the 10th Army Corps, again in the same Brigade with the same Regiments. It appears much like old times to meet with so many old associates in arms as the reunion brought about. I hope to be able to write you before long that our efforts in Va have been successful. I started out this morning with 660 men and Officers, more men that I have had in line before since I took command of the Regt. . . .[17]

STEAMER JOHN TUCKER—*May 5, 1864*

We are above City Point on the James River, some eight miles above Harrison's Landing. The troops are debarking as rapidly as possible on the south bank of the James. This is a sensible move, and one that has commended itself to my judgment for a year and a half. If the enterprise should fail it will not be because the plan is not a good one.

The operations of the army so far as I can judge from the few indications made indicate a sound policy on the part of the War Department. Concentration and strength are the predominating ideas. Before, our operations have been so divided and weak that we have accomplished but little east of the mountains towards bringing the war to a successful end. But why theorize on the present plan of operations when so soon we will be compelled to demonstrate its practicability by the terrible arbitrament of the sword.

The struggle is over with me now. It has been a terrible struggle, but I am calmly prepared for anything the fate of battle or campaign may prepare for me. I have the cheering hope that I shall triumph over all the trials and hazards of the coming struggle, and return to the bosom of my dear family to compensate them with my care & company for all the wearing anxiety my absence has caused, & with a good Government to protect us & a restored country to be proud of. Cheer up now. Remember I am trying to do my duty, that I am cheerful, and mean to come out of the campaign with the approval of my conscience and so as to win the pride of my own dear wife and our dear children.

Now for business. The Government owes me for all pay and allowances since the 31st day of Dec last, making almost $800 due me. . . . I owe nothing in the Regiment, nor any one connected with it. I owe Koch & Myers for clothing, the only bills I think of due in Akron or elsewhere.[18] My personal effects with me consist of the following: Rob Roy McGregor, [horse] worth $300, saddle and furniture $40, saber & pistol, field glasses, rubber coat, pant & blanket worth $15.00. Trunk and clothing. The horse, horse furniture and rubber goods will be sold here. The other property will be sent home to be disposed of as I have indicated heretofore indicated. As to that you may do as you please, as I have the fullest confidence that your love for our dear children will influence you to do for them all in your power. . . .

This is written in case I should be unfortunate. . . . The telegraph may reach you with news before I write again. But you have had enough experience as to the uncertainties of telegraphic reports not to make yourself unnecessary trouble till time enough has elapsed to settle questions of doubt.

It is now my turn to be lucky. I have been hurt twice. It certainly now is my turn to get through without being hurt. . . .

IN THE FIELD, MILES BELOW RICHMOND—*May 8, 1864*

I take it you will not be at all surprised to learn that we are a few miles below Richmond on the south bank of the James River. From my old letters you are appraised that I had no attachment for campaigning in Virginia, but since I have been relieved from my anticipated merger in the Army of the Potomac I am tolerably well contented to go any place else.

Since leaving Ohio on the 28th of Mch till this time we have had comparatively easy times, but now we are roughing it in real campaign style. Hard tack, salt meat & coffee, the damp ground for a bed, a single blanket for covering and a little shelter tent that I carry on my horse for covering. Thursday we passed Harrison's Landing when I saw the chestnut tree where I had Regimental head quarters nearly two years ago. But how changed the appearance. It was all activity & life with a hundred thousand men when I saw it then. Now it is as quiet and lonely as when Capt John Smith first visited the area.[19]

We are in the woods doing about the same kind of work we did in the first days of July 1862. It is warm, yes hot here. I saw say a half a dozzen men of the two Regiments in the fight suffering from Coup de Salient,[20] a thing unheard of for the 7th of May in northern Ohio. I lay out all night with no covering except my usual suit of clothing on the 6th Inst., and suffered no inconvenience from it after the fatigue & want of sleep had been satisfied.

I begin to think that I can go light and not suffer. I do not feel half the dread of the trial, fatigues and deprivations of an active campaign I did when you left me. My hammock makes me a good bed, a tolerable seat. My little trunk carries all my necessary for clothing & toilet, and is carried in our Regimental wagon. (We have only one wagon for all of the Officers of the Regiment). My horse carries my bed and little tent & myself when I want to ride. Bob is getting over his lameness, at least is not worse. I have cast off my sword entirely, so that I may not suffer more than absolutely necessary from that old wound. I do not feel much trouble from it though I must be careful about straining or unusual fatigue.

The 2nd Brigade of this Division had a little fight on the railroad yesterday with a little loss on our side. We could see the smoke & hear the musketry, but did not participate in the fight. The railroad was destroyed for a mile or more, our bridge cut down, a saw mill burned, but no decisive results were secured as far as I can learn. We hear ill defined rumors of the advance of the Army of the Potomac, but nothing that we can gain anything that shows what is being done. We have the papers of the 5th, but they are no better informed than we are and we know absolutely nothing at all.

We think the rebels were taken by surprise by our advances so far up the James, as no opposition was offered us till we struck the railroad above Petersburgh. We are fortifying a place rendered strong by nature and in a few days will be able to resist any pressure the rebels can bring against us. I see more difficulty in keeping our long line of communication open from Fort Monroe to this place, 100 miles, than any danger from the front. I feel tolerably secure here, but I feel constant solicitude being so near the enemy & may at times be involved in a struggle with them. I never however hard we may be put to it expect to be placed in as desperate an affair as that assault on Fort Wagner.[21]

It has been quite hot for a few days. Our men suffered from the heat quite as much as they did in South Carolina. For me this is not as disagreeable as for many because I feel better in warm weather than in cold. This Sunday has been one of constant effort on my part. The men have been at work on the rifle pits all day. I with my coat off have been with them a good share of the time to aid by counsel and example. . . .

I am in good health and fine spirits, and want you to be so too. I have heard nothing from you since I last saw you. Write me frequently. Kiss the children for me. I will go to sleep now & dream of you and ours.

BERMUDA HUNDRED—*May 10, 1864*

I have been in more dangerous campaigning than we have had for the last two days but never more annoying or worrying on the men. We have constantly been on hard duty night and day almost ever since we landed here the morning of the 6th, I think. Fought one hard contested battle and been on picket in front of the enemy, with almost uninterrupted firing one half the day and nights since that time, and one of those nights we were in imminent danger of being gobbled up and sent to Richmond before our time.

I never experienced a more anxious night in my life and my feeling was intensified in the apprehension of my Officers & men. We supposed we were surrounded & every few minutes the guns of my pickets indicated that they were feeling my position. Then to add to my perplexity I was supreme in the command of the given place & entirely separated from our forces.[22]

Officers urged me to fall back, men looked frightfully anxious, and all of us were entirely ignorant of the country, much of which was a dense forrest. I put on a cheerful face, told all that we were secure against surprise, that we could strike consternation with any force that dared approach us in the night and that I should have support by daylight. I placed 2 companies out a 1/4 of a mile on each of the 2 roads leading to my place & kept 4 as a reserve at the road crossing. I layered the men in two ranks . . . with adequate guards to keep watch, and put myself in the middle of the road just to the front of my men. Whenever a gun would fire my men would spin to their feet ready for an attack.

That is the way I prepared my men for the fight of the 10th. In consideration of that fight we were left to guard camp when our army started to attack Richmond and fortunate for us was it, as the army got badly cut up, but we had constant picket duty to perform while it was gone. I have been on the picket lines the last 48 hours. The first day as Officer of the Day & today with my Regt I stayed in camp, however, last night, being out all the night before. It was the most shocking picket service I ever saw. Our lines were close together, & a constant skirmish was going on between the lines and this morning the rebels shelled my lines in the most savage manner. I had only four men wounded. How they escaped is unaccountable to me. Trees were cut off, lines falling and fragments of shell scorching through the air enough to terrify the stoutest heart.[23]

I can fight a battle. The occasion brings support along with it. But to deliberately go into unseen danger without the means of protection with the terrible uncertainty surrounding your every movement, unaided by the reflection that you cannot do anything to overcome the designs of the secret enemy, are complications of difficulties I can hardly bear. I hope the campaign will soon end. I know it will not be so verry long. But how much misery may be caused before it ends I cannot discern. I have been fortunate so far and hope for the future.[24]

My baggage is all back a mile, but I could not forego the desire to write you though I had only this little bit of paper. I hear the shrill music of canon shot in the air as I write this. I am as well as could be expected.

IN THE FIELD NEAR DREWRY'S BLUFF—*May, 11, 1864*

I am verry tired and so much prostrated that I would do nothing in this world but go to bed at this late hour, eleven o' clock P.M., save to write you my dear wife and fight a battle in case of great emergency. Since I wrote you last I have passed through another battle, in which my glorious old veteran Regiment covered itself all over with glory and that splendid flag of yours was in the fight from beginning to end, and that Col husband of yours was there too. Though I am no Brigadier and never commanded a Brigade for an hour till yesterday, I can now say what few Brigadiers can say, that I have not only commanded a Brigade but I have commanded one of the most desperately fought battles of the war. It was not a great battle on account of the numbers engaged, for I did not have 2,000 men in all in the fight, and some fifteen or sixteen Regiments of the enemy were repulsed.[25]

Gen A. H. Terry, Comdg Division, came up with three Regiments of infantry, say 1,500 men, after I had made all the dispositions of my forces and the battle had been opened and assumed command, but he told me to go in & put the thing down, and I did. After the fight was all over Gen Ames came up with reinforcements and reported to Gen T.[26] On inquiring of him about the fight he told him that the 67th had done nobly. Said General Ames, 67th what? The 67th Ohio was the reply, and that Col Voris had made a most desperate fight. Who is Col Voris? was the next question. "The Col of the 67th Ohio and the Officer who commanded this battle." This conversation was had in the presence of the Adjutant. Is not this quite complimentary, and does it not show a record that many a political Brigadier might be proud of?

The 67th, 13th Ind and 169 New York Vols aided by a battery of light artillery did most of the fighting. I had these troops under my command before reinforcements came up or Gen T arrived, and added to these was 1,200 Negro Cavalry.[27] I made but little calculation as to their value in a fight, but I so displayed them that they made quite a formidable show to the enemy & probably saved my left flank, though they never fired a piece.[28]

I have no time now to enter into details but the 9th and 10th were really days of intense anxiety and peril to me and my Regiment. The 67th lost 71 in killed & wounded, 13th Ind 163 in killed, wounded & prisoners, the 169th New York 51 killed, wounded & missing. Old Bob had a 12 lb solid shot pass between his legs and completely gave out on the field. I broke down the second horse before the fight was over, and then played out the day. My side became quite irritable and the loss of sleep & want of other rest & food in connexion with the excitement, labor and the heat of the day, completely overcame me. I lay down in the shade a while and when I got up I was so prostrated in my nervous organization that I sunk to the ground as helpless as a new born baby. Rest and sleep are making me as good as new.[29]

I got four letters from you this forenoon, Blessed good letters they were to me. I am always cheered when I get letters from you. I must go to bed now. I have been so busy since I saw you last that I have had no time for to be lonesome or homesick. Lts Wallick & Ballard were instantly killed doing their duty like heroes.[30]

Morning 12th. I am up and busy as ever. All my men are at work on the trenches, fixing for defensive operations to open at any time. I saw a paper of the 10th yesterday (The Richmond Examiner). It speaks boastingly of repulsing the Yankees, but at the same time shows that the battles are drawing constantly nearer to Richmond, a fact significant of their inability to hold their advanced positions. . . .

IN THE FIELD NEAR RICHMOND, VA.—*May 12, 1864*

I am getting somewhat rested, have done as little work as possible today and freed my mind from all cares of trouble from the reb or anybody else, except such as daily attach to a Regimental command. I have done this evening what I never did before in the field except the two nights you were with me, made up my hammock bed with clean white sheets and intend to take my clothing off and go to bed as I do at home. . . .

I have no tent now, nothing but the fly as it is called, which is open at both ends & the sides, being simply a canvass roof, put up in the same manner a tent is. It is raining & has been most of the day. My Regt has gone to the picket lines, but I am not feeling able to lay out all night long on the wet ground with the rainy clouds pouring out their contents on my poor exposed body.

Before you get this you will have learned that I have been in the battle of the 10th Inst. and had a sharp fight. Whether you will learn anything about my operations or not I don't know, probably not, for there are so many envious Eastern troops here, besides lots of ambitious Officers who would do nothing to promote the prospects of an Ohioan Officer, who hold the whole Eastern press in subservience to their selfish ends and there are no Western journals represented here. I presume my heroic Regiment and myself will be totally ignored. Well, suppose I am. What does it signify? I have more to boast of than 99 out of a hundred of them have, or ever will have. I commanded & planned a battle, did it well and successfully, a thing very few Brigadiers have done.[31]

Gen Gillmore did a good thing for me. He intentionally placed no seniors over me, & gave me some of the best troops in the Department to aid me and I tried to make such use of them that he should not feel as if I had misused the confidence reposed in me. O! you would feel proud if you knew in what estimation the 67th is held here. . . .

There is no Regiment in the Department that today has as flattering notoriety as the glorious 67th. May I not feel proud that my fortunes have been cast with this Regt? And you as my own dear wife may feel proud, doubly proud, because your own husband has been the commanding Officer of the same almost since it first entered the field, has always been with it in its worst trials and dangers, and by the magnetism of example tried to inspire the men & Officers with the buoyant confidence that they were invincible. The twenty six months I have commanded the Regiment you have never heard ought to detract from its honor, but on the contrary many things that give undying honor & glory to its fame. I know your heart will swell with emotions of pride as you learn of the new honors now by <u>my</u> old Regiment.[32]

Col Commager commanded the major part of the Regt in the fight and did himself, the Regiment and the country great honor. He is a <u>credit</u> to the service and deserves a better place than Lt Col. When danger thickens and desperate chances are to be taken, he like a hero bears his own breast to the strong and eloquently says, "boys do as I do and we will win."[33]

Major Butler is personally a man of great courage. He is what the world calls a game man, and is perhaps the best example of that type of a man in the Regiment. He did a magnificent thing for me the night before the fight by going after midnight [from camp], when we had every reason to believe the road was intercepted by the rebels, some five miles off for reinforcements, a truly hazardous enterprise.[34]

The Adjutant is of another type of the heroic, cool, dispassionate, but as energetic, pertinacious and sincere as mortal can be. His conscience gives to him a personal worth that makes him to me one of the best men I ever knew. I love him, admire him, scold him, praise him, still he does not become puffed up with praise nor sorrow with reproof. He is a little hero, a brick.

My Officers without exception perform their duties with an ability and will that never was excelled by the same number of men like situated in any army. My men were not to be outdone by the Officers. Everyone appeared to feel the inspiration of duty and heroism, and went in & held out for some four hours as if there was no such thing as fail. Ohio may indeed feel proud of her 67th Reg Vet Vols. The new recruits fought side by side with the veterans without a flinch. I hesitated much about using them, but my hesitancy is all gone now. Nobody but ourselves knows but the Regt is all veteran.

Friday evening, May 13. It has been raining most of the day and appears so much like Sunday that I have been all the live long day calling it so. My Regiment being on picket some two miles from camp, and all the other forces of the command are off to the front some three miles beyond where I had the fight last Tuesday morning. . . .

Fancy me in a low pine woods under the edge of a tent fly with a little brush fire built to the front on the ground, reading the papers of the 10th Inst. detailing the horrible slaughter of the battles of the 5th and 6th between Lee and Grant, & you will have me as I sat a few minutes ago.[35] Then I thought of my lonely wife at home and her dear little ones & how they longed to see the soldier husband and father at home, and concluded I would add another half sheet to the letter I commenced last evening. . . .

The only wonder is that I have written as often and much as I have. Night & day without facilities I have been in these ugly woods of Va almost constantly hearing rebels guns near me. There has been less demonstrating on our front today than at any other time since we landed at Bermuda Hundred. And not being verry well I have had on the whole a very quiet day. I am going to bed early and try to sleep off my dull feeling. I know I should be happier by far if I could do it at my own home with my own dear family than in this dense forrest below the rebel City of Richmond.

I sometimes think I have had enough of military glory and will quit, though the last week has been perhaps the most propitious for me since I came into the field. As soon as this campaign is over I will let you say whether I shall leave the army or not. If we are successful I think the great movements of the armies will be substantially closed this spring. If not the North will want peace. In either case there will be no great demand for more men. But I do not want to be at home and placed where I must urge my fellow citizens to go & fight when I can not set them the example. Keep the children for me, take care of yourself and a good night.

Saturday morning. Am better this morning.[36]

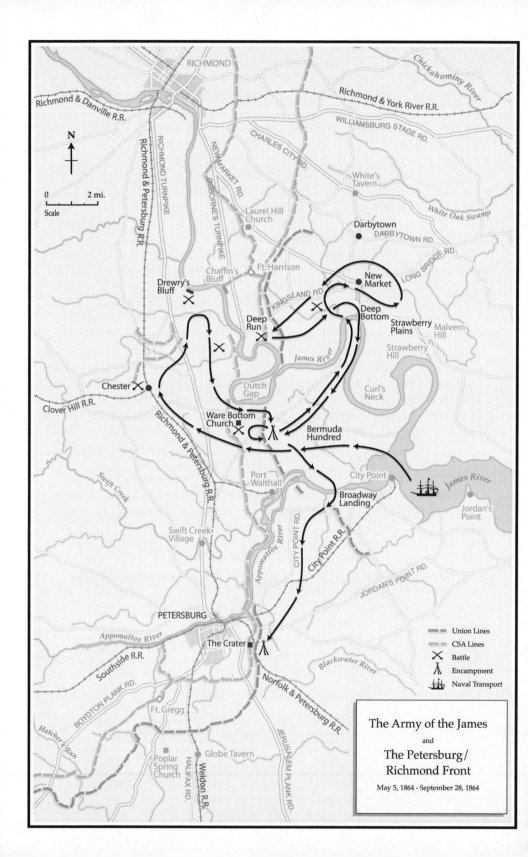

The Army of the James
and
The Petersburg /
Richmond Front

May 5, 1864 - September 28, 1864

"Constantly under Fire"

[On May 12, 1864, Butler deployed 15,000 infantry from two corps, Gillmore's Tenth and Maj. Gen. William F. Smith's Eighteenth, toward Drewry's Bluff on the James River, five miles below Richmond. After intense fighting ended by May 17, Confederates under Beauregard had forced Butler to retreat and bottled his forces along the neck of Bermuda Hundred, effectively preventing the Army of the James from achieving its objectives. The 67th Ohio was not engaged at Drewry's Bluff. Gillmore held it in reserve along a defensive perimeter, south of the battlefield, performing picket duty. Not until May 20 did the regiment again see combat. In the short but deadly melee at Ware Bottom Church, the 67th helped regain ground lost earlier and captured a number of prisoners, notably Brig. Gen. William S. Walker. By the end of June, while the front shifted to Petersburg, a railroad center southeast of Bermuda Hundred, about twenty miles from Richmond, the 67th remained in place, apparently stalled and destined to remain in a backward area, vexed by changeable weather, nightly artillery bombardments, and occasional but deadly skirmishes along its picket lines.]

BERMUDA HUNDRED—*May 15, 1864*

. . . As I think of the horrors of this campaign my heart sinks. I read the news with anguish and look into the future with melancholy forebodings, not for myself but for my bleeding sorrow stricken country. After I came out of the fight of the 10th I felt exultant, proud, wanted to try it again, was not at all satisfied with what we had done. But after I had reflected on what had been done, the sacrifices it cost, the misery it entailed, I began to regret that I had been a prominent actor in the struggle, and now I hate the thought of taking my men where they will slaughter & be slaughtered.

Wherever they go I have no doubt of their doing credit to themselves and the service & of adding honor to the Officers that command them, but who wants honor at so fearful a cost.

We have the Eastern papers of the 13th, and frightful indeed are they with the horrid recitals of war. Never did a people fight as do these Americans. They are heroic, sagacious and tenacious beyond parallel, and the latter quality is being wonderfully developed by the war.

While I am writing this I hear the continual reports of heavy artillery from the rebel ranks between here and Richmond and of our own light artillery. My Regiment is fortunate in being left here on picket just outside the intrenchments, a service that gives them rest and is free from the dangers of the forces before the rebel forts covering Richmond. Our army is some eight miles to the front toward the rebel capital, and is pushing its way to the I hope doomed City by hard fighting.

Col Osborn 39th Ill came in this morning with his right arm shattered by a shrapnel shot. He was chafing a good deal this morning, because he was wounded before he had even a chance to use his Regiment in a fight.[1] For two & a half years the Col has been with his Regt and never has yet had it in a fight. . . . I tell them they have great cause to be grateful for their good fortune, but they can't see it in that light. They are spoiling for a fight. One battle will cure them of that. Night before last they went out to the front, and in all human probability will have abundant opportunity to gratify their longing for a fight with the rebels. . . .[2]

I don't expect there is a Col in the Department who will have as fortunate a chain of circumstances occur to him as already have to me; for no one unless a regular army Officer or a Brigadier would have been placed in my position on the 10th had not the force of circumstances compelled it, and good fortune attended me to a successful accomplishment of all that anyone under the circumstances could have accomplished.

I saw the comparative merits of the Eastern and Western troops well illustrated in the fight. Half of the 6th Conn could not be driven into the work. They would lay on their cowardly bellies and hurrah at inducements to move them into line of fire, but not a man would start. Our men stuck to it with the most dogged tenacity. If either the 67th Ohio or 13th Ind had been left out at the beginning of the fight and their place supplied with any of the Yankee troops there, the battle would in my humble opinion been lost at the first shock.[3]

I may feel compelled to ask to be relieved from my duties in the field, as my side annoys me more on account of exposure than the labors of the campaign. I shall not certainly hang to the delusion of being a great military man at the expense of my future health. I am willing to meet the usual *consequences* of the service, but I do not feel as if I ought to add to these the constant annoyance of injuries already acquired in the service. I do not expect permanent injury from the Wagner wound, but it does make me a good deal of trouble.

My pride makes me dislike to ask to be assigned to lighter duties while the whole army and country are in the struggle. Still I shall do so or ask to be discharged altogether if I do not feel better at the end of the month. My side is more of an annoyance than anything else to me, but it is of that nature as *not* to destroy my efficiency for command. Then you know I have been harassed almost to death in my effort to reorganize my Regiment, and the want of co operation in that behalf. I hope for easier times for the future. . . .

BERMUDA HUNDRED—*May 16, 1864*

While battle is raging with great fury some eight miles from here toward Richmond, I am permitted to sit in my tent entirely secure from present danger. I was stopped here by orders to go to the front, but shortly rapid firing to our left made it expedient to keep my command in camp. There is a lull now all along the front. 10 o'clock A.M. How long this may continue I don't know, as we are constantly on the lookout for demonstrations from the rebs. We have a position here that we can hold against great odds, so you need not expect to hear of my going to Richmond a captive unless I get taken by accident. And as a good Christian <u>I mean to watch and pray.</u> I am sitting in a large rocking chair that accidently came into camp, not on its own legs.⁴

I have just received orders to stay with my Regt in camp. This means rest. But the Lord only knows what will be the next order, nor when it will come. Perhaps I had better continue this while we are waiting orders. Everything is quiet all around us now. Our troops are coming back to camp, having accomplished what was intended, so rumor says. My men have been saved much fatigue and danger by being placed on picket duty (some two miles to the front of this camp), and I have been saved all by staying within the intrenchments and gaining what strength I could against the time of trial which may at anytime be precipitated on me. I feel quite much recovered, and by careful usage can do field duty again. Have been on horseback most of the day. (12 1/2 P.M. now.)

I see by the New York Herald of the 14th that Col Voorhies's [sic] Brigade had a sharp fight at the Junction, but my Regiment is hardly mentioned while notice is given to Regiments that did not lose five men and 3/4 of whose strength could not be forced into the fight. I am satisfied that the Western troops may make glorious fights on the field and Eastern Regiments on paper, and the country will never know but what the cowardly blovating shirks are the best & most self sacrificing part of the Army. But we know the difference. As the mail goes out pretty soon I must hasten to close this.⁵

I see poor wounded men going past my quarter with broken arms and lacerated bodies, who have walked eight miles to get to a place of safety. I learn that we had a seriously disastrous morning, that a whole Brigade was gobbled up with Gen Heckman its commander, that the 39th Ill, that Regt I wrote you of spoiling for a fight, was frightfully cut to pieces.⁶

We always get such rumors from the first stragglers from the battle field. Frequently what is represented as a disastrous defeat is a glorious victory as soon as the full accounts are given. My Regiment has been gobbled up several times, if rumors were true. Yet the 67th never lost a score of prisoners since it appeared in the field. Still I know enough to be assured that the rebels were too much for us this morning.[7]

The army is coming back of the intrenchments. I feared this. We might have given them a heavy blow ten days ago, but we demonstrated before them for several days giving them time to mass enough troops against us to at least check our advancement. I hardly think we will try to take Richmond from the south side of the James, and this may compel our forces to fight on the defensive rather than on the aggressive as it started out.

Our army here is too light to do anything more than threaten their weak points and destroy their lines of communication. This the papers say has been effectually done, but I don't think so. I am afraid the work has not been thoroughly done. If not all our operations this side of the James is for nought but a temporary purpose.

I do not feel afraid on account of myself. . . . I feel indeed thankful to an All Wise Providence for the good fortune that has attended me. I have indeed been blessed with the preservation of His strong hand. I send you persimmon seeds taken from my battle field, the day before the fight. Mine has as yet been the only one of unquestioned success since we landed here.[8]

BERMUDA HUNDRED—*May 21, 1864*

I recd your letter of the 14th and 15th last evening just as I got in from another battle. The picket lines were assaulted in the morning by the enemy, and our Brigadier needed to open them again. Col Howell comdg our Brigade wanted to try the mettle of his boys, get the honor of trying the rifle pit, a very foolish whimsy of a very foolish old man who is better fitted for the mad house than the command of troops in the field. If I am not verry much mistaken he was quite drunk during the fight. If I did not have good Officers to assist me, and did not know that a Regimental commander had little to apprehend from the interference from his superiors, I should be completely discouraged. <u>But my experience has taught me that a good Regimental commander has matters pretty much his own way in a fight.</u> I know that yesterday I had more to do with the disposition of the forces in the field than the senior Officer charged with the work.[9]

We are awfully tired and used up for want of rest and sleep. We slept in the trenches last night, after being up most of the time for the previous three nights. I was so exhausted that I could not sleep, was up three or four times during the night. I slept some today, a poor dreamy sleep that failed to rest me. What I want is undisturbed quiet sleep that brings refreshment with it, but that is out of the question here. Matters cannot continue after this style verry long. Human endurance cannot bear it. Sickness and demoralization follow in the wake of long protracted efforts of this kind. I had 13 men killed and sixty wounded yesterday. Capt Emmerson will die. Lt Minor has a frightful wound of the side of the head, and Lt Cochrane lost his left foot, taken off just below the knee.[10] I went to the hospital this morning. A horrible sight presented itself to me, maimed, perforated and lacerated bodies in every possible stage of wounds from the slight to the most frightful.[11]

I will say for your benefit that you need not worry because you may think that we are going on to the defenses of Richmond from this way. That has been tried and abandoned as impracticable. Unless a much larger force is brought here we will be compelled to hold the place we have forti-fied, keeping ourselves within our intrenchments.

My boys [Company C] took Major Gen Walker yesterday, breaking his leg so as to require amputation. I have his sword as a trophy of the fight.[12] I will send it to you as soon as opportunity offers. The mail is just closing and being desirous that you should get this early I will close right here. I can't write any more today. We have great cause to be thankful to the All Wise for His protection through my late trials.

BERMUDA HUNDRED—*May 22, 1864*

I cannot permit this Sabbath day pass without an effort on my part to al-lay your anxiety on account of my nearness to the enemy and my constant liability to personal danger. This has been the most quiet day we have had for a long time, yet all hands have been at work. We are getting matters in such shape that we can easily defend ourselves against a large army and with comparative safety to us. Picketing is the worst duty we have to per-form. Our lines are in the woods, and in close proximity to those of the en-emy and the constant fear of attack from both parties keeps up almost a continuous fire, not verry dangerous to be sure but verry annoying. And al-most every night a panic will seize some timid Regiment and a general firing will ensue from both sides for a short time at the imagined advance of either party or both. Then the artillery must pitch in with aimless fire, but with great noise and magnificence. A few men only suffer from this, but it keeps our troops from the much needed rest so essential to the morale of an army.

We must be ready in case of an attack. As a consequence all of us fit for duty sleep on our arms, with our heavy accoutrements fixed to the body, a verry poor preparation for repose. I was out to the front a few nights ago when our folks made one of these night attacks upon the rebel lines. I not being a party to the affair took proper precaution to keep out of harm's way. A few hundred troops & two mountain howitzers made enough noise for a big battle. The stillness of night and the thick nature of the woods combined to make it an imposing affair, if not verry decisive or hazardous. There is something so uncertain about night attacks that one involuntarily feels a dread of them.

I see by the papers that the people in Ohio did not know that the 67th had been in a fight till the 18th inst. . . . Great solicitude will be awakened when they learn that again we have been in a desperate fight and lost as heavily as we did in the others. These two battles cost my Regt as much as the assault on Wagner. I had nearly twice as many men to begin with this time, still the loss is a great one in the 74 killed & wounded, in the latter 69, in all 143 men, of these 25 number among the dead and 65 or 70 severely wounded.[13]

What a horrid thought to contemplate. 143 victims in my own Regiment, many of them my comrades through the terrible trials of this cruel war for most of three years, all of them allied to me by the obligations of duty, honor and affection. It makes me heart sick to reflect on the terrible inroads this campaign is making on my men. . . .

I am sorry to learn that you are sick. I hope it will not continue long. . . . Tell the children I will write them soon as I get time. I sent by Mr James Ballard of Toledo the rebel Gen Walker's sword to be expressed from Toledo to you. I want it preserved as a trophy of the battle of the 26th. May God bless you.[14]

BERMUDA HUNDRED—*May 24, 1864*

Matters are becoming more settled here than they heretofore have been. My men have had a little time for rest, which has been verry much needed by them. We are still on the extreme front, and in range of both their artillery and musketry, but have a thick abatis to our front and sufficient earth works constructed to hold a strong force at bay.[15]

We are in a place of comparative safety, but this is not what we come here for. I fear this movement has been a sad failure. Instead of having accomplished the substantial results I see spoken of in the news journals, we have failed in everything except gaining a position and losing some six thousand men in killed, wounded and prisoners. All you have seen in the papers about our having cut the rebel communications to Richmond south of the James is substantially untrue. Three days after what had been accomplished on their railroads and so vauntingly published to the world the enemy were running their trains past our position & not three miles off.

I am fearful that Gen Butler is a failure, nor is this to be wondered at. He has had no military experience in the field. His operations in the early stages of the war were not of such a sort as to develop skill & ability for operations of the kind undertaken by his army. That he has acquired reputation as a General is true, but it has been rather on account of administrative ability connected with civil than military matters. To me it is singular that the War Department should entrust to such a Gen the supreme command of as important an enterprise as this against whom it could only have expected that the best talent of the Confederacy must be arrayed, fortified by the practical experience of three year's service in the field. It was easy to gain reputation in the earlier stages of the war. The blunders & want of experience in our commanders was overlooked by equally blundering and inexperienced tyros in the Confederacy. But it is not so now. Three years have made an array of military commanders for the South against whom no inexperienced man, however much a genius can expect to succeed unless by the merest luck, chances upon which no wise government would for a moment rely.

We are virtually besieged on the little isthmus known as Bermuda Hundred. All I have to do is to step a few paces from my fly shade, and I can see the enemies works bustling with artillery & musketry so near that their musket shot wound our men daily. This has been so for five days, and for his life Gen Butler cannot tell whether there are five thousand or twenty five thousand troops surrounding us. If we come here to command their communications southwardly through Peterburg we have failed in that, because the enemy have it is said two strongly fortified lines between us and the railroad which is not three miles off.

With the labor we have already expended here we might have made a chain of fortifications, equally adapted to defense as our present works and at the same time completely commanded the railroad & turnpike. This was so patent to me when we first came here that I supposed that course was being pursued, but upon going to the front I was greatly disappointed at finding nothing done. As a matter of ordinary precaution this ought to have been done. If the capture of Richmond was the grand object of the campaign the tables are fairly turned upon us, as we were driven from before Richmond by hard fighting and are much more closely besieged than the rebel capital.[16]

This is anything but encouraging to us, and not verry flattering to the pride of the good people at home who have been reading Gen Butler's dispatches almost exulting in the realization that Richmond was ours. This indicates a want of a well defined policy, and that the command is not controlled by clear notions as to what ought to be done and the manner of doing it.

Again the troops. Many of them are not verry reliable. In my fight of Friday last I charged with my Regiment over the prostrate line of the 6th Conn to get at the enemies position. In the battle of the 10th I saw the same thing substantially manifest itself. All parties here concede that our Western Regiments here are superior to any other troops in the Department. We are in high repute, but this is rather dangerous honor for fearful responsibilities follow in the wake of a good fighting reputation.

Do you see Mr Upson? If so I wish you would ask him what he had done with my papers [applying for promotion to brigadier general]. I heard nothing about them since I left. The last time I saw Judge Spalding he told me he had not read them. I wrote Mr U while at Washington, but learn nothing. I do not expect anything whatever I may do. Merit is worth a great deal more in the hands of some negative man who has political power or strong friends than in the possession of only a genuine meritorious soldier. I am quite well.[17]

BERMUDA HUNDRED, VA.—*May 26, 1864*

I am tired, have the headache, need rest, good sweet repose verry much. How I wish I could take my place in our home far away from the terrible alarms that constantly excite the most anxious feeling our part in this damnable place. Clean clothing, good food & drink and above all quiet rest in a soft tidy bed are luxuries that I would give most anything for. But here we are in the close forrest of Va with cruel rebels close to our front, with none of these comforts and perplexed by cares and danger, labors and watchings till poor humanity feels like sinking under the burden. No one knows but the soldier what we suffer and are required to do in the field while prosecuting active campaign operation in the face of a vigilant enemy. War is an awful calamity let it come ever so lightly, but let all the energies of a whole people be aroused to give efficacy to its horrors and no tongue can tell nor human pen describe the miseries that follow in its wake.

My experience in the field would make me a good legislator. I should never vote for war unless upon the most urgent necessity. I have no private ambition to gratify at its fearful cost. No position in the circle of military power, and nowhere is it more absolute, offers inducements strong enough to lead my judgment from the opinion above expressed. Should I live to old age I shall never feel otherwise unless I become forgetful of the lessons of the past.

I pray God this year may see the return of peace, blessed peace, but I dare not hope with any degree of fervor because I see so little that indicates that decisive results are necessarily going to flow from the prodigious efforts now made by both parties. The South are far from being reduced, either by famine, stress of war or broken finances. They show the means of producing subsistence and clothing for their army, the ability to efficiently arm and equip all the arms bearing men in the Confederacy, and their peculiar productions go verry far to supply the place of their broken currency. Cotton is so high that they can use the small quantities they get into market to supply them with munitions of war, and with their wide range of productions they can live almost entirely independent of the outside world. We did not know how cheaply a people could live and live comfortably till the war taught us a lesson of practical economy. The South have learned this and submitted to their fate with a zeal and fortitude that challenges my admiration and certainly worthy a better cause.[18]

I commenced to write this just at evening, but an order coming requiring me to go on picket with my Regt and act as Gen Officer of the Day for the whole line [forced me] to quit in the middle of a sentence on the second page of this letter. But going from my quarters to my place for the night, it being verry dark, I fell into a ditch of one of the forts I had to pass and well nigh broke my leg. For sometime I thought it was broken, it pained me so, but I soon rallied and got to my place, where I stayed till 3 A.M., but feeling verry uncomfortably from my accident I concluded to go a mile to the rear out of harm's way & nurse my left knee. I gave it as bad a wrench as I had some years since. I certainly have been quite fortunate so far, have suffered none from the enemy while one fourth of my command have been in some way visited by their shot & shell. . . .

I was disappointed in not getting anything from you for I am anxious to hear from you. Your last signified that you were sick.

Saturday. 28 May. . . . I hope this period of extreme anxiety will soon be over, <u>but terrible struggles must ensue first.</u> The late papers indicate that Gen Lee is very much annoyed by the movements of Gen Grant, and is probably within the defenses about Richmond. But that only signifies that we will have more terrible fighting before the ends of the campaign are accomplished, unless Lee intends to evacuate Virginia. I hardly can imagine that the enemy think of abandoning their capital without a desperate and protracted struggle, for they can escape with their army after the adversities of a siege without much danger of annihilation, and nobody can tell what they may accomplish by tenaciously resisting our efforts. They know it is a long way to the last ditch.

I wrote Mr Chamberlin day before yesterday. He is one of my most ardent friends, does more for me than many who talk more. So far as terms of social intercourse are concerned I have reason to feel well towards my neighbors and former associates at the bar, but I am under no sort of obligation to [any] one of them for anything under Heaven, further than their *social* amenities bestowed on me. . . . Nevertheless I do feel that if my friends had made an earnest effort in my behalf I might have a better position, and compared with hundreds of others I feel as if I had richly earned promotion.

I have no doubt but that political jealousies have their weight. Ambitious aspirants who <u>could not find it convenient</u> to go into the field and who have great weight in the administration of public matters are not anxious to aid in building up successful rivals, & while they are willing to laud the acts of good men in the field they are not over zealous to give them more substantial support. I do not know as I have any reason to complain, for my gallant Regiment has done more for my welfare than most Brigades would have done. But my friends at home are certainly entitled to no credit for that. The ability of my Officers, the heroism of my noble men & my good fortune in being their Commander are entitled only to my gratitude for this. May the day grow dark and the Heavens pitiless when I presume to ignore the well earned claim of my men to the honor I have acquired in this war.

If the choice was given me between a Brigade made up of many Regiments I know and the command of the glorious Old 67th, I would unhesitatingly seize the higher honor of casting my lot with my old veterans. If I could have a Regiment a thousand strong of such men as five hundred of my men were on the 1st of May Inst. I would not be afraid of the best Brigade in the Confederacy.[19]

In that affair of the 20th Inst. the rebels admit that they were terribly punished. A Lt who met the flag of truce says that there was a great many dead gray backs directly to the point of the line occupied by my Regt. I knew that we delivered a terrible oblique fire upon them while they were trying to flank our right. We occupied a favorable position to give them a demonstration of our ability to use powder and ball <u>and they got it.</u>

My boys are not old Hunkers, but resort to any feasible means to accomplish the great end, whip the rebels. On the 10th inst. at the fight in the pike, the gunners of the 4th N J Battery had been driven from one of their pieces.[20] The Sgt like a true hero, stayed by his gun, and called on the infantry for help. Lt Kief my Regt had some thirty odd of my men as provost guard & by my order had gone to the front and finding one of my Caissons in the hands of the enemy, rushed on them, took it and converted part of his guard into artillery men and fired shot shell and grape at the columns of the rebs that soon made them skedaddle. It is said they used the saber, ammunition & reamer as if they were also veterans in the artillery service.[21]

On the 20th I got very much out of patience with the 6th Conn Vols. I found them spread out flat on the ground under a slight elevation to the front that substantially shielded them from the enemies fire. My men formed immediately in their rear and commenced a rapid fire over their prostrate bodies. They at once set up the cry "you are firing on your own men, we have skirmishes in front." Upon viewing the field I could see nothing but gray backs. Saying to the Yankees, "All right your skirmishes are in very bad company. Boys! charge over these cowardly scamps and give the rebs H——L."

Pell mell our boys dashed over the prostrate line of the 6th Conn, and charged on the rebel rifle pits which we occupied in less time than it takes me to narrate it. I did brandish my pistol about the ears of the ranking captain of this Regiment, making some allusion to the fact if he did not move his men at once there would be a Yankee captain reported among the list of Killed In Action. The craven pocketed the insult, and probably feels as if he got off well in not having a barbarian Buckeye Col knock his brains out. Some of his men talking to my boys about the affair said Col Voris might get himself into trouble if he assumed to dictate to their Officers, whereat my boys told them that they would get into trouble, Officers and all, if they got "Old Promptly" after them, that next to rebels he wanted to annihilate cowardly soldiers.[22]

But this is an awful recital. Still it is one of the *incidents* of war. I am glad I did not do what I threatened, which I certainly should had he not obeyed me. I want to come out of this war without having the reflection to haunt me that I have taken the life of a human being. Riding by a strange Regiment the other day, I heard the boys say, "that is the Col of the 67th Ohio. He is a very Devil to fight. <u>I saw him in a fight.</u> I wish we had such a Col," and the like expressions as I passed them.

When I heard that I began to dream of a star till a whole constellation began to cluster on my devoted shoulder, but soon the spell broke and I realized that I was only an Ohio Colonel and had only done my duty, and that they little knew what an awful effort it cost me to do it. My God, deliver me from any more fighting. Others may think me a brave man, but I know I am not. I know I feel that terrible agony that so distresses the timid man, but my will and pride partially lift me over the terrible sensations that fear and danger force upon one. Gen Terry told me a few days since that it was easy enough for me to go through a fight. I presume he thought so for he had seen me all energy and absorbed with the will to conquer in the fight of the 10th. I told him of the thought so he will understood the terrible struggle that well nigh overthrew my courage and manhood.[23]

Well, dear wife, I hope to escape in future, but God only knows what is in store for me. I am better today. My side does not pain me much & will be gone in a few days.

BERMUDA HUNDRED—*May 30, 1864*

Grant is on the Chickahominy today. We have heard heavy and almost constant artillery firing in the neighborhood of Richmond ever since morning with the strong indication that the conflict is approaching the <u>doomed</u> City. We don't know as much about Gen Grant's movements as you do as we do not get the papers as regularly as you do, but this demonstration is an item of news that cheers us with the belief that Old Unconditional Surrender has flanked Gen Lee and moved his army within a few miles of Richmond. Now mark what I have written, that on the 30th of May Gen Grant was on the Chickahominy.[24]

Whatever may be the ultimate fate of his campaign against Richmond all must concede that he is one of the most persevering men of the age. What most men would shrink from he takes hold of with a steady unyielding confidence and triumphs over difficulties where most others would fail. No man since the days of Washington has handled an army in whom the people had as much confidence as in Grant. His unassuming energy, perseverance and unselfish devotion to the work before him assures us that the country not Grant is the great object of all his endeavors. We will honor him though he fails. You know I am not much of a man worshiper, and when I say this of another you will certainly understand that I am a great admirer of the man.[25]

I admit that I have had and still have unpleasant reflections as to the ultimate success of his present effort, for I know something of the desperation with which the rebels fight. I have always told you of the unanimity of Southern sentiment, the self sacrificing feeling of all and their deep seated hatred of the Yankees and their institutions, and of their unyielding determination to never yield to our arms so long as a desperate hope is left them. The three years has intensified rather than abated these feelings, and

at the same time has accustomed them to bear with patience the deprivations & tribulations consequent on the war, and really has developed a better military spirit than the North can acquire as long as shody, political
stock gambling and money speculations *overrun* the loyal states.[26]

I grant the Confederacy has become an overwhelming and unmitigated
despotism, tyranising over the person and property of every man in it, but
it [contains] elements of strength, which enables one master mind to combine all the power of the new government and direct the same in a single
channel, if need be. They see the necessity of this, and yield, whilst the
North, hardly realizing that we are in a state of war, will discuss every question, determine upon the specific policy to be pursued in each case, will
cheerfully aid where convenience, interest or pride are secured, but will
fight the same with bitter hostility if their caprice is against the measure.
With us cowards, speculators, demagogues and traitors are permitted to
give aid and comfort to the enemy by factions opposition to the measures
of the Government with almost as much latitude as if we were not in a
state of war.

The Administration is too unselfish and kind hearted to assume to itself
the powers it ought to exercise, to give the war that vigor it ought to have,
to make it so sweeping a terror to the enemies of the Government. No great
war can be a success without becoming absolutely despotic in its administration. War is a state of social revulsion, the foundations of society are broken up and no people should ever think of engaging in a great general warfare, unless they are prepared to yield everything to its demands.[27]

If Grant should fail in this campaign I fear that the North can never be
brought to that submission essential to a successful prosecution of the war.
Nothing but a successful invasion of the North could bring about such results. But why moralize on this subject. Sufficient for the day is the rest
thereof.

I myself feel as if I had done about enough, suffered about enough in
this struggle for the integrity of the original Union. It is more a question of
pride than national existence. The North can live separated from the South
and still be a powerful people. The Continent is certainly broad enough.
We have people enough and resources enough to make us the envy of the
world still. Yet I am so much a lover of the old Union that I cannot bear to
think of a dismembered country. But what will it be if we should conquer
the South? When under Heaven will the bitter rancors of this terrible conflict be obliterated from the minds of the people? Hate, cruel hate will em-
bitter our intercourse for years. How I wish we were not so foolish and
wicked. O! once happy America, how art thou fallen.[28]

I suppose you will say that the rattle of musketry and the thunder of artillery are making quite a philosopher of your soldier husband. That may be
so but it is the philosophy of peace. My experience in the field makes me
abominate war. I wish everyone in the land North & South felt as I do about
it. The war would soon end. . . .

May 31st. . . . Five month's pay & allowances are due me today from the Government, four months of which I hope to get before long. . . . It is not verry flattering to the Pay Department that the soldiers of the country are compelled to go so long without their hard earned wages. It is more embarrassing to Officers, as they have need of money to meet their current demands for subsistence in the field, and this cannot be done without money. The soldier is supplied without the cash. But their families must feel the want of the little allowance the state should pay her troops every two months if the periods of payment are extended to four and five months. The soldier will fight better if he feels that his personal rights are carefully guarded by the representatives of the Government.

I saw surgeons operate in case of amputation of the hand for the first time this morning. The subject was placed under the influence of anesthetic, and slept as quietly through the whole operation as if he were having nothing more than his hair cut or nails filed. This success of saving pain in such operations is one of the wonders and blessings of this wonderful age. I believe I would have made a surgeon had I given my attention to it in my younger days. The most heart sickening features of this war are seen in the hospital after a battle has been fought. I visited some of my unfortunate boys in the field general hospital the morning after our fight of the 20th, and found one minus a leg, another minus an arm, another less a hand, yet another dying from a wound received in both legs, one of which had been amputated, the other shockingly lacerated by a rifle shot. It makes me melancholy indeed to pass through these scenes of distress when but the day before all was animation and healthful vigor. I am losing all courage for a soldier. I fear it will drive me from the army. I feel now like leaving the service as soon as this campaign ends so that I can do so honorably. I will write you more fully in a few days. . . .[29]

BERMUDA HUNDRED, VA.—*June 2, 1864*

I see by the papers as well as your letter . . . that you had no knowledge of my participation in the engagement of the 20th May up to the date of your letters, only as the same might have been inferred from the decease of Capt George Emmerson. Lt John Cochrane is reported dead, and so far as I can learn I suppose the report to be correct, thus making four Officers killed & died from wounds during the month of May last. All of them first class Officers and gentlemen of real worth. They are a great loss to the Regiment and to the country. How thankful I am that I have passed unharmed through these battles. Lt Minor is doing well, and will soon return to his company.

Being on the extreme front all the while and on picket every third day, you may be assured that I get enough of the war. Almost daily we have skirmishes with the enemy and every day we are compelled to submit to an artillery demonstration. This *occurs* at night as well. To escape evil consequences from this I have my bed in a pit with a high earth bank to the front and on both flanks and overhead a perfect bomb proof. The way the rebs make their fragments of iron fly round our ears is anything but desirable. The boys have their knapsacks, tents and other warlike paraphernalia knocked about at a wild rate by their unmannerly projectiles. The cook of one of the companies had a kettle of fresh beef cooking today when a fragment of shell knocked the kettle, meat and gravy beyond the reach of the hungry boys without so much as an apology. Another shell penetrated a knapsack, making fine fragments of its contents carrying a pair of shoes off several rods. We are on the skirts of a heavy forrest, through which the enemies shot & shells are frequently thrown with a terrific momentum, of which the uninitiated have no conception. Large trees are cut down by them. The crashing of limbs, the screeching sound in the air, their awful explosion and the tearing whirl of the fragments are awe striking indeed.

Let some twenty guns *as is frequently the case* play over your position in the night time, so that you may see the track of the shell by the burning fuse and hear the explosion of each with the hollow echo of the report of both the pieces and the projectiles that only the night can give, together with the phantomic impressions that darkness produces, and it takes stronger nerves than mine to calmly rest in those hours designed by nature for repose. I grant I have been so tired as to sleep under this but it was not that refreshing kind of sleep a man gets in his own domicile. I tell you I hug the ground verry closely and keep snug to the leeward of my subterranean palace.

Our sojourn here for the last four weeks has been perfectly awful. The hope that matters will soon change for the better is the only thing that keep many of us up. We are much safer than we were a while ago, but God deliver me from our present security, if this be security. I really think the last month has been worse than in the trenches before Fort Wagner last year, for here we come unawares upon the rebs daily, & then we pitch in & had a fight; then we knew where to find them, there then was no possibility of a surprise; here it is impossible to avoid them.

My camp is in a peculiar locality and appears to be the subject of their peculiar attentions. When the rebs open a shot on our lines the way the boys break for the breast works is <u>more</u> than lively. With all their haste I have lost some unfortunate fellow members almost daily. The camp is not more than ten rods from the earth works.

I had hardly closed the three first pages of this last evening & got myself fixed for the night, which was a very dark one, when a terrible musketry fire was opened on our front and knowing that six companies of my Regiment were in the immediate locality of the shooting you can imagine that I felt anything but comfortable. It was so dark that I knew that no demonstration of the enemy in force could be made, but the awful confusion that would ensue if our folks believed an attack was being made might be as disastrous to us as the worst demonstration of our enemy.

In a little time Col Commager sent in news that one of his companies had been attacked & half of them taken prisoners and asked for reinforcements. The rebs at quite a distance delivered heavy volleys of musketry but were careful not to come close to us. We have this consolation, that they are as much afraid of us as we are of them.[30]

We can hear the heavy artillery fighting of Lee and Grant night and day. What will be the finale of the investment of Richmond God only knows. But if mortals ever prayed, we pray for the success of the enterprise. I am better. Have got almost rested and well from my fall. . . .

BERMUDA HUNDRED, VA.—*June 5, 1864*

This is really a quiet Sabbath morning, the first we have had for many a long week. You were with me the last, and that was anything but a quiet Sabbath to you. Since midnight Friday to this hour, 9 A.M., we have been perfectly free from rebel annoyance. Since last evening we have not so much as heard the distant booming of Grant's canon. The gun boats are still, the picket lines are still and so far as my feeble senses go all the world is still.

But how soon this may be changed I cannot tell. We are not apprehensive of any determined effort on the part of the enemy to drive us from our present position, and everyday makes the probabilities less, as we are making our position stronger. The enemy are making corresponding efforts on their part all along our front to prevent our egress toward their capital. Friday skirmishing was kept up during the entire day, we losing say two hundred in killed, wounded and prisoners, 1/2 being prisoners, the enemy losing quite as largely with a greater proportion of killed. The enemy supposed we were evacuating the Hundred pitched in with a view to capture our rear guard and such public property as had not been removed.

In their conjecture they were slightly mistaken, and before they got through the affair they also found that it was not safe to meddle with the Yankees. For a while the enemy threw their metal at a furious rate about our heads, but I kept myself at a safe proximity to Mother Earth with a heavy bank between me and the direction from whence came their projectiles. In the night they opened musketry fire on our picket line, the balls whizzing over my camp at a malicious rate. A captain of the 39th Ills only a few yards from my quarters was shot through the thigh by one of their random shots.

These ugly little messengers of wrath from the rebs are anything but agreeable to us, especially when we are anxious to get a night's sleep. The first shot brings my men to their feet, and a continuance sends them to the parapet at a double quick. Last night there was no firing of any kind in hearing, and all hands embraced the respite to take a good snooze. I slept better last night than at any other time for a whole month. When I lay down I made up my mind there could be no attack, and should the rebs let loose their artillery or musketry I could lay in my den safe from their worst efforts.

The moral effect of canonading is much greater than the physical. Verry few are hurt, considering the noise and weight of metal projected. The effect is terrific enough to appearance, still when you look at the results to a command you would be astonished at the few persons injured. This is true of all long range efforts, but get within canister range and the distinction is frequently awful. Ft Wagner for instance.

You would think this awful living if you had to live as I have done for the last month, in the woods, with poor food, little shelter, no rest, awful danger, the severest labor, interspersed with daily affairs with the enemy, constantly under fire and twice desperately engaged in battle. All these my men have borne with fortitude, heroism & cheerfulness never excelled by any troops in any service. I honor them for it. The people at home never will know how much they owe to the common soldier who does and suffers so much for the good & honor of the country.

It has been raining for the last twenty hours, not hard but enough to make it unpleasant. This is the worst country in the world for rain. The soil is made up largely of clay, and passing over it a few times in the rain makes the most horrible mud under the sun. . . .

By this morning's report, I am two hundred men and some ten Officers short of what I had a month ago. Of these 30 are dead, as many more permanently disabled from wounds, enough more *from sickness* to make a hundred permanently disabled. The ballance will get back to the Regt sometime or other.[31]

I see so much of horror and suffering in the army that I sometimes wish for peace at almost any terms. I sometimes feel as if ultimate success is going to be too expensive to warrant the cost. I know this war *would* never have been had the people anticipated half the evils it has already entailed. But being in it, when I think earnestly, I of course insist that we must punish the enemy till we crush out all opposition to the just requirements of the Government. We have expended too much to quietly yield now. But I do wish I could see a speedy solution of this question. I want to get home. I want to see and realize the fruits of peace. I am becoming a great peace man, and am willing to fight for it if necessary. But I want to see the necessity.

BERMUDA HUNDRED, VA. — *June 13, 1864*

. . . The hundred day men are reaching here. We have a Regt of them in our Brigade. Good hearty fellows, and for ought I can see as good food for gun powder as the three years volunteers. This may not suit the Guards, or their dear friends far off at home. I tell them I think they can fight as well as we can, and that I hope that *they* may an opportunity to distinguish themselves, that there are several "hundred days" campaigns in history memorable for their achievement and I hope they may do much to make them notorious in history.[32]

Tuesday morning. The nights are quite cool, and I want to sleep under double blankets to make me comfortable. I get fair sleep being only occasionally disturbed of nights now. The pickets are quiet now, and let each other alone. This is much better for all parties. This picket firing is barbarous and does no good. I am out of patience with such cruel and useless efforts that exert no influence on the results of a campaign, *nor the termination of the war. . . .*

BERMUDA HUNDRED, VA.—*June 17, 1864*

I do not feel in writing mood today as I am feeling verry dull from the twenty four hour duty ending with dark last night. But you are anxiously looking this way for intelligence from me, and more so as you before this time have learned that Gen Grant is on the south side of the James. . . .

Grant's army taking position on this bank of the James will most likely change the location of our command from this place. When we will go or where are matters not even of conjecture. For the present we may not go for any length of time from this place. It is hardly contemplated to move the army far from the City of Richmond, and the line of our operations against the City is limited. Therefore I judge we shall not be sent far from here. I do not expect any more hazards than I have experienced for the last month & a half, indeed I think the increase of our strength will diminish our risks. . . .[33]

I was up all of night before last and in the field from this A.M. till 9 P.M. of the succeeding day, actively engaged most of the time in the affairs of a command before the enemy. My Regiment is divided into two commands, four companies under Maj Butler are holding a redan to the front of our works, the other six companies are only a command for a Lt Col, which I leave to Col Commager only as I rest him.[34]

I look after the administrative affairs of the Regiment and do the duties of an Officer of my rank in other respects. When on the field I have the fortune to have a good command given me. Yesterday I was Gen Officer of the Day & had three Regiments under my command. I handled them like an old veteran, Lt Col [Commager] commanding the six companies of my Regt. These companies had eight men wounded in the fight yesterday, none killed. Sgt Major Rampano was shot again. He was acting as Lt having been promoted by appointment of the Gov. . . .[35]

Mr Buttles of Columbus Ohio has been with me all the week; will not go away till tomorrow, unless we go away from him. He went out on the field yesterday to see what a fight developed, rather dangerous curiosity, but still he indulged in it and to his satisfaction. Before I had been in battle I would have taken a good many chances to have seen a battle, but since I have had the honor of participating in nearly a half a hundred fights and a half dozzen battles I have lost all desire to gratify my curiosity at the risks a battle furnishes. I know the popular mind is that we become accustomed to the dangers of the field and as a consequence cease to be sensitive on that account. But that is a delusion. We may meet these dangers more calmly, but we appreciate them more accurately than the initiated. . . .[36]

All is quiet to our front now, but was rather turbulent last night. My boys are all out who are able to shoulder a musket. I hope you will write me more frequently. If you want to do me good while in this terrible place write often.[37]

BERMUDA HUNDRED, VA.—*June 19, 1864*

Comparative quiet again reigns in camp after four days of constant excitement and toil. My poor men have been on duty all the while night and day in face of the enemy. The mental anxiety and constant watchfulness with the privations the men must suffer under such circumstances tell severely on my men. I have not lost more than a dozzen men in action during this time, but they nevertheless have been terrible days and distressing nights.

A Regt of 100 day men were with us one day. They thought it a terrible trial, and to them it was a terrible ordeal, but my men so far as the fighting was concerned thought it fine fun. The Johnny Rebs making an attack on our line, my boys met them with a volley and returned hearty cheers for their yells. The 100 days fellows hearing my men cheer and deliver a heavy fire thought the rebs were on them and cut for camp as if the very D——l was after them. Gen Foster and myself undertook to stop this stampede, but the only persuasion I could find that did any practical good was the support of my revolvers. O! what horrible things we are frequently compelled to do. . . .[38]

Capt Childs has just called in. He had his sword struck by a rifle ball which fastened the scabbard on it so that he cannot draw it. He also had a shot through his pantaloons & another in his rubber blanket. These are the little incidents our men have to recount after having been on picket.[39]

Many of my men fired over a hundred rounds of ammunition yesterday killing quite a number of the *enemy* and taking over a dozen prisoners. They do not seem to feel badly on being taken prisoners. This is true however much the fellows may be wedded to the cause of the Confederacy. The terrible realities of this campaign have made them feel that almost anything is a relief to them. Being a prisoner of war assures them that they will have enough to eat, and that they will be well treated and placed beyond the reach of the dangers of the field, all of which are not undesirable conditions for the common soldiers of the South.

Still I do not believe they are on the starving point. So far as my observation goes, I am satisfied their resources are by no means exhausted. They are raising crops for the year to come and in great abundance. They clothe their army comfortably, arm them well and supply them with as good ammunition as we have. The troops from the Army of the Potomac report that all the regions of country through which they passed from the Rappahannock to the James is well cultivated and gives evidence of abundant crops, and report the Virginians now have everything to live on the country produces & that the promise is good for the ensuing crops.

I have no doubt this is substantially true, for I see their army looks strong, and the fellows feel well. The producers in the South are well off. The "poor *white* trash" probably suffer for many of the wants of life, the better class for the luxuries, but who cannot dispense with the latter if the disposition is rightly inclined. The poor idea that the South is on the verge of starvation is entirely exploded in the army. The campaigns of Grant & Sherman have [uncovered] at many places large depots of supplies not at all in keeping with the idea that they had nothing on which to supply their army. I am suspicious that Gen Grant is beginning to think that it will be a fruitless effort to fight his way into Richmond. He at least is trying to accomplish the same end by strategy.

You would never know this was the Lord's own day by anything associated with it if you got your impressions from what you see. Soldiers in motion, bustle, confusion & *activity* of army details are the only things that occupy our attention. . . .

You know I am not much of a Sunday man. Yet I like to have the day for repose and communion with you and our little family. I hope Eddie will soon be well. I have no doubt my Pet will be down with the measles before you get this. You may tell her papa has another pet now, "Little Bunny." He eats nuts from my shoulder with as much composure as if I was an old Oak. If I can get him home I mean to do so. A squirrel from Bermuda Hundred would be a great curiosity at home. . . .

BERMUDA HUNDRED, VA.—*June 21, 1864*

. . . I am getting such a disgust for the horrid operations of the field as well as awfully tired of its labors that I fear I am becoming misanthropic. I would scold outright if any sort of excuse offered itself, and occasionally I do indulge a little without provocation. For instance some luckless New Yorker of less manners than curiosity was standing before my quarters talking to his comrade longer than I liked. Requesting them to disperse, this vagrant did not clear out. I thereupon rather sharply told him to leave. Off he started with an oath saying "ye needn't be so d——d mad about it." I collared Mr New Yorker, took him to the guard and had him tied to a tree for an hour, when I ordered his release with the admonition that he had better let "Old Promptly" alone if he wished to live in peace near my quarters. Well, it had the desired effect. I have had quiet quarters since. . . .

My unsteady habits (which are forced on me by the demands of the service) are not comparable with the best flow of spirits [and] cheerful action. When a man feels well he is courageous, when he is tired, hungry and prostrated he has but little spunk. I can fight when I feel myself, but I had rather let the job out when I am out of sorts. Healthy men can fight, half sick ones can run and live to run another day, if they don't get better. Health is *an essential* condition for the soldier.

We are having a repetition of Morris Island this afternoon. A rebel battery with at least two heavy guns and three of their rams are playing away at our iron clads, but at such respectful distance that both parties are quite sure nobody or boat will get hurt. This heavy artillery practice is not at all up with the standard of advancement and practicality of the present age. It sounds big, there it ends. This is true for all military purposes, except for battering fortifications where the momentum gives it terrific force. I had rather stand all day long before a battery of one hundred pounders than be compelled to face light artillery that threw only one fourth the amount of metal. Twelve light twelve pounders would do more mischief to infantry than six one hundred pounders as they are generally used. The rebels once had great horror for our big guns and gun boats, but I think much of this has abated. I certainly can see no reason why they should entertain their former notions about the terrible Yankee guns.

Our Morris Island campaign taught me a lesson of admiration for these big displays of pyrotechnics, but not of fear. The spade is more powerful than the canon, and we are learning that from the progress of the war, and the rebels would be great fools not to have learned this from the many not verry damaging demonstrations we have given them. I like to hear these great iron bolts hurled through the air and crashing in the woods when I am assured I am not in particular danger. . . .

We have been working as hard as ever for the last week, as hard as we ever worked. If this will bring matters to a head I am satisfied, but I see so much that is not sustained by good sense. Last Thursday we occupied the rebel works to our front, but on Thursday evening we were ordered to abandon them. In less than twenty four they were re occupied by the rebs and strengthened & supplied with artillery, hedging us in again so that twenty thousand men may not be able to dislodge them. With five thousand men we could have had their works and secured a position within fifteen miles of Richmond. The policy that led to the abandonment of their works by us would ruin any other people than ours. When I see well directed efforts *though* they are expensive to us I feel satisfied, but when I see great advantages thrown away I feel discouraged. I do not know the plans of the Gen, nor have I his knowledge of the whole field, and therefore do not feel like finding fault at many things I think so wrong, because I may be mistaken though judging correctly from my limited standpoint

Noon. President Lincoln has just passed my quarter. I hear the boys still cheering way to the left. He looks better in the field than in the White House.[40]

BERMUDA HUNDRED, VA.—*June 26, 1864*

No tidings have come to me of a later date than a week ago Thursday. You can appreciate my anxiety when you remember that your last letter I received conveyed the unpleasant information that Pet was sick and Eddie had not recovered from the measles. I do not fret and make myself miserable about matters I cannot controll, but I do confess to a good deal of anxiety in regard to my dear ones at home. . . .

When I look back [to] the fifty four days we have been here and realize what we have endured and suffered, and then imagine what have we accomplished towards bringing the rebellion to a close, I am not encouraged. I feel as if much we have done and borne was thrown away. Yes, worse than thrown away because valuable lives have been thrown away, much misery caused, and no good accrued to anybody. I can bear all this horrid war demands when I can see substantial good resulting from it or a fair prospect of it, but when I see stupidity and personal ambition controlling our affairs without any reasonable prospect of good to the great cause flowing from it, I wish the war might be ended at once. The only consolation I can derive from all this is that the enemy are as unwise in their policy as we are, that they make as grievous blunders as we do and that they are wearing away in great if not greater ratio than we are. And this is war.

It is not so much the capacity to win battles as it is the ability to bear grief that ultimately gives victory to a people. The South have made up their minds to bear with fortitude what the North never will bear unless a question of national existence is forced upon them, an issue this war has not even as yet intimated. . . .

I will send you copy of recommendation Gen Terry gave me to the Secy of War. Gen Gillmore has given me assurance that he would do something of the same sort. Here is a copy. "Head Quarters, 1st Division 18th A. C. Bermuda Hundred, June 22, 1864. Hon. E. M. Stanton, Secy. Of War. Sir: I have the honor to bring to your most favorable notice Colonel A. C. Voris of the 67th Ohio Vol., a Regiment which is a part of my Division, possessed of the first soldierly qualities and of unusual natural ability. Col. Voris has rendered to the country service which deserves not only recognition but reward. . . ."

Be that as it may I am gratified to find those who have been in command over me think so well of my abilities and services. Aren't you proud that you have such a husband? It is not every wife even who has a husband in the army that can boast of such a Colonel as Gen Terry represents me as being. Then you know that I have Gen Seymour's and Gen Gillmore's opinion to the same effect addressed to the Governor of Ohio. I also see by a report from the Cincinnati Commercial that the State Agent in making his report to the Ohio troops in the "Army of the Potomac" gives a verry flattering report of my Regiment, as well as a high compliment to the Colonel commanding. This being official and going to the Chief Executive Officer of the State is quite consoling to one who loves flattery as well as I do. I have felt as if it was true, but had my fears as to whether my views would ever receive the recognition of others.

But these compliments are poor pay for considering the terrible cost. For it we hazard life, health and danger, lose home and its comforts, society and its pleasures and endure the discomforts of a soldiers life. If I get home safely I shall look back on all my hardships as of little moment, perhaps will be proud that I had met them, but I am free to confess that I dislike them verry much while I am bearing the realization. . . .

It has been verry hot for several days and is becoming exceedingly dry. We long for rain to cool the earth and moisten the sky. My side has annoyed me for several days, feel much as it did last November and about the 1st of January. The muscles about the old wound are weak and quite irritable. It may all go off in a day or two & may trouble me for some time. Hard labor and the want of rest induce the trouble. I mean to take such precautions as will not make it worse, and try and avoid in future anything that will be likely to induce a return of the difficulty.

Two months ago I hoped that the 1st of July would see the successful end of this campaign, but I now look into the future with no hope that we are able to take Richmond by storm, and have doubts about our being able to do it by strategy, the latter course evidently being Gen Grant's present plan. The South are relatively stronger today than they were when the war was commenced. This may appear strange, but the history of the war demonstrates this. . . .

"A Desolated Country
Cursed by Slavery and Slavery's War"

STALEMATE AND MONOTONY AT BERMUDA HUNDRED

JUNE 29, 1864 – AUGUST 12, 1864

[The defensive works constructed by each side at Bermuda Hundred blocked any decisive breakthrough. While the Army of the Potomac had crossed the James River and begun a siege of Petersburg, Voris and his men fell into a humdrum routine during the hot and rainy days of July and August 1864. This lull ended in early August. The 67th Ohio became part of a new tactical thrust toward a bend of the James River at Deep Bottom, halfway between Petersburg and Richmond.]

BERMUDA HUNDRED, VA.—*June 29, 1864*

You have read so many letters from me written within the canon's roar that if I should tell you that I am hearing the deep boom of heavy artillery every minute this is being penned you would not be in the least surprised. How soon novelties wear off and become the natural concomitants of our existence. At one time I could no more write a letter with the terrible realities of a battle going on within hearing than I could write in the bottom of the Ocean! But now I can do it and it hardly furnishes me a single thought with which to give spirit to this letter.

The bombardment of Petersburg is going on some *10* miles to our left, the musketry fire of which was distinctly heard here today. But what is really being accomplished we cannot tell more than you can. Perhaps [we] do not know as much about it as the editors of New York do. I have educated my nerves so that I can write a message or order under the exploding shells of the enemy batteries or the volleys of their muskets, or both, and not forget to cross a T or dot an I, especially if they are capitals. I have frequently done this when, as the poets say, distance lends enchantment to the view. I wrote an official report of my tour of duty as Gen Officer of the Day for the 23rd Inst. on the ensuing day while the rebel shells were exploding overhead and about in every direction at a furious rate.

I of course did this in my little fortification I had thrown up for the protection of myself and the precious body of Col Commager. This was covered with a strong canvass roof that weighs say ten ounces to the sq yard, & first rate protection against the sun's rays and does verry well against the rain when it is not too much commingled with special case and shrapnel. My tent floor caught several pieces of iron flung here without ceremony by the rebs & an awful gash was made by a piece of shell the other day that dashed through aforesaid roof.

How would you relish a sleep in a log pen built up some five feet on three sides & open on the other with three logs for top opposite the open side, with canvass stretched from these logs front & covering the open side, with the three timber walls banked up some half dozzen feet thick with earth, with a tolerable top dressing of the same sort some three feet in thickness, & an excavation two feet deep, with awful canon balls dashing by, cutting off trees & exploding against this little castle & scattering their fragments all about you? Do you think you could lay quietly at my side under this? I have done this. . . .

For two weeks I stretched my hammock between two trees in the open woods, and let the rebs whack away. But I must confess it was rather comfortless and when the fire came too close I would take the lea of the earth works to our front, but since I got my new place fixed I lay as comfortably on my bed as if we were having nothing more than a thunder storm. By the way we have had no thunder storms since we came on to the James this time. We had a severe storm while at Gloucester Point, but none since. It has been threatening rain for some three days but has not made it out yet. It is much cooler today. . . .

Thursday. I had a decent sleep last night, but nothing to boast of. Was up at sun rise and soon found a letter from you mailed the 23rd. This has been longer coming than usual. I occasionally get them in three days. . . .

It has been quiet with us for several days. My boys are getting rest again. We are taking care of the fortifications on the Bermuda Hundred and will probably occupy them till Gen Grant develops some new movement. I am waiting hourly to hear that he has flanked them to our left and is moving in to their lines of communications. He is evidently endeavoring to compell Lee to evacuate Virginia without being compelled to fight before the strong forts protecting Richmond. Heavy canonading has been heard all day towards Petersburg till within the last hour. Why it has ceased [I] can form no opinion.

You say you have seen Mr. Upson but you tell me nothing about what he did for me while at Washington. . . .

BERMUDA HUNDRED, VA.—*July 3, 1864*

A quiet Sabbath day is again upon us. It has reached four o'clock P.M. and not a gun has been fired in my hearing but once or twice today, an unusual circumstance for the last two months with us. You may be assured that I am glad to have the repose of a quiet day once and awhile. Fighting for some days has been transferred to the left, Grant's Army.

The weather has been too hot for heavy work, but so far as I can learn the body of both armies has been compelled to work upon earth fortifications in spite of the high temperature. It has been verry dry for a long time, this with the heat makes it almost insupportable. It is so oppressive that I cannot write. To tell the truth nobody else under the sun but my dear wife could get a letter out of me today, so hard is it for me to even write a letter. . . .

We were much surprised to learn this morning that Secy Chase had resigned and that his resignation had been accepted by the President. He loses in Secy Chase the ablest member of his Cabinet. I know of no man in the range of my acquaintance the President can call on to fill his place. Gov Tod certainly is not the man. If I was called on for advice I would say Gov Brough. Gov B has ability, force, will and integrity. But such men will be appalled at the task of conducting the finances of the country through this war while so many selfish men are permitted to assume controll in the affairs of the Government.

I believe that the demagogues about the Capital compelled Gov Chase to resign. The people entrusted them with responsibility of acting for them either as Legislators or executive officers. They have used their influence to break down a most valuable man struggling under the almost insupportable weight of the finances of the Government, instead of supporting him, because they dared not do what they knew to be their duty for fear of offending the people who hold the votes.[1]

The mail is about to go out, and requires me to close this or wait another day. This would hardly do. By the way tomorrow is the famous 4th of July, but how different from the evening of an Independence Day prior to 1861. I fear we will never have such 4ths of July again. Two years ago I fondly hoped that this 4th would see the country in peace, but how have my hopes been realized? I am a thousand miles from home with a hundred and fifty thousand armed rebels surrounding me, in the midst of the most desperate campaign of modern times and no near a successful solution of our troubles than two years ago. . . .[2]

BERMUDA HUNDRED—*July 4, 1864*

. . . The resignation of Secy Chase is a most untoward circumstance. Taken in connexion with the extraordinary appreciation of the precious metal shows that the finances of the country are in a verry unsettled condition. Chase was the ablest man of the Cabinet. . . . I have great confidence in the integrity and unselfishness of the President, but he is lacking in force. He is controlled by circumstances instead of taking them by the forelock & give direction to them. . . .

BERMUDA HUNDRED, VA.—*July 6, 1864*

I wrote a letter to Mr. J. H. Chamberlin on the 4th, not a verry cheerful letter but as good a one as I could write under the circumstances. I will inclose it with this and send to you to let you see how I feel about matters in the field.[3]

The 4th formerly was a glorious day to me. I have in my drawer two old speeches written full of laudations of the day, the American people, 76 and "God and Liberty" etc & etc. But this three year's fighting has taken much of the romance from the glorious 4th of July. . . .

Now you must not say I am not a patriot for my hard lot in the field for most three year. My dangers and wounds are sufficient evidence to satisfy you and all whose ópinions are worth anything that I am not unpatriotic. But the distress that hovers over the nation at this time makes me feel sad, and the future makes one feel almost discouraged. I could fight the world if I was the person beside my adversaries that had to suffer. But when I think of the terrible sorrows and casualties the war produces I am anxious to see it ease.

This plan of using the state militia for a hundred days to the front will make many peace men. They affect to feel sold, say they did not agree to leave the state when they joined the militia, and when they consented to go for the hundred days they were told it was for garrison or guard duty, but the idea of going to the front, digging rifle pits, throwing up breastworks & forts, doing picket duty under the guns of the rebs, and above all to be put where they must fight if the ugly rebs forced a fight *never entered their heads*. The three years troops and the army came out for all these purposes, and they say let them do it, they are used to it. <u>Well that is cool, patriotic and sensible.</u>

The poor fellows count the days they have to serve with as much care and accuracy as do our poor convicts in the penitentiary. If they grumble at the heartlessness of the Government at putting the Nation Guards to the front for only one hundred days, what will the patriotic creatures do when they are asked to fork up as the law directs for three years or the close of the war? The 100 days will only give them disgust for the field. Their time of service is too short to make the man accommodated to the life and discomforts of the soldier. When Nov comes I am thinking may of them will vote the peace ticket. . . .

They of course think my standard too high. I admit it is high, but not too high for the 67th Regt. I went out on the picket line to the left on the Appomattox and found a corporal on duty. He's a hundred day man. I gave him some instruction that made him unquestionably think that I been in the service long enough to know how to command. It is rather amusing to see these new fellows on duty. It furnishes a practical chapter of what we were when we first entered the service. . . .

We have had comparatively quiet. Our boys hobnob with the secesh as much as they dare for fear of their Officers. Rebel deserters are constantly coming into our lines. This makes the enemy verry vigilant. They shoot every man of theirs they discover making efforts to get into our lines.[4]

The President has announced a proclamation declaring to the rebels that they will not be compelled to serve in our army if they desert & come into our lines. I have been arranging to get copies of the proclamation into the hands of the rebel soldiers. This is to counteract the impression existing among them that we force them to take up arm against their friends, which never has been true.[5]

It still continue verry warm. I could barely endure the heat in the middle of the day. It has tried to rain today but the dust is not layered yet. I suppose poor Pennsylvania is all excitement again for fear that the rebels are invading their state again. We learn that *Early* is in the Va valley with a large force threatening Pa.[6]

Well let her put her hundred days men or National Guards to work in good earnest in the defense of the state. I think I am doing better service in guarding my own state by fighting the enemy on the south side of the James than on the north side of the Ohio. That costs us only what we personally risk, while if it was done at home the State would bear all the disabilities and horrors of war within her borders, which are the most calamities of a state of hostility. . . .

We have just learned that Harpers Ferry is in the hands of the rebs. This will alarm the North again, but if we manage well we will take the invading army. I am as well as usual but my side troubles me terribly.[7]

BERMUDA HUNDRED, VA.—*July 12, 1864*

. . . The bugler has just sounded the Surgeon's Call, and the lame, halt & blind are thronging about him for their allowance of drugs. The bugler says: "Come and get your quinine; Come and get your quinine; You whose heads are sore, have crippled toes; The bellyache or other woes; It's good for soul and body both; Come and got your quinine."

I am not absolutely certain I interpret the bugle correctly, but as near as I can understand the old tune I have written what it is said about every morning for the last 2 1/2 years. The Surgeon's Call always brings together the poor, the absolutely poor man of a Regiment, perhaps more feeble ones in mind than in body. In fact they are associates. A weak mind is verry poor support to the body which verry frequently fails for want of mental support. You say where there is a will there is a way. So it is with Surgeon's patients. A battle, hard picket, or fatigue duty always makes the call largely attended, if this poor class of humanity have any premonition of what is to come. More are sick to fear than are broken down by the reality. A few men consistently answer this call. Should they omit it I should be alarmed for fear that it augured some great physical revolution that might set all our calculations awry. . . .[8]

Matters have been quite easy with us for some days. But poor Maryland & Pa may not be satisfied at this. We learn that Gen Wallace has been defeated. Well, who expected anything else.[9]

BERMUDA HUNDRED, VA.—*July 16, 1864*

How rapidly time wings its way into the past. It is indeed the middle of July again. This time last year we were in sight of the rebel City of Charleston and hourly expecting to make an attack on Fort Wagner. When I *casually* look back it seems but a little time, but as I combine the events as they are recalled by memory the year does appear longer than a casual retrospect indicates. . . .

In that time 325 of my men have been wounded in battle, and a hundred have been killed or died of disease. What an amount of suffering, sorrow and anguish it has cost my command and their friends. Most of it has been cheerfully borne, encouraged with the hope that the country would derive benefit therefrom and that a speedy and honorable peace would be the result. But I am now free to confess that our expectations have not been realized, that much of our pains have been for naught, and that the future is not as big with hope as we ought to realize.

I presume the nervousness of the North at the late raid of the rebels about Baltimore and Washington has put a gloomy aspect on affairs upon the fickle public mind of the loyal states. Our communications north have been somewhat interrupted by the rebels the last ten days, yet we got our mail with some regularity. But the Northern papers have not reached us as speedily as heretofore, leaving us in doubts as to what the news was, not much improved when we get the dailies the day after they are printed. This may not be verry flattering to the truthfulness of the newspapers, but certainly leaves enough margin for their capacity in the line of invention.

July 17th. A delightful Sunday morning has again opened on us. At this time a murmur is heard. The buzz of the flies & the trembling leaves hardly create a vibration on the auditory nerves. This quiet certainly is not in keeping with the hostile emotions of the two hundred thousand belligerents arrayed against each other and each other's engines of war.

I just heard the notes of a cornet band floating off in the breeze. Well it may be music, but my poor soul does not dance with pleasure at mere attempts at music. It must be genuine to get my attention. . . .

BERMUDA HUNDRED, VA.—*July 19, 1864*

I have dated all my letters from this place to you as "Bermuda Hundred." Our orders read at "Near Hatcher's," but I am inclined to think the former to be right. At the time Virginia was first settled England was divided into what was called hundreds, a subdivision not unlike our townships. The section of country lying between the James & Appomattox rivers, forming a small peninsula as large as our township on the [Western] Reserve was called Bermuda Hundred, and still should retain the name if it really does not now.

A paper of the 18th Inst. has just been handed to me and I must read the news even at the expense *of waiting to continue* writing to you for the present. Now that I have read the paper it is too late to write you further & therefore consign myself to my couch and will couch a little for the good of my not verry tired nature. It has rained all day long & I have lazed away the day betwixt the bed and a rocking chair. . . .

Wednesday Morning, July 20. It has quit raining. All night we could hear heavy artillery firing and occasionally volley of musketry would announce that warm work was going on beyond the Appomattox in the neighborhood of Petersburg. Have had no news yet but presume somebody was hurt. It is as quiet now as if no hostile armies were near each other. . . .

You appear to feel unhappy about Washington. We have had no serious apprehensions about its safety here. We know that Lee dared not move a large force from this place. The rebels never had a large army there.[10] Our conduct there has been disgraceful to our history. Of the half a dozzen Generals about Baltimore not one of them has capacity enough to command the confidence of the people. Everyone should be discharged and give place to men who have richly deserved promotions, but cannot get the places they have well earned, because the Government early in the war adopted the trifling and wicked policy of giving impudence and falsehood the place of merit. The universally recognized claim to promotion for meritorious conduct in the field are set aside by the Government because there is no place left open for them. . . .

Yet the meritorious are told that good conduct is its own reward, that the places they have earned are already filled, and that too big a class of men exists who the Government does not trust to discharge the duties of the places usually assigned to their rank, and that the unpromoted man is required to do the labor, perform the duty and assume the responsibility of the place, while the other is monopolizing the emoluments and the honor the other is fulfilling.

Such conduct on the part of the Government is outrageous. It is disgraceful to the Government and unjust to the meritorious officer in the field. The Government should dismiss inefficient and trifling officers, and make way for those who have given evidence of their ability & fidelity. But on the contrary the good for nothing Generals are permitted to idle away their time at the expense of the people and at the same time bulge up the way to all successful competition. Men of such stupid business sense as have brought about and continue to keep up such a state of things ought to be hurled from power, and forever afterward kept from mal administering the affairs of the Government.

Well I won't grumble any more in this letter. I rode down to Department head quarters this morning to see Gen Butler, but was disappointed in not seeing him. From what I see at present, I am satisfied that it is not the intention here to act on the offense for the present. We may be compelled to fight, but I hardly think so. Our fortifications are too formidable to be taken by the enemy unless they have a vastly superior force, which they have not. I feel a good deal discouraged as to the final results. We all hoped in the spring to be able to see the prospect of a speedy solution of this difficulty by the 20th of July Inst. But we are up to this date and matters are as uncertain as ever.

My general health is much improved of late. I have had rest for some three weeks, so that I could get my meals and sleep regularly. I hope to get home before long. Tell your father not to work too hard.

BERMUDA HUNDRED, VA.—*July 22, 1864*

Col Commager starts for the North in the morning on twenty day leave of absence on account of disability. He probably will stay longer than that time as it takes some time to recuperate after the fatigues and prostration of such a campaign as we have had, especially after the system has received as severe a shock as his has been from gun shot wounds. I shall expect to see him back here by the 1st of September a strong, hearty man, when I hope to be able to get out of this miserable war. The 2nd of October next will make my three year's service in the army when the good Lord and the rebels willing I mean to get home to stay. I feel lonesome enough to think of the good time Col C will have at this own home. Three years is long enough for any man to be exiled from his home, society and the comforts of civilization, & I mean to act with that view unless circumstances make it an imperative duty for me to stay longer in the field. What may occur in that time we do not know, but I hardly dare hope that the war will be ended by that date. . . .

Saturday Morning. The weather has modulated considerably, making the mornings quite cool and the days more comfortable. I am afraid of August and September here. I expect to see bilious disease prevailing to a considerable extent. Our location here is much better than at Harrison's Landing so far as health is concerned, but that is not saying that it is positively healthful. . . .

Since City Point has become a safe base for the Christian Commission, I have not seen a single representative of the <u>very Christian institution.</u> All hail to this benevolent institution.

You appear to feel melancholic. You ought not to feel so. <u>I am happy as can be,</u> and you ought to be more so. . . . We are safe here. Love to the children. . . .

BERMUDA HUNDRED, VA.—*July 23, 1864*

. . . It is a delightful summer evening, cool enough to be comfortable; but what surroundings! A desolated country cursed by slavery and slavery's war, now occupied by two hundred thousand men in deadly hostile array within an area of territory not larger than the County of Summit, a major part of whom are so near to their opposers that no change of position is necessary to bring them in range of the ordinary engines of war.

I presume the enemy have thirty pieces of artillery that could play on my quarters whenever they wished and thousands of muskets that need only to be discharged to rake my camp. I see the Johnny Rebs every day by hundreds. . . . The picket lines of the contending armies are so near each other that in many places the men of the opposite parties converse with each other. I thought today as I looked at them from a point where I could hit them with our Springfields, what infernal work it was to labor day after day to take the lives or cripple the fine specimens of manhood I saw quietly awaiting the day when we should meet in hostile array. In the heat of battle I can keep an eagle eye for an opportunity to disable these fellows. . . , but when my manhood has full sway I utterly deprecate the war in all its bearings. . . . The exaltation of battle lifts me . . . above all considerations of sympathy for the evils of war for the moment. I feel like "giving" them a little more grape, but when quiet reflection rules I feel an abhorrence for the cruelties I am compelled to inflict that frequently almost drives me from the field.

Today is no more like Sunday than most of the days we have had this month. I think we have hardly had a gun fired during this month excepting the 4th of July all along our front from the James to the Appomattox. Heavy artillery fighting occurred in the after part of the night in the neighborhood of Petersburg with some musketry with what results I am unable to say.

We got the news yesterday that Sherman had repulsed the enemy in three charges on his line the 21st Inst., and that he was occupying positions in easy range of the City of Atlanta, that he intended to attack the City the next day, that he was on the railroad leading northwardly to Richmond etc & etc. To offset against this the rebels set up enthusiastic cheers at Tattoo last evening all along their lines to celebrate the success of Gen Hood over Gen Sherman at Atlanta, as they say. They claim to have routed Sherman driving him back of Marietta, and that he has lost 50,000 men in killed, wounded and prisoners, and that war will close in three month, & etc & etc. Somebody is badly sold. Judging from former reports I must think it must be the rebels.[11]

I got a note from Judge Spalding that was twenty days reaching me. He said be <u>had handed</u> my recommendation with my other papers to the Secy of War. Verry well for him, but not quite as much as I expected. Some impudent fool that never has been in a fight might get his kind offices with a pressing recommendation from our Congressional delegation to back him unless matters have vastly changed since the last Congress. I may speak too harshly, but the hasty and unjust manner in which general officers have been made gives color to the insinuation. I hope before many days to see you at home with the prospect of staying with you for a while at least. I do not propose staying in the army longer than my three years, which ends Oct 2, 1864. So far I am happy in being under no obligations for the place I hold. I am a free man & hope to get out the army as such.

BERMUDA HUNDRED, VA.—*July 30, 1864*

It is a pleasant Saturday evening after a verry hot day, the temperature of which I have tested on horse back along our picket line as Corps Officer of the Day. I went over to Gen Meade's Hd. Qrs. yesterday with Capt Lewis Cass Hunt of my Regiment to see Gen Henry J. Hunt, Chief of Artillery of the Potomac Army, and cousin of the aforesaid Capt, who is a nephew of Gen Lewis Cass.[12]

I started for Petersburg in the hope that I might see or hear something that would inspire me with hope for our speedy success, but I came back to my camp with the idea that our campaign would be protracted for a long time to come. I do not expect great results without a corresponding effort, and am prepared for a desperate struggle before the successful accomplishment of the great ends of this campaign. As a matter of course [I] am not disappointed at many of the results of this campaign. But the lack of men to prosecute *something like success* after so much has been to do so does annoy me exceedingly, and the policy of begging for men, new Regiments, hundred day men and one year's volunteers and conscripts disgusts me at the trifling policy that controlls the Government.

My God, don't the President know that the rebels are in earnest yet? It does look to me as if the experience of the three last years had been thrown away, and a miserable hand to mouth policy adopted for one of vigor and utility. I seriously doubt the capacity of the present Administration to bring the war to a successful close. Old Abe is honest, but I fear he lacks that force and directness necessary to crushing out of this rebellion. I do not know but you have set me down as a gambler, perhaps a Copperhead. I am quite sure the partizan Republicans of the North would if they knew how I felt and wrote. But I am as patriotic as any of them and most earnestly want a policy pursued that will not make useless all the toil, suffering and bloodshed the more than three years of this war has caused. I am so selfish that I want what I have done not to be trifled away by the folly of the Government. I grant the President has an awful burden on his shoulders, that it is easier to find fault than to remedy the evil, and that I might do infinitely worse. Nevertheless I do think that we have good right to expect more forethought and vigor in the Administration.

July 31st. Sunday morning. In nine weeks more I shall have served in the army three years. What anxious terrible years they have been for both of us. But you and I have suffered no more than thousands of others. This is the terrible penalty we are paying for our follies and political delinquencies, perhaps I should say crimes. No people under heaven have been more blessed than the American people. None have abused their blessings more, and now in sorrow are they reaping the reward for their reckless ingratitude. . . .

I have just had a call from Col Bell, 4th N.H. who gave me an account of our operation before Petersburg on Saturday morning last.[13] We blew up a rebel fort and its contents, took their lines for some distance, which were occupied by the colored soldiers. But the black rascals got scared and dashed back on our troops with fixed bayonets, and so disorganized the white troops that the rebs retook a great part of their last works. All join in saying the "nigger" did verry badly and had no excuse for it. I fear that the expectations of the people at home are to be disappointed as to the taking of Petersburg until new combinations and additional forces are put into the field. This is a terrible war & full of terrible blunders. . . .[14]

The weather is intolerably hot. I have suffered today doing nothing as much from the heat as I did in South Carolina. . . . I look out on the poor miserable country about us, and feel the miserable monotony of our field operations with a longing for the beautiful scenes of our own favored Akron and wish I could enjoy them again. . . . The more I see of this continent the better am I suited with the section of country I have chosen for my home. If we were only at peace again I know I could enjoy our own dear home. . . .

Aug 1st. . . . Has been threatening rain, but none came. I am getting so lazy that I want nothing at all to do. When I have nothing to do I am dissatisfied for want of employment. When I have employment I am too inert to want to take hold. So betwixt the two I am a miserable creature. . . .

BERMUDA HUNDRED, VA.—*Aug 4, 1864*

. . . This is the President's Fast day. I am keeping it in the style it ought to be kept here by taking my ordinary meals with a thankful heart that it is no worse with us than it is. Worse is the rule, and worsely has it been lived up to. I suppose old Abe hopes to make it better by a little hunger and a great deal of prayer. So far as we are concerned we have fasted enough since we came into the field without it necessary for the President to fix upon any special times to go hungry. Perhaps he has only intended the fast for the people at home. From what I have seen and heard I am inclined to think those at home fast enough. Look at their extravagance, and again they are so fast that neither enormous bounties or drafts can get them from their homes. Perhaps that is not the kind of a fast he means. . . .[15]

What we want is the fast & prayer of an intense purpose, a vigorous policy and a comprehensive appreciation of the wants and dangers of the times. I am appalled when I see the temporizing expedients the Government resort to, to bring us out of the terrible troubles that are overwhelming the nation. . . .

I do not believe the President is enough for the place he holds in times like these. My sympathies are all with him. His has been the most unthankful task of any President of the United States. None other ever had such weighty responsibilities on him. In none was greater confidence reposed nor was any more ever abused. In all he has been patient, unselfish and devotedly honest to the great work before him. Yet he has been too unsuspecting, too easy, too confident of success, and never energetic enough. He never will take the liberties from the people, but by him they may lose them for want of proper effort. While I greatly distrust his adequacy to the occasion I do not know who I could vote for in his stead. I would like "Old Abe" if he meant to close the war in the next year, rather than to hope him to get through with it in the same time. Purpose is what we want, damn the hope. Hope will do well enough for lovers, but is entirely too frail a release to help us through a war like ours.

We were disgracefully repulsed before Petersburg last Saturday. The President was not to blame for it either. I am glad it was no blunder of his. Gen Grant finds the Army of the Potomac a different body than the dashing impetuous Western men he had under him in the Mississippi Valley. Gen Hunt, his Chief of Artillery, told me that the Army of the Potomac had been defeated in every battle from the Peninsula to Petersburg except the one at Hanover Court House, verifying what I have always said that army could not be relied on. The whites blame "the niggers," "the niggers" the Yankees for the defeat of Saturday last. I am led to think both were much to blame. But all troops are learning to dread to assault fortified positions. And for the future I will predict that but few such enterprises will be ordered. The Army of the Potomac is now learning what we learned last year on Morris Island. But every army must learn for itself. They must see the folly of it before they can realize what others have learned by experience.[16]

It is evening now, I have spent the day as I indicated this morning. The days are intolerably long but somehow or other the weeks are short. I am in tolerable health, am a little inclined to bilious difficulty.

BERMUDA HUNDRED, VA.—*Aug 7, 1864*

. . . Everything is quiet at this of our line. While the army to our left has been laboring hard and bearing disaster here we have been reposing quietly since the 20th of June, with hardly a shot being fired across the picket line from that date to this. I hardly think we will be disturbed at this place, but we may be sent from here at any time. The 2d Ohio Cavalry started for Washington night before last. Until the army is largely augmented we will be doing well to hold our position intact. Many of the old three years troops will be leaving constantly until the end of the year, every hundred of whom are worth three or four times their number in new recruits.[17]

The weather still continues verry hot with verry little rain. This with the monotony of our stay here makes it mighty hard for me to fill up this letter. . . . An infernal fly just bit my ankle clean through my stocking with such fury that I said by D——n and put myself in the most artistic attitude for self defense. The flies are terribly vicious. Two years ago at Harrison's Landing I saw horses and mules that were literally killed by these pestiferous creatures. If a poor horse got the skin knocked off ever so little, the flies would collect on the sore and eat at the poor creature till he was eaten up. . . .

The boys are being paid today for six months hard services [in] greenbacks as money. Officers get no increase of pay but to the contrary are required to pay five per centrum instead of three on that part of their wages liable to taxation. . . . I am reconciled to taxation, but at the same time I want then to accomplish something with the men and means they employ. The reckless extravagance of the managers of this war is shocking. It reaches to the lives and future of the men as well as public property.

I hope you and the children can live comfortably through the war. Everything a family consumes to live is becoming enormously dear, and non producers will be in a bad fix unless wages rise in some ratio to gold. . . . .

BERMUDA HUNDRED, VA.—*August 9, 1864*

. . . I commenced this last evening, but the arrival of the papers demanded a perusal. In the field is found as much anxiety to know what doing in the outside world as among the people at home. We read the papers when we can get them with as much care, except the political news which does not receive much attention. We are vastly more concerned about putting down the rebellion than we are the candidates of the opposition party. We don't care who is nominated if the man is only sound on the goose and capable. I am heartily sick of the twaddle I see in the papers about this or that candidate or this or that man who wants a nomination. An earnest united effort to bring the war to a successful end is all were are looking for and laboring for, and all the issues outside of this are too trifling to be talked of in this the time of our country's tribulation. . . .

I am going down to the Hospital to see Miss Barton, a kind lady who visited the army for the last three years for the good of the suffering soldiers. She tells me that she saw me once when I did not know it, the dreadful night of the Wagner tragedy after I was wounded, that I had fallen asleep & she thought it best to let me rest. She says she knows more about me than I do about her. I told her verry likely, but I hoped she thought well of me on account of that knowledge, which I think she does as she is coming up here to see my boys and make me a visit. When I learn more about her I will write you of her kind good acts. I think her to be a good girl (a little odd to be sure) but this is the fate of all those who have the good fortune to live long.[18]

BERMUDA HUNDRED, VA. —*Aug 12, 1864*

I wrote you a letter closing it Monday or Tuesday last, can't say which, but somehow it appears to have been a long time since. . . . I was stopped here by the lusty cheers from the rebel picket line to our front some half mile. Our boys took up the shout and for a whole mile the shouts of rebs and Yankees made the whole country ring. It may mean that the rebs have read some good news, it may be the result of some patriotic speech making. We learned of the death of Gen McPherson from the rebel picket line the day after it occurred.[19] We verry frequently get the news of important events in the South and Southwest from the enemies papers two or three days before they reach us from our papers. . . .

Saturday afternoon. All day long we have been preparing to leave this accursed place. Where we are to go the Lord only knows, but I think I shall be nearer home in a few days. It will not be safe to place any reliance upon present suspicions. You know the fate of the soldier too well to be troubled at a move. I am quite sure it cannot be worse than it was here the first six weeks we occupied the Hundred. I have become so accustomed to the associations of this place that I cannot feel a sort of regret at leaving. But why I should feel so I cannot tell. The uncertainties of any other place cannot be worse to bear or more full of danger than this place has been. . . . I will write you from the transports.

Saturday Evening. It is dark now and all hands are waiting to move. The boys are singing as merrily as if the breaking up of camp was a desirable event. The soldiers' life is full of more cheerfulness than the folks at home are want to believe. The men have no care but for themselves, no responsibility but to obey orders. The moment they are out of danger they take to rest and amusement and soon dull care is far away. Not so with the officer. He has a duty to perform beyond personal enjoyment and preservation, verry frequently after the hard days work is done. All night long is spent in anxious solitude over the condition of his men. I am more than an ordinary sleeper. I can rest when most of the men will be too excited to sleep, yet I have seen many nights where for hours I dared not sleep for fear some accident might happen that my vigilance might avoid. Again I have frequently tried to assure my command that we were safe when I knew that we were liable to be overwhelmed at any moment. This I did that my men might rest, and be prepared for trouble if it came. I would lay down awhile now, however, and take a nap if I had not taken my beds all down and rolled all the beds up, making too much trouble to unfold for a little "cat nap."

I forgot to tell you that I had Miss Barton here <u>to tea</u> last Wednesday evening. . . . After tea I took her home by moonlight, not alone for I had my orderly with me. I think her to be a verry good old girl, say 32 years of age. She was old enough at least to admit that she was an old maid.[20] I wrote her a little note today saying that we were off, and should she come where I was & I should be so unfortunate as to get disabled, I hoped she or some other kind angel of mercy would look after me. . . .[21]

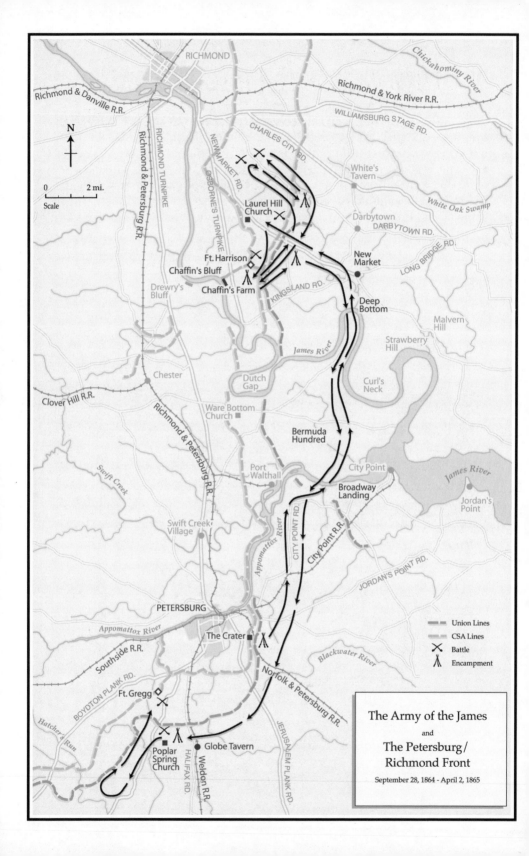

The Army of the James

and

The Petersburg/
Richmond Front

September 28, 1864 - April 2, 1865

RICHMOND

Richmond & York River R.R.

Chickahominy River

Richmond & Danville R.R.

WILLIAMSBURG STAGE RD.

N

CHARLES CITY RD.

White's Tavern

White Oak Swamp

NEWMARKET RD.

0   2 mi.
Scale

Laurel Hill Church

Darbytown   DARBYTOWN RD.

OSBORNE'S TURNPIKE

RICHMOND TURNPIKE

Ft. Harrison

New Market

LONG BRIDGE RD.

Chaffin's Bluff

Chaffin's Farm

KINGSLAND RD.

Drewry's Bluff

RICHMOND & PETERSBURG R.R.

Deep Bottom

Malvern Hill

Strawberry Hill

James River

Curl's Neck

Chester

Dutch Gap

Clover Hill R.R.

Ware Bottom Church

Richmond & Petersburg R.R.

Bermuda Hundred

City Point

James River

Swift Creek

Port Walthall

Jordan's Point

Broadway Landing

Appomattox River

CITY POINT RD.

City Point R.R.

Swift Creek Village

JORDAN'S POINT RD.

PETERSBURG

Appomattox River

The Crater

Norfolk & Petersburg R.R.

Blackwater River

Southside R.R.

Union Lines

CSA Lines

BOYDTON PLANK RD.

Ft. Gregg

Battle

Encampment

Hatcher's Run

Poplar Spring Church

Globe Tavern

HALIFAX RD.

Weldon R.R.

JERUSALEM PLANK RD.

"I Would Not Feel It Any Degradation
to Command Colored Troops"

[*From August through November 1864, Grant attempted but could not break
Confederate lines on the Petersburg-Richmond front and suffered high casualties with each effort. Even so, the attacks forced Lee to extend his defensive
perimeter, leaving the position thin and vulnerable. During this period, Voris
commanded and led two brigades in battle, the First Brigade, First Division,
Tenth Corps, and the First Brigade, Third Division, Tenth Corps, an African
American unit. Although physically worn by his unhealed wound, Voris also
headed the First Division, Tenth Corps, for a brief time in November. As cold
weather settled in, the First Brigade went into winter camp. Voris took advantage of this situation, and on December 13, 1864, he left for Akron on a thirty-
day recuperative leave.*]

IN THE FIELD, NORTH OF THE JAMES—*August 18, 1864*

I have an opportunity to send you a note, but not to write you a letter. I
am safe and doing well. Been in one skirmish and one terrible battle, the
14th and 16th Inst. As well as could be expected. I have great additional
cause to be grateful to a Good Providence for His care the last five days. I
will write you as often as possible. This is rebel paper and envelope. . . .[1]

NORTH OF JAMES—*Aug 19, 1864*

I wrote you a short verry short note yesterday morning to announce to
you that I was then safe after the terrible danger of the 14th and 16th Inst.
In fact for all the time since Saturday night till this time has been one of

great danger and fatigue. You have before this time learned that I have again been in battle again. Sunday I led in a charge on the rebel rifle pits, and assisted in taking them.[2]

This was accomplished with little losses to us. On Tuesday again I led the advance of one brigade in the assault on the rebel works and saw the 67th first occupy their line of breastworks. This was a terrible thing, the most destruction I have seen for the time it took. The shock was over in two minutes but cost the little Brigade of 700 men 250 of their number, fifty of whom were instantly killed. The ground for a space as wide as our lot and front of the house had 200 dead and wounded men lying on it.[3]

I must say that I can find nothing in the terrible work of war that is pleasure. I am on the contrary more than ever disgusted with everything I see on the field. I will not write more till I get to some convenient place. You may indeed feel grateful for my preservation in this struggle. I presume we will go back to camp in a few hours, but this is all matter of uncertainty for we know not what an hour may bring forth.[4]

I am verry much fatigued but in good health. I got your letter of the 9th this morning. My love to the children.

24th morning. It is wet. I am dry. Otherwise all right.

BERMUDA HUNDRED, VA.—*Aug 24, 1864*

We got back to our old camp this morning about 4 o'clock after one of the hardest weeks of toil and exposure, danger and discomfort I ever experienced. The weather has been excessively hot and close, and our operations have been confined chiefly to the thick wooded country some ten miles below Richmond and on the north bank of the James. . . .

The 67th has again been unfortunate. Of the four companies that went out with about 150 men, thirty were prostrated with sunstroke and forty were disabled on the field or were taken prisoners by the rebs. The 67th again had the fortune to kill a rebel General (Chambliss) and took one stand of Colors.[5] My Regt was fortunate in having no more than four companies in this short campaign for had they all been together and suffered in like ratio I should now have hardly a show for a Regiment.[6]

We will have a few days rest. . . . I am as well as can be expected.

PETERSBURG, VA.—*Aug 25, 1864*

I have been so awfully busy this week so far that I have had neither time nor temper to write you a letter, for when I was not actually engaged in active services I have needed rest so much that I could not write worth anything. The Regiment moved to this place yesterday. I came down this afternoon after having served as Corps Officer of the Day for the preceding thirty hours, all which was put in active duty, & this morning in making dispositions for the picket line, which was driven in by the rebs [just] before daylight. After demonstrating pro and con for some four hours quiet was restored after a loss of some forty men on our side. The 67th of course was not in it.[7]

We are having Morris Island re enacted here. Shot shell and musketry are constantly disturbing the peace of the locality and its occupants, but the heavy earth works makes it as safe as it was at our picket line and defenses at Bermuda Hundred. I have been blessed with good fortune amid many dangers the last two weeks for which I hope I am grateful to the all Wise and Good Providence that so carefully has preserved me. A terrific canonading is going on to our left, some eight or ten miles off. All the men are in the trenches. . . . I can get no sleep. Have not slept two hours consecutively since a week ago last Friday, with the exception of one night. . . .

PETERSBURG, VA.—*Aug 26, 1864*

I have been sleeping part of the day and taking rest and quinine in the hope that by tomorrow morning I shall be a man again. I don't know as I ought to write you a full account of the last two weeks operations so far as they have passed under my observation for they have been so full of the terrible evils of war that you will be rendered unhappy by their recital. If I was at home and out of the war I would gladly tell you all, for then you would not be disturbed by any unhappy reflections as to my personal safety.

While I am writing this I hear rifle balls striking against the trees all about me. I have taken my bed to a bombproof to sleep for the night, and think it is best to put myself there soon as I want to save my precious body from any more rebel marks[men]. I will finish this page and skedaddle to a place of safety. Whew I just hear one tearing through the woods.[8]

Saturday 27th. . . . Miss Barton [is] the only lady I have seen worth seeing since I came to the Hundred. . . . Well, I must tell you a little of Miss Clara H. Barton. In appearance . . . she [has] a large head, black hair, little frosted with grey, strong features, well developed muscles, so far as I could see them, strong vital organization, dark complexion and awfully afraid to contradict anybody. Lord! what a woman. Afraid to contradict, kind in manner, easy of address and unaffected & frank in action. Too good a girl by all odds to be scattering her good qualities over the wide world (I mean after the war for she is an angel of mercy here). . . .

NEAR CEMETERY HILL PETERSBURG, VA.—*Aug 29, 1864*

. . . Ever since we came to this point no moment has passed either night or day but one could hear the discharge of the deadly rifle or the loud canon or mortar throwing their almost irresistible bolts in our midst. This however is not met with as much personal danger as the uninitiated would suppose as we have learned the art of war so well that with the axe and spade [in] a few minutes we can make ourselves comparatively safe from shot shell or musketry fire. A rifle ball just clicked among the trees to my right, two overhead since I began to write this sentence, but my stockade behind which I have planted my tent is bullet proof—two more are just passed—another and yet another, and the artillery is roaring away at so great a rate that the sound appears almost continuous. My whole camp is entrenched, each man has his bunk and shelter tent behind an earth work six feet high and thick enough to resist ordinary light artillery firing.[9]

We are in a pine forrest, and pleasantly situated near enough to the enemy to see their eyes when they dare show their heads. I mean half the time on the picket line, the other half of the time we are to the rear 1/2 a mile where the Regimental camp is located but this close enough to the rebel lines to make one feel as if fiery billows rolled <u>above our heads.</u> . . .

I have just received a letter from you mailed on the 25th Inst. I will now open it. I have read it, and find you have been somewhat in the dark on account of my letter announcing that the Regt was on the move on the 13th Inst. As it finally turned out only four companies went. We crossed the James with 140 men, charged twice on the rebel rifle pits, lost 41 men killed, wounded and missing & had some thirty 30 odd prostrated <u>coup de soleil.</u> I have had six men killed and forty five wounded & taken prisoners within the last two weeks. Last Thursday morning I was in command of the picket line on Gen Butler's front through which my Regt had gone the day before Thursday last when our picket line was practically driven in by the enemy. I ordered the picket line to retake their former position, reinforcing them with a few hundred men which they did with but little loss. We took two Officers and fifty nine men from the enemy. Our loss was some twenty killed & wounded, and as many prisoners captured by the rebs. That made me three fights in two days. I pray to God they may be my last.[10]

The terrible artillery fighting that is at this moment going on to my immediate front out to my right is poor realization of my prayer. But this latter fighting is so usual here as to hardly attract attention. The men hug their earth works and let the big guns shoot. . . .

NEAR PETERSBURG, VA.—*Sept 2, 1864*

. . . You know I am not a vain man, one that never indulges in self laudation, but to be honest don't I write the <u>goodest</u> letters you ever read? And am I not the most <u>nice</u> man in the world to take so much pains to please one little woman? I confess to a weakness in that direction. I love to please the ladies. It is a rare treat for me to get in a <u>tete tete</u> with them. . . .

But somehow or other the Sanitary Commission understands my weakness and that of my class, and send such *plain* looking old girls here that their faces freeze all sorts of magnetism out of my senses. Now I got a piece of pie at a certain place by the favor of a good lady of whom I have written before (Miss Barton), and found two other <u>real old girls</u>—good at heart, no doubt, but with awfully *unattractive* outside arrangements. They were not to blame for this, but I tell you I was for once lost for words of admiration and like the lamb led to slaughter was dumb. The first time in my life I ever failed for want of utterance before the fair daughters of Eve.

Now there is good policy in all this for such a physiognomy is a protection to the virtue of the possessor, another illustration of the wise laws of nature's God and the discrimination of the Sanitary Commission. Else how could the Army Hospitals be supplied with the tender assiduities of the affectionate sex? Miss Barton understands this perfectly. She means to have no one under her careful supervision who can fall from grace, or bring the sisters of the Army into any danger of departure from the most virtuous walk with God and man.[11]

Now I admire Miss Barton for her sacrifices for the comfort of the soldier, but vastly more for her discrimination in selecting female subjects for her helpers. You, dear wife, know I am a man of keen discernment in estimating the qualities of the ladies, or how on earth could I ever have selected so fair and precious a jewel for my dear wife, and when I say I admire Miss B I say so for her good qualities which shine out from no bad arranged mortal tenement, & in a most beneficent manner toward the sufferers in the Army. . . .

I have made a safe place to rest and sleep. I am not afraid of rebel shot and shell while I keep my quarters, but when I step out I am constantly reminded that the rebs are neither quiescent nor peaceable. Night and day they keep up a constant fusillade of musketry or artillery practice. I visited the whole line of trenches day before yesterday to the front of our camp being about three miles of earth works. I got along unhurt but several sentries became the mark for their sharp shooters. Artillery is banging away at this moment. We are directly to the rear of the fort blown up by Gen Burnside. I passed within 150 yards of it day before yesterday.[12] I am well. Be careful of yourself.

NEAR PETERSBURG, VA.—*Sept 4, 1864*

The Lord's day has again appeared and partly passed with almost an entire cessation of hostilities on our lines. My Regt is on the picket line within 150 yards of the rebs, both parties being buried in deep angular trenches to save themselves from the fire of the other. It is really quiet for this place. This morning Surg Westfall & myself took a stroll through the zig-zag covered ways to the front to see how matters looked in rebeldom.[13]

The boys were exchanging papers with the "Johnnies" as they call the Confederate soldiers. Both parties had so much confidence in the other that for the time being they showed themselves from behind their entrenchments which an hour before would have cost the life of the party who dare make the exposure. On this verry line the most spiteful musketry fire has been kept up since we came here till today with the exception of an occasional armistice to exchange papers. The opposing parties are so close to each other that a man's head is a fine mark to shot at. I don't mean mine, though it has several times been the objective point of some keen sighted rebel.

If the men take care of themselves here there is not much danger as veterans rate danger, but an awful amount of hazard as the hundred day men would estimate it. I am comparatively safe in my quarters, entirely so as against musket practice and tolerably so against shot and shell. I can sleep verry comfortably in it, though constant firing that has been keep up less than a half mile to the front.

Last night mortar practice was kept up from both sides with great spirit and fair success an hour & a half or two hours. "Nobody was hurt." The fiery track of these projectors through the air after night gives a splendid sight to one so situated that he has no serious solicitude for his personal safety. Occasionally the artillery suddenly opens and for half an hour a perfect storm of canonading rages. Enough noise is made to keep the surrounding country reverberating with continued and unbroken thunder. If sound did anything one would think all rebeldom knocked into a cooled hat, but after all is over and a count is made both sides are as strong numerically as when the thunder commenced.

Of course the men lie low at such times, and the entire surface of the country for miles around Petersburg is cut in every possible direction by covered ways, mines, parallels, approaches, ditches and forts. All you have to do to keep your body whole is to follow the labyrinthine ways that surround the doomed City. While I am writing this I hear frequent reports of their canonading and occasionally a report of the rifle musket, but it is so much tamer than usual that it is hardly worthy of notice.

Our Division, Gen Terry's the 1st Div 10th Corps, has about a mile of front to protect. Our Brig, the 1st, has the grounds immediately opposite and not more than 150 yards from the Crater as it is called (the fort blown up by Gen Burnside) and is the most exposed part of the line. My Regiment stays there half the time, two days on and two days off. The boys rather like the fun as they get a frequent shot at a Johnny and if they take care of themselves are as safe as in camp.

No place here is perfectly safe, and when are we so? If we are to be taken out of this world by violence, how can we escape our fate? I suppose you have the news that Atlanta is in our possession. We had a telegram the evening of the 2nd announcing that fact, and another last evening confirming the same and further announcing that Sherman had fought another battle and been successful, no particulars given. We shall hear [more] in a day or two.[14]

What Gen Sherman's army will do next, I cannot divine. Probably will rest awhile. What a pity it is that he did not have a fresh army of a hundred thousand to follow up the success he has already gained. He is so far from his base that he must be embarrassed greatly to keep his communications open. We ought to have Charleston now. That in our hands we could keep the Southern Confederacy cut into by way of Chattanooga, Atlanta, Macon & Charleston.[15]

That Western Army is a better fighting army than the Army of the Potomac. The East may say what they please. The Potomac army has had a great deal of hard marching hard work and fighting to do, but somehow or other the fates have been against it. Jealousies among Generals and want of capacity & loyalty among too many of the Officers, and a desire to make a grand army instead of a fighting victorious battles for the country have stood in the way of its success. There has been more effort at organization than to inspire the rank & file with the idea that hard knocks were *required* to do the work . . . for the great end for which the Army was called into being. The Brigade Band are just passing my tent to get a good place to give a few patriotic touches to their big brass horns. "Blow ye the trumpet blow."

I saw a capital execution yesterday from my front door. A soldier of 3th N. H. had deliberately shot a comrade in the battle at Olustee, Fla, for which he had been tried, sentenced to be hanged till <u>dead—dead—dead</u> in the language of the old judges. The gallows was erected some thirty rods from my quarters. With my glass I could see all I wanted of the terrible scene. The poor fellow was almost gone with anxiety and fear. He showed none of that firmness we so frequently hear of being exhibited on the gallows. He appeared to have so little strength that he had to be partially supported on the scaffold.[16]

I have always felt as if I did not want to see an execution of this kind, but this was thrust on me and finally I concluded I would see it with the eye of a philosopher, that is see how I felt & judge how the convict felt. But this kind of philosophy has no charm for me. I have no doubt but he deserved to die a felon's death. Yet I could derive no satisfaction from the fact that he was justly punished. I have seen death in many horrible forms, but this was the most disagreeable to me of all. . . .

NEAR PETERSBURG, VA.—*Sept 8, 1864*

. . . I am writing under the same flattering auspices of my last. I mean under the angry guns of the rebs. . . . Everything is quiet now. I do not hear anything but a drum bang to remind me that we are in close proximity to the rebs. Some crazy Johnny has broken my spell by firing his shooting iron at the exposed head of a Yankee. These compliments have been constantly passing so that I have become so used to them that I do not hear them, or pay any more attention to them than the striking of the family clock, unless I pay particular attention to this condition of affairs. All forenoon both sides were banging away with little guns and big guns—howitzer & mortars—to pay for which we are having for a few moments almost a perfect lull in hostilities. It is surprising how much ammunition is used upon these fusillades and so few persons hurt. One would think a terrible battle was raging and not a man be injured. The shovel has done much to make it so, however. . . .

I do not know what is to be the next act in this war tragedy. I am thinking Father Abraham will put all the vigor into the war his conservatism will allow till the end of the fall campaign. The fall of Atlanta will make new combinations and require much effort in that direction to keep matters in good shape for us.

The Chicago Convention is over. The ignoble peace men controlled it, and took "Little Mc" for their standard bearer with Pendleton of Cincinnati for his 1st Lieutenant, a rampant original anti war man. In Congress he voted with Vallandigham & the Woods, and was ever ready to extend the hand of sympathy to the haters of his country and willingly stab every effort for the salvation of the Government offered by the political friends of the Administration. Shame that so great a party with such a history as it had fairly won in the annals of the country and with the splendid talent it combined should thus prostrate itself to such base purposes as are developed in their platform. I did suppose the war democracy of the country had enough of spirit and loyalty to spurn such an alliance as they make at Chicago with the Copperheads.[17]

Whatever of personal objections I may have for Mr Lincoln I shall lay them all aside and do all in my power to give him the hearty and united support of the Union men of the country. I am astounded at the demagogism of the Democratic Party, and look upon their advent under the leadership of such men as controlled the Chicago Convention as a great national calamity, too dangerous to be thought of being bourn. The rebels are rejoicing over their action. Only night before last long loud and hearty cheers went up for McClellan for miles on the rebel lines. Now I am not in favor of doing what the enemy wants me to do in my military matters and think it quite as safe to act on the same principle in political affairs.[18]

It is evening now, I have just returned from the trenches to see what is going on to the Brigade front for which I am responsible. I take good care to keep my head out of the way of their wicked bullets. Since the first of May I have seen war, but this is not entirely a novelty to me as the Dept of the South. But my wound of the 18th of July 1863 saved me from much of the hardships and dangers of the siege on Fort Wagner. This cool damp weather makes me feel a little anguish. Am well though.

NEAR PETERSBURG, VA.—*Sept 11, 1864*

I am Corps Officer of the Day for the 24 hours ending tomorrow morning 9 A.M. (Monday). As this involves special privileges, I cannot let the day pass without remembering you by letter at my good fortune on the Lord's day. You may ask what is there in the special privilege of being Corps Officer of the Day? Well, I will tell you. It gives you two mounted orderlies to wait on you, gives you a ride of five miles from camp, a visit to Camp Holly twice with a chat with the General and the high honor of being shot at ever so many times by the sharp shooters of the ugly rebels.[19]

I had a tall orderly to go with me through the trenches. As his head would stick up above the earth bank to the front occasionally, whiz would fly a minnie at his head. Soon the rebs discovered my red sash close to the tall orderly, and all along the line whenever an exposed place exposed either of us, bang went the rebels at us. I ran for the first time to escape their bullets today and I ran with a will and who would not. I have a holy horror for their blazing power and balls.

We have grand times here almost daily, sometimes several times a day. You may be awakened in the night with the belief that Mars has broken loose with the D——l and all pell mell at his heels. Ye Gods, what can the matter be? Bang, Bang, Bang, whiz, whirl, whew, Bang, Bang, Bang, whirl. Thunderation, earthquakes, trumpets, tornadoes and volcanoes. What are you here for? What on earth does all this mean, bang, bang, bang, bang, bang, bang? Gods & bomb proofs protect us. Ye bloody sons of Mars, why torment a fellow so, tell me what all this terrible breaking up means—whir, whiz, bang! bang! bang! bang! Aren't the nights hideous enough in these accursed trenches without adding the spleen of devils to the fury of rebels? "Oh! What are you fretting about?" This is all nothing but a bit of an artillery duel, with a slight sprinkling of musketry practice thrown in gratuitously with a bit of a charge on the picket line, to give point to the entertainment, that is all. . . .

Nevertheless I cannot be thus rudely wakened without feeling horrors confirmed and wonder what it will all amount to. Yet it is nothing, only a nightly attack of artillery duel, a big talk of the great guns aided by the little guns & mortars interspersed with the spiritual accompaniment of the venomous Springfields. "My God! Nothing?" Nothing but an artillery duel & its accompanyments. . . . If this is nothing what is war?, the civilian would say, and well he might say so till he got accustomed to it. . . .[20]

My puppy, the nicest black & tan terrier, has just bounced into my tent and broken the thread of my horrible discourse and by animated barks says I must give a little attention to "Black and Tan." I lost my squirrel on the expedition over the James, & have made up for it by the acquisition of a puppy. . . .

I see by the Ohio papers that there is not much likelyhood of the draft being enforced in our State. I am satisfied the war is going to be prolonged, the Lord only knows how long, and more for the want of men and vigor than for want of ability to crush out the rebellion. I wish I was in a place to exercise my notions fully as to the means of doing this work. I would organize an army that would make the rebels trouble. I am afraid for the country's politics, "party politics" will absorb everything till it is too late to do anything before winter.[21]

I am an Old Abe man but from force of circumstances, rather than the belief that he is a fit man to give us victory. He is a good man, and will not do or suffer wrong to be done if he can help it. I am in usually good health.

NEAR PETERSBURG, VA.—*Sept 15, 1864*

I do not write you in the most happy mood. Mollie wrote me so that I got it last evening that poor Rossie had died in some Southern prison from depravation and cruelty. Thus has fallen a martyr to his country, a noble boy whose age would have protected him from the ravages of this cruel war but his heroism and patriotism would not. I hope it will yet fall in my power to avenge this outrage on humanity. It is not enough for these traitors to destroy our Government and deluge the country with the woes of war, but they must murder our children by the tortures of a lingering death. Make peace with such devils by permitting them to have a voice equal to mine in the settlement? No! Never! Never!! Never!!! The man who makes the proposition is wanting in an appreciation of what constitutes national honor and political self respect. Alas! poor Rossie, your life and hopes, all are swept away by this cruel, cruel war. . . .[22]

I sent you a portrait of Col Joshua B. Howell of the 85th Pa Volunteers who for a year has been the commanding officer of the Brigade, a heroic patriotic and zealous officer whose remains we deposited in the dark narrow tomb this afternoon with the rites of the Masonic fraternity. Col H accidentally lost his life by the fall of his horse, he falling under the animal, and was so injured internally as to live only a few hours. I know he had much rather fallen in battle than thus accidentally meet his fate.[23]

But for me if I am to die, I cannot say that I want it to be in the din of battle in deadly conflict with mortals, the children of the same "Father of us all." I assure you I do not wish to be ushered into His presence with my hand reeking with the warm blood of my fellows. When I die I want to be in the quiet seclusion of my family in the full possession of my faculties, that I may appreciate the realities of the great change from mortality to immortality. I never did want to live to an extreme old age. Once a child is enough for me, but I have a dread of a violent death that no education can overcome. I don't know that I have great fear of death. I think I could meet the so-called King of Terrors with firmness, grace, composure. Yet I am exceedingly desirous of living until my children, your dearest treasures, are grown up to the estate of manhood & womanhood and are fitted from age and education to meet the realities of human existence with credit to themselves, usefulness to the world and a full discharge of the obligations of manhood.

What a bubble is a human being on the great ocean of eternity. . . . We scarcely know what we are before we plunge into the unfathomless depths of eternity of which we know nothing, into that tomb from whence no traveler returneth. I have the faith that the great author of our being has wisely arranged in the infinitude of His wisdom and goodness to support us in the great unknown of the future, for how could he give a momentary existence to finite beings and erring mortals and then hurl them from His influences forever? Shall the goodness of the creator be turned to the reck-lessness of eternal abandonment? God is good, and high over all His quali-ties *with Him* justice reigns supreme. I never could believe that all those qualities that so appeal to our gratitude so far as we are concerned are to drop with us into eternity never again to reach us. It is not Godlike. I sup-pose I would not be considered orthodox by verry many erring mortals in that respect, but I am willing to leave these matters with the great author of my existence.

You write me when I am to be at home. I am awaiting the action of Gen Grant on the question whether Officers mustered of a new grade during ser-vice are to be retained after they have served for three years. If he insists that we must serve three years of the new grade, I may be delayed till the close of this campaign. And nobody knows when that will be unless it be with the close of the war. I came verry nearly getting home on duty a few days ago, but being the only Colonel in the Brigade for the time being it was thought not best for me to make the effort. I thought so too, and let the matter pass. It is no great matter to command a Brigade now as a Brigade does not frequently number as many men as a full Regiment. . . .[24]

NEAR PETERSBURG, VA. — *Sept 18, 1864*

I have nothing interesting to write you today. The dull routine of trench life is gone through today with nothing more than a little shoot-ing from the picket line with only an occasional mortar shell or shot from their big guns. In fact the last twenty four hours has been the most quiet twenty four consecutive hours we have had since the command left Bermuda Hundred. What it means I of course cannot imagine. I see them continually working to our immediate front making new works and strengthening old ones, mounting new guns and opening new embra-sures with a zeal that indicates that they are not going to be taken at this point without an effort. I certainly admire their zeal and industry in their unholy efforts. I never had any patience for passive men and as a natural consequence must admire the opposite, though the activity was not al-ways guided by wisdom or justice. Not that I have admiration for wrong doing because it was wrong, but because of the energy put forth. I am for go ahead men. . . .

I have seen brave men cut some queer antics in their anxiety to [take] cover from the exploding projectiles from the enemy. The 6th Corps oc-cupied my camp for a few days at Bermuda Hundred in June last. They laughed at my boys on account of their bullet proof, saying they were a nice thing for 100 day men (whack struck a bullet against my shebang). My boys humored the joke, saying that veterans like the 6th Corps might possibly find them comfortable if they stayed in the locality long. In a few hours the rebs opened a tremendous artillery fire on my camp. When this ceased we found 6th Corps huddled as thick as pork in a barrel in our bomb proof and in our ditches, slop holes, swills and even stinking sinks. This amused our boys vastly, as they asked our 6th Corps veterans what they now thought of the hundred days men idea of bomb proofs. . . .

This infernal shooting annoys me. It is as constant as the tick of our clock and so close that one can hardly stir without imminent peril to life or limb. Col Commager returned this evening from a long stay at home. He is not improved in health as much as I had expected to see him. His nervous organization is much impaired. He is not much pleased with the statement of the people at home. Thinks they are not alive to the great interest at stake.

I shall know verry soon whether I am to get away from the army on the 2d next month. If Grant says Officers of my class stay, I shall, but he has not yet announced his intentions yet. My health is fair.[25]

NEAR PETERSBURG, VA.—*Sept 22, 1864*

. . . I hope never to see again such a five months as the last have been, but when such times will end I cannot tell. I fear the Lord in His wisdom has further tribulations for this verry wicked nation. This war is only one of the many ways the nation has of exhibiting its wickedness. It is a natural result of the corruption of the people and the diseased moral condition of society. It might have been averted for a few years, but it was as natural a result of our way of acting as the fever and ague is of miasmatic atmosphere.

If the war does not cleanse out the system we cannot long expect a healthy body though we should agree to peace. I know many feared the consequences resulting from a general state of war, but I think its tendency is to soften and purify rather than to make desperate and wicked men. The discipline of the army makes good men none the worse, while it restrains the vicious and keeps them away from verry many of the vices of civil life.

I know that the veterans are not half so cruel and reckless as the new recruits. The hardships, trials and dangers of the field have a tendency to chasten the heart and give healthful reflection to the brain. The motive for conducting the war on our part is certainly praiseworthy. The end is one of the most glorious political conceptions ever entering the heart, to wit the restoration of the best Government ever bestowed by a beneficent Providence upon erring man.

Friday afternoon. . . . I am awaiting Gen Grant's order for the muster out of Officers after having been in the service three years. If the order is approved at the War Dept as it ought to be, I shall be able to get home by the middle of Oct. But this matter of getting home is not so easy a matter. But out of regard to you I mean to make an effort. If the order is announced as I expect I can retire from the service without dishonor. I feel as if I had done my duty. Three years is a good long time for service in the field, away from home and to bear all the disabilities of the service. If every good patriot does as much as I & we then fail, I shall be willing to seek peace. I do not know what it is to be idle, and shall feel uneasy at what is being done in the army if not in it, but I know I shall not be without useful employment if I do get out of the army.[26]

Saturday morning. . . . We have just finished firing a salute on Gen Sheridan's second victory in the Valley.[27] It looks as if the rebs were getting slack. I hardly think Gen Lee will make a fight here. He will withdraw his army from Va to save it from destruction. Still they may see fit to risk a battle. If they do it will be a big one. But we are fast accumulating the means of cutting and holding the enemies communications, the accomplishment of which would compel his abandonment of Richmond and vicinity or the surrender of his army. Faragut, Sherman, Sheridan & Grant are verry strongly admonishing the rebs that the way of the transgressor is hard.[28]

Saturday afternoon. This letter drags out but you see that I am most through with it. We are feeling well over the news from Sheridan. He is giving them all they can now afford to take and a little more. It is raining but is warm and pleasant. More like spring than fall rains.[29]

NEAR PETERSBURG, VA.—*Sept 25, 1864*

I have been too busy all the live long day to write you, as we have moved our camp from the front to the rear some two miles. Was up all of last night till 3 1/2 o'clock A.M. when I lay down on the open field and slept till sunrise. It was rather cool for the naked ground as a bed, but I could not do better. This made my side ache all day, but feels better now. I am not sure how it will operate with me to lay out these cool nights. If it should trouble me as it did last night and today I shall be under the necessity of avoiding the exposure incident to an active fall campaign. I hope this matter will not be forced on me as I expect to get out of the service soon. . . .

IN CAMP NEAR PETERSBURG, VA.—*Sept 28, 1864 11 A.M.*

It has been all confusion and hurry since Saturday noon preparatory to a movement of our Corps, the 10th. We are under orders to move at 3 P.M. this day. Where we are destined to go and on what service are matters beyond rational conjecture ever so carefully have the objects of the move been kept within the knowledge of the commanding Generals.

As a good soldier I ask no questions. "Go it blind" is the motto of the Army. Some say Bermuda Hundred, others West Point up the York, others North Carolina, but all are in the dark and have few reasons for their theories. Now I do not want you to fret on my account as my time is so near out, and I learn that our orders have been announced by the War Dept that will admit of my being mustered out on the expiration of my three years. I have no regrets at keeping my promise to you that I would retire from the service as soon as could do so honorably. My three years are ample certificate of my discharge of duty in this struggle, unless new and more desperate developments are made. I of course do not know what this movement signifies. But I have made so many such that it occasions me no concern beyond the ordinary operations of active field service. The Good Providence that has protected me thus far through the war is the same ruler of the universe. He always has been & does not permit a sparrow fall without His notice.

Col Commager goes home in the morning to recruit up the Regiment. This was due to him as he expects to become the Colonel of the Regt before long. A long time ago I promised to resign in his favor as he had tendered me his resignation and withheld it on my procuring for him leave of absence and promising to resign so that he could leave the service finally of the rank of Colonel.

I have no regrets at being ordered away from here wherever we may go, as I doubt if we can find a more unpleasant place taking everything into account about Richmond & Petersburg. The fall will soon be cool and stormy, the winter dreary enough and the infernal clay soil here is the worst in the world after a little rain. The only evidences of humanity we find here are confined to the army and "niggers." The chivalrous Southerners are all beyond our reach and could we meet them our associations would be exceedingly unpleasant. They hate us with a cordiality that makes us feel like avoiding them as far as possible.

I might have enumerated another thing that has a human manifestation about it, that is the railroad and trains that pass over it almost hourly. Gen Grant has made a new railroad from City Point to the left of his line for the transportation of supplies. You have no idea of the immense wagon trains an army like this army requires to keep it supplied with supplies, & the vast array of water craft needed to bring troops, munitions of war and other articles for the consumption of the army. The former is measured by miles & hundreds of miles, the latter by hundreds.

Uncle Sam is a bully fellow. Has lots of men, lots of supplies and lots of transportation. He has more than the rebels have, but they have learned to do without and learning to do without have saved themselves much that has troubled our army. Ours has been a monster of baggage, theirs of poverty, ours of stability, theirs of mobility. They have been at home, we abroad. They have had earnestness, we pride. They have fought for national existence, we for *national unity*. They are deluded and infatuated, we *inspired by a proud sense of duty,* and when the differences are all weighed, we all wonder why we fight so, or even why we fight at all. I must stop here and pick up as we are to get ready immediately. I will write you as soon as I can.

NEAR RICHMOND—*Oct 1, 1864*

Here we are six miles from Richmond. Had no hard fighting with this Corps. Was within three miles of the rebel Capitol night before last. It has been raining the last 18 hours and is rather cool, but we all take it as a matter of course as a part of the program in taking the place. So far everything has gone on well. I will write you as soon as opportunity offers. I will get home as soon as I can get away, but that will be some days yet.

NEAR CHAFFIN'S FARM—*Oct 4, 1864*

The rain is over, so is the fight for some days. I have sent up my papers for discharge. The Gen [Butler] says he cannot spare me. I told him that I knew what I was entitled to. He says I must hold on for the present, which I feel as if I ought to do, but do not at all waive my right to discharge when I may ask for it.

I got a note from the Treasurer of State, Mr. G. Volner Dorsey, saying he had as chairman of the state Union Central Committee written the Secy of War for leave for me till after the elections to take part in the political campaign. What this may result in I do not know, but I shall write you soon what I am to do & when I may get home. I am as well as could be expected.

SIX MILES FROM RICHMOND, VA.—*Oct 5, 1864*

I am still near the rebel Capitol, but will most likely leave this place for one further to the rear in a few hours. With all the bluster made over this movement it has not cost us as much as our expedition to Deep Bottom on the 14th of Aug last, proximity to the City of Richmond being popularly taken as evidence of the amount of labor and fighting done by the army. So far as my Regiment is concerned I have felt as if it at all times has been in less danger than while we were in the trenches before Petersburg. Have lost only two men since we started, one killed & one wounded. This is the lightest loss I have sustained for a like period since the first of August last.[30]

I think I wrote you that I had applied for my discharge. I went to see Gen Butler last evening about it. He told me that I could not be spared, that he would not let me go at present, that such men as I had proved myself to be must under no circumstances leave now, that I should have the Brigade, the bully 1st Brig, & that he had forwarded my name with Gen Grant's approval and that I would be a Gen in a few days. Of course I did not feel verry much flattered at this, as I had compelled them to do something by my determination to leave the service. . . .[31]

I do not feel as if I had been well treated & so feeling think my obligations to the service are not as strong as if I had what was my due fully accorded me. I have strong suspicions that Mr Upson did not do as he led me to suppose he would. I relied upon him to act under his voluntary offer and lost time by his not doing what he might have done. My facilities are so poor for writing that I must close. . . .[32]

HD QRS 1ST BRIG 3RD DIV 10 CORPS
— *6 Ms from Richmond, Oct 9, 1864*

This Sunday has been put in verry much as last Sabbath was with the scenes and solicitude of close proximity to the rebels. I have no tent, no transportation except my horse, not even a clean plate, knife & fork. No nothing, everything to the rear & on the other side of the river. I broke my pocket inkstand on the way here, & have no means but the pencil to write you.

The cool weather of fall is upon us, but my rubber leggings and overcoat keep me dry & the big woods here keeps up the fire so that I do not suffer. The equinoctial rains are over indicating that we will have fair weather for some time. . . .

HD QRS 1ST BRIG 3RD DIV 10 CORPS — *Near Richmond, Oct 11, 1864*

Today is the first time for two weeks I have had the facilities for writing you a letter & with pleasure do I embrace this opportunity. I had hoped to have been home before this time, but the decrees of fate are not aiding me in the accomplishment of that end. I have heard nothing of my application to be mustered out of the service, and what its fate will be I am unable to tell. I know this, there will be a strong effort to keep me here.

I told Gen Butler whatever inducements he might offer I must go home & would not determine what course I should take till after I had been home. He says that I will be a Brigadier and that ought to be sufficient inducement with duty to keep me. I have heard nothing from that either. As you see I am not with the Regiment now. In fact I have been away from the 67th most of the time for the last two months. At present I have nearly 3,000 Africans under my immediate command, real black shiny fellows.[33]

Wednesday 12. . . . I would have finished this last evening but my tent is jointly occupied with two of my staff and being rather cool we take to the fire outdoors to keep ourselves comfortable.

Friday evening. I had to break off this letter as you see to go out on an expedition towards Richmond and to make everything ready I had to be ready to march at a moment's notice. It commenced to rain soon after and a sweet time we had of it. We got back to our quarters by 9 P.M., & had to take rest by little snatches till 3 A.M., when we were again on the move. By daylight were on the Darbytown road five miles from Richmond & in the face of the enemy.

My Brigade was verry fortunate, only losing 15 men. The old Iron Brigade lost heavily.[34] The 67th lost some sixty men. Lt Ward, now Capt, loses a leg, Rampano an arm.[35] It does appear as if the 67th was fated to be used up. It is a splendid Regiment, the best I ever knew. I do feel proud of it. My Adjt Gen had his horse shot. "Old Rob" went through safely. . . .[36]

I am waiting awhile to see if I get my appointment as Brig Gen as Gen Butler told me I should have it soon. I should like to be recognized before I leave the field. I certainly think I ought to be. We have a rumor from the rebel lines that Sherman has again whipped Hood, but as yet we have no reliable information. We also learn that Pa, Ohio and Indiana have laid out the Copperheads in the elections of Tuesday last. The election passed off verry quietly here. I voted and took no further notice of the day. You know I never was anything of a hand to hang around the polls, and here I had no inclination to interfere with the vote of a single soldier. They know what it costs to give substantial support to a nation in such a trial as ours. I believe they are patriotic and most cheerfully concede to them the fullest exercise of their preferences and judgment. . . .

HD QRS 1ST BRIG 3RD DIV 10TH—*Oct 21, 1864*

I have not written you a letter for six long days, but for three or four days I was so much occupied with business that I could find no time to write in the daytime and the evenings were too cool to write in my tent, the only place I could keep a light. To obtain this we built up a big fire to the front of our tents and sit before it dodging the puffs of smoke till bed time when we roll ourselves up in our blankets and sleep the best we can. . . . I will write more next time.

HD QRS 1ST BRG 3RD DIV 10 CORPS—*Oct 23, 1864*

. . . I am recovering from my cold, but as fully as I should like. My left shoulder is rheumatic enough to twinge considerably if I keep the same position too long in bed and on getting up this morning had considerable difficulty in getting my coat on. My scalp is not in good order being affected with something like the erysipelas. It is not the scurvy and certainly cannot be the itch, for the itch does not attack the head to begin with. . . .

I see somebody in the [Cleveland] Herald has been writing that Col A. C. Voris of Summit County ought to be made a Brigadier. Who that somebody is I do not know, but I most certainly think he is right. If I should get the honor of representing a Gen in my own person I probably will be no better suited than I was with the glorious old 67th Regt, than which there has not been a better Regt in the service. I feel proud of having had my fortunes in the army cast for so long a time and under such trying circumstances with this noble band of civilian soldiers.[37]

I never expect to command the Regt again as its Col, but have the assurance that I may command it as the component part of a Brigade I am to command. This may not be under all circumstances the most agreeable to all parties as I until the decease of Col Howell was the junior Colonel in the Brigade, Col Osborn & Col Pond yet being my seniors. But my services have such a nature as to entitle me to promotion if it placed me over them, a fact they will not like to recognize. Col Pond has not sustained for himself a good reputation as an officer, [because of] neglect of duty and indifference to the discharge of his duties to his men & fellow Officers. I hardly think he will remain in the service after the expiration of his three years service as Col, the 18th day of Dec 1864.[38]

We have been having a good time rejoicing over the victory of Sheridan won last week on Cedar Creek below Winchester. I recollect well the place having at three different times encamped for the night on the grounds where the battle was fought. So far as we can judge this last fight of his has been productive of one of the most decisive victories of the war.[39]

My cold and indisposition make it the hardest work in the world for me to write a letter. I just finished one to Mr. F. A. Nash, Provo Marshall 18th Dist, thanking him for his kind offers in the Herald of the 19th in which he sticks my name up for Brigadier for 18th Dist.[40] I wondered who had been taking this trouble, but a letter from him this morning opened my eyes to the fact that it was a good Summit Co man. . . .

HD QRS 1ST BRIG 1ST DIV 10—*Oct 26, 1864*

I am back to my old Brigade again and in command of the same by order of Gen Butler. This will please you as I see by your last letter you do not like my being in command of the Africans. When I went among them I did not expect to stay long, but I can assure you I was not ignobly disappointed in my uniform and command in Ethiopia. On the whole I regretted leaving as I found verry pleasant associates among the Officers. If I am not unsuccessful or unfortunate I shall probably remain in command of this Brigade for some time. . . .[41]

I am not pleasantly situated here, as Col Pond is my senior and as such is entitled to the command. . . . I will write more when I get the time.

HD QRS 1ST BRIG 1ST DIV 10TH AC—*Near Chaffin's Farm Oct 30, 1864*

I have a comfortable tent of my own again for the first time since the movement on the 27th of Sept last. I did not feel like fixing up much in Ethiopia as I did not expect to stay there long, being assured that I should have the command of the 1st Brig 1st, Div 10 A. C., the old Brigade to which I had been attached with slight changes most of the time for the last two & a half years. The copy of official communication from Gen Terry to Gen Butler & Gen B's endorsement thereon enclosed will explain why I wrote you so little about my command in the African Division.[42]

I should say however that my stay & command in the 1st Brig of the colored troops in this Corps was a verry pleasant time to me. Officers treated me verry kindly, the men were civil and obedient, and my staff especially were gentlemen of ability, culture and aimed to make me feel at home among them. I commanded the Brig in one fight, that of the 13th Inst., and was highly gratified with the bearing of both men and Officers. I must admit on the whole I was sorry to leave the Brigade. If I sought personal ambition alone I would prefer to take my chances among the colored troops, for less is expected of them and what they do is more noticed than what is done by veteran white troops. Everybody knows that the latter will fight, while with the former it is yet a matter of experiment. Where troops are to be used in masses, the colored troops make as good troops as the whites, but where individual effort & qualities are required such as the skirmish line, picket post and even the battle line they are far inferior to the <u>Yankees.</u> This Officers who have had the most experience with the <u>darks</u> admit.[43]

Now for my quarters. I have a rough board floor with a log foundation two & a half feet big, hewed of course, on which is stretched my tent making it high, air tight and warm. The chinks are all filled up with mud. Then I have a nice brick fireplace that makes the whole radiant with light and hot of an evening, a luxury that I verry much appreciate for night before last, no the night of the 27th Inst., a dark stormy rainy October night, I lay out in the woods near the enemies lines in battle array, the live long night on the bare ground with naught but my clothing to protect me from the chill, stormy night. . . .[44]

I assumed command of the Brigade on the 26th. On the 27th at 4 A.M. started to the right to fight the rebs with three Regts of my Brig. Did not have any verry severe fighting. The 67th lost in killed, wounded & missing in the aggregate 26 men. One Officer killed and 3 men, 2 missing, probably taken prisoners, ballance wounded.[45]

Lt. Ward is dead. Died from his wound received the 13th Inst. from gangrene. He ought to have recovered and had he been treated properly I think he would. I am not a surgeon, but I dare utter the opinion that hospital gangrene ought not to be a serious bar in the way of recovery from wounds at this season of the year. Mrs Ward will indeed feel sadly as she was expecting her husband home shortly.[46]

I have not seen the papers for the last two days, but learn that we have been successful in Missouri.[47] I hope this is true, for we have not done enough before Richmond during all the last long six months to encourage the notion that the rebellion must soon be crushed. . . .

I have drawn nine months pay for this year of which you have $1,400.00, "the Lion's Share," a flattering compliment to your financial skill and the estimation you are held by your husband.

I am at work trying to make a full Brigade.

IN THE FIELD BEFORE RICHMOND, VA.—*Nov 3, 1864*

I am astonished to find it is Thursday again, but time flies so swiftly that I at time do not keep up with it, though I am considered by you a considerable of a rusher. We have had another rain storm for the last twenty four, commencing with little hail & sleet, and continuing all this day with misty rain making it verry unpleasant for the men. The old soldiers have made themselves quite comfortable considering the outfit the Government furnishes them with for field operations, to wit clothing, one blanket, one rubber blanket and one piece of shelter tent. The men have laid contribution on all the buildings for miles round for boards, timber, brick, windows and doors. The pine forrests furnish material for huts & with what the buildings supply enable the men to make quite comfortable huts. Every four men have a little house about 8 x 10 ft in area with a little fire place & chimney. The shelter tent for roof which not only keeps off the rain but answers for lighting the room in the daytime.

I rode through the camps of my Brigade this morning to see how matters were progressing in the storm. I found but few lazy heedless fellows who were caught by the storm without shelter or fire, but most of the men had been preparing for the cold storms of Nov. It is indeed singular that men who have brains will so far neglect their comfort as to let the nasty weather of fall and winter catch them entirely unfitted for what the seasons must bring. My old Regiment is better fixed up than either of the other three Regiments of the Brigade. I think my thorough way with them and my example has been of real worth to the Regt. I never did have any patience with a slouch, and while I had the command of the men I took pains to prevent the manifestation of slouchiness. I had when I had the means the best and neatest camps of any troops in the neighborhood. A tasty camp made the men have a regard for their personal neatness and comfortable quarters gives them a more contented valuation of the service.

I feel more at home again than for a long time. I have my tent all to myself, and can sit much of the time during the day undisturbed. This gives me time to read and brush up in the <u>tacticks</u> which I again need. I never drilled a Brigade, though tolerably well posted in the evolutions of the line. I must rub up to be the instructor for its enlarged duties. . . .

HD QRS. 1ST DIV. 10TH A. C.—*Nov 5, 1864*

. . . [A year ago] this time I was making one of the prettiest camps ever made on Folly Island. . . . That year has passed into the forever gone realities of the past, and what an awfully anxious year it has been for us; and *still* all the horrors of this infernal war instead of being closed are intensified and multiplied upon us.

O! Unhappy times! O! Unhappy people! Will you never learn wisdom from experience? But we are in the fix, and must fight our way out. I sometimes fear the people instead of learning wisdom from the sad experience of the past few years are preparing for themselves additional troubles. The traitors at the North act to me as if they were ready to plunge the free states into the turbulent gulf of revolution. I am indignant at their course. When I read of the exposure of their traitorous combinations at Indianapolis last summer, I felt happy at the thought that I was in the army and fitting myself to successful resistance to such scoundrels in case they should rise. Really I have a much stronger desire to fight those fellows than the rebels of the South who are fighting with some show of consistency.[48]

Eddie writes me his boy notions of the election. Little he knows of the vast import of the approaching election. I sometimes fear the total breaking up of society and government before we get out of the war. I pray God it may not be so, but I am not, I cannot be confident. If "Honest Old Abe" is elected I hope he will convince all political disturbers that there is a Government. I would do it if I had to write every word in blood and furnish the stationery at the expense of the confiscation of all the property of those who stand in the way of the supremacy of law. . . .

Sunday . . . It is evening now and I must hurry this off if I get it into the mail tonight. It has been a pleasant day, but too cool to sit in my tent without a little fire. I have busied myself in the saddle enough today to make the time pass off rapidly.

I mean to make me a little log house if I can find windows and boards enough anywhere within our lines. This is pretty hard to do as the whole community has been ransacked for boards, doors, windows & brick. You have no idea of the total destruction to property when an army is encamped expecting to stay for the winter. The sickly idea that rebel property is sacred *long ago* departed this army and combined with our wants has revolutionized the ideas that followed McDowell & McClellan's campaigns. We fully recognize the doctrine that rebels have rights that white men are bound to respect, but Gen Lee is looked upon as being the conservator of those rights for the present, and so far as their vitality is concerned is held in abeyance subject only to the Constitution.

I must say that I am not satisfied with the wholesale destruction of private property wherever the army goes, but it appears to be the way of all armies in the field & it makes but little difference whether it is the rebel or Union army that occupies. When I look over the Virginia valley, the fairest portion of fair Virginia, I feel sadly at the ravages the rebellion is making. No state of the Old Union has paid so dear a penalty for bringing on this war as Old Virginia. I wish they could see the folly of their ways and lay down their hostility to that Government that once gave them complete protection and is anxious to do it now.

I am having rather quiet times now. The command of a Division does not require as much personal effort as that of a Regiment. . . .[49]

HD QRS 1ST DIV 10 A.C.—*Nov 6, 1864*

Dear Jane[50]

. . . I expect to be the future commanding officer of the 1st Brig unless I am unfortunate or am transferred to another command. I was assigned to the command of the Brig by the order of Gen Butler, though I am the junior Col save one in the Brig, but I have good reason to suppose that I rank most Cols in the army. I am certainly junior to several Colonels in the Division but by order from Army Hd Qrs am commanding Division.

I have fought in a good many battles, been under fire say two hundred times, have commanded a squad, a Regiment, a Brigade and a Division in battles, and on a review of my efforts in the army I think I make as good a Regimental commander as they often make. I do think the 67th Ohio to be the best Regiment taking for all purposes I ever knew. I know it has made its mark in several Departments and stands "A No. 1" here. Its summer casualty list numbers 3/5 the new men for duty at the opening of the campaign, and on the 27th Inst. it did its duty as vigorously & faithfully as it did on the 10th of May last.

Not least among the exploits of which I feel proud is my command of a colored brigade on the 13th of October last in an attack of the rebel intrenchments on the north side of the James (where I now am). The fighting was light when I was there, but I had an opportunity of seeing "Africa" in a fight. I tell you they will fight. I am glad that the Government is giving them a chance to fight & make men of themselves. If I had to leave my old Brigade I know of none that I would sooner take than one of the Colored brigades in the 3rd Division of this Corps. . . .[51]

HD QRS 1ST DIV 10TH A.C.—*Nov 10, 1864*

The presidential election is over and so far as I can learn "nobody is hurt" unless it is "Little Mack" and his friends. In the army the elections passed off verry quietly. No noise, no excitement and so far as I could judge no great anxiety was manifested by the soldiers or Officers as to the result. It appears to have been a foregone conclusion amongst all classes that "Honest Old Abe" had the inside track and would beat the "Great Unready" by a long way, perhaps distance him.

We are assured that he has done this handsomely. As early as yesterday noon we had it announced to us that Mr Lincoln was elected by a large majority. What surprised us most of all was that Baltimore City should give him 15,000 majority. I have not studied party politics since I became a part of the army. As a matter of course I cannot claim much for my opinions, but I think such a revolution in public sentiment is verry remarkable. In Baltimore was spilled the first loyal blood in this war. The City was closed against the passage of our troops, even to save the national capitol from the possession of traitors. It was only by the most wise & potent means that saved the City from going with the rebellion. Now after a lapse of three & a half years the man who had to pass through this City in disguise to reach the federal capitol to be inaugurated as the Chief Magistrate of the nation now gets fifteen thousand majority of the votes of that City for the presidency. And the state then holding over 80,000 slaves now is free not holding a single slave, having in the meantime voluntarily manumitted all her slaves. This is indeed a revolution, and big with glorious associations and prospects for the future.[52]

Pecuniarily the South in fighting for their peculiar institution have lost more than the entire worth of her human property at its most extravagant value, while in national honor, strength & social grandeur she loses the great benefit of the general independence, intelligence, trust and affection of her population. How much to the strength and glory of the South might her four millions of unfortunate and abused slaves have added had they been humanized & Christianized by education and encouraged to enterprise by giving to them the care and protection of law. The citizen statesman & philanthropist of the South must have been blind not to see it. What a blot these poor millions of degraded inhabitants have cast not only on the fame but material status & prospects of the country. You cannot dry up the enterprise and manhood of so many human beings in any country and not feel the damaging consequences of this folly & wickedness.

It is a gratifying reflection that out of the misfortunes of war the nation is awaking to a realization of the beneficence of freedom and the inconsistency and poverty of slavery. I am glad the Union Party put the emancipation doctrine directly in issue, and am doubly glad the long and sorely tried judgement of the people has in the election of Mr Lincoln sustained this great measure of justice, and proclaimed to the world that they knew & dared to do what justice and their great interest demanded.[53]

To the people at home who through this campaign have heard the negro question harped upon with so much zeal & perhaps has furnished more bitter food for fierce denunciation than any other subject ever agitated, it would be astonishing to learn that in the army the prejudice heretofore existing against the negro has almost entirely died out. Officers return the salute of the colored soldier with cordiality, and treat them with kindness, and the soldiers are glad to welcome them as comrades in arms. I do not mean by this that they make them their social associates, but they are not ashamed to recognize them as fellow soldiers and entitled to all the honors of veterans.[54]

While I had rather command white troops I would not feel it any degradation to command colored troops. I have heard our men cheer the negroes for their exploits as heartily as if they belonged to the rapacious Europe & American race. The North will soon come to this, and in a few years will wonder why they ever were so unwise and unjust as to curse the colored man and damn his friends. . . .

Friday. . . . I am building me a house, 12 by 16 ft, one story high. I send you front & end projections. I am ornamenting the door & windows by combinations of crotches with the rough bark on. The boys are making for me a grand affair. Would you like to live in it?

HD QRS 1ST DIV 10 A.C.—*Nov 14, 1864*

I ought to have written yesterday as I intended to have done, but the papers, Jeff Davis's Message and other things kept me from it. . . .[55] Since the election matters have been so quiet here that I could write you nothing about our operations of interest unless I indulged in the license of fiction, which for the sake of truth I dare not write.

I ordered a review of the 1st Brigade for this afternoon. I as division commander did the review with great <u>dignity</u> and <u>grace.</u> I had a dashing staff of Lieutenants, Captains and Medical Officers. Then I had volunteer Colonels and other Officers on fiery steads. I on my <u>"best horse"</u> followed by this grand pageant, rode to the front and rear of a line a half a mile long and looked every soldier in the eye. <u>I did.</u> Little Mack in his palmiest days couldn't <u>did it</u> better. Before starting I cautioned my staff to frisk up their horses and look ferocious as I was bent on making the review an event of historic importance. Well, they frisked their charges, looked ferocious as they could, and made a grand display of horseflesh, blue cloth, brass buttons, gallant Officers and I as the big man of the day in my slouch hat (rather rusty by the way) felt as if I had done a big thing. The review was a good thing. The command appeared better than I supposed it would with the disadvantages of an active campaign constantly on our hands since the 1st of May last.

There was one drawback and what rose has not its end. I was so lame from my old wound that I could hardly sit on my saddle. For some unaccountable reason my side has twice this fall become quite irritable, remaining so for several days, the result of cold no doubt but goes off without serious results. It feels better today. I hope to be right in a day or two. These old bullet holes are bad things. I want no more. It is rather capricious for at times when I labor hard and expose myself the most I do not suffer from it again. Without any apparent cause I suffer severely. I mean to get leave of absence by and by, when I hope to see you for a few days at home. But the winter is a bad time to visit in the North. . . .

It is Tuesday evening and this letter is not off yet. By the aid of a little time I will make it go before the mail gets away. Lt. Hathaway goes tomorrow with half a dozzen Captains of the 62d Ohio.[56] Officers are leaving verry generally. I can't say as I blame them much, but many are leaving for place and position offered during the war. Many of them most likely will never see as good an opportunity for personal advancement in their lives.

I am trying a cigar sent me a few moments ago. It is called good but since I quit smoking entirely tobacco has no charms for me. We had ice Sunday morning, the first I have seen this year. I washed my face & hands in the slush, for the novelty of the thing, felt better, & took my breakfast with a relish. . . .

Miss Barton sent me a cup of butter, real nice Northern butter, a doz of eggs and two big apples a few days ago. I sent her some of my boys to fix her up for the winter. She was so much pleased that she tried to reward <u>me instead of the boys.</u> Perhaps she rewarded them too, for they were much pleased with what they did for her & with her kind treatment to them. I have seen but little of her since last summer. She is not more than a mile off doing lots of good for the poor boys who get sick & wounded.[57]

HD QRS 1ST DIV 10TH A.C.—*Nov 17, 1864*

. . . I had a good deal of inflammation in my groin for some eight days, but since Monday has gradually become easier so that I can walk without much trouble. I think the whole trouble arose from taking cold, a liability to which has troubled me more this fall than at any other time since I came into the army. Otherwise I have stood the wear and tear of this year's operations without serious detriment to health. . . .

I have read the news since commencing this letter. Had the New York papers of yesterday morning, find but little in them. We get the news here nearly as soon as you do in Ohio, frequently sooner as we get the rebel papers through the picket lines. Important war news is brought to us by telegraph directly from Washington, giving us the news twenty four hours in advance of the papers. . . .

HD QRS 1ST BRIG 1ST DIV 10 A.C.—*Nov 20, 1864*

Today has been really the most dreary of the most dreary months of the year. For two days we have had nothing but rain and mud and fog in this most muddy country in the world. Va east of the Blue Ridge excepting on the sea coast is the muddiest country I ever saw. How much better we were off in South Carolina with all our hardships than in this rebel cursed country. The summer has been as oppressive here as there, with a prospect ahead of a dreary winter, which never reaches Hilton Head. If it was not for the James River we would be compelled to abandon this place on account of the mud (unless we made railroads).

It is half past four P.M. and with all the ill luck of weather I have managed to get through so much of the day without feeling time hang heavily on my fingers. I got up verry late, on account of being called up several times during the night. The naughty rebels will not let us sleep quietly only part of the night. I sleep more like a civilized being than formerly. I remove my clothing & tuck my body between two sheets of nights unless the Johnnies are unusually troublesome. . . .

I wish the war would end, but I can see no prospect of its speedy close. Still, Sherman may make them great trouble the ensuing month. We are not going to take Richmond by storm. Sherman's movement, however, may have much to do in determining whether we take Richmond at all or not. . . .

IN THE FIELD NEAR RICHMOND—*Nov 23, 1864*

Here I am quietly waiting for Thanksgiving. Not an old fashioned New England Thanksgiving, with turkey, pumpkin pie, hard cider and all the family at the same table, but an army Thanksgiving with reveille at 5 1/2 A.M. & all hands under arms, and drum & fife, and shoulder arms, and hard tack, perhaps a turkey for the men cooked in a camp kettle stew style. I understand 1,300 turkeys have arrived for the boys—hope it is true. It will be a splendid treat for them. . . .

Thanksgiving morning. A bright cold wintry morning. The ground is frozen quite hard. . . . I had an elegant piece of custard pie last night. I took dinner with Dr Kittenger of the Flying Hospital. Miss Barton had made some bully pies, and boarding at the Dr's table we had a chance at the pastry. I praised her pies. Mr Wardell of the N.Y. Herald said they were splendid, Dr Leach, first rate, Dr Kitlinger, the best he ever ate.[58] I, the last man, said I would beat them all in my praise of the custard so I called it "stupendous." All hands agreed that the first one had no chance. Well I made stupendous use of my knife & fork, & demolished lots of the stupendously good thing. . . .

HD QRS 1 BRIG 1 DIV 10TH A.C.—*Nov 27, 1864*

. . . I had a little bit of a ride yesterday. I sent a carpenter to Miss Barton's cabin to put a window in. To do this he had to cut a big hole in the side of the wall. While he was doing this I had her come and stay in my new house. . . .

My brigade staff was here this afternoon to our Thanksgiving dinner. We had turkey, pumpkin pie and cake, in addition to the usual allowance of things. Friday afternoon the men had their dinner, turkey, geese, chickens, pies, cakes, fruits & lots of good things made up their repast. It did them lots of good to eat this supply of good things from the kind hearted friends at home. I know that the good women who did the work would have been repaid a hundred fold if they could have seen the boys enjoy the meal. It is not so much the material as the realization of the thoughtfulness that prompted the people of the North to do a kind act for the soldier. Kind words, kind thoughts and kind actions in themselves trifling are of great consequence to the soldier, especially if they come from home. They long to be remembered and remembered with attention and affection from those that hold the relation of kindred & friends out of the army. . . .

I hear heavy canonading at Dutch Gap, some three or four miles from here.[59] The air is damp and otherwise all is quiet so that sound is coming with great distinctness. Those heavy guns make a verry fair substitute for thunder. The reverberation along the hills is heard for several seconds and is hardly distinguishable from distant thunder.[60]

I mean to make application for leave of absence before long. But when I cannot say for there is a great demand for Officers at present.[61] We got 270 new recruits for the two Ohio Regiments last week. These need much attention. If it was not so far and the way of getting here so bad and the operations of the campaign so uncertain, I would ask you to come and share my new house with me. But the winter and my way of living would hardly be compatible with your health. . . .

HD QRS 1 BRIG 1 DIV 10TH A.C.—*Nov 30, 1864*

. . . I ought to have finished this so as to have sent it by this evening mail, but being on duty as Corps Officer of the Day yesterday and not relieved till 9 1/2 A.M. today and then my Brigade drills are to be looked after, with the general duties of my place, has kept me fully engaged the live long day. . . .

I just *read* a telegram from Gen Scofield, Franklin, Tenn that the enemy had been badly repulsed on the 30th at that place. Poor Hood has made a great mistake in trying to get Sherman from Atlanta by making a campaign in southern Tennessee, & an equally bad mistake in trying to defeat Thomas's Army. I wish we could speedily whip those fellows so that they would give up the rebellion. If that army is badly defeated, the Cotton States will feel verry despondent as they placed great hopes on the efforts of Beauregard and Hood's Army. We learn but little of Sherman's operations but so far we feel quite confident that it has gone well with him, for we hear no exaltation within the rebel lines as would if they had good news from that quarter.[62]

I find a general good feeling in the army as to the results of our summer's operations with the hopeful prospects before us. I am inclined to the opinion that we are doing quite as well in keeping Lee's Army in Virginia as if we took Richmond and he escaped with it to the South as he could easily do.

I am enjoying good health, & suffer no inconvenience from old wound at present. Love to all.

IN MY OWN ARMY HOME—*Dec 4, 1864*

. . . [Miss Barton] said she was glad to see me. I told her I was gladder, & told her if she was really in earnest I would take her on a bit of a ride. She said she was in earnest. I believed her and we did take a ride. She on Rob, the wicked horse that broke my wagon to pieces, I on one not half so good or ugly. We both rode on separate horses of course. I said all my funny, winning sayings in my best style, she like a polite lady said yes to everything. We went to Fort Harrison, saw the rebels, then rode along our line. . . .

Miss Barton is a real good woman, full of kindness of heart and thinks I am a better man than I am. I have been doing little acts of kindness for her through my men for which she is mindful. She sent me a beautiful cup of butter & some pies a few days ago & occasionally a few splendid apples. I like butter, pies, apples & above all a nice woman. I know you think so.

BEFORE RICHMOND, VA. —*Dec 9, 1864*

. . . The President's message, meeting of Congress, army news and all such are hardly matters of passing notice since the reaction of the excitement of the great political campaign has taken possession of the country. Well, I like Old Abe's plain way of telling the rebels they can have peace if they want it, and if not they can have war to their hearts content. I like plain talk. It is encouraging to find after four years experiment the President has come to the earnest conclusion that the Confederacy mean something and that there is so much earnestness about their meaning that the most energetic measures are essential to the successful conviction on their part of the error of their ways.

In truth I should admit that our operations of the past six months have been of that demonstrative kind that must convince them that the way of the transgressor is hard. The devastation of the Virginia valley, and the destruction accompanying Gen Sherman's columns show vigor and emphasis on the part of the Government that will do more than all the executive bullying & coaxing of his Administration towards bringing these rebellions madcaps back to their sober senses. . . .

Has been cold today, freezing in the shade and thawing little or none in the little sun shine we have had. I had a Brigade drill this afternoon, rather cold work, but I double quicked the boys and made them warm while the mounted Officers shivered as if they had never seen cold weather. . . .

Saturday evening, Dec 10th. I was too tardy in writing last night to get your letter off and today the naughty Johnnies have kept me so busy that I could not attend to wife at all. While at breakfast this morning I heard musketry on the picket line. I dropped knife and fork & ordered everything into the trenches at once, was on my horse in double quick, had orderlies flying and staff Officers on the wing to get matters in shape & ascertain what was the matter.

It has been an exceedingly uncomfortable day, some two inches snow on the ground with slush enough to make it intolerable walking or horse back riding. All day long had the poor men to stand in the snow and mud waiting for an opportunity to shoot the rebs or get shot themselves. I am not sure but it would have been a good thing to have had a little brush with them. The accelerated flow of blood would have done to give warmth to the shivering lads who had all this miserable day to dance attendance to the orders of "Bob Lee." Winter comes later than winters in Northern Ohio, but when it does come it is as mean and nasty, excepting is not so intensely cold verry often and does not remain cold so long. I am better fitted in mind for cold weather than the two last winters.

Sunday morning. We were out under arms at 5 o'clock this morning and moved a mile below through the slush & mud and stayed out till after eight o'clock, when we were permitted to return to camp with a whoop & holler. To uninitiated this looks like pretty hard soldiering. Well it is, but it doesn't come so every day, and many of us are old soldiers and know how to take such things. . . .[63]

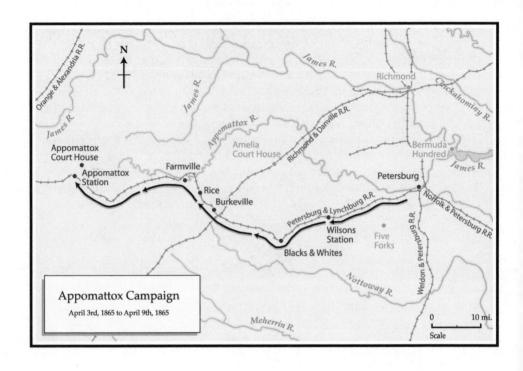

N

Orange & Alexandria R.R.

James R.

James R.

James R.

Appomattox R.

Appomattox
Court House

Appomattox
Station

Farmville

Rice

Burkeville

Amelia
Court House

Richmond & Danville R.R.

Petersburg & Lynchburg R.R.

Wilsons
Station

Blacks & Whites

Five
Forks

James R.

Richmond

Chickahominy R.

Bermuda
Hundred

James R.

Petersburg

Norfolk & Petersburg R.R.

Weldon & Petersburg R.R.

Nottoway R.

Meherrin R.

Appomattox Campaign

April 3rd, 1865 to April 9th, 1865

0   10 mi.

Scale

"Each Day Brings the War So Much Near a Close"

[*On January 16, 1865, Voris returned to the 67th Ohio, camped on the north bank of the James River. For nearly the next two and a half months, the regiment drilled, took turns on picket duty, observed peace commissioners pass through its lines, and awaited improving weather for the start of the spring offensive. On March 27, the 67th Ohio swung into action. Reacting to Lee's attempt to break the Union's siege, the regiment joined the onslaught against the Confederate left as Grant's forces applied massive pressure along the entire front. Over the next two weeks, the 67th Ohio helped rupture Lee's lines and pursued the enemy following their evacuation of Petersburg and Richmond. The chase ended April 9. Confederate surrender ended Voris's war.*]

NEAR RICHMOND, VA.—*Jany 16, 1865*

I arrived here safely last evening. Had nothing on the way after leaving Akron of more than ordinary interest except, when near Massillon in the night of Wednesday, a rail broke and spoiled the forward passenger coach. "Nobody hurt" & but a short delay. I stayed in Washington part of two days, and found matters as favorable for me as I had any reason to suspect. I find the men in good heart and quite comfortably fixed for the winter. . . .[1]

Judge Spalding was anxious to have me return & take the place of Mr Nash at Cleveland. I declined to take the appointment, as it would reduce me in rank instead of giving me what I should have, promotion. I finally told him that I would not object to being detailed for that duty until after the present draft if he desired, provided it did not impair my chances for promotion & did not affect my rank and pay.[2]

He means to apply to the Secretary of War, as soon as he returns from Savannah for an order detailing me for duty at Cleveland till after the draft. If Mr Stanton is willing that an Officer of my rank should fill the place designated, I shall be sent there till the opening of the campaign in the Spring. . . .[3]

NEAR RICHMOND, VA.—*Jany 1865*

I have been considering your letter requesting me not to drink intoxicating liquors. The reasonableness of the request and the kind manner in which it is urged have caused me to think of the matter seriously. Now you know that I never was in the habit of drinking alcoholic liquors when I lived at home. Nor have I acquired the habit since I came into the field except when I went to Folly Island, S.C. I have used it in small quantities almost daily during the hot weather, excepting for a few weeks the last summer, to fortify my system against the miasmas of the various places I have been.

I feel as if I ought to gratify you in your request so long as I can do so without inconvenience to myself. I perhaps might say it gives me pleasure to gratify your wishes when I can. I therefore will do as you ask of me and will abstain from all alcoholic drinks for the mere gratification of appetite, or habit as a matter of social observance or claim. By this I mean that I will not drink unless under such circumstances as a prudent person would take it to preserve health. . . .

We are rejoicing over the taking of Ft Fisher. Gen Terry has knocked Gen Butler so far into the shade he will never recover as a military character. . . .[4]

NEAR RICHMOND, VA.—*Jany 21, 1865*

. . . Fort Fisher is ours but it cost us terribly. I see in the list of Officers killed quite a number of valuable men. But this is the price of our success. The loss of Wilmington is a severe blow to the rebels, the most damaging of the war save the taking of New Orleans. I have no doubt but that we will be able to completely blockade the port of Wilmington & thereby to a great extent stop blockade runners from access to the South.[5]

NEAR RICHMOND, VA.—*Jany 24, 1865*

. . . We have been quite excited over the destruction of the rebel iron clads that attempted to pass our batteries this morning. We blew one up and beached the other two in such a place that they will be unable to make any use of them hereafter. We have also been under lively orders for the last twenty four hours on account of activities on the part of the enemy. It is awfully muddy making it almost impossible to move troops and entirely so in most places for artillery. The rebels are much exercised on account of our late success and may do desperate things to turn the tide of affairs. The loss of Wilmington and the destruction of their iron clad fleet in the James are disasters that the whole Confederacy must greatly feel.[6]

Mr Blair's second visit to Richmond has a plausible significance. It certainly looks as if Mr Davis was anxious to negotiate with the Government for peace. If the two contending parties can meet for the purpose of adjusting our difficulties with the unmistakable demonstrations we have been making for the last six months, I shall begin to hope for the speedy close of the war.[7]

While the South have the means of doing us immense amount of harm and of delaying our ultimate success, they must feel that while they are doing us much harm they are doing themselves an injury without any adequate compensation. They cannot be so unwise as to waste their energies and resources without realizing any prospect of good therefrom. Deserters have come in lately in increased numbers. Some days it is reported as many as fifty or sixty with no day short of ten or a dozen. This is on our front and does not embrace the Army of the Potomac. The steady decline in the value of gold with this shaky tendency of the secesh soldiers is a striking indication that confidence with the permanency of the Confederation is becoming weaker and weaker as we push the cause of victory forward. . . .[8]

NEAR RICHMOND, VA.—*Jany 30, 1865*

. . . The James is frozen nearly over many places, but the rise of the tide prevents it from filling entirely up. For a week we have had snowy winter weather for Northern Ohio. It is milder this morning and promises to be a pleasant day.

The rebs have done an immense amount of work since last summer along James River above the Bermuda line. A great deal of it will never be of any use to them or anybody else under the sun, but to the contrary will be a great nuisance to the owners of the soil. This is true of a great deal of work done by the army. . . .

They have not been as destructive with rebel property as we have, but they have enough to impoverish the country where their army lies. It matters little whether the army is friendly or hostile, a winter campaign demands the resources of the people and the demand is made inexorable either by order or permission tacitly recognized. The enemy are beginning to recognize that the war has been a mistake, and we think are trying to devise means to get out of it. Their papers are discussing the possibilities of their defeat, are awfully afraid that the states will hold conventions to deliberate upon the state of the country and find bitter fault with their Congress and especially with Jeff Davis for their blunders and inactivity, all which indicates that their troubles are making them think and fast pushing to action.

Mr Blair's second mission to Richmond so soon after his late visit is significant of a disposition on their part to wish to get out of the troubles occasioned by their rebellion. I should not be surprised if peace should soon be secured. But of this I am not very sanguine. They are too strong yet to feel like submission. Yet they must see the inevitable consequences of a protracted prosecution of the war. We can conquer them and they know it. They last year relied on the want of harmony in the North and the events of our presidential election for peace. Now they have neither foreign hope nor distraction in our councils to encourage them. We mean war, unyielding and irresistible, and with our means we can make it so & they begin to feel it. . . .

NEAR RICHMOND, VA. — *Feby 2, 1865*

. . . We are all excited over the peace question. The Commissioners have gone through our lines on their way to Washington to see what can be done to settle the awful troubles now distracting and distressing our country. Vice President Stevens, Ast Secy of War Campbell and President of the Senate R. M. T. Hunter are the parties delegated to represent the Confederacy. The selection is probably as good as could be made by them. I am not verry sanguine as to the practical results of this conference. Still it can do no harm.[9]

I do not believe the South are whipped enough yet to compel them to relinquish their idea of Southern independence. Still they must see that we are relatively becoming stronger every day while they in fact are becoming much weaker, and the unanimity with which Mr Lincoln was reelected to the presidency must show them that the people of the loyal states are determined to vindicate the entirety of the Government.

I hope we may have honorable and enduring peace. The sooner the better. But so much ill feeling has grown up between the two sections of the county that I fear that much more blood must be spilled before we can secure we so much desire, peace. I see that the rebel papers are defiant and impudent over the peace proposition, but this indicates nothing as to the policy of the Confederacy for their puffing and blowing may be to keep up courage till negotiations are concluded. . . .

We have a rumor tonight that Charleston is ours. This is not reliable nor is it improbable as Sherman has had time to reach the City before this. The rebel papers of this morning say nothing about it. They experience as much difficulty in getting news from the South as we do in getting our mail matter from the North. Should Gen Sherman operate awhile longer they will find still greater difficulty in hearing from their dear sisters in the far South. . . .[10]

IN THE FIELD NEAR RICHMOND, VA. — *Feby. 5, 1865*

. . . I see by the Northern papers that the whole community has been turned upside down by the rumors of peace by the peace Commissioners sent by the rebel authorities to confer with the old Government. It has been rather amusing to us to see the contradictory statements made as to the fact of Commissioners being sent. We know here last Tuesday that such Commissioners had started on their mission and that they were recd at City Point by our military authorities.[11] And to get during the week papers saying that Mr Blair's mission had all failed because Commissioners had not been appointed to return with him and therefore that there was no prospect of peace looked to us as if all that had been said by the papers on either side had been the most baseless conjecture. Which in fact they were.

These Commissioners did go to <u>Ft Monroe</u> and were met by Secretary Seward and finally by Honest Abe we believe to be true, and that each have returned to their respective capitals. It is said that the President verry unceremoniously left Washington at 10 A.M. of Thursday last Feby 2, with only one person in a special car for Annapolis, & thence to Fort Monroe. . . . I am glad the President has taken it upon himself to see these Commissioners face to face and find from them by his own observation what the wishes of the South are in this matter. Mr Lincoln possesses a rare amount of shrewdness and strong hard sense, perhaps I ought to say sagacity, and having more at stake than any other man living in the solution of this matter would be more likely than any other to act with great circumspection. It would be the crowning glory of his life if he could announce to the Country & world in his next inaugural address that during the first four years of Administration the rebellion had been put down and that the country was restored and again in peace. . . .

But God only knows what is in store for us. I am afraid the rebels are not satisfied on such terms as the Government will accept. We will verry soon know. I should feel verry much provoked if all this passing to & fro between the rebs & Uncle Sam should end in nothing more than idle curiosity on both sides to learn what the other had to say. I can't think our Government so trifling as that. The South might make capital out of it, but it would be damaging to us. I shall hope for the best for the present, praying devoutly that asking Providence will so direct the deliberations of our rulers that justice will be done. We have punished ourselves enough.[12]

NEAR RICHMOND, VA.—*Feby 9, 1865*

Your letter dated Jan 31 but mailed the 3rd Inst. reached me this morning. I have several letters at the same time, one from Gen Curtis written by his wife who is taking care of him at Chesapeake Hospital. He was wounded in the assault on Fort Fisher, loses an eye and is somewhat disfigured in the forehead. He expects to go home in a few days. Fort Fisher will be long remembered as being the place of one of our most splendid victories. . . .[13]

NEAR RICHMOND ON THE JAMES—*Feby 12, 1865*

. . . I thought it quite probable a few days ago that we would be ordered to Wilmington but I now think differently. We learned that Gen Terry was verry anxious to get the First Division with him (his old Division), and supposed that his wish would be gratified, but we learn that Gen Scofield has gone there with a considerable force and assumed command.[14]

Without a transposition of forces we will be needed here, as our line is not any too strong to take care of itself. I expect that our force will take Wilmington before long. Charleston will soon be ours. Then all the seaport towns on the Atlantic Coast will be in our hands and all the railroad lines leading to the Cotton States and the S. W. will be completely severed. Poor

Dixie certainly will know what it is to have Uncle Samuel standing between the extremes of the Confederacy, spreading himself over the whole interior armed with a mighty long sharp stick, too strong to be taken by rebel hands. Bully for <u>Uncle Samuel.</u> . . .

The failure of the Peace Commissioners to secure any substantial advantage for the South has made a great howl among the leading men of the South. A great effort is made to fire the Southern head. Let it burn! A little more of Grant, Sherman, Sheridan and Ft Fisher will put the fire out. . . .

You may expect to see hard fighting and a good *deal* of it before the South are ready to relinquish the idea of a separate government. Their slaves and two thousand millions of their capital of other sorts will be lost to them if they return to the Old Union, much of which will be saved if they should soon secure peace on the basis of independence. The men who have slaves and large amounts of promises to pay of the Confederate Government are the last ditch fellows and will exert a great influence on the people. I am glad the President sympathizes with these last ditch fellows. He means to let them have their way to the last ditch. . . .

NEAR RICHMOND ON THE JAMES—*Feby 16, 1865*

. . . I have been engaged in a trial before a Gen Court Martial as counsel for a young Lieutenant who had the misfortune to accidentally kill one of his men on picket duty by the premature discharge of a Springfield Rifle. The accused is a mere boy 18 1/2 years old, about as much of a child as Eddie, as thoughtless and guileless as he. I found him on the Brigade staff when I was assigned to the command of the 1st Brig. His boyish manner and capacity led me to soon send him back to his Regiment. But when he got into trouble I felt as if he needed help, which I afforded him by way of appearing as his friend before the court. Night before last I sat up till after midnight preparing a written argument for him. I worked with that earnest zeal I formerly manifested when engaged in my profession. . . .

NEAR RICHMOND, VA.—*Feby 19, 1865*

. . . Here it is about as quiet as it in Akron town. Nobody is hurt unless it be the few fellows that catch their death for desertion and other verry aggravated crimes. The 10th Connecticut Vols had a deserter shot Friday and two hung yesterday. Two of the cases were proper subjects for the gallows, the other was one of those doubtful cases that could only be hung for the effect on others. He was a mere boy, and Irish at that, who had been forced into the service by the fraud of those bounty brokers about our metropolitan cities who resort to the most abominable frauds to fill the quota for those verry loyal subject of the draft who can preach patriotism but dare not fight.

I am led to think that some of the Eastern states that have been the most eloquent declaimers against the South for her crimes against the poor African will have as dark a list of crimes to answer for as ever did the South for the infamous wrongs they have resorted to fill their quotas. Nor does this wrong stop with the unfortunate subjects they have thus put in the field. It is outrageously unfair to those states that have fairly filled their quotas with their good men who means to see this rebellion put down.

This Brigade has had hardly a case of desertion to the enemy during the three and a half years it has been in the field, while several of the Eastern Regiments here have had more desertions from a single Regt this winter than we have had since ours came in the field. I know Regiments that cannot be trusted on the picket line without an extra line of men stationed immediately in their rear to watch them with loaded muskets to keep them from desertion. I need not say to you these are not Western troops. I am proud of what the great West has done for the country in this mighty struggle for the nation's existence. . . .[15]

I see by the papers that Portage Township have a much larger quota to raise of the 300,000 more than it was expected. This will make a shaking among the dry bones that for a long time had been slumbering in the assumed security of freedom from the draft. The amendments to the enrollment acts will make many who fancy they have done their whole duty by procuring a worthless substitute contribute in person or by an acceptable substitute who supposed they were free.[16]

I see by the papers I am confirmed Brevet Brig Gen, which reads Bobtail Brigadier General. There is one good thing to be said for the bobtails, they can be trusted in the field. This cannot be said of many of the full Brigs.[17]

IN THE FIELD NEAR RICHMOND, VA.—*Feby 23, 1865*

. . . Yesterday we celebrated the anniversary of Washington's birthday by doing nothing in particular and many things in general. . . . In the evening at the chappel of the 199 Pa Vols we had a formal meeting to give the men an opportunity to celebrate and a few us an opportunity to blow off patriotic steam for the amusement & edification of the aforesaid men. We had a band of music, two chaplains, three Colonels & a <u>Bobtail</u> Brig Gen to do the talking. Your most reticent husband spouted for nearly 3/4 of an hour upon almost a thousand & one subjects—God & liberty, pluck & patriotism, firmness and fight, and no back down were made the superlatives upon which the boys hung their applause.

24th. . . . We are rejoicing over the announcement of the fall of Wilmington, another <u>blessing in disguise</u> for the rebels.[18] We also hear the rumors from the other side of our lines that there was a great bread riot in Richmond Thursday (yesterday) and that the rebs had to bring their canon to put it down. We heard canonading in that direction yesterday and have reason to believe the rumor is true. The poor Johnnies are having a hard time of it with no verry flattering prospects for the future.

A splendid opportunity is now offered for the last ditch fellows to show their grit and fortitude. They can patriotically belch forth grape and cannister upon their women and children who are made frantic by famine and neglect. These are the beauties of secession, the fruits of that glorious independence the South was going to establish as against the despotism of the Old Union.

While we rejoice at the great success we have been lately gaining and encouraged over the severe disasters the Confederacy have been suffering we should not be too exultant, for the war is not ended yet. The rebellion has an immense amount of power left, and can make us a great deal of trouble before the war is ended. The evacuation of Charleston, Columbia & Wilmington are part & parcel of matured plans of the rebels, however doing this no faster than they are compelled to do and not lose too many men and too much materiel. By this course they gain time, waste our energies and prepare a place inland where they mean to make a stand and desperately resist us. In all their operations east of the mountains they have been careful to lose but few men and while they have been losing positions and munitions of war, they have not lost much that will make them weaker in the field.

The heavy ordnance taken at Savannah, Charleston & about Wilmington is only useful for siege purposes. It could never be taken into the field. Men are liberated from the defense of these places that may be used in the army and was it not for the moral effect on the Confederacy and in the eyes of the world, I should say that these victories are not half as damaging to them as people generally suppose. The worst blow they have received in all this is the destruction to their lines of travel and their inability to reach the great sections of their supplies. The loss of their principle railroads and the destruction of their rolling stock is a loss they cannot supply. It may compell them to entirely change the theater of war. Sherman may have to fight before he gets to Virginia.

Col Commager goes home in day or two. He has been mustered out of service to accept appointment in the 184th Reg Ohio Vols, a one year Regt. I am exceedingly sorry to lose him. I am quite sure the Regiment shares my feelings in that matter. . . .[19]

We are having much warmer weather than you have been having in Ohio if the papers are to be credited. The roads are becoming somewhat settled so that we are able to get out of doors again without stilts. . . .

NEAR RICHMOND, VA.—*Mch 1, 1865*

. . . I have been back here over six weeks and must say that they have been the longest six weeks I have experiences for many a day. . . . I dislike to have the time drag so heavily on my hands, but I do not know how to remedy the evil only to take the days as they come and sleep the nights away as they arrive and make the most of what is brought with them. I have this to console me, each day brings the war so much near a close.

Nor am I sure that time is doing quite as much as our fighting to bring about final peace.

I occasionally see in the papers threats that when we have put down this rebellion we will pitch into France and England and pay them off for their neutrality. This is all verry fine talk, but I am not one of those that are in favor of the next war, nor are those noisy patriots in favor of the present war enough to risk their precious selves to it. I might possibly permit them to propose this matter if they only put their shoulders to the wheel until we got out of this trouble. Then if they had exhausted their pugnacity I could say to them I will hold your hats and coats while you pitch in and give old John Bull a few punches in the ribs. . . .

Mch 5th. We are having all the mud we need and a good deal more, but we have got used to it. For three days have had more or less rain (one of the incidents of winter climate in southern Virginia). . . .

I would have been pleased to visit Washington on the morrow and taken part in the ceremony of inaugurating the President for the next four years, but duties in the field and the miserable poor pay given to Officers make it impracticable. . . .

I have not received official notification yet of my confirmation but I am satisfied that it is all right. I almost wish I had stayed at home when I was there, but the war will soon be over. The South are quarreling among themselves and are becoming quite despondent. I am more hopeful than I have been for a long time.

The Brigade has been on review this afternoon (Monday) and made a verry fine appearance. Quite a number of general Officers were in the field. I would write to the children but I will not have time before the mail closes. This mud is drying up so that we can get about a little easier.[20]

NEAR RICHMOND, VA.—*Mch 16, 1865*

. . . [I] am far from home, mud bound on the miserable soil of Old Virginia that for two centuries has been worn out and cursed by African slavery. Would to God the curse had stopped with the soil, but Alas! it did not and does not stop there. It poisoned all who came in its reach. The slave was degraded, the master debased and the political conscience of the country almost destroyed. Outrage and cruel wrong was not satisfied by its visitations in the miserable victims of this infamous crime but the country, the free North, have had to suffer all the horrors of this wicked war to satisfy its demands.

Perhaps we have been enough to blame too for tolerating the evil to demand this great punishment. But then it effects so many who are entirely innocent of its wrongs. Those who denounced it and did all they could to stay the evils are suffering equally with the supporters and apologists for this accursed institution. You may not thank me for an abolition speech, for you get enough of that in the public lectures at home, but you must pardon me. I must write as I think at the time of the writing and I should keep my hand in to enable me to do credit to myself in the future if I should be so fortunate as to get out of the war safe and politically sound. . . .[21]

I understand the Government has increased the pay of Officers in the field a trifle to meet the increased expense of living. We are not certain of this however. . . .[22]

NEAR RICHMOND, VA.—*Mch 17, 1865*

. . . From what I can learn of the feeling at home I am satisfied that many believe the war almost ended. It is well enough for them to feel so while the 300,000 call is being filled, but to be able to successfully resist the means of the rebels to make the war yet a terrible reality they should not feel too confident. A want of preparedness for the future has already protracted the war much longer than it need have existed if the Government had only prepared itself to take advantage of the many successes it has gained during the war.

The South have an array of resource and strength that is not to be trifled with. If our armies are well managed I do think we must be successful in our efforts to bring the war to a speedy close, but we may yet suffer such losses and be so delayed in our efforts that this campaign may not be the decisive one. I nevertheless have strong hope that a few months will see us out of this accused war with an honorable peace as the reward for our many hardships and deprivations.

Grand Reviews have been all the rage for the last fortnight. Friday the Corps was reviewed by Gen Grant and Secy Stanton. Everything passed off finely. A review of an army Corps is a splendid sight. I often wish McClellan's plan of closing out the rebellion by Grand Reviews a splendid scheme, but the ugly Johnnies would make him fight. What awful work it has made for us. . . .

Two old soldiers have just returned to the Regiment, one left us at Morris Island, the other at Alexandria. They were discharged on the expiration of their three years and have reenlisted and come back to the old Regiment. Most all of the old soldiers get uneasy after being at home for a while, and get back into the service. One of these boys says he got a $550 bounty. That is as good as the increased pay now given to Officers in the Army. . . .

March 23, 1865

. . . The mud has dried up, making it quite comfortable getting about so long as we do not go into the woods. We are making arrangements to be in working order as soon as the season becomes enough settled to make it judicious to operate against the ballance of the rebellion.

Three years ago this day I was in my maiden battle (Winchester). When I look back to that event I feel proud of the day and the sturdy men who sent "Stone Wall Jackson" whirling up the valley. Both armies fought differently than now. Officers had no experience, the men were undisciplined and both parties pitched in without system or organization. Our men fought with great vigor and tenacity that day. It was as fair a fight as I have ever seen. How few of those men are now in the army. Of the Officers in the 67th in that battle, only Capt Childs and myself are with the Regt now. I should have perhaps named Dr Westfall, but being a noncombatant I can not strictly say he was in the fight. Maj Bond was promoted to the Colonelcy of the 111th Ohio; Capt Spiegel to the Colonelcy of the 120th O was killed last April in Louisiana; Maj Butler to the Colonelcy of the 184th O; and Lt Col Commager to the Colonelcy of the 184 Ohio, and since Breveted Brig Gen. Quite a number of them have been discharged on resignations and expiration of their terms of service and several of them have fallen victims to the cruelties of the war. The Regiment has never lost any field Officers by battle casualties, Col Commager and myself being the only ones ever wounded. We have had two Officers taken prisoners, one at Ft Wagner, the other on the 13th Oct last in the front of Richmond. Between six hundred and seven hundred battle casualties have occurred to the Regt since it came in the field.

We have say 175 of the men who belonged to the Regt at the date of its organization. All the others have not marched to that bivouac from whence there is no return, many having been discharged on account of disabilities frequently contracted in the service, and others from wounds and a few from the expiration of their terms of service.[23]

Again a few have been transferred to the Invalid Corps, an organization that has grown into existence on account of the great number of disabled soldiers who had no means of earning a livelyhood, but who could do many offices in the army that able bodied men had been detailed to perform, such as orderly duty at hd qrs, clerks at the offices of the many administrative departments and frequently garrison & light guard duty at the posts to the rear of the armies operating in the field. Men do not recover from their wounds rapidly. For months and years they are partially disabled, but eventually will almost entirely recover from their wounds. This Corps is well fitted for a certain class of maimed soldiers, such as have lost a leg or arm, foot or hand & etc. Uncle Samuel is a kind old gentleman even if he has a big load on his shoulders. Think of it, an army of 30,000 cripples & disabilities. But 30,000 is no expression for the number of disabled ones of our mighty army. It will not express the number of the permanently disabled. Our hospitals have their thousands and tens of thousands. It is said that we have had 30,000 prisoners of war die in the hands of the enemy, ten times as many as ought to have died with humane treatment. . . .

Mch 26, 1865

. . . By an order from the War Department, Washington special in my case I will not be retained in the army after the 29th of July next, unless a new tenure of office is created for me at which time I will be mustered out of the service and be permitted to come home. . . .

[I] will finish this by saying that we are soon going to leave our comfortable quarters. I am called to duty and must close.[24]

ON THE LEFT NEAR HATCHER'S RUN—*Mch 30, 1865*

We broke up our old camp on the left of the James Monday evening last and started for this place just at dusk, 27th last, just six months after leaving the Petersburg front, occupying the same camp for that length of time being the longest time the Regiment ever stayed at one place unless we call our stay on Folly Island & Morris one place. . . . The men made themselves verry comfortable in front of Richmond on the north bank of the James, having fine houses & easy times generally with the exception of a few fights it made the most comfortable place the men ever enjoyed in the army.[25]

Soldiers live much better now than they did three years ago, having learned how to take care of themselves. Soldiering is an art as much to be learned by experience as any other. The new men who came in the field now have the experience and example of the old veterans. It is much easier now to become a soldier than when I came into the field. . . .

You will hear of something big before long from the Army of the Potomac unless all Gen Grant's calculations fail. Sherman, Sheridan & Meade are at work. May God speed the right. You may not hear from me for several days for we may cut loose any day. I am quite well. It has been raining hard for last twelve hours but is not cold.

IN THE WOODS BELOW PETERSBURG, VA.—*Apl 3, 1865*

We are after the rebs ten miles below their line of fortification made for the defense of the rebel capitol. On Sunday morning, Apl 2nd, we assaulted and carried their works in splendid style, making the Johnnies scatter in double quick from Hatcher's Run to the Appomattox.[26]

I led in the charge on Fort Gregg near Petersburg, losing over 60 men of the 67th. Col Hunt & myself sought shelter in the ditch of the fort filled with water & mud waist deep where I remained for a half hour with shot & shell flying in a terrible hurricane from all points of the compass. Had it not been for this ditch we would in all probability all been slaughtered or disabled. The ditch was so full water at one end that the men had to swim across.[27]

When reinforcements came up the boys lifted me up the sides of the ditch or scarp so that I crawled into the fort, perhaps the first man of the Regt. We are doing finely, are marching into Dixie as we did in the spring of 1862 in the Valley. It seems good to get from behind these dirty earth works and roam over pleasant fields again. The war will soon end. We have used up 20,000 rebels in the last two weeks with small loss to our army. Many will now desert. I cannot see how Lee can keep together an army large enough to long resist our armies.[28]

20 Miles below Petersburg, Va Apl 3rd afternoon. I am all right, passed through the fights of Sunday safely. The Regt lost heavily, all being done in

a few minutes. I wrote you this morning but having an opportunity to send this I take [another] opportunity. The enemy are on the biggest kind of a run for further South. Of course all of you have heard the news. I was in the charge on Fort Gregg before Petersburg.[29]

FARMVILLE, VA. —*Friday, Apl 7, 1865*

We have marched here and driven the rebs at a great rate. We occasionally skirmish with them, say 2 or 3 times per day. We are going to be home in sixty days. Have plenty coffee, chicken and hard tack. I am well.[30]

APPOMATTOX COURT HOUSE, VA. —*Apl 10th, 1865*

I suppose you have learned before this of our fights and marches that have led us into the heart of the Confederacy and that had enabled us to annihilate the army of Gen Lee in Virginia. Yesterday the 9th of April we so completely surrounded his army that he sent in a flag of truce asking for cessation of hostilities long enough to agree upon terms of capitulation.

We were in hot pursuit of the enemy when the flag came in. On the news being announced our army sent up such shouts us we have not been heard since the war began. The army looks upon this as being the end of the war. I expect no more fighting, for if their best army could do nothing against us what can the few fragments do against our combined armies?

I see by the papers of the 4th Inst. (the latest we have) that the whole North in a blaze of glory over the taking of the works about Richmond and Petersburg. Well they may for the evacuation of Richmond and Petersburg opened the way for an almost unmolested march of our army towards Lynchburgh. Since the 3rd Inst. we have had a hasty chase with the Johnnies for that place. Saturday we marched thirty miles. Yesterday morning we struck their advance and stopped them.

Thursday the 6th we fought them but they had the start of us and got away. I have been remarkably fortunate. I was struck yesterday by fragment of rebel shell, but received no hurt from it. I have felt perfectly confident that I would get through all right. As matters now look I think I am through the woods. Won't the day of assured peace be one of unspeakable glory and happiness? I hope soon to be able to write you that our political troubles are happily adjusted. Sixty days will see the major part of the men at home. We have passed the last ditch, the enemy gave up whipped. I am well.

APPOMATTOX COURT HOUSE, VA. —*Apl 13, 1865*

Your last letter that reached me was dated the 26th of March last. I think I got a Cleveland Herald of the 28th, the last news of anything I have had from home or the West.

Saturday evening, Apl 1st, we broke up camp and started for the left and massed to the front of our works within rifle range of the enemies position, laying on our arms for the night, ready for an assault on their works at 4 A.M. of the 2nd. During the night heavy musketry fire & some canonading was heard to our right. A little after day night we learned that the 6th Corps had pierced the enemies lines about five miles from Petersburg, when we were ordered to march to their support. We marched at a distance of eight miles in rapid style, the men flinging away knapsacks, overcoats, blankets & frequently haversacks to enable them to get along more rapidly. By 8 A.M. we reached the enemy and soon charged after them, driving them at a furious rate within their works about Petersburg. We charged on Fort Gregg, taking it after a terrible slaughter. It was an earth work surrounded by a deep ditch and partially filled with water, and garrisoned by 350 picked men who were to hold the fort to the last extremity. How well they did this is told by the fact that of this number fifty five were killed in the assault.[31]

I saved myself by taking to the ditch, middle deep in mud & water where I remained some half an hour before reinforcements came up and relieved us from our not verry pleasant position. I might also say not a verry safe one either, for shot and shell and projectiles from small arms were flying about & over the ditch from both the assaulting and assaulted parties. Next to Ft Wagner it was the most trying place I ever was in while in the field. I think the old barge was in the tightest fix. After taking the fort we lay in front of Petersburg till the next morning when we started for this place. I was well satisfied as soon as the fort was taken that Petersburg would be evacuated during the night and perhaps Richmond, both of which events did take place.

On the ensuing evening, Thursday, Apl 6th, we ran against Gen Lee's columns near Highbridge, skirmished in the evening till after dark. In the morning following, the rebs were all gone. Sheridan had been into them the day before taking some 40 pieces of artillery, 12,000 prisoners & a dozen Generals. Friday morning had a fight on the banks of the Appomattox not far from Farmville, which lasted but a few minutes.[32]

Saturday we marched from Farmville to near Appomattox Station 30 miles off. The men were encouraged to make this as they learned that Sheridan had captured four rebel supply trains on the railroad & that we were needed to support them against the enemy. At 11 P.M. we bivouacked in a wood to be up at 3 A.M. and on the march again. This we did and by 7 A.M. were in advance of the rebel army and soon had their only road for escape blocked up by the confounded Yankees. Then a bitter fight was opened in which our artillery & cavalry stampeded at a wild pace. Our infantry opportunity took their places and soon the Johnnies were whirling on the back-track when we again took up the advance, but before going a mile a suspension of hostilities was ordered because of negotiations going on the overture of Gen Lee to surrender up his army. The moment the men got the news, the wildest enthusiasm seized them, and cheers & yells and guns mixed with each other to see who could make the most jubilant noise.[33]

The men on both sides look upon the war as over. The entire army of "Northern Virginia" with all its materiel and the army of the Confederacy with the Generalissimo of the *broken* concern are all in our hands. This with the crushing losses they have sustained during the last year must from necessity end the rebellion. Their supplies are gone, munitions of war captured, their soldiers thoroughly demoralized, the inhabitants discouraged with an utter prostration of business and no public treasure. We may materially look for no more fighting. I do not see how they can organize a new army. As for guerilla warfare they dare not resort to that, for our armies can devastate any section of the country where they have the temerity to try this dangerous experiment.[34]

I suppose you have been quite anxious about me, but I have had no opportunity to send letters since we left on the 1st of Apl only as I got a line on the express sent by some of the newspaper correspondents. I have two letters in my pocket I wrote for you but have had no opportunity for sending them. I am quite well and bear the wear and tear of campaign life better than I expected. . . .[35]

We have been resting since Sunday and guarding the Johnnies. I should say that we have taken 35,000 prisoners of war, 200 pieces field artillery and three hundred wagons, four trains of cars and lots of pigs, chickens and other contraband truck. If my speculations are correct about the end of the war & I do not see how they can be incorrect you and I will always be proud that we have contributed so much to the restoration & support of this good Government of ours. May all wisdom come from the follies & disasters of the past. . . .

"A Black Woman Had Rights"

RECONSTRUCTION IN VIRGINIA

APRIL 16, 1865 – DECEMBER 1, 1865

[Voris had an opportunity to help define the meaning and consequences of victory as the first stage of reconstruction unfolded in Virginia. From May 4, 1865, to three weeks before his discharge on December 15, 1865, he served as commander of a military subdistrict consisting of Albemarle, Fluvanna, Goochland, and Louisa Counties plus parts of Hanover and Henrico. Despite a number of restraints, both local and national, Voris formulated a program to deal with the war's heritage that he advocated for the remainder of his life.

APPOMATTOX COURTHOUSE—*Apl 16, 1865*

I had the good fortune to get from you two letters today, the one with the pictures and other of the 2nd Inst. This is the first mail we have had for more than two weeks. And what weeks they have been, painful marches and awful battles have kept us on the highest point of human endurance and danger and anxiety.[1]

We are this morning startled with the intelligence that Mr Lincoln was assassinated Friday evening last at a theater in Washington & that Secy Seward & son were dangerously wounded. This is bad business for us just now and may complicate our settlement with the rebels.

I must think it was done by some half crazzed zealot who is seeking immortality by some grave act of infamy because of want of ability or character to write himself a name in history by the merit of his conduct. Desperate indeed is the cause that can only be supported by the dark deeds of the assassin. This is the legitimate fruits of the teachings of the heroic chivalrous Southern slave holding society. The beauty of their system consists in the exercise of the higher assumptions of crime under the garb of right. I am well. We go towards home in the morning. I will write as soon again as I can.

BURKEVILLE, VA.—*Apl 19, 1865*

We are approaching civilization again. Today at noon we reached this place with a mail waiting for us. I got your letter of the 8th and have seen the papers of the 17th NY Herald with full particulars of the assassination of Pres Lincoln. We also got the news of the fall of Mobile, a result that was accomplished on the day Gen Lee surrendered his army. When we go from here I do not know nor when. . . .[2]

This has been the pleasantest campaign I ever made, easier and more significant of results. The men feel as if their fighting was done & that a little more will close their labors in the army. I really hope so. I fear the death of Lincoln will complicate matters, but that the rebellion has gone under I do not at all doubt. . . .

BURKEVILLE, VA.—*April 20, 1865*

We have been resting here for the last twenty four hours and will stay overnight, but how much longer I cannot tell. When we left Appomattox Courthouse we expected to march to Richmond before stopping for any length of time, but we now hear of rumors of changes of organization and our recent signal successes have thrown us into such chaos that nothing pertaining to the army is certain. The New York papers indicate that Gen Johnston has surrendered his army on the same terms as Lee did the Army of Northern Virginia. We know that Mobile is taken and that there is no army of much significance in existence against the government anywhere east of the Mississippi except Johnston's and Gen Sherman is more than sufficient to smash that army into fragments.[3] The war is over, though the army may not be disbanded for some time yet. . . .

I do not think I would experience much trouble in getting out now, but having stayed so long and expecting the army to be soon disbanded for want of its further services I prefer to go home with the boys. If I stay till the close of the war I will be entitled to three months extra pay. . . . This being the only bounty I can get for my services, I would like to get it. I grant that this is not much, but I can put the $285 in something that you and the babies & myself will always be pleased with. Dr Westfall goes to City Point in the morning with the sick and disabled men of the Corps to be gone a few days. I would like to go along and see the fruits of the many toilsome & terrible days & nights the army has suffered before Richmond & Petersburg.

This spring has been perfectly delightful compared with the awful realities of last year's operations of the Army of the James. I might also say the Army of the Potomac. We have had so many verry hard marches, but the men were inspired with the confidence that their efforts were of irresistible effect upon the crumbling and fleeing army of Gen Lee, and cheerfully did they march thirty miles one day to head off the old rebel captain. They now are proud of their blistered feet and tired limbs. We get bacon, corn-meal, chickens, turkeys, lamb, pig, milk occasionally and lots of delicacies such as camp behind breast works does not furnish. . . .[4]

I am writing this on a cracker box in a little shelter tent, where I sleep all alone with a little young rabbit that stayed with me last night. It awakened me by licking my eyes last night. . . .

By the way I have not seen the Beacon for four weeks, but have had almost every number of the Cleveland Herald. I got half a dozzen yesterday. My address was published in the Herald of the 8th Inst. Mr B gave it quite a flattering notice. . . .[5]

RICHMOND, VA.—*Apl 26, 1865*

I am now writing you from the fair City of Richmond, the late Confederate capital which to us for the last three & a half years has been a City of "magnificent distances," if the miles marched to gain it are to all determine its distance. It is indeed a beautiful City, surrounded by a beautiful country, its location and immediate surroundings with what has been done for it by art & capital has made it one of the finest cities I ever visited. It is a seven hill City & has the advantage of the James River to give vivacity and picturesqueness to its scenery.[6]

. . . The rebels as they evacuated the City burned the richest portion of the place, destroying the most parts of eleven blocks. . . . They also destroyed the three bridges across the James leading from the City to Manchester. All the property destroyed in and about Richmond was done from the most foolish and unphilosophic idea possible, for they destroyed nothing that could be of present use to us against them but what might have been of good to the country and to Va, particularly after the war in aid of the development of her resources after the return of peace. It does appear as if the leaders of the rebellion had lost their reason simultaneously with the fall of their baseless fabric, an independent government. I never saw so poor a people as live here. Business prostration has exhausted everything but their fixtures and furniture.

There is more aristocratic beggary here today than can be found in any other city on the globe. I saw a rich poor old woman today trying to sell a few silver wine goblets at the Provost General's office. She had not courage to ask for a long time, & when she did she burst out in tears, pride & poverty having a terrible struggle in her bosom when want came to the rescue and forced poor pride to the wall. . . .[7]

Apl. 27. Today is the anniversary of my birthday. I am fast becoming an old man. 38 years have consumed the childhood, youth and the elasticity of much of my manhood. I frequently ask myself am I enough wiser & better to take pride in the years that the revolutions of time add to my earthly existence. I dare not say that I am satisfied with myself. To be sure I feel complacently enough after a good, hearty dinner and I am ready to swear to the world and all that therein is bully, but my digestion is so rapid that I soon begin to feel regret that I was not a bigger man. This is the fifth anniversary that I have been from home. I hope to be at home the next. . . .

I hope to be assigned to such duty now fighting is over as will take me away from a command. I may come home soon. Everything and everybody public & private are afloat. The country is in a transformation state. All will be soon settled. Then there will be no use for me and a large part of the army in the field.

RICHMOND, VA.—*May 4, 1865*

I am quite tired tonight having been busy all day long doing not much but preparing to do. My old Regt, the 67th, started for Beaver Dam some *40* miles north of this City. I have had a district assigned to my command consisting of the west half of Henrico & Hanover counties and the whole of Goochland, Louisa, Fluvanna and Albemarle counties. My duties are of an infinite and multitudinous sort that embrace the promotion of order, protection of darkies, development of loyalty, etc, etc, etc, & everything else. I start for the interior in the morning. . . .[8]

BEAVER DAM, VA.—*May 7, 1865*

. . . I am occupying a house for an office and have a soft bed to sleep in, but I am compelled to enjoy it all alone unless I beg or borrow somebody else's wife or other woman for a bed fellow, a thing that could not be tolerated even in loose Old Virginia unless that woman was of the "visible admixture" sort, an alternative I have never elected to take. I find many persons here have been of a different opinion, whom for the honor of the ladies I will call men, for I see every shades from the jet black to the fairest white. This blending . . . has been made so perfect that for the life of me I frequently saw groups in Richmond that I could not tell where the African ended or the lordly white man began. Nor was this the work of the nasty abolitionists.

I stayed with Col. E. Fonntaine, Prest of the Va Central R. R., night before last in the country forty miles from Richmond with a guard of a corporal and just three men.[9] I felt just as secure as if I had taken lodgings in the City of New York and slept quite as soundly. The 67th came up the next day. I have a few cavalry at my disposal, and a whole people anxious to be relieved from the vexations of a state of war. . . .[10]

I am doing all sorts of duty, being sort of a military governor, police officer and judge, being to this people what Moses was to the children of Israel. I of course mean the other Israel, not your paternal Israel [Allyn]. I expect to go up to the mountains in a few days as far as Charlottesville, the county seat of Albemarle County. The railroad will soon be opened to that point. There is no danger now in going there and I shall take sufficient force to take care of my precious body. I suppose you are making some arrangements to come down and see me. I want you to do this but you may be disappointed for I may be so much of a peripatetic concern that you cannot find me. . . .

Monday afternoon. I have been awfully busy all day making Union men and have no time to finish this letter.

LOUISA C. H., VA.—*May 14, 1865*

. . . I am living in sight of the mountains sixty five miles from Richmond in a beautiful but poor country. Tobacco culture, slave labor and the war have made what was once one of the finest countries in the world a verry poor country indeed. I think I can see here developed one of the great causes of the fearful rebellion we have just put down. The thriftless manner of developing the natural resources of the South with the depressing influences slavery had upon the white population permitted the old settled part of the South to retrograde as soon as the virgin soils were exhausted, while at the North the stimulant of free labor and free institutions constantly increased the North in all the elements that give strength, wealth and influence to a people. The contrast became so apparent to the South and they not reasoning correctly could not or would not attribute the causes to themselves & their organization of society, attributed their want of success to our extraordinary growth & prosperity to the selfish unfair discriminations of the Federal Government against them & and in favor of the North, when in fact just the opposite policy had been true.

To escape from a government that they supposed was used to do so much for the free states and so little for them was made a high political virtue, and many, verry many believed they had good reasons for agitating discontents and urging revolution. They should have known that political causes had verry little to do with their or our national condition. Domestic institutions and personal enterprise are the grand elements that produced the diverse results for the two sections of the country.

I thank God for myself and my children that I was not a slave owner. The burdens & disabilities it throws on the owner in Virginia never compensated the community for the costs even when the individual owner made it profitable, which cases are rare, and in all cases the want of thrift, spirit, character & intelligence of so large an element in society spread a blight over the whole community. Honest thinking persons tell me that they no doubt that Virginia is better without slavery than with it, but all feel as if at this time it is costing an insupportable burden on them. All are poor here.

Persons with pockets full of what was used for money one year ago are absolutely penniless. Those who have their hundreds of thousands of Confederate government bonds are as poor as if they had the same weight in paper rags only, and the owners of real estate have few horses, no other kinds of farm stock, hardly grain enough to keep themselves and their negroes from starvation till after harvest, and everything in the nature of home or domestic supplies are so battered and worn under the pressure of four years of war and a searching blockade that all are compelled to begin almost anew. The colored people in many instances are as well off as the whites with the advantage of knowing how to work. . . .

I do not expect that we will be mustered out of service for some weeks. I think the 24th Corps is fixed for the present, and will not be liberated till a new organization is perfected or Virginia is fixed in her political relations. I have written you that you and Eddie might be invited to see me at Richmond. I do not go there often now, am living in the country. I go to Charlottesville in the morning. I think you can come here and stay a while if you want. You must provide yourself with enough money to carry you both ways and support you while here, for I do not know when I shall be able to get any money again from the government as the troops being mustered out are taking all the funds of the government, and no pay masters are visiting the army now. You should provide yourself with a riding dress as you may be compelled to join the cavalry arm of the service. Edwin can march with the infantry. I will know more about it by the middle of the week. . . .

LOUISA C. H., VA.—*May 21, 1865*

I have had a verry busy week in my little kingdom. I have been up to the mountains staying three days at Charlottesville, one of the finest towns in Virginia, the county seat of Albermarle, the seat of Virginia University and the *former* home of Thomas Jefferson, third President of the United States.

It is beautifully located almost among the mountains, the Blue Ridge lying to the west and the spurs thereof rising from the plains of Eastern Va on all sides of it. The Blue Ridge makes a single chain of mountains of many hundred miles in length of rare regularity and beauty running parallel with the sea coast and about a hundred and fifty miles from it, rising beautifully from the plain lands next [to] the Atlantic. To the front of the Ridge next [to] the Atlantic coast regularly formed spurs or isolated mountains rise from the plain lands breaking the abruptness of the scenery upon the elevation of a mountain chain from almost a level country. I have never seen more beautiful scenery than presented in Eastern Virginia, except in the valley of Virginia of which I have years ago written you.

Tuesday evening I rode up to "Monticello" the former residence of President Jefferson, which is situated above the Rivanna River on the pinnacle of a small mountain that gradually slopes off in every direction, giving to the old mansion a beautiful view of the mountain scenery on one side, the plain lands toward the ocean on the other. Time, neglect and this terribly cruel rebellion have made sad havoc with this once magnificent home of the father of the Democratic party. The estate was sequestered and sold by the old and damned Confederate government. Whatever was left of the personal effects of Thos Jefferson was at the commencement of this war was sold under the greedy hammer of the auctioneer to furnish funds for the prosecution of the late wicked rebellion and against the institutions this great man had so long and faithfully labored to establish. The verry bed upon which he died and which till the commencement of the war had remained as he left it went into the rebellion fund. The estate at that time belonged to the United States by virtue of a will from the late Commodore Levy.[11]

The mansion house is much dilapidated. In its structure and arrangement it shows the peculiarities of Mr Jefferson's mind. He not his wife made the plans. The interior arrangements are plain, odd and anything but modern. . . .

Monday morning. I made a visit to the country yesterday afternoon, took tea and had a pleasant visit with a Union family. The head of the family is an elderly young lady who loses over a hundred negroes by the close of the war. She has been a decided outspoken Union lady since the commencement of the war, been threatened with caste thunder, confiscation, mobs and all sort of terror restored to by the cruel authors of the rebellion. . . .

LOUISA C. H., VA.—*May 28, 1865*

. . . I find the people here much disposed to peace and verry anxious to convince us that they want no more of the evil consequences resulting from internal quarrels. The whole country is satisfied with the war lessons, and are anxious to cultivate good relations for the future.

I have *just* made a short visit into the country, some 7 miles off to a Mrs James Baker's. Had a good dinner and pleasant visit. The slavery question was the all absorbing topic of conversation. I told them I talked it every day and every hour in the day till I got heartily sick of it & hoped they would talk of something else, but for the life of me I could not get out of hearing of the <u>"inevitable nigger."</u> Former slave owners feel sore at the loss of their slaves, money, horses, crops and the blessed Confederacy. All have gone. These losses have made them poor indeed and poor prospects for the coming year. . . .

LOUISA C. H., VA.—*May 30, 1865*

. . . Kirby Smith having surrendered his army we may say the war is entirely over. Thank God for peace. I see in the terrible fruits of this war that peace is going to be appreciated and preserved with jealous care by the American people. God grant that the peace may be enduring & fruitful of good to this once so bountifully blessed people.[12]

I am trying to do good here. I am a sort of middle man between the former poor, helpless slave and his owner, to see that his rights are respected and when it is needed to compel respect for his rights. I do not allow these chivalrous lords of creation to scourge women anymore in my district. If by my efforts I can leave these poor creatures in a better condition for my having been among them, I shall feel bountifully paid for the sacrifices I am making in their behalf and count the pains in feeling I am compelled to undergo as well borne.

I suppose I might make more of fame for myself if I courted the favor of the powerful lords who have so long compelled the country to recognize *and uphold* the stupendous wrongs of slavery instead of holding out a helping hand to the poor man who has no power to help me nor hurt me. But their good is more to me than *the flattery or* hate of their former masters.

Today a poor old woman of 60 years came 12 miles to tell me of a cruel beating she had received from a <u>strong man</u> and was stripped for another flogging because she said she would see the General. In the presence of several F.F.V. I kindly heard her tale of wrong & outrage, & told Capt Childs to make a memorandum of the matter & send for the creature who had maltreated her. An old gentleman who had not lived long enough in a <u>free America</u> to know that a black woman had rights & that she would be protected against the white brute that would scourge her volunteered to tell me how respectable a man her brutal owner was. I verry plainly told him that I would call on him when I needed his services, and that I wanted them to understand that the rights of humanity would be recognized in my command and that I had just as high a regard for the rights of a poor colored woman as of any *other* person in Virginia, and that I would use my power to compell others to respect their rights. When they act meanly I mean they shall know that the tables are turned, that right not might rules. I try to be kind & just. I am well.

June 4, 1865

. . . I am about to build a few school houses for the contrabands & hope to get a few nice school "Marms." Won't I have a nice time twixt the whites, blacks and the school "Marms." Now dear puss don't get jealous of me on that account, for think how much of a philanthropist I will be if I lay the foundation for the education of the little contrabands in this part of old Virginia. . . .

Only eight weeks from yesterday and I will be permitted to go to my Ohio home. . . . I hope to be able to do some good in these eight weeks to a poor class of heretofore abused people. I had rather have the satisfaction of having done them permanent & substantial good than have the honor of fighting a battle, and the good I do for them no one can attribute to selfish motives for they have nothing to bestow on me save their poor gratitude for anything I may do for them. . . .

LOUISA, C. H., VA.—*June 15, 1865*

. . . The 67th is in camp near Richmond. I called on them a hour yesterday, when to my horror I was called out to make a speech in reply to a few verry happy remarks from Surgeon Westfall, at the conclusion of whose remarks a magnificent sword, sash and belt was stuck at me as a testimonial of the approval of the men and Officers of my old command. These articles were enclosed in a splendid case beautifully inlaid with appropriate military devices. $500 worth of trappings only for show were thus lavished on your dear soldier husband. . . .

The 67th is one of the verry best Regiments the world ever saw. I have always tried to secure its honor and I believe the command appreciates my efforts. I have always tried to honor them & I believe they have tried to honor me. . . .

LOUISA C. H., VA.—*June 18, 1865*

. . . The new relation between the once master & his slaves occasions much perplexity. I must confess to verry vague ideas as to what ought to be done. Under our form of government and looking at the matter as strictly a political question, not as a matter of political necessity, efforts made by the military authorities to regulate the domestic relations and internal affairs of a community must be looked on as being an assumption and should not be resorted to only as a matter of necessity. The General Government never has regulated the details of social life & obligation. These have been left to the states as the special subjects for their controll and to the common law. The relations of husband & wife, parent & child, master and servant have been defined by the states without let or hindrance on the part of the General Government.

I have urged upon the property owners the humanity and necessity of devising some systematic plan by which the labor of the freed population may be advantageously used, but system is almost entirely out of the question. Everybody and every economic relation are in a state of shocking chaos. The want of money, subsistence and facilities for working the land is exceeding embarrassing to the immediate application of productive labor.[13]

The price to be fixed for the labor of the freed man is a difficult matter to fix. The landholders will not develop their agricultural resources unless they can secure labor on advantageous terms. The freed man will not unless he can be satisfied that he is securing an equivalent for his labor. If this matter of price be left to the caprice of each employer great variations will exist & in many instances gross injustice be done to the laborer. If association of effort is secure there is great danger of combinations of capital against labor, leaving the relation of master & slave only changed in name. If the General Government assumes to make a tariff of prices for labor, the objection will be fairly made that it is interfering arbitrarily with the laws of trade and the domestic relations of the citizens of the state, the practical bearing of which interference would unquestionably bring disappointment and dissatisfaction. I am well as the basic question here discussed demonstrates, and moderately inclined to do something as this dissertation on the negro question indicates. . . .[14]

HD QRS MILL SUB DIST SOUTH—*June 20, 1865*

. . . The Secesh women here think they spite me terribly by refusing to receive us into their society. At my boarding house the other day two ladies were sitting on the stoop when I rode by with my staff in full dress. I rode so near to them that they thought it best to go in, but I saw their inquisitive eyes peeping through the lattice blinds. . . .

LOUISA C. H., VA.—*July 2, 1865*

. . . The 67th Regt O. V. reported back to me the past week with largely diminished numbers. All hands appeared glad indeed to get away from Richmond. Whether they are pleased with my command or not is indicated by a petition signed by every Officer of the Regiment, asking of me that I should use my efforts to get them back under my command, which I succeeded in doing. . . .[15]

We understand arrangements are making to make the 4th one of the grandest hollidays the world has ever witnessed. Well may it be so. The most cruel and destructive of wars is just over, the best Government in the world just established and twenty millions of free men rejoicing over a peace that must be permanent and overflowing with blessings. . . .

LOUISA C. H. VA,—*July 16, 1865*

. . . I am getting along as pleasantly as could be expected in my command. Have to interfere frequently to save the poor darkies and occasionally put some poor offender through for petty offenses, but on the whole have but little trouble. . . .

LOUISA C. H., VA.—*July 20, 1865*

. . . I was at Richmond day before yesterday. Gen Terry is anxious to have me stay in my place for the present. I told him I had no desire to remain in the Army and would not make an application to be an army officer in any event, but that I would not object to staying for the time being if I did not have to muster again. I should not object to staying in my present capacity till the end of the year. I shall of course know whether I am to remain in the army till the winter verry soon. I suppose you would not object to my staying a few months longer now that the dangers and hardships of the field are passed through.[16]

I am sorry you write me such savage letters about hanging traitors. I am quite sure you would not do so if you had your own way. . . . While I would hang a verry few of the rebels, those who were most instrumental in precipitating the calamities of revolution on our nation, I would extend generous clemency to the great body of the people of the revolting states. I had rather heal up the wounds made by this cruel rebellion than irritate the festering sores *which* will soon enough kill treason without hanging all of them on the sour apple tree. . . .

LOUISA C. H., VA.—*July 31, 1865*

. . . I can take care of you and Eddie verry well here and I shall be so happy to do it. If you see Mr Chamberlin say to him I will write him soon. You may say to him I have been recommended for promotion as Brvt Maj

Gen, and pressingly urged to stay as Military Gov of my Dist & this because my Dist makes less difficulty at Hd Qrs than any other in the State.[17]

LOUISA C. H., VA.—*Aug 5, 1865*

. . . I am fearful from what you write that your health is not good. I do not want you to risk your health, but if you are careful I do not think a trip here will be injurious. You may rest at Washington and at any other place you may feel as if rest would do you good. You may come prepared to stay a long time. I can't say how long for I do not know how long I may stay in the army, but you can go here to New England and that way home if you get tired of staying with me. I sent Capt Childs up to Charlottesville on Monday to see if he can find a good place there for us to live. . . . I probably will not write again unless I get a letter from you saying that you cannot start the 15th.[18]

RICHMOND—*Oct 30, 1865*

I sent my sword and case home this morning by "Adams Express." It will probably reach home by the last of the week. I did not pay the charges as they did not know how to rate them at Charlottesville. I am better than when you left. I speak to the colored ministers at Hanover C. H. tomorrow. . . .

CHARLOTTESVILLE—*Nov 26, 1865*

You will be pleased to learn that the 67th Ohio Vols is ordered to be mustered out of the service. We start for City Point Wednesday next to be mustered out, from thence we will proceed to Ohio to be disbanded. This will consume say two weeks time, perhaps more. . . .

CITY POINT, VA.—*Dec. 1, 1865*

We reached this place preparatory to be mustered out of the service last night. All hands are actively engaged in making out proper papers to make that desirable end as soon as possible. I hope we will be able to start for Ohio by the middle of next week. This is Friday eve. If so we will be paid off and get home the next week after. . . .[19]

I am highly gratified at the expression of feeling the citizens of my district manifested on my leaving. The whites and colored people gave me the kindest expression of regard. I feel as if I had done the colored people good without having done any injustice to the whites. The Chronicle gave me a verry favorable notice. . . . I am well. Tell Pet papa is coming home now for sure unless accidents occur.[20]

Notes and Sources

INTRODUCTION—*"I Cannot Bear to Think of a Dismembered Country"*

1. Alvin Coe Voris to Lydia Allyn Voris, June 22, 1862, Allan Johnson Collection, Akron, Ohio.

2. Voris Family History, 1890, Johnson Collection; William Henry Perrin, *History of Summit County: With an Outline Sketch of Ohio* (Chicago: Baskin & Battey, 1881), 786.

3. Perrin, *History of Summit County*, 786–87. Voris's parents left Akron in 1857 and resettled in Mattoon, Ill. Julia Coe Voris died from undisclosed causes on Aug. 4, 1858. Peter Voris remarried four years later, started a new family, and died Aug. 8, 1880 (Mattoon County Historical Society, Mattoon, Ill.).

4. Oscar Eugene Olin, *Akron and Environs: Historical, Biographical, Genealogical* (Chicago: Lewis, 1917), 521. Frances Dana Gage used the pen name of "Aunt Fanny" for her advice column in the *Ohio Cultivator*. She presided over the 1851 women's rights convention in Akron when Sojourner Truth made her declaration against slavery and for women's rights. Timothy L. Smith, *Revivalism and Social Reform: American Protestantism on the Eve of the Civil War* (New York: Harper & Row, 1957), evaluates the religious milieu that influenced Voris.

5. Perrin, *History of Summit County*, 787; Francis R. Aumann, "The Development of the Judicial System of Ohio," *Ohio Archeological and Historical Quarterly* 41 (1932): 216. In December 1838, Bierce, a brigadier general of Ohio militia, led a group of volunteers in an abortive attempt to liberate Canada from British control. Barely escaping capture, Bierce returned to Akron as a hero. During the Civil War, he served on the Ohio adjutant general's staff. See Karl H. Grismer, *Akron and Summit County* (Akron, Ohio: Summit County Historical Society, 1952), 664; George W. Knepper, *Summit's Glory: Sketches of Buchtel College and the University of Akron* (Akron, Ohio: University of Akron Press, 1990), 66–67.

6. Voris to Samuel Voris, July 21, 1865, Johnson Collection; Oscar Olin et al., *A Centennial History of Akron, 1825–1925* (Akron, Ohio: Beacon Journal, 1925), 14–92.

7. "Marriage Licenses, 1840–1865," 2:V-7, Summit County Archives, Akron, Ohio; Samuel A. Lane, *Fifty Years and Over of Akron and Summit County* (Akron, Ohio: Beacon Job Department, 1892), 712; Ruth A. Clinefelter, "Calendar of the Israel Allyn Papers" (master's thesis, University of Akron, 1953).

8. Lane, *Fifty Years*, 583; J. G. Adel, *Official Report of the Proceedings and Debates of the Third Constitutional Convention of Ohio* (Cleveland: W. S. Robinson, 1874) (hereafter cited as *Proceedings*), 1:824, 2(pt. 2):1816, 1821.

9. Voris to Lydia Voris, May 12, 1865, Johnson Collection; *Summit County Beacon* (hereafter cited as *Beacon*), Oct. 18, 1860. See Eric Foner, *Free Soil, Free Labor, Free*

Men: The Ideology of the Republican Party before the Civil War (New York: Oxford University Press, 1970), for these principles.

10. *Journal of the House of Representatives of the State of Ohio for the Second Session of the Fifty-Fourth General Assembly, Commencing on Monday, January 4, 1861, Being the Fifth Legislature under the New Constitution* (Columbus, Ohio: Richard Nevin, 1861), 47:14–15, 18, 22–23, 34, 47, 52–53, 55, 81, 124, 134, 217–19, 224–30, 487–88.

11. *Beacon,* Sept. 19, 1883, July 29, 1904.

12. Voris to Lydia Voris, Jan. 5, 9, 13, 30, Feb. 3, 17, 20, Mar. 11, 16, 20, 1861, Johnson Collection.

13. Ibid., Feb. 23, 1861; *House Journal,* 47:77–78, 118–19, 121–23, 216, 493–94, 497–503, 509–12, 526–27, 530, 539–40, 634, 637; Eric J. Cardinal, "The Ohio Democracy and the Crisis of Disunion, 1860–1861," *Ohio History* 86 (winter 1977): 19–40.

14. Voris to Lydia Voris, Apr. 10, 14, 16, 18, 24, May 5, 1861, Feb. 1, Oct. 24, Nov. 13, 1863, Sept. 22, 1864, July 2, 1865, Johnson Collection.

15. Ibid., Mar. 27, May 1, 1862, June 7, Sept. 2, 1863, Feb. 10, Apr. 8, May 28, Nov. 10, 1864. Only one letter from Lydia has survived in which she explained her position. On October 11, 1861, she wrote an aunt in Connecticut that "my husband has joined the army." Admitting that she initially opposed his decision and would miss his absence "more than I can bear," Lydia nonetheless now supported Alvin's determination to defend "this Government which our forefathers fought and died to establish." Lydia A. Voris to unidentified woman, Oct. 10, 1861, Dibbert Collection, Akron, Ohio.

16. Voris to Adj. Gen. Catharinus P. Buckingham, Aug. 19, Sept. 10, 16, 23, 24, 1861, "Correspondence to the Governor and Adjutant General of Ohio, 1861–1866," Ohio Historical Society, Columbus, Ohio (hereafter cited as OAGC); *Cleveland Morning Leader* (hereafter cited as *Leader*), Nov. 4, Dec. 2, 1861, Jan. 3, 4, 11, 10, 1862; Lane, *Fifty Years,* 358; *The Biographical Cyclopedia and Portrait Gallery, with an Historical Sketch of the State of Ohio,* 6 vols. (Cincinnati: Western Biographical, 1883), 1:257.

17. Voris to William Dennison, Jr., Sept. 16, Voris to Buckingham, Sept. 26, Oct. 21, 23, Nov. 2, 6, 18, 20, Dec. 31, 1861, Feb. 4, 1862, Henry S. Commager to Buckingham, Dec. 4, Morrison R. Waite to Buckingham, Dec. 24, 1861, OAGC.

18. *Daily Toledo Blade* (hereafter cited as *Blade*), Aug. 30, Sept. 29, Oct. 19, Dec. 5, 18, 23, 26, 1861; Voris to Dennison, Nov. 29, 1861, Ohio Governor Papers, OHS; Voris to Buckingham, Nov. 30, Dec. 13, 15, Burstenbinder to Dennison, Dec. 8, Burstenbinder to Buckingham, Dec. 15, Dec. 20, Heckman to Buckingham, Dec. 17, 1861, OAGC; Alvin Coe Voris, Dec. 18, 1861, Alvin Coe Voris, "Service File," National Archives, Washington, D.C.; "Regimental Order Book, 67th Regt," Center for Archival Collections, Bowling Green University, Bowling Green, Ohio (hereafter cited as CAC); *Cleveland Daily Herald* (hereafter cited as *Herald*), Mar. 8, 1862; Whitelaw Reid, *Ohio in the War: Her Statesmen, Her Generals, and Soldiers,* 2 vols. (Cincinnati: Moore, Wilstach and Baldwin, 1868), 2:392. Toledo had a population of 13,768 in 1860.

19. Isaac N. Hathaway to Buckingham, Oct. 9, 10, 16, 21, 29, Burstenbinder to Buckingham, Nov. 4, 29, Morrison R. Waite to Dennison, Nov. 8, Burstenbinder to David Tod, Jan. 15, George Baxter to Tod, Jan. 15, John A. Simon to Buckingham, Jan. 15, 1862, OAGC; *Blade,* Oct. 19, 1861, Jan. 9, Feb. 5, 1862; Frank L. Byrne and Jean P. Soman, *Your True Marcus: The Civil War Letters of a Jewish Colonel* (Kent, Ohio: Kent State University Press, 1985), 16–17.

20. Voris to Lydia Voris, Jan. 17, Sept. 12, 1862, Johnson Collection; *Beacon,* Jan. 23, 1862; Lane, *Fifty Years,* 351.

21. Description derived from a photograph of Voris taken sometime during the war (Johnson Collection). See also Voris to Lydia Voris, Feb. 23, 1863, ibid.; and *Akron City Times* (hereafter cited as *Times*), June 22, 25, 1890.

22. This sketch of Voris's military career is drawn from his letters and pertinent primary and secondary documents listed in these annotated endnotes. Wartime relations between husbands and wives are discussed in Reid Mitchell, *The Vacant Chair: The Northern Soldier Leaves Home* (New York: Oxford University Press, 1993); Jeanie Attie, *Patriotic Toil: Northern Woman and the American Civil War* (Ithaca, N.Y.: Cornell University Press, 1998); and Carol K. Bleser and Lesley J. Gordon, *Intimate Strategies of the Civil War: Military Commanders and Their Wives* (New York: Oxford University Press, 2001).

23. Voris, "Service File," NA; *Beacon*, Dec. 8, 1873; *Biographical Cyclopedia*, 259; Lane, *Fifty Years*, 395. A special act of Congress on June 20, 1874, compensated Voris with a pension of $30 per month (*Beacon*, Nov. 14, 1883, Nov. 1, 1895).

24. *Beacon*, July 3, 1866, June 2, 1875.

25. "Record of Deaths, Probate Court," 1:104–95, #346, Summit County Archives; "Cemetery Lot Record," The Akron Rural Cemetery Association, Akron, Ohio.

26. *Beacon*, Apr. 19, May 3, 10, 1866, Mar. 21, 1867, Nov. 4, 1879, June 22, 1887; *Times*, Aug. 14, 1872, Apr. 7, 1880, May 15, Aug. 6, 1889; "Index to Marriages, Summit County," 1:134, Summit County Archives. "Lizzie" Voris lived until Sept. 15, 1931, dying at 83 (Voris, "Pension File," NA). Lane, *Fifty Years*, notes a number of Voris's major cases. *Illustrated Summit County, Ohio* (Akron, Ohio: Akron Map and Atlas, 1891), 77, 94, 102, 113, 128, 134–35, lists most of Voris's real estate holdings.

27. *Beacon*, Mar. 21, 1867, Nov. 15, 1876, July 11, 1883, July 29, 1896; *Times*, Aug. 7, 1889; "Records of the Akron Bar Association, Organized February 20, 1875," document the range of Voris's professionalism. Stephen H. Paschen, *Order in the Court: The Courts and the Practice of Law in Akron, Ohio, 1787–1945* (Akron, Ohio: Summit County Historical Society, 1997), is useful for background information.

28. *Beacon*, July 30, Aug. 1, Sept. 22, Nov. 3, 7, 1890, May 9, 1896; *Times*, Oct. 29, Nov. 5, 1890, May 6, 1891.

29. *Beacon*, July 5, 12, Nov. 29, 1871, June 25, 1895, June 20, 1904; *Times*, July 11, 1872; Alvin C. Voris, *Address before the Students of Buchtel College, Akron, Ohio . . .* (Akron, Ohio: Canfield, 1889); "Record of the Executive Committee of the Board of Trustees of Buchtel College. From Jan. 29, 1889–Feby, 15, 1917," 2, 43, 81, 86, 115, 130, University of Akron Archives; George W. Knepper, *New Lamps for Old: One Hundred Years of Urban Higher Education at the University of Akron* (Akron, Ohio: University of Akron Press, 1970), 5–57.

30. *Beacon*, Apr. 6, 1874, June 2, 1875, Nov. 1, 1895.

31. *Times*, Feb. 14, 1872, Apr. 22, 1888, Jan. 23, June 22, 25, 1890.

32. *Beacon*, Nov. 1, 1866, Jan. 11, Mar. 21, 1867, Feb. 18, 1868, Jan. 31, May 31, June 2, 1872, Aug. 25, 1880, Apr. 2, 1884, Nov. 1, 1886, Nov. 9, 1887, Aug. 29, 1888, May 8, 1889, Aug. 1, 1904; *Times*, Feb. 14, 1872, May 8, 1889, Jan. 23, June 24, 1890; Alvin C. Voris, *Our Memorial Chapel: Dedicated Tuesday, May 30, 1876, with the Life and Service of Col. Lewis P. Buckley, and a History of Buckley Post, No. 12, G.A.R.* (Akron, Ohio: Beacon, 1876); Lane, *Fifty Years*, 249–54; Olin, *Akron*, 220–21.

33. For a general discussion of this topic, see David Thelen, "Memory and American History," *Journal of American History* 75 (1989): 1117–29; Carol Reardon, *Pickett's Charge in History and Memory* (Chapel Hill: University of North Carolina Press, 1998); David W. Blight, *Race and Reunion: The Civil War in American Memory* (Cambridge, Mass.: Harvard University Press, 2001).

34. *Beacon,* Jan. 10, Apr. 11, 1867, Apr. 2, 1873, June 2, 1875, Sept. 21, 1881, May 30, 1888, July 5, 1895; *Times,* July 3, 1878; Alvin C. Voris, *Address Delivered by Gen. A. C. Voris, Memorial Day Tuesday, May 30th, 1871 . . .* (Akron, Ohio: Lane, Canfield, 1871), 7–8; A. C. Voris, *Memorial Address: Under the Auspices of the G.A.R., Delivered at Pittsburgh, Pa., May 30th 1878* (Akron, Ohio: Beacon, 1878); A. C. Voris, *A Soldier's Duty . . . Address Delivered at Perrysburg, Ohio, September 4, 1879, at the Reunion of the 67th O. Regt, by Their Late Commander* (Akron, Ohio: Canfield, 1879), 1–8; Alvin C. Voris, *National Unity: Memorial Address of A. C. Voris . . .* (Akron, Ohio: Paul E. Werner, 1882), 3–12; Alvin C. Voris, *Charleston in the Rebellion: A Paper Read before the Ohio Commandery of the Military Order of the Loyal Legion of the United States, March 7, 1880* (Cincinnati: Robert Logan, 1888), 35; Alvin C. Voris, "The Battle of the Boys," Military Order of the Loyal Legion of the United States, Ohio Commandery, *Sketches of War History, 1861–1865: Papers Read before the Ohio Commandery of the Military Order of the Loyal Legion of the United States, 1890–1896* (Cincinnati: R. Clarke, 1896), 87–88.

35. *Beacon,* Apr. 11, 1867, Oct. 4, 1871, June 26, 1872, Aug. 29, 1883; *Proceedings,* 1:824; *Harper's Weekly* 28 (Aug. 18, 1883): 525; Voris, *Memorial Address,* 12–15; Voris, *Soldier's Duty,* 8; "The West in the War of the Rebellion as Told in the Sketches of Some of Its Generals: General A. C. Voris," *Magazine of Western History* 4 (August 1886): 511–512, 514; Felice A. Bonadio, *North of Reconstruction: Ohio Politics, 1865–1870* (New York: New York University Press, 1970); Robert D. Sawrey, "Ohio and Reconstruction: The Search for Future Security, 1865–1868" (Ph.D. diss., University of Cincinnati, 1979).

36. *Proceedings,* 1:358, 388, 2(pt. 1):567, 2(pt. 2):1816–23, 1946, 1973–77, 1980, 2(pt. 3):2747–50, 2800–2808, 2842, 2853–54, 2861, 3313; *Beacon,* Mar. 29, Apr. 9, June 4, Sept. 29, 1873, Feb. 4, Mar. 11, 25, May 20, 29, June 10, Aug. 5, 26, 1874; *Times,* Jan. 28, Aug, 26, 1874, May 8, 29, 1888, June 10, 1889.

37. For samples of Voris's political activities, see *Beacon,* Apr. 19, July 3, 1866, Aug. 27, 1868, Sept. 25, 1872, Sept. 20, 1876, Oct. 6, 1896; *Herald,* June 2, 8, 1880; Alvin C. Voris, *Address Delivered at Akron, Ohio, Sept. 30th, 1880: Labor and Its Protection as Affected by the Two Great Parties* (Akron, Ohio: Canfield, 1880).

38. *Beacon,* May 5, 1896, July 11, 20, 22, 29, Aug. 1, 1904; *Akron Press,* July 28, 1904; William E. Barton, *The Life of Clara Barton, Founder of the American Red Cross* (1922; rpt., New York: AMS Press, 1969), 139–40.

39. *Beacon,* July 28, 29, Aug. 1, 1904; *Leader,* July 29, 1904.

CHAPTER 1 — *"Soldiering Is Romantic Indeed"*

1. The Vorises ignored Victorian norms that frowned on public displays of affection. They clung together in visible distress at the railroad station when he left Akron (Byrne and Soman, *Your True Marcus,* 20). Nancy F. Cott, *Public Vows: A History of Marriage and the Nation* (Cambridge, Mass.: Harvard University Press, 2000), elaborates on these Victorian standards.

2. Voris probably referred to Marcus M. Spiegel, Company C. He became Voris's closest friend in the 67th Ohio (Voris to Tod, Sept. 12, 1862, OAGC).

3. Bierce was 61, overage for active military service.

4. On Sept. 5, 1861, "Fusion" Democrats and Republicans created the Union party, dedicated to supporting the nation and defending the Constitution. David Tod, a Youngstown, Ohio, Democrat, the incoming governor, won on this gubernatorial ticket. See Reid, *Ohio in the War,* 2:64–82; George W. Knepper, *Ohio and Its People* (Kent, Ohio: Kent State University Press, 1997), 233.

5. A "Toledo" was a generic term that Voris used to describe a superior sword or sword blade, originally fabricated in Toledo, Spain. His use of this term may also have been a play on words.

6. In 1857, Gov. Salmon P. Chase had appointed Henry B. Carrington to reorganize the Ohio militia. During the war's early months, Carrington dispatched nine Ohio regiments to reinforce Brig. Gen. George B. McClellan in western Virginia (Reid, *Ohio in the War,* 2:931–932).

7. William Dennison, Jr., a Columbus Republican, the outgoing Ohio governor.

8. Col. Lewis P. Buckley commanded the 29th Ohio Volunteer Infantry Regiment, which contained three companies from Summit County. Buckley to Assistant Adjutant General Rodney Mason, Dec. 29, 1861, OAGC; *Beacon,* Jan. 23, 1862; *Herald,* Jan. 23, 1862; Ohio, Roster Commission, *Official Roster of the Soldiers of Ohio in the War of the Rebellion, 1861–1865,* 12 vols. (Akron, Ohio: Werner, 1886–1895) (hereafter cited as *Roster*), 3:353.

9. An anonymous member of the 67th Ohio confirmed Voris's statement: "I do not think there is a man in the regiment who does not love and respect [Voris]. He may at all times be seen among his men, talking and joking with them" (*Beacon,* Feb. 6, 1862).

10. Lieutenant colonels in 1861 received a base pay of $90 per month plus allowances for incidentals and servants. See *Revised United States Army Regulations of 1861. With an Appendix containing the Changes and Laws Affecting Army Regulation and Articles of War to June 25, 1863* (Washington, D.C.: Government Printing Office, 1863), 361. Both Buckley and Burstenbinder "feared" that if "unpaid companies" did not receive "funds," some "trouble might" erupt (Buckley to Buckingham, Jan. 16, Burstenbinder to Buckingham, Jan. 20, 1862, OAGC).

11. Before leaving Columbus, Voris had warned the state judge advocate general and Governor Tod about Burstenbinder's "inability to command" the regiment (Voris to Tod, Jan. 21, 30, 1862, OAGC). Otto Burstenbinder Court-Martial File, Record Group 94, B1205 (VS), 1862, "Records of the Office of the Judge Advocate General," NA, contains full material on this issue.

12. Brig. Gen. Frederick W. Lander. Gary L. Ecelbarger, *Frederick W. Lander: The Great Natural American Soldier* (Baton Rouge: Louisiana State University Press, 2000), is a recent biography.

13. As Voris noted, Burstenbinder lost his nerve when six unpaid companies refused his order to cross the river. According to the *Beacon's* anonymous correspondent, Voris indeed rose to the occasion. "Lt. Col. Voris addressed the men with one of the most patriotic speeches I have ever heard" (*Beacon,* Feb. 6, 1862). "TJC" added in the *Blade* that Voris's words "were fit and fitly spoken" (*Blade,* Feb. 1, 1862; *Leader,* Jan. 31, 1862).

14. Maj. Gen. Thomas J. Jackson.

15. In common with other Union officers, Voris overestimated Confederate combat strength. Jackson had less than 4,000 troops under his command. Total Union forces numbered slightly more than 6,300 (*Leader,* Mar. 29, 1862; Gary L. Ecelbarger, *"We Are In for It!" The First Battle of Kernstown, March 23, 1862* [Shippensburg, Pa.: White Mane, 1997], 268–72).

16. Col. Harry Anisansel led the 1st West Virginia Cavalry (*Herald,* Feb. 8, 1862).

17. Voris's rank allowed two servants. Although the record is unclear, he probably had one, whom he called an "African gentleman." Voris helped this person, likely an escaped slave, gain his freedom (*Army Regulations of 1861,* 361; Voris to Lydia Voris, Feb. 10, 1862, Johnson Collection).

18. Alfred P. Girty, Company G, became a first lieutenant on Dec. 18, 1861. Promoted to captain on May 13, 1862, he received a medical discharge, Apr. 25, 1864 (*Roster,* 5: 604).

19. Edwin F. Voris was six months short of his eighth birthday.

20. These men were from the 29th Ohio. See *Blade,* Jan. 21, 29, 1862; J. Hamp SeCheverell, *Journal History of the Twenty-Ninth Ohio Veteran Volunteers, 1861–1865* (Cleveland: n.p., 1883).

21. Col. Erastus B. Tyler. His brigade consisted of the 5th Ohio, 8th Ohio (three companies), 62d Ohio, 67th Ohio (seven companies), 13th Indiana, 14th Indiana, and 84th Pennsylvania. See *Beacon,* Mar. 13, 1862; *The War of the Rebellion: A Compilation of the Official Records of the Union and Confederate Armies.* 128 volumes. (Washington, D. C.: Government Printing Office, 1880–1901) (hereafter cited as *OR*), ser. 1, 12(pt. 1):341.

22. Tyler lived in Ravenna, Ohio, the county seat of Portage County, located near Akron. Voris and Tyler were fellow attorneys and had likely met on legal business. Tyler became a brevet major general of volunteers in March 1865.

23. Henry Steele Commager was a successful Toledo lawyer and Democratic politician and a forefather of the historian by the same name. Commager received promotion to lieutenant colonel in August 1862. See Voris to Charles W. Hill, Sept. 11, 1862, OAGC; *Herald,* May 28, 1864; *Roster,* 5:565; Neil Jumonville, *Henry Steele Commager: Midcentury Liberalism and the History of the Present* (Chapel Hill: University of North Carolina Press, 1999), 6.

24. Voris admired the editorials and war coverage in the Republican *Cleveland Daily Herald* and was friendly with George A. Benedict, the paper's editor. In turn, Benedict lauded Voris as a "prominent member of the Summit bar" and "one of the ablest and industrious" men in the legislature, who had enlisted for "patriotic reasons" (*Herald,* Apr. 1, 1862; *Beacon,* May 17, 1876).

25. This movement culminated in the Battle of Bloomery Gap, Feb. 13, 1862, halfway between Paw Paw and Winchester. In his report to McClellan, Lander noted the infantry was "not near enough to support" the attack (*OR,* ser. 1, 5:405–6).

26. Lander termed this battle "a complete victory" (ibid.; *Herald,* Mar. 1, 1862; *Beacon,* Mar. 6, 1862).

27. The 67th Ohio had one assistant surgeon, Dr. James Westfall (*Roster,* 5:565).

28. A rod measures 5.5 yards, or 16.5 feet.

29. Based on Voris's recommendation, Capt. Eddy D. Mason, Company F, became acting regimental adjutant (Voris to Hill, Nov. 14, 1862, OAGC; *Roster,* 5:597).

30. Confederate troops surrendered at Fort Donelson to Union troops under Brig. Gen. Ulysses S. Grant, Feb. 16, 1862.

31. Maj. John B. Bond had been adjutant of the 29th Ohio until he joined the 67th Ohio. Promoted to lieutenant colonel on July 20, 1862, Bond assumed command of the 111th Ohio Volunteer Infantry Regiment in February 1865 (*Roster,* 5:565).

32. The 67th Ohio left the state without a regimental flag. Burstenbinder boasted that "he would take the first Secessionist flag we see—and that is our motto for the present." On Feb. 28, 1862, Toledoans presented the regiment with a more appropriate Union flag (*Blade,* Jan. 29, Feb. 28, 1862).

33. Voris inflated Confederate forces by about two-thirds (*Leader,* Mar. 29, 1862).

34. Lander had been ill since the campaign began and died Mar. 2, 1862, likely from pneumonia. Col. Nathan Kimball, who led the division's First Brigade, took Lander's spot on a temporary basis. Shields became Lander's permanent replacement

(*OR,* ser. 1, 5:405; *Blade,* Mar. 3, 1862; *Leader,* July 8, 1862; Ecelbarger, *"We Are In for It!"* 50–51). Douglas L. Wilson, "Lincoln's Affair of Honor," *Atlantic Monthly* 281 (February 1998): 64–71, details Shields's prewar rivalry with Lincoln.

35. Located in Stark County south of Akron, Canton had a population of 12,260 in 1860. See William H. Perrin, *History of Stark County: With an Outline Sketch of Ohio* (Chicago: Baskin & Battey, 1881), 209–10.

36. Voris's letter appeared in the *Herald,* Mar. 13, 1862, under the pseudonym of "X."

37. Maj. Gen. Nathaniel P. Banks, a prominent prewar Massachusetts Republican, headed the newly created Fifth Army Corps. Brig. Gen. James Shields's division in this corps included the 67th Ohio (*OR,* ser. 1, 5:22). For more on Banks, see James G. Hollandsworth, *Pretense of Glory: The Life of General Nathaniel P. Banks* (Baton Rouge: Louisiana State University Press, 1998).

38. Brig. Gen. Alpheus S. Williams, a Mexican War veteran, led the First Division, Fifth Army Corps.

39. This phrase reflected Voris's use of irony or sarcasm to convey the exact opposite meaning to his words.

40. The 67th Ohio had 587 troops available for battle, out of an aggregate 896 (*OR,* ser. 1, 12[pt. 3]:4). The remainder were ill with "measles and severe coughs and colds" (*Blade,* Feb. 28, 1862).

41. Bunker Hill was south of Martinsburg and some twelve miles north of Winchester. Voris's comments about Manassas concerned Gen. Joseph E. Johnston's withdrawal of Confederate forces toward a more secure line along the Rappahannock River.

42. "JMR" wrote home that Voris "is in command of the 67th now, (Col. Burstenbinder being under arrest)" (*Beacon,* Apr. 10, 1862). Whether Voris would continue was already a matter of controversy. At least three other aspirants, citing Voris's lack "of military experience," had begun lining up support to replace Burstenbinder (Thomas March to Tod, Feb. 15, Robert Lemmons to Tod, Feb. 17, 1862, James T. Asper to Tod, Feb. 18, OAGC).

43. Cedar Creek.

44. Voris's manner impressed his command. "JMR" observed that in Voris "we had a leader who would be cool and brave in action" (*Beacon,* Apr. 10, 1862).

45. Perhaps Voris read the "JMR" letter before that writer sent it to the *Beacon* for publication.

46. Dr. Samuel F. Forbes, the 67th Ohio's surgeon, a frequent field correspondent for the *Blade* until he resigned from service on Oct. 7, 1863, wrote: "The gallant 67th had marched 30 miles" to reach the battlefield before fighting began. Even so, its men "were the first in battle" (*Blade,* Apr. 1, 1862; *Roster,* 5:565). Lydia was likely relieved when a local reporter confirmed that Voris's wound was minor. He was hit "in the foot, during the fight, but is doing quite well" (*Beacon,* Apr. 3, 1862).

47. Capt. Hyatt C. Ford, Company B, died on Mar. 23, 1862. Corp. Jacob Lantz, Company C, recovered, but his wound led to his discharge, June 20, 1862 (*Roster,* 5:572, 580).

48. Details of the battle may be followed in *OR,* ser. 1, 12(pt. 1):340–41, 350, 360, 376–77; and the *Blade,* Mar. 25–27, 31, Apr 1, 10, 1862.

49. The 67th Ohio suffered 47 casualties: 1 officer and 8 enlisted men killed; 2 officers and 36 enlisted men wounded (*OR,* ser. 1, 12[pt. 1]:326, 12[pt. 3]:19).

50. Sgt. James E. Bruce, Company C (*Roster,* 5:578). Philander D. Hall was the senior partner in a prominent Akron mercantile and dry goods store (Lane, *Fifty Years,* 334, 363).

51. Voris recopied parts of this letter in his reminiscence "Battle of the Boys," *Sketches of War History*, 87–100.

52. Voris's official report to Kimball appears in *OR*, ser. 1, 12(pt. 1):370–71. Voris's complaint about the lack of coverage had some merit. For instance, the *Blade* editorialized, "That such neglect should befall the Regiment *first in the field*, and the first to drive back the rebels . . . is not a little strange" (Apr. 1, 1862).

53. Ecelbarger, *"We Are In for It!"* 157–59, 191, 265, covers Voris's participation in the battle.

CHAPTER 2 — *"The 67th Has Not Been Stationary"*

1. This skirmish took place at Stony Creek.

2. 2d Lt. Edward H. Baker, 67th Ohio, Company A, was just as realistic. Describing an army hospital in the battle's aftermath, he wrote: "In the corner lie pieces of amputated flesh and limbs. Better to be dead than to live as some must" (*Herald*, Apr. 3, 12, 1862). Gerald F. Linderman addresses the widening gulf between civilians and soldiers that Voris mentioned in *Embattled Courage: The Experience of Combat in the American Civil War* (New York: Free Press, 1987), 80–133.

3. In 1860, 3,520 people lived in Akron.

4. Some of these reports appear in *Blade*, Mar. 25, 26, 29, Apr. 3, 7, 1862; *Leader*, Apr. 17, 1862; *Beacon*, Apr. 17, 1862. Local interest in Kernstown became secondary to the larger and bloodier battle at Shiloh (Pittsburg Landing), fought on Apr. 6–7, 1862, which engaged more Ohio regiments.

5. Some 7,000 Confederates at Island No. 10 on the Mississippi River below New Madrid, Mo., surrendered Apr. 8, 1862.

6. McClellan launched his long anticipated offensive on Mar. 17, 1862. By April 5, the Army of the Potomac began an almost monthlong siege of Yorktown.

7. The 67th Ohio's movements can be traced in *OR*, ser. 1, 12(pt. 3):16–41.

8. Capt. Josiah J. Wright (*Roster*, 3:378; Buckley to Buckingham, Jan. 8, 1862, OAGC).

9. *Beacon*, Apr. 17, 1862, carried several such letters, along with a widely circulated reprint from the *Cincinnati Gazette* that asserted Voris had "pressed forward where the fight was the fiercest."

10. *Blade*, May 14, 1862, carried this notice.

11. On the same day, the *Blade* published a letter, written by 1st Lt. Joseph Seiter, Company K, that must have pleased Voris: "Gen. Shields accorded more praise to the 67th than any other Regiment that distinguished itself in that bloody fight."

12. Information about Colonel Burstenbinder's forthcoming court-martial appeared infrequently in Ohio newspapers, except for an aside 1st Lt. Sheldon Colton, Company K, made in the *Blade*. Burstenbinder, Colton wrote, "was confined to his room by sickness" (May 31, 1862). Betsey Gates, ed., *The Colton Letters: Civil War Period, 1861–1865* (Scottsdale, Ariz.: McLane, 1993), 70–125, has more information about Colton.

13. A brigadier general in the Ohio militia, Charles W. Hill had served in western Virginia during the war's early months, but he alienated McClellan (Reid, *Ohio in the War*, 1:814). Even so, Hill informed Adjutant General Buckingham that he expected "further military service" in the "field" as a brigade commander once the state formed "more Ohio regiments." If the governor asked him to take command of the 67th, Hill added, he would accept, provided he could train the regiment for at

least a month, settle his expenses, and await the disposition of his application for a brigade (Hill to Buckingham, Jan. 3, Feb. 4, 1862, OAGC).

14. Voris strengthened his claim by emphasizing the prerogatives of a commander. In a letter to Governor Tod, Voris listed certain officers and men who deserved commendation, promotion, demotion, or court-martial for conduct at Kernstown (Voris to Tod, Mar. 31, Apr. 29, May 31, 1862, OAGC).

15. For a time, Ohio imprisoned Confederates at Camp Chase. See William H. Knauss, *The Story of Camp Chase: A History of the Prison and Its Cemetery, Together with Other Cemeteries where Confederate Prisoners Are Buried, Etc.* (1906; rpt., Columbus, Ohio: General's Books, 1990).

16. An abbreviation denoting the First Families of Virginia. Some Union troops, as Voris, used FFV as a sarcastic pejorative (*Herald,* May 14, 1862).

17. By May 1, 1862, the Union had captured New Orleans, controlled the Mississippi River except for a corridor around Vicksburg, and extended the blockade along the southern Atlantic Coast. In the east, McClellan's forces outnumbered Confederates, but his hesitation, perhaps indecision, allowed Confederates to reinforce their defenses. What Voris termed a victory eventually proved a Union setback.

18. Cuyahoga Falls, northeast of Akron, numbered 1,516 in 1860 (Perrin, *History of Summit County,* 466).

19. In campaigning for local support to retain his command, Voris repeated these observations in a public letter to Samuel A. Lane, the *Beacon*'s editor, which he published May 8, 1862. For further civilian reaction to Union forces, see Margaretta B. Colt, ed., *Defend the Valley: A Shenandoah Family in the Civil War* (New York: Orion, 1994), 110–65.

20. Maj. Gen. Irvin McDowell's troops were located at Fredericksburg and expected to join McClellan in a concerted attack on Richmond. Jackson sought to prevent this linkage by attacking Union forces in the Shenandoah Valley. See Herman Hattaway, *Shades of Blue and Gray: An Introductory Military History of the Civil War* (Columbia: University of Missouri Press, 1997), 83–85.

21. Voris referred to either McClellan's communications about his lack of action after he became commander of the Army of the Potomac or to a sentimental song of that name popular among troops on each side.

22. Voris took advantage of President Abraham Lincoln's inspection of McDowell's command to complain to the president about the regiment's inadequate provisions, partially the lack of shoes. McDowell did not appreciate Voris's conduct, but the incident increased his standing in the 67th Ohio and among appreciative Ohioans (*Blade,* June 18, 1862; William H. Hamby, *Sixty-Seventh Ohio Veteran Volunteer Infantry: A Brief History of Its Four Years of Service in the Civil War, 1861–1865* [Massillon: Ohio Print and Publishing, 1922], 6–7). William C. Davis, *Lincoln's Men: How President Lincoln Became Father to an Army and a Nation* (New York: Free Press, 1999), deals with Lincoln's intent for such inspections.

23. On May 31, 1862, the 62d Ohio (Col. Francis B. Pond), 67th Ohio (Lt. Col. Alvin Voris), 39th Illinois (Col. Thomas O. Osborn), and 13th Indiana (Lt. Col. Robert S. Foster) joined the Department of the Rappahannock under McDowell, in the First Division, Second Brigade, led by Brig. Gen. Orris S. Ferry, with Shields in divisional command (*OR,* ser. 1, 12[pt. 3]:309).

24. An anonymous member of the 67th Ohio reiterated Voris's comments: "March! March! March! has been the order" for "nearly three weeks past. Not less than 240 or 250 miles have been tramped over by [Shields's Division] in that time" (*Blade,* May 18, 1862).

25. Voris wrote such a letter to Tod. Praising the regiment for its hard marching despite "the evident neglect" of its "supplies," Voris grumbled that the 67th Ohio deserved better than its present "unsettled status." For those reasons, "I expect to see to some of these matters in person before long" (Voris to Tod, June 8, 1862, OAGC).

26. Medical "disability" led to Priv. Charles W. Beecher's discharge, Sept. 16, 1862 (*Roster*, 5:580).

27. Robert G. Tanner, *Stonewall in the Valley: Thomas J. "Stonewall" Jackson's Shenandoah Valley Campaign, Spring 1862* (Garden City, N.Y.: Doubleday, 1976), covers Jackson's campaign.

28. Shields reported that his "command marches with nothing now but arms, ammunition, subsistence, cooking utensils, blankets, and shelter tents" (*OR*, ser. 1, 12[pt. 3]:358).

29. Maj. Gen. Henry W. Halleck, heading the Department of the Mississippi, matched McClellan's caution in the advance toward Corinth, Miss.

30. Brig. Gen. Erastus Tyler commanded the Third Brigade; Col. Samuel S. Carroll, the Fourth. *OR*, ser. 1, 12(pt. 3):316–436, 906–14, notes the demoralized condition of Shields's division.

31. Lt. Col. Thomas Clark and Maj. John S. Clemmer (*Roster*, 3:353, 378). Confederates captured Clark but eventually exchanged him (*Herald*, Aug. 26, 1862).

32. Voris had originally enlisted in the 29th Ohio.

33. Jackson's victory at Port Republic on June 9, 1862, ended this phase of the war in the Shenandoah Valley. See *Herald*, June 17, 1862; Robert K. Krick, *Conquering the Valley: Stonewall Jackson at Port Republic* (New York: William Morrow, 1996).

34. Maj. Gen. Nathaniel Banks.

35. "Observer" shared Voris's optimism. Within days, "Observer" predicted, the troops would be "re-clothed and re-shod," ready to march "on to Richmond" (*Blade*, June 18, 1862).

36. Governor Tod had just named Charles W. Hill as Ohio's adjutant general.

CHAPTER 3: — *"Terrible Realities of a Protracted and Savage War"*

1. Maj. Gen. John E. Wool, commanding the Middle Department, had ordered the 67th Ohio to Martinsburg and New Creek on June 22, 1862 (*OR*, ser. 1, 12[pt. 3]:424–25).

2. The First Battle of Bull Run (Manassas), July 21, 1861. William C. Davis, *Battle at Bull Run: A History of the First Major Campaign of the Civil War* (Baton Rouge: Louisiana State University Press, 1977), notes this terrain.

3. In common with other officers, Voris disdained journalists. He considered them little better than sensation-seeking hacks at best—and traitors at the worst—for publishing information about troop movements and battlefield casualties. John F. Marszalek, *Sherman's Other War: The General and the Civil War Press* (Memphis: Memphis State University Press, 1981), presents the best example of this attitude.

4. For more on how Voris's observation typified this new attitude toward the conduct of war, see Mark Grimsley, *The Hard Hand of War: Union Military Policy toward Southern Civilians, 1861–1865* (New York: Cambridge University Press, 1995).

5. Capt. Sidney G. Brock (*Roster*, 5:565).

6. *Beacon*, June 19, 1862, and *Herald*, June 26, 1862, noted Akron's elaborate arrangements for the "Glorious Fourth."

7. Jacob Goldsmith established his Akron clothing store in 1861 (*Beacon*, June 20, 1861). Spiegel, who had been on leave, returned with letters and packages for

various personnel, Voris among them (Byrne and Soman, *Your True Marcus,* 108–9).

8. The War Department did not accept Buckley's resignation until June 26, 1862, when he left the service for "failing health." Buckley subsequently became assistant doorkeeper of the House of Representatives. He died June 25, 1868. Local veterans named the Buckley Post No. 12, Akron, Ohio, Grand Army of the Republic, in his honor (*Beacon,* Aug. 14, 1862, July 2, 1868; *Roster,* 3:353; Lane, *Fifty Years,* 358).

9. The tiresome pursuit of Jackson had "so weakened the 67th," a report went, that the regiment "expected to relieve" rested troops in the "forts" around Washington (*Leader,* July 3, 1862).

10. Secretary of War Edwin M. Stanton came from Steubenville, Ohio.

11. The barge, *Delaware,* "Observer" wrote, was "a two-deck concern, very old looking and not presenting many agreeable features" (*Blade,* July 5, 1862).

12. "GLC" corroborated Voris's description of the panic aboard the barge and hailed his efforts in calming "the excitement of the men." Even more courageously, Voris "was the last man to leave the wreck, directing the delivery of his men till all were safe before he thought of himself" (*Herald,* July 24, 1862).

13. On July 2, 1862, President Lincoln assigned each state a quota to raise 300,000 new three-year volunteers, "chiefly of infantry." See James D. Richardson, *A Compilation of Messages and Papers of the President, 1789–1908,* 11 vols. (Washington, D.C.: Bureau of Literature and Art, 1909), 6:115–16.

14. 1st Lt. Alfred R. Girty, Company G (*Roster,* 5:604).

15. On July 11, 1862, the 67th Ohio, 39th Illinois, 13th Indiana, and 62d Ohio joined the Third Brigade, Second Division, Fourth Army Corps, Army of the Potomac, under Maj. Gen. John J. Peck (*OR,* ser. 1, 11[pt. 2]:218).

16. Stephen W. Sears, *To the Gates of Richmond: The Peninsula Campaign* (New York: Ticknor & Fields, 1992), replaces Alexander S. Webb, *The Peninsula: McClellan's Campaign of 1862* (New York: C. Scribner's Sons, 1881).

17. Voris agreed with Halleck's critics that the Corinth campaign was a tactical setback, because Maj. Gen. Pierre G. T. Beauregard's forces had avoided capture. See Stephen E. Ambrose, *Halleck: Lincoln's Chief of Staff* (Baton Rouge: Louisiana State University Press, 1962), 51–54.

18. David P. Crook, *The North, The South, and the Powers, 1861–1865* (New York: Wiley, 1974); and Dean B. Mahin, *One War at a Time: The International Dimensions of the American Civil War* (Washington, D.C.: Brassey's, 1999), discuss Civil War diplomacy.

19. William Henry Harrison, ninth president of the United States.

20. "Gus" was more pessimistic about the 67th Ohio's "effective" manpower. Only about 300 men were available for combat. The others were "either in the various hospitals scattered all over the country or home on sick furlough" (*Herald,* Aug. 2, 1862).

21. Voris's emphasis on concentrated, offensive warfare to destroy the enemy, not merely occupy its territory, reflected a growing consensus in overall Union strategy. See Herman Hattaway and Archer Jones, *How the North Won: A Military History of the Civil War* (Urbana: University of Illinois Press, 1983), 300–337, 375–416.

22. Thomas M. Key.

23. Voris increased the pressure, especially on Hill. Emphasizing "the good of the service," he sent Hill recommendations for promotion, headed by "Lt. Col. *Alvin C. Voris*" to "the colonelcy of this Regiment." Voris was more coy with Tod but no less forceful in laying out a brief for Burstenbinder's court-martial. As for Hill or others who might seek the regiment's command, Voris contrasted their lack of combat experience with his battlefield record (Voris to Hill, July 22, Voris to Tod, July 23, 1862, OAGC).

24. Burstenbinder remained on active duty, pending his court-martial. The *Blade, Herald,* and *Leader,* each representing large blocs of Republican voters, strengthened Voris's claim. The *Leader* in particular urged Voris's promotion to "full Colonel." Ohio "has sent no man to the field who has better done his work than Col. Voris" (*Leader,* cited in *Blade,* Aug. 8, 1862).

25. John Crabbs, the 67th Ohio's chaplain, praised regimental physicians, Surgeon Forbes and Assistant Surgeon Westfall, for improving "sanitary conditions." Despite their efforts, Crabbs admitted, some men were still "unwell and need rest during these very hot days" (ibid., July 23, Aug. 8, 1862).

26. On July 20, Voris requested a twenty-day leave of absence for recruitment duty. The 67th Ohio, he informed Brig. Gen. Seth Williams, assistant adjutant general, Army of the Potomac, was far below strength, numbering 474 enlisted men and 29 officers. Voris also had another purpose. With Burstenbinder's court-martial imminent, Voris explained to Williams, the regiment was demoralized. As a result, Voris intended to meet with the governor so "that a permanent organization can be given to the Regt." Voris received his leave the following day (Voris to Williams, July 20, Williams to Voris, July 21, 1862, Voris, "Service File," NA).

27. Voris assumed command of the 67th Ohio at the rank and pay of a colonel on July 29, 1862. A special order, cut the same day "under the direction of the President," dismissed Burstenbinder from "the service." He appealed, claiming an undisclosed illness prevented him from fulfilling his duties. But McClellan, the commanding general, accepted the court-martial's finding and refused to reconsider the matter (Ferry to Suydam, July 20, Townsend to Ferry, Voris to Suydam, Aug. 22, McClellan to Williams, Sept. 27, Tod to Burstenbinder, Oct. 4, 1862, Burstenbinder Court-Martial File, RG 94, NA; Voris, "Service File," NA).

28. Voris spent part of his leave in western and northern Ohio seeking recruits in Toledo, Cleveland, and Cuyahoga County. He also found an agent, George L. Heaton, to raise others. The *Leader* sought to aid Heaton by extolling Voris for his "soldierly qualities" and calling the 67th Ohio a "'crack' regiment, and well officered throughout." Heaton, however, confessed that local residents considered the 67th Ohio "a foreign regiment" and were not "disposed" to lend it their "aid and influence." In the end, he managed to enroll only twenty-two men (*Leader,* July 10, 17, 31, Aug. 20, 22, Sept. 3, 1862; *Blade,* Oct. 4, 1862; Edwin S. Platt to Hill, Oct. 6, 1862, Voris to Hill, June 3, 1863, OAGC).

29. Maj. Lewis Butler, Company I, was Burstenbinder's chief supporter and Voris's most persistent critic. A resident of Toledo, Butler sought promotion, one that he eventually earned, and ended the war as a brevet brigadier general of volunteers (Butler to Hill, July 1862, OAGC; *Blade,* July 28, Sept. 16, 1863, Feb. 13, 1864; *Roster,* 5:565, 616). Perhaps encouraged by Butler, a clique of anti-Voris officers requested an official inquiry into his conduct based on a number of charges and specifications. Three charges were serious: mishandling regimental accounts, absence without leave, and lack of "military abilities." After freezing Voris's pay and investigating the situation, a three-man court of inquiry issued a stinging rebuke to his critics. The court found the accusations "untenable" and "manifestly frivolous" and concluded that the entire episode stemmed from personal malice, not "zeal for the service." With this exoneration, Voris retained command, and his pay resumed. He did not mention the episode to Lydia (Capt. John R. Spafford to Maj. Benjamin B. Foster, Nov. 25, Nov. 26, 1862; Ferry to Spafford, Nov. 26, 1862, Peter Bell to Hill, Jan. 15, John Faskins to Hill, Feb. 11, Commager to Hill, Mar. 15, 1863, Capt. Samuel Breck to Voris, Oct. 19, 1863, Voris, "Service File," NA; *Army Regulations of 1861,* 499–501).

30. The Fourth Army Corps, Department of Virginia, including the 67th Ohio, 62th Ohio, 39th Illinois, and 13th Indiana, occupied Suffolk, Va., southwest of Norfolk. Suffolk controlled navigation on the Nansemond River, a winding, marshy stream with deep channels sufficient for gunboats. This assignment improved morale. "Before leaving Hampton," a soldier wrote, "our brigade received an entire new outfit of 'dry goods,' and we are no longer the hungry, ragged, and worn out 67th" (*Herald,* May 15, Sept. 16, 1862; *OR,* ser. 1, 18:377).

31. Maj. Gen. Charles Cornwallis, 1st Marquess Cornwallis, 1738–1805.

32. Maj. Gen. John B. Magruder led "Magruder's Command," Department of Northern Virginia, Apr. 12–July 3, 1862. See Paul D. Casdorph, *Prince John Magruder: His Life and Campaigns* (New York: John Wiley & Sons, 1996).

33. The call for volunteers was not popular, largely because of a rising antiwar sentiment that grew out of mounting Union losses (*Herald,* Nov. 4, 1862).

34. Voris touched on the Union defeat at the Second Battle of Bull Run (Manassas), Aug. 29–30, 1862. See John J. Hennessy, *Return to Bull Run: The Campaign and Battle of Second Manassas* (New York: Simon and Schuster, 1993).

35. Maj. Gen. Robert C. Schenck, a Dayton, Ohio, lawyer, suffered a crippling wound at the Second Battle of Bull Run. He resigned his commission, Dec. 5, 1863, to take a seat in the House of Representatives. See *Herald,* Sept. 2, 9, 1862; James R. Therry, "The Life of General Robert Cumming Schenck" (Ph.D. diss., Georgetown University, 1968).

36. By Aug. 3, 1862, Ferry had 3,868 troops at Suffolk (*OR,* ser. 1, 18:377, 396).

37. Voris's remark dealt with Gen. Robert E. Lee's setback at Antietam (Sharpsburg), Sept. 17, 1862. See John M. Priest, *Antietam: The Soldiers' Battle* (New York: Oxford University Press, 1993).

38. Maj. Gen. Joseph K. F. Mansfield commanded the Twelfth Army Corps at Antietam. He died of wounds, Sept. 18, 1862. See John Mead Gould, *Joseph K. F. Mansfield, Brigadier General of the U.S. Army: A Narrative of Events Connected with His Mortal Wounding at Antietam, Sharpsburg, Maryland, September 17, 1862* (Portland, Maine: Stephen Berry, 1895).

39. Jackson had captured some 12,500 Union soldiers and a large amount of supplies at Harpers Ferry (Chester G. Hearn, *Six Years of Hell: Harpers Ferry during the Civil War* [Baton Rouge: Louisiana State University Press, 1996], 169–99). Stephen W. Sears, *Landscape Turned Red: The Battle of Antietam* (New Haven: Ticknor & Fields, 1983), is the standard work on this battle. Gary W. Gallagher, ed., *Antietam: Essays on the 1862 Maryland Campaign* (Kent, Ohio: Kent State University Press, 1989), offers other useful interpretations.

40. Chaplain Crabbs agreed with Voris about the destitution so evident among the poor of both races. Crabbs also described an "unusual African stampede" of escaping slaves who sought freedom behind Union lines (*Blade,* Oct. 21, 1862). At first, many of these African Americans came from the area near Suffolk, but others from North Carolina soon joined them. While few Union troops were abolitionists, "GLH" thought their firsthand experience with slavery, especially after viewing the plight of these "most pitiable looking beings," would convert the men into making the end of slavery a war aim (*Herald,* Sept. 23, Nov. 22, 1862). For more on these points, see William W. Freehling, *The South vs. the South: How Anti-Confederate Southerners Shaped the Course of the Civil War* (New York: Oxford University Press, 2001), 96–121.

41. A member of the 67th Ohio had a different impression of Voris. He was "in good health and fine spirits. We all think the 'Spread Eagles' become him much" (*Beacon,* Sept. 11, 1862).

42. Voris waited more than a month after assuming command to reorganize the officer corps. He sent Hill a list of men he wanted to promote, with precise seniority dates, and others that he did not favor, chiefly Burstenbinder's allies (Voris to Hill, Oct. 18, 1862, Ohio Governor Papers, OHS).

43. By Oct. 12, 1862, "about 12,000 troops" were in Suffolk, "well-entrenched" and capable of defeating "any force the rebels are likely to gather there." New volunteers also arrived daily, bringing the 67th Ohio to near "full" strength (*Blade,* Oct. 10, 1862; James F. Fisher to Hannah Fisher, Nov. 8, 1862, Marilyn Clay Papers, CAC).

44. When Union forces occupied Suffolk, local "citizens shut up their homes and refused to open them," "JCC" wrote. The situation changed when the "commanding general" ordered "that they should open their homes on a certain day, or he would order the troops to take possession of them" (*Blade,* Sept. 5, 1862).

45. Capt. James Adair, Company G, 62d Ohio (*Roster,* 5:357).

46. Voris, Chaplain Crabbs wrote, had indeed supervised the construction of a formidable defensive perimeter, "at least a half-mile in length," protected "by fortifications and rifle-pits of the most superior construction" (*Blade,* Oct. 13, 1862).

47. Maj. Gen. John A. Dix, head of the Department of Virginia (*OR,* ser. 1, 18:377).

48. Lincoln removed McClellan from command of the Army of the Potomac on Nov. 7, 1862. See Stephen W. Sears, *George B. McClellan: The Young Napoleon* (New York: Ticknor & Fields, 1988), 337–343.

49. Democrats made strong gains in the fall elections of 1862. They won several key gubernatorial races and netted an increase of thirty-two congressional seats, including prominent Peace Democrats from Ohio and New York. See Joel H. Silbey, *A Respectable Minority: The Democratic Party in the Civil War Era* (New York: W. W. Norton, 1977), 142–46.

50. Lincoln had named Maj. Gen. Ambrose E. Burnside as McClellan's successor. In late November 1862, Burnside launched another invasion of Virginia, culminating in his defeat at the Battle of Fredericksburg (Dec. 13, 1862). See William Marvel, *Burnside* (Chapel Hill: University of North Carolina Press, 1991), 151–217.

51. Chaplain Crabbs, aware that such boredom might breed immoral behavior, assured Toledoans that, "Even though men are free from constraints of home, little viciousness, drunkenness, or profanity" existed in the regiment (*Blade,* Dec. 3, 1862).

52. Edward Zane Carroll Judson, an adventurer and writer, adopted the pen name of "Ned Buntline" and became a founder of the "Dime Novel" genre. He served in the Union army Sept. 25, 1862–Aug. 3, 1864. See *Herald,* Dec. 27, 1862; Jay Monahan, *The Great Rascal: The Life and Adventures of Ned Buntline* (Boston: Little, Brown, 1952).

53. For details of this expedition, see *OR,* ser. 1, 18:483–86; Simeon Barton to Mary Barton, Nov. 25, 1862, Borton Family Papers, CAC.

54. The bloody loss at Fredericksburg indeed eroded confidence among Northern civilians and made plausible Peace Democratic demands for negotiated peace. See *Leader,* Dec. 12, 15, 19, 22, 1862; A. Wilson Greene, "Morale, Maneuver, and Mud: The Army of the Potomac, December 16, 1862–January 26, 1863," in Gary W. Gallagher, ed., *The Fredericksburg Campaign: Decision on the Rappahannock* (Chapel Hill: University of North Carolina Press, 1995), 171–227.

55. On Dec. 30, 1862, Ferry ordered the 610 officers and men in the 67th Ohio, with their "ammunition and garrison equipage," to Norfolk and "the transport expected there" (*OR,* ser. 1, 18:495). Steven A. Cormier, *The Seige of Suffolk:*

The Forgotten Campaign, April 11–May 4, 1863 (Lynchburg, Va.: H. E. Howard, 1989), covers the Suffolk campaign.

CHAPTER 4: — *"Never Ceasing Scramble for This Bauble Glory"*

1. "Observer" assured Toledoans that the *Morton,* unlike the *Delaware,* was "a fine sea vessel" (*Blade,* Jan. 31, 1863).

2. The First Brigade, Third Division, Eighteenth Army Corps, contained the 62d Ohio, 67th Ohio, 39th Illinois, and 176th Pennsylvania. Colonel Osborn, senior to Voris, commanded the brigade; Ferry, the division; Maj. Gen. John G. Foster, the corps. The corps had five divisions, one cavalry unit, and the 1st North Carolina (Union) Volunteers (*OR,* ser. 1, 18:548).

3. The Battle of Stones River (Murfreesboro) took place on Dec. 31, 1862, and Jan. 2, 1863, ending with a Confederate withdrawal on the night of January 3–4, 1863. Although the battle was a tactical draw, the Union chose to interpret it as a victory. Even so, Voris was correct. Both sides had severe casualties. The Union lost 31 percent; the Confederates, 33 percent. See Peter Cozzens, *No Better Place to Die: The Battle of Stones River* (Urbana: University of Illinois Press, 1990).

4. Michael C. C. Adams, *Our Masters the Rebels: A Speculation on Union Failures in the East, 1861–1865* (Cambridge, Mass.: Harvard University Press, 1978), analyzes the defeatism rife in the Army of the Potomac.

5. President Lincoln issued the Emancipation Proclamation on Jan. 1, 1863.

6. For a discussion of loyalism or "Unionists" in North Carolina and the Confederacy in general, consult William C. Harris, "Lincoln and Wartime Reconstruction in North Carolina, 1861–1863," *North Carolina Historical Review* 63 (April 1986): 149–68; Wayne K. Durrill, *War of Another Kind: A Southern Community in the Great Rebellion* (New York: Oxford University Press, 1990); and Richard N. Current, *Lincoln's Loyalists: Union Soldiers from the Confederacy* (Boston: Northeastern University Press, 1992).

7. The *George C. Collins* was a converted merchant ship. See John D. Hayes, ed., *Samuel Francis du Pont: A Selection from His Civil War Letters,* 3 vols. (Ithaca, N.Y.: Cornell University Press, 1969), 2:225, 3:99.

8. "JCC" also lamented that officers and men in the 67th Ohio had not been paid "a cent" for six months. "How does the government expect us to live? We cannot live on hope much longer" (*Blade,* Jan. 30, 1863).

9. Ferry's Third Division, Eighteenth Corps, was on detached duty in the Department of the South at Hilton Head. The 67th Ohio was now in the second brigade under Osborn (*OR,* ser. 1, 18:577, 678, 738, 14[pt. 1]:144).

10. Rear Admiral du Pont, head of the South Atlantic Blockading Squadron, had captured Hilton Head Island, between Charleston and Savannah on Port Royal Sound, after his victory at the Battle of Port Royal, Nov. 7, 1861. See Howard P. Nash, Jr., *A Naval History of the Civil War* (South Brunswick, N.J.: A. S. Barnes, 1972), 56–64.

11. "Brother Jonathan," a caustic term implying Yankee meanness, applied first to New Englanders and then to Americans in general. The phrase evolved into a complimentary nickname synonymous with the New Republic and America's citizens.

12. The USS *Monitor,* the prototype for similar ironclads, had sunk in a gale off the North Carolina coast, Dec. 31, 1862.

13. An armored gunboat under Capt. John Rodgers, the USS *Galena* was covered with three-inch iron plate. Du Pont used the ironclad steam frigate USS *Ironsides* as his flagship. See William H. Roberts, "A Neglected Ironclad: A Design and Constructional

Analysis of the *U.S.S. Ironsides," Warship International* 26 (June 1989): 109–34.

14. During the War of 1812, Commodore Oliver H. Perry had defeated the British on Lake Erie at Put-In-Bay, near Sandusky, Ohio, Sept. 10, 1813,

15. The USS *Wabash,* a steam-powered frigate mounting forty-four guns, served as du Pont's flagship at the Battle of Port Royal.

16. The largest of the Sea Islands, St. Helena lay between Charleston and Savannah. Du Pont's victory at Port Royal caused Confederate troops and most St. Helena slaveholders to abandon the island, along with their slaves, for Charleston. The Union used St. Helena as a staging area for the attack on Charleston. See Guion Griffis Johnson, *A Social History of the Sea Islands with Special Reference to St. Helena Island, South Carolina* (Chapel Hill: University of North Carolina Press, 1930), 3–130.

17. In introducing Gage to his regiment, the admiring Voris called her "the law-giver, protector and guide of these unfortunate beings who have just fled from bondage." See *Herald,* Dec. 20, 1862, Mar. 26, 1863; *Leader,* Mar. 4, 1863; Willie Lee Rose, *Rehearsal for Reconstruction: The Port Royal Experiment* (Indianapolis: Bobbs-Merrill, 1964), 191–92; Wendy H. Venet, *Neither Ballots nor Bullets: Women Abolitionists and the Civil War* (Charlottesville: University Press of Virginia, 1991), 99, 114.

18. Laura Towne, a young Northern idealist who worked with freed African Americans on these islands, confirmed Voris's stricture (Rupert Sargent Holland, ed., *Letters and Diary of Laura M. Towne; Written From the Sea Islands of South Carolina, 1862–1884* [1912; rpt., New York: Negro Universities Press, 1969], 102–3). Thomas P. Lowry, *The Story the Soldiers Wouldn't Tell* (Mechanicsburg, Pa.: Stackpole, 1994), 34, 84, 123–30, 165, 174, notes these sexual tensions.

19. Du Pont used the *Arago* for transport.

20. The USS *Augusta Dinsmore* gave du Pont logistical support.

21. Stephen R. Wise, *Gate of Hell: Campaign for Charleston Harbor, 1863* (Columbia: University of South Carolina Press, 1994), 26–27, explains the mistrust and lack of cooperation that existed between Union naval and army officers over tactics and personalities.

22. "Observer" agreed. Half the fleet had not arrived, "and it will probably be a week, at the rate things usually move in the army, before we are ready for an offensive operation" (*Blade,* Feb. 13, 1863).

23. Voris had written his first "Mary Jane" letter on Jan. 8, 1863, to "friend Lane" (*Beacon,* Feb. 5, 1863). The letter repeated much of the observations Voris had made to Lydia,

24. Using the pseudonym "Vox," Voris again reiterated themes he had developed to Lydia (*Herald,* Mar. 3, 1863).

25. Located on Port Royal Sound, Parris Island was separated from St. Helena by the Beaufort River on the southwest.

26. Lincoln signed the "Act for Enrolling and Calling out the National Forces" on Mar. 2, 1863. As Voris noted, most volunteers scorned conscripts as unpatriotic slackers. To avoid this stigma, many potential draftees volunteered. See Eugene C. Murdock, *One Million Men: The Civil War Draft in the North* (Madison: State Historical Society of Wisconsin, 1971), 3–90; James W. Geary, *We Need Men: The Union Draft in the Civil War* (DeKalb: Northern Illinois University Press, 1991), 48–91.

27. A number of journalists, including Fletcher Harper, managing editor of *Harper's Weekly,* and Henry J. Raymond, the owner and editor of the *New York Times,* had arrived on the *Arago* for firsthand observations of operations around Charleston (Hayes, ed., *Du Pont,* 2:521).

28. Maj. Gen. David Hunter commanded the Department of the South, Jan. 20–June 12, 1863. See E. Milby Burton, *The Siege of Charleston, 1861–1864* (Columbia: University of South Carolina Press, 1970), 100, 135, 141–44.

29. Wise, *Gate of Hell*, 25–32, deals with this point.

30. A cousin of the more famous Rear Adm. John Rodgers, Capt. Christopher R. P. Rodgers had extensive prewar service. See Robert E. Johnson, *Rear Admiral John Rodgers, 1812–1882* (Annapolis: United States Naval Institute, 1967), 52, 172.

31. The USS *Patapsco*, under Comdr. Daniel Ammen, mounted one fifteen-inch smoothbore and a 150-pound Parrott rifled gun (Nash, *Naval History*, 185; du Pont, *Letters*, 2:32).

32. Du Pont attacked Fort McAllister, an earthen fort near Savannah, to test the monitors' ability to bombard Charleston into submission. When the ships failed this trial, du Pont concluded that the navy needed infantry support to capture the city. The *Nashville*, a Confederate blockade runner, ran aground, Feb. 27, 1863. John L. Worden, captain of the USS *Montauk*, seized the opportunity to destroy the *Nashville*. See Stephen R. Wise, *Lifeline of the Confederacy: Blockade Running during the Civil War* (Columbia: University of South Carolina Press, 1988), 313; Ivan Musicant, *Divided Waters: The Naval History of the Civil War* (New York: HarperCollins, 1995), 384.

33. Gen. Pierre G. T. Beauregard, heading the Department of South Carolina, Georgia, and Florida, was in charge of Charleston's defense. See *OR*, ser. 1, 14:503–6, 514–16, 603–4, 685, 781–83, 786; Alfred Roman, *The Military Operations of General Beauregard in the War between the States, 1861 to 1865* (New York: Harper & Bros., 1884), 20–80.

34. Commander Ammen was an Ohio native.

35. Col. Francis P. Pond, 62d Ohio, Second Division, Second Brigade, Department of the South (*Roster*, 5:325; *OR*, ser. 1, 14[pt. 1]:443–44).

36. Gage persuaded Clara Barton to support equality for freed African Americans. See Elizabeth Brown Pryor, *Clara Barton: Professional Angel* (Philadelphia: University of Pennsylvania Press, 1987), 120–22.

37. Such frustration also characterized 1st Lt. Orville M. Eddy, Company F. In a letter from St. Helena, he told Toledoans that the 67th Ohio awaited orders for "an expedition" to an unknown target. In the absence of facts, the troops relied on gossip, "and those are so numerous that it would be useless to mention any" (*Blade*, Mar. 21, 1863).

38. Many Civil War soldiers escaped the tedium of camp life by writing letters home. For example, the *Arago* left Hilton Head on one trip with 5,110 letters (*Leader*, Mar. 12, 1863).

39. Located where the Stono River entered Stono Inlet, Cole's Island guarded the southern route to Charleston. Although Confederates had built strong fortifications on the island, their unexpected and controversial decision to evacuate allowed the Union to occupy nearby strategic sites, mainly Morris, James, and Folly Islands (Burton, *Siege of Charleston*, 63, 92, 100, 115, 148).

40. Du Pont's reluctant attack on Charleston miscarried with heavy damage to his nine ironclads, especially the USS *Keokuk*, and to his career. Secretary of the Navy Gideon Welles refused to admit any defect in his strategy. He made du Pont a scapegoat by declining to authorize an official inquiry that du Pont requested, and ultimately Welles replaced him (*Blade*, Apr. 13, 15, 18, 1863).

41. Voris's second "Mary Ann" letter once more contained ideas that he had emphasized to Lydia, chiefly his abolitionist and free-soil beliefs. "America," Mary

Ann's servant and a recently freed African American, Voris wrote, sought personal betterment through education, an opportunity available to him only in a free-labor society. Voris also touched on another evil that slavery created, white hypocrisy about the sexual exploitation of slave women. "America is hardly black and is certainly no other color, what made him so, I can't tell as he was produced in that good Democratic state of Virginia, where *is said* to exist the most uncompromising hostility to amalgamation" (*Beacon*, Mar. 12, 1863).

42. The popular nickname for Secretary of the Navy Welles.

43. *OR*, ser. 1, 14:440–47 covers the attack. Gideon Welles, *The Diary of Gideon Welles: Secretary of the Navy under Lincoln and Johnson*, 3 vols. (Boston: Houghton Mifflin, 1911), 1:263–67, 276–77, recalls the Lincoln administration's reaction to this setback.

44. Brig. Gen. John G. Foster had directed the Department of North Carolina during the 67th Ohio's stay at New Bern.

45. Voris probably admired Hunter's strong commitment to abolition. See Dudley T. Cornish, *The Sable Arm: Negro Troops in the Union Army, 1861–1865* (New York: W. W. Norton, 1966), 15, 31–55.

46. Confederate drubbing of the ironclads created two significant personnel changes. On June 12, 1863, Brig. Gen. Quincy Adams Gillmore, an Ohioan, took over the Department of the South. Less than a month later (July 5, 1863), Rear Adm. John A. B. Dahlgren replaced du Pont. See Robert J. Schneller, Jr., *A Quest for Glory: A Biography of Rear Admiral John A. Dahlgren* (Annapolis: Naval Institute Press, 1996), 231–73.

47. Brig. Gen. Israel Vogdes had replaced Ferry (*OR*, ser. 1, 18:439).

48. Brig. Gen. Alfred H. Terry commanded the First Division, Tenth Corps, Department of the South.

49. The 67th Ohio was on Folly Island in the Second Division, First Brigade, under Col. George B. Dandy, a West Point graduate, from the 100th New York. The brigade also listed the 62d Ohio, 39th Illinois, 3d New York Artillery, and a company of engineers (*OR*, ser. 1, 18:439, 444).

50. Fort Moultrie.

51. Although Voris had more combat experience, Osborn was senior by date of rank. See Charles M. Clark, *The History of the Thirty-Ninth Regiment Illinois Volunteer Infantry Regiment (Yates Phalanx) in the War of the Rebellion, 1861–1865* (Chicago: Published under the auspices of the Veteran Association of the Regiment, 1889), 369–370.

52. Army regulations allowed officers of Voris's rank two servants. He had one, likely the model for "America."

53. Capt. Bazell Rodgers, Company H, 62d Ohio (*Roster*, 5:367).

54. Capt. John B. Chapman, Company C, 67th Ohio (ibid, 5:578).

55. These differing accounts related to Gen. Lee's victory over Maj. Gen. Joseph Hooker's forces at the Battle of Chancellorsville, May 1–4, 1863.

56. Maj. Gen. John Pope owed this derisiveness to his boastful and unfulfilled pronouncements prior to his loss at the Second Battle of Bull Run. For more on Pope, see Peter Cozzens, *General John Pope: A Life for the Nation* (Urbana: University of Illinois Press, 2000).

57. "Furlough Papers, Ohio Volunteers, 1862–1865," ser. 2445, OAGC, contains records of such leaves.

58. The Invalid Corps consisted of troops who, for various medical or military reasons, were unfit for combat. Rather than receiving a medical discharge, they performed garrison or hospital duties, often freeing able-bodied men for other service. See *Herald*, June 9, 1863; *OR*, ser. 3, 3:171–72; George W. Adams, *Doctors in Blue: The Medical History of the Union Army in the Civil War* (New York: Henry Schuman, 1952), 187.

59. An anonymous member of the 67th Ohio qualified Voris's opinion about the likelihood of an imminent attack. Union forces could renew the offensive "possibly in a few days, but probably not under three or four weeks." A successful assault was contingent on organizing "a strong land force" that would "co-operate" with the navy (*Blade,* May 18, 1863).

60. In a period before combat photography developed, *Frank Leslie's Illustrated Newspaper,* a pictorial that utilized a number of field artists, impressed readers with firsthand images of war. See W. Fletcher Thompson, Jr., *The Pictorial Reporting of the American Civil War* (New York: Thomas Yoseloff, 1960), 20–24.

61. By June 10, 1863, Vogdes had 4,711 officers and men on Folly Island from the 62d Ohio, 67th Ohio, 6th Connecticut, 39th Illinois, 4th New Hampshire, 85th Pennsylvania, and 100th New York (*OR,* ser. 1, 14[pt. 1]:461, 468–69).

62. Lydia Allyn Voris was born June 16, 1831, making her 32, not 33.

63. Voris referred to Maj. Gen. Edward Braddock's failure in 1755 during the Seven Years' War to follow the advice of a young George Washington about proper troop movements in American Indian territory.

64. Burnside, now heading the Department of the Ohio headquartered in Cincinnati, had issued General Order No. 38, which banned traitorous conduct, especially sympathy for the enemy. Clement L. Vallandigham, a Dayton, Ohio, Democratic politician, defied the edict in a conscious attempt to appear a martyr to civil liberties. His subsequent arrest, military conviction, and later banishment to the Confederacy ignited an antiwar backlash that led to his nomination for governor. See *Herald,* May 9, 14, 19, 1863; Frank L. Klement, *The Limits of Dissent: Clement L. Vallandigham and the Civil War* (Lexington: University Press of Kentucky, 1970), 128–89; Mark E. Neely, Jr., *The Fate of Liberty: Abraham Lincoln and Civil Liberties* (New York: Oxford University Press, 1991), 65–68, 174.

65. Brig. Gen. John H. Morgan's cavalry had raided Ohio and panicked many citizens. See *Herald,* July 2, 1863; Edison H. Thomas, *John Hunt Morgan and His Raiders* (Lexington: University Press of Kentucky, 1975), 72–85.

66. As a prewar reformer, Voris had opposed the liquor trade and avoided alcohol. Although he strayed from his teetotaler habits under the strain of command, Voris had little sympathy for Colonel Dandy, who had gained a reputation for excessive drinking and lack of self-control (Wise, *Gate of Hell,* 39).

67. The War Department combined units on Folly and "adjacent islands" into the First Brigade, Second Division, Department of the South. This brigade, under Vogdes, held the 62d and 67th Ohio, 4th and 7th New Hampshire, 39th Illinois, 100th New York, 85th Pennsylvania, and 4th New York Independent Battalion. The brigade also had detachments from the 3d New York Heavy Artillery, 3d Rhode Island Heavy Artillery, 1st Massachusetts Cavalry, and 1st U.S. Artillery (*OR,* ser. 1, 28[pt. 2]:8, 13, 15).

68. Gillmore planned to capture Charleston by moving his infantry from Folly Island across Lighthouse Inlet to a staging area on the southern side of Morris Island. His troops, after a bombardment, would take Fort Wagner and Fort Gregg at the island's northern end. With those secure, Gillmore would use rifled artillery to reduce Fort Sumter. Once Gillmore accomplished these aims, he counted on Dahlgren's monitors to force Charleston's surrender without "a land attack." On July 10, Gillmore opened with the bombardment, followed by an infantry assault, but his indecision allowed the defenders to regroup. The following day, Gillmore ordered an unsuccessful attack on Fort Wagner. During this phase of operations, the 67th Ohio was unengaged and remained on Folly Island. See James Fisher to Hannah Fisher, July 14,

1863, Clay Papers, CAC; *Blade,* July 16, 1863; *OR,* ser. 1, 28[pt. 1]:3–13. Gillmore explained his plans in his *Engineer and Artillery Operations against the Defenses of Charleston in 1863: Comprising the Descent upon Morris Island, the Demolition of Fort Sumter, the Reduction of Forts Wagner and Gregg: With Observations on Heavy Ordnance, Fortification, Etc.* (New York: D. Van Nostrand, 1865).

69. Fort Wagner, Fort Gregg, Fort Johnson, and Cumming's Point Battery were south of Charleston harbor.

70. Although the news was nearly two weeks late, Voris learned that Grant had captured Vicksburg on July 4, 1863, a day after Maj. Gen. George G. Meade had repulsed Lee's final thrust at Gettysburg.

71. On July 18, Gillmore ordered a heavy bombardment of Fort Wagner that lasted from noon to the early evening. At 7:30, Brig. Gen. George C. Strong led the first wave of infantry, spearheaded by the African American 54th Massachusetts, supported by Col. Haldiman S. Putnam's brigade, consisting of five undermanned regiments, the 67th Ohio among them (*OR,* ser. 1, 28[pt. 1]:16).

72. The 67th Ohio moved against Fort Wagner with 210 officers and men. In his formal report, Maj. Lewis Butler, who assumed command when Voris fell, detailed the regiment's role in the battle and counted 124 casualties (5 killed, 76 wounded, and 43 missing), a rate of 59 percent (the regimental order book listed 136 casualties). Moreover, Butler noted that after Voris and Commager, the second in command, were wounded "before reaching the fort," he had led "a portion of the 67th" into Fort Wagner and remained there "nearly two hours—fighting hand-to-hand with the rebels." On that basis, Butler staked his claim for either his own command or replacing Voris on a permanent basis (*OR,* ser. 1, 28[pt. 1]: 210, 344, 347, 363, 53:5–8, 10–11; "Regimental Order Book," CAC; *Blade,* July 28, 1863; *Herald,* July 30, 1863.

73. Lydia Voris likely had to wait nearly two weeks before reading a full report about her husband's role and wounding in the attack (*Leader,* Aug. 3, 1863).

74. The *Cosmopolitan* was a transport steamer.

75. Jean Margaret Davenport Lander, "an actress of celebrity" and Brig. Gen. Frederick Lander's widow, was a nurse at Port Royal. See *Herald,* Mar. 4, 1862; Charles A. Hibbard, "Diary," Dec. 22, 1863, CAC; Esther Hill Hawk, *A Woman Doctor's Civil War Diary: Esther Hill's Diary,* ed. Gerald Schwartz (Columbia: University of South Carolina Press, 1989), 48.

76. "GLH" wrote that Voris's "many friends in Ohio will be pleased to learn that his wounds are doing as favorably as could be expected." Surgeon Forbes supplied further information. Voris was shot in the "abdominal wall" on the left side but improved each day. Capt. Lewis C. Hunt, Company A, added that Voris had conducted himself with "courage and coolness" (*Herald,* July 18, 28, 1863; *Blade,* July 22, 30, Aug. 1, 1863).

77. Chaplain Henry Clay Trumball, 10th Connecticut.

78. Clara Barton and Mary Gage, Frances Gage's daughter, were the only women on the battlefield. Voris was among the wounded Barton tended, and, according to a biographer, he "would have died but for her ministrations" (Barton, *Life of Clara Barton,* 249; Stephen B. Oates, *A Woman of Valor: Clara Barton and the Civil War* [New York: Free Press, 1994], 173, 446).

79. Voris, *Charleston in the Rebellion,* 33–43. When Voris detrained in Cleveland, a reporter wrote that he still "is suffering from his injuries. He is however in the best of spirits, and his general health is very good" (*Herald,* Aug. 4, 1863). "A grand reception of friends and the Akron Silver Cornet Band" turned out the next

day to greet Voris when he was scheduled to return home. He was not on the train. Instead, he had gone to Toledo "to see the wounded men." Next evening, Voris came home without fanfare (*Beacon*, Aug. 6, 1863; Voris, "Service File," NA).

CHAPTER 5: — *"Old Promptly Has Returned"*

1. John H. Chamberlin, an Akron businessman and politician, operated the Best-City Mills in Akron and had a branch office in New York City. See *Bailey's Akron Directory, 1871–1872* (Akron, Ohio: Akron Publishing, 1871), 208; Perrin, *History of Summit County,* 295, 328; *Times,* Sept. 11, 1872.

2. During Voris's convalescence, Gillmore had moved his heavy guns within range of both Fort Wagner and Fort Sumter and began a bombardment of Charleston. On Sept. 7, 1863, Confederates withdrew from Fort Wagner, because its usefulness had ended, and took new positions on James Island. The following day, Dahlgren tried but could not sustain an effort to capture Fort Sumter (Augustus F. Bull to Roxanna C. DeWitt, Aug. 15, 1863, Augustus F. Bull Papers, CAC; *Blade,* Sept. 8, 11, 16, 1863; *Leader,* Sept. 14, 23, 25, 1863).

3. USS *Weehawken.*

4. Details of these operations may be found in *OR,* ser.1, 28(pt. 1):622–26, 666, 718–27, 28(pt. 2):89–96, 100–101.

5. The 67th Ohio indeed gave Voris a rousing welcome. According to an on-looker, Voris seemed "fine as usual," although somewhat wan "from his late illness." Despite a "hoarse" voice, Voris raised morale "in this tired band" when he read Lydia's letter. She praised its "admirable" combat record and expressed her hope that the men would be "safely returned" to their homes. Voris then presented her regimental flag, an action that stimulated "long and loud cheers." Her flag, a bystander added, was "superior" to all others on "this Island. It bears upon its folds in letters of gold the names of the battles the 67th was participated in, as follows: Bloomery Gap, Feb. 14, 1862. Winchester, Mar. 23, 1862. Morris Island, July 10, 1863. Fort Wagner, July 18, 1863. Charleston is yet to be added" (Simeon and Silas Borton to Mary Borton, Sept. 16, 1863, Borton Papers, CAC; *Herald,* Sept. 24, 1863; *Beacon,* Oct. 8, 15, 1863).

6. Voris would have been relieved if he knew that Governor Tod decided to avoid consolidating "any Ohio Regts. now in the field until the war is over" (Tod to Stanton, Sept. 15, 18, 1863, OAGC).

7. The 67th Ohio was in the Second Division, Second Brigade. Led by Col. Joshua B. Howell, the Second Brigade also held the 39th Illinois, 62d Ohio, and 85th Pennsylvania (*OR,* ser. 1, 28[pt. 2]:74, 137).

8. Sen. Benjamin F. Wade, from Canfield, Ohio, chaired the influential Joint Committee on the Conduct of the War. A prowar Republican from Ravenna, Ohio, Rufus P. Spalding represented the Eighteenth Congressional District, which included Summit County. Salmon Chase, Ohio's leading Republican, was Lincoln's secretary of the treasury.

9. A prideful Voris wrote Toledo Mayor Charles M. Dorr that "The [old] flag has never been disgraced" (*Blade,* Sept. 25, 1863).

10. A shell fragment killed Capt. Joseph Woodruff, a native of Ottawa, Ill., Sept. 23, 1863 (Clark, *Thirty-Ninth Illinois,* 527).

11. Even though equally disturbed by the "slow progress at Charleston," Welles continued the bickering that marred the campaign. He blamed Gillmore for the delay and defended Dahlgren (Welles, *Diary,* 2:449).

12. Capt. Alfred Girty might have run the advertisement for innocent amusement, or an escape from boredom, but he was hardly fair to many lonely young women, especially those who had lost a loved one in the war. "A gentleman, and an officer of the Army of the Union, who has served his country for two weary years, and is now in the trenches before Charleston, wishes to correspond with some intelligent and accomplished young lady, with a view to fun, love or matrimony. Please address, with a Photograph, George I. Yates, Co. G, 67th Ohio Vols., Morris Island, South Carolina" (*Herald*, Sept. 26, 1863).

13. Gillmore was a native of Black River, Ohio.

14. Major Butler probably had another reason for disliking Voris. Butler opposed abolition and belittled African American troops in the attack on Fort Wagner (*Herald*, July 30, 1863; *Blade*, Sept. 8, 16, 1863; *OR*, ser. 1, 53:5–8).

15. "GLH" remarked that Voris's resumption of command improved discipline, an observation that likely further estranged Major Butler (*Herald*, Oct. 13, 1863). Another soldier also noted that, because of Voris, "We have a middling nice camp now, not sand about shoe top deep" (Simeon Borton to Mary Borton, Nov. 8, 1863, Borton Papers, CAC). The 67th Ohio's aggregate strength stood at 30 officers and 551 enlisted men (*OR*, ser. 1, 28[pt. 2]:108).

16. Probably Capt. Charles C. Lewis, Company K (*Roster*, 5:623).

17. After his successful Tullahoma campaign (June 23–July 3, 1863), Maj. Gen. William S. Rosecrans pushed on to Chattanooga. At the Battle of Chickamauga, Sept. 19–20, 1863, Gen. Braxton Bragg defeated Rosecrans. See William M. Lamers, *The Edge of Glory: A Biography of William S. Rosecrans, U.S.A.* (New York: Harcourt, Brace, and World, 1961), 274–400.

18. Voris's partisanship was palpable in the volatile Ohio gubernatorial race between John Brough, a fusion prowar Democratic-Republican candidate, and Peace Democrat Clement Vallandigham. In a speech to his troops that was reprinted throughout the state, Voris urged them to give "a vigorous and united support" to all prowar candidates. Directly censuring Vallandigham, Voris charged that the "peace party" would make all their sacrifices meaningless (Simeon and Silas Borton to Mary Borton, Sept. 16, 1863, Borton Papers, CAC; *Leader*, Oct. 17, 1863; *Herald*, Oct. 24, 1863; *Beacon*, Nov. 5, 1863).

19. From Sept. 29–Oct. 3, 1863, Union artillery fired 560 shots at Fort Sumter, and 324 struck the fort (*OR*, ser. 1, 28[pt. 1]:660).

20. A New York War Democrat, Gov. Horatio Seymour became an important national figure by criticizing the Lincoln Administration for its purported infringements of constitutional liberties. See Stuart Mitchell, *Horatio Seymour of New York* (Cambridge, Mass.: Harvard University Press, 1938), 231–364.

21. Voris's xenophobia toward Irish Americans was common in this period. "GLH" shared this prejudice. "Not a single native born citizen in the regiment voted for Vallandigham" (*Herald*, Oct. 24, 1863). For more on this topic, see Dale T. Knobel, *Paddy and the Republic: Ethnicity and Nationality in Antebellum America* (Middletown, Conn.: Wesleyan University Press, 1986).

22. Voris's partisanship worked. Brough received 233 votes in the 67th Ohio; Vallandigham, 29. Other Ohio regiments also had scant support for Vallandigham, giving him 2,298 to Brough's 41,467. Brough won the overall election, 288,374 to 186,492 (*Blade*, Oct. 21, 31, 1863; *Leader*, Oct. 26, 1863; Arnold M. Shankman, "Soldier Votes and Clement L. Vallandigham in the 1863 Ohio Gubernatorial Election," *Ohio History* 82 (winter–spring 1973): 88–104.

23. Maybe as a Republican election ploy, Chase had released $25,000,000 for unpaid soldiers (*Leader,* Oct. 17, 1863).

24. In teasing Lydia, Voris might have been reacting to a public letter that Capt. Sidney Brock, Company D, had written her about the flag: "We look upon it with pride and gladness, because we remember that the donor is watching us, and looks to us that it shall be borne in honor, and because it is the beautiful symbol of our country" (*Beacon,* Oct. 15, 1863).

25. Ohio and Pennsylvania gubernatorial elections were equally critical. In Pennsylvania, Andrew G. Curtin, the prowar Republican incumbent, beat antiwar George W. Woodward by 15,325 votes out of 529,992 cast. See Arnold M. Shankman, *The Pennsylvania Antiwar Movement, 1861–1865* (Rutherford, N.J.: Fairleigh Dickinson University Press, 1980), 122–28.

26. Gillmore had ordered the Second Brigade to Folly Island on Oct. 28, 1863 (*OR,* ser. 1, 53:94).

27. Voris likely repeated army gossip. Rather, Lincoln feared that the defeat at Chickamauga had immobilized Rosecrans. With that in mind, Lincoln appointed Grant head of all Union forces in the area bounded by the Appalachian Mountains and the Mississippi River. Grant took personal charge of military operations around Chattanooga and replaced Rosecrans with Maj. Gen. George H. Thomas. See Wiley Sword, *Mountains Touched with Fire: Chattanooga Besieged, 1863* (New York: St. Martin's Press, 1995).

28. Union shelling of Fort Sumter grew more intense from Oct. 26–Nov. 30, 1863. Weapons of various calibers sent 18,320 shots toward the fort, hitting it 13,436 times (*OR,* ser. 1., 28[pt. 1]:650).

29. On Oct. 28, 1863, Bragg approved a night attack under Lt. Gen. James Longstreet against an extended Union division at Wauthatchie, Tenn., near Hooker's main base. Although Bragg and Longstreet later disagreed about this attack's exact details, it resulted in a costly Confederate loss. See Judith L. Hallock, *Braxton Bragg and Confederate Defeat,* vol. 2 (Tuscaloosa: University of Alabama Press, 1991), 123–25.

30. By November 1863, Ohio had an estimated 400,000 men fit for military service (*The Union Army: A History of Military Affairs in the Loyal States, 1861–1865: Records of the Regiments in the Union Army, Cyclopedia of Battles, Memoirs of Commanders and Soldiers,* 8 vols. [Madison, Wis.: Federal Publishing, 1908], 2:337).

31. Not everything was so serene on Morris Island. High waves in late October nearly swamped Union positions (*Blade,* Nov. 11, 1863).

32. Sgt. James E. Bruce, Company C, and Priv. Charles F. Eurimius, Company E (*Roster,* 5:578, 594).

33. Voris additionally sent a brick to Governor Tod as a souvenir (*Blade,* Nov. 24, 1863).

34. The Akron Rifles, a prewar militia unit, had earned local plaudits for showy drills (Lane, *Fifty Years,* 351).

35. Voris was too optimistic. By Dec. 1, 1863, Meade's maneuvers south of the Rappahannock River, near Mine Run, a creek that flowed north into the Rapidan River, ended with little accomplished. See Freeman Cleaves, *Meade of Gettysburg* (Norman: University of Oklahoma Press, 1960), 201–13.

36. Ohio's quota was 29,352. Governor Tod suspended the draft until the state received full credit for its aggregate enlistments (*Leader,* Sept. 18, Oct. 22, Nov. 4, 1863; *Herald,* Nov. 2, 1863).

37. The role of African American troops from the 54th Massachusetts Volunteer

Infantry Regiment in the assault on Fort Wagner moderated the racialist assumptions of many white Union troops. See Joseph T. Glatthaar, *Forged in Battle: The Civil War Alliance of Black Soldiers and White Officers* (New York: Free Press, 1990), 135–43, 164. Voris discussed this attitudinal change in his postwar memoir: *Charleston in the Rebellion,* 35.

38. Grant ended the Chattanooga campaign (Oct. 26–Nov. 26, 1863) by his victory at Lookout Mountain and Bragg's retreat toward Dalton, Ga. See Peter Cozzens, *The Shipwreck of Their Hopes: The Battles for Chattanooga* (Urbana: University of Illinois Press, 1994).

39. Voris's admiration for Grant reflected a growing Union belief that he had become the Union's preeminent field commander. See Harry Williams, *Lincoln and His Generals* (New York: Knopf, 1952), 284–96.

40. For more on Voris's observations about the need for total war, see Hattaway and Jones, *How the Union Won,* 465–702.

41. The example that Voris had in mind was the destruction of Nineveh, the ancient capital of the Assyrian Empire, leveled by the Medes in 612 B.C.

42. *OR,* ser. 1, 28(pt. 2):137.

43. By December 1863, Ohio had enrolled 200,453 men in 129 often shorthanded infantry regiments (*Union Army,* 2:337).

44. Voris might have reacted to reports that appeared in many Ohio newspapers during the late fall about inhumane conditions facing Union prisoners of war. For instance, a *Leader* editorial about Libby Prison in Richmond stressed the Confederacy's "systematic brutality toward our brave and patriotic soldiers" (Nov. 14, 1863).

45. Frederic Augustus James, *Civil War Diary; Sumter to Andersonville,* ed. Jefferson J. Hammer (Rutherford, N.J.: Fairleigh Dickinson University Press, 1973), is a representative example of reminiscences written by Union prisoners of war. See also William Marvel, *Andersonville: The Last Depot* (Chapel Hill: University of North Carolina Press, 1994); and Lonnie R. Spears, *Portals to Hell: Military Prisons of the Civil War* (Mechanicsburg, Pa.: Stackpole, 1997).

46. On Dec. 8, 1863, President Lincoln pleased both abolitionists and conservatives when he issued his Proclamation of Amnesty and Reconstruction. Abolitionists admired Lincoln's praise of African American troops and his determination to make emancipation a precondition for reconstruction. Conservatives appreciated his promises to restore the seceding states without property confiscation (beyond African American freedom), no prosecution of Confederates for treason, and the use of labor contracts for freedpersons to cushion the economic consequences of emancipation. See David H. Donald, *Lincoln* (New York: Simon & Schuster, 1995), 469–74. Chase's well-known ambition to supplant Lincoln in the 1864 presidential race disillusioned many Ohioans, including Voris. See Frederick J. Blue, *Salmon P. Chase: A Life in Politics* (Kent, Ohio: Kent State University Press, 1987), 220–35.

47. The abolitionist in Voris likely found Lincoln's position especially apt regarding African Americans.

48. George Benedict was an army paymaster during this period.

49. Much of this land, which sold below market price, ended in the hands of Northern speculators rather than freed African Americans. See Elizabeth Ware Pearson, ed., *Letters from Port Royal, 1862–1868* (1906; rpt., New York: Arno Press, 1969), 25; Rose, *Rehearsal for Reconstruction,* 199–216.

50. Joseph E. Stevens, *1863: The Rebirth of a Nation* (New York: Bantam, 1999), reviews the events in this momentous year.

51. A conscript could avoid military service by either finding a substitute or

paying the government a $300 commutation fee. These provisions created resentments that crossed class, ethnic, religious, and occupational lines, much to the benefit of Peace Democrats. See James W. Geary, "Civil War Conscription in the North: A Historiographic Review," *Civil War History* 32 (September 1986): 208–28.

52. The competition among northern Ohio regiments for new recruits became intense. In one typical advertisement, 2d Lt. Charles F. Minor, the 67th Ohio's main recruiter in Cleveland, mixed patriotism and economic self-interest with a way to escape Cleveland's harsh winters. Promising that volunteers would receive "the largest bounties paid," Minor asserted that the regiment was stationed "where we have a mild climate, plenty of food, good clothing and regular pay. Come and assist us in the capture of Charleston" (*Blade,* Nov. 25, 1863, Feb. 13, Mar. 7, 24, 1864; Reid, *Ohio in the War,* 2:174–75; *OR,* ser. 3, 3:415–16, 2084, 1155–56, 1172–73, 1179–80; *Herald,* Dec. 8, 1863, May 7, 1864).

CHAPTER 6: — *"Days of Intense Anxiety and Peril"*

1. What became of "America" is unknown. Based on information in Voris's letters and his family's oral history, "America" probably settled in Akron and worked on a farm owned by Voris's sisters. Voris's activities, recruitment effort, and the 67th Ohio's movements from Jan. 4–Feb. 20, 1864, may be found in Voris, "Service File," NA; relevant northern Ohio newspapers; and *OR,* ser. 1, 35(pt. 1):30–32, 456–464, 35(pt. 2):36, 50, 59, 53:477–78.

2. Voris issued strict orders to maintain discipline and prevent drunkenness on this troop train. Enlisted men had to remain on assigned cars, even when the train stopped at a station. Voris also barred "the use of intoxicating drinks" and "hoped" officers would set an example of "this very wholesome prohibition" (*Herald,* Apr. 9, 1864). Charles E. Finsley, ed., *Hannah's Letters: Civil War Letters of Isaac E. Blauvelt, Friends, and Other Suitors* (Cedar Hill, Tex.: Kings Creek Press, 1997), presents another view of the events Voris discussed. Margaret Leech, *Reveille in Washington, 1860–1865* (New York: Harper and Bros., 1941), traces wartime life in the nation's capital.

3. Senator Wade garnered the nickname "Bluff Ben" because of his often crude manner and aggressive abolitionism. See Hans L. Trefousse, *Benjamin Franklin Wade: Radical Republican from Ohio* (New York: Twayne, 1963).

4. Voris and former Congressman Sidney Edgerton had been fellow attorneys in Akron. Wade had become a derisive figure when he joined the sightseers who fled the battlefield in panic.

5. The Christian Commission, organized in 1861 by Protestant ministers, the Young Men's Christian Association, and the American Tract Society, distributed religious material to the Union army, held revivals, and sponsored military relief under George H. Stuart's stewardship. See William Q. Maxwell, *Lincoln's Fifth Wheel: The Political History of the United States Sanitary Commission* (New York: Longmans, Green, 1956), 191–92; George M. Fredrickson, *The Inner Civil War: Northern Intellectuals and the Crisis of the Union* (New York: Harper & Row, 1965), 107.

6. Francis Pond, the 62d Ohio's commanding officer and senior to Osborn and Voris, headed the First Brigade.

7. John L. Motley, an American historian, wrote *The Rise of the Dutch Republic* in 1856. Perhaps unaware of the extent of his Dutch ancestry, Voris probably drew a parallel between his motivation for military service and one of Motley's major themes, the conflict between despotism and human freedom.

8. Noah H. Swayne was a Supreme Court associate justice, 1862–1881. Maj. Gen. James A. Garfield, the future president, entered the House of Representatives in December 1863. A staunch abolitionist and newspaper editor, Henry E. Peck, an Oberlin College academic, raised troops for the 41st Ohio Volunteer Infantry Regiment. James C. Wetmore, a member of Ohio's Sanitary Commission, was the state's military agent in Washington.

9. Volunteer officers with little or no military background relied upon Maj. Gen. Silas Casey's *System of Infantry Tactics,* usually known as *Casey's Tactics.*

10. Casey informed a glowing Voris, "The 67th Ohio is an admirable Regiment—your marching was excellent" (*Blade,* Apr. 27, 1864). Such praise compensated for the complaints of one private that "Colonel A. C. is stricter than hell" (Simeon Borton to Mary Borton, Mar. 27, 1864, Borton Papers, CAC).

11. The 67th Ohio, 62d Ohio, 39th Illinois, and 85th Pennsylvania formed the First Brigade in the First Division, Tenth Army Corps, Army of the James, Maj. Gen. Benjamin F. Butler commanding (*OR,* ser. 1, 33:1005).

12. Gloucester Point on the James River, across from Yorktown, became the staging area for Tenth Corps. *OR,* ser. 1, 36(pt. 2):44, lists the Tenth Corps's itinerary from May 4–June 9, 1864.

13. Brig. Gen. Alfred Terry was Voris's division commander. Maj. Gen. Quincy Gillmore led the Tenth Corps.

14. The First Division, outside of the largely western First Brigade, contained eight eastern regiments. This mixture often acerbated the sectional rivalries that Voris noted (*OR,* ser. 1, 36[pt. 2]:13).

15. Capt. Sidney Brock, the 67th Ohio's adjutant.

16. The *John Tucker,* a converted merchantman.

17. Although partially recovered from his multiple wounds at Fort Wagner, Lt. Col. Henry Steele Commager rejoined the 67th Ohio with Company A, which had been on leave in Toledo after reenlisting (*Blade,* May 13, 1864; *Herald,* May 28, 1864; *OR,* ser. 3, 53:482–483).

18. Koch & Myers, an Akron mercantile store.

19. Capt. John Smith's efforts at Jamestown during the early colonization of Virginia had become the stuff of legend.

20. Sunstroke. This malady, unusual for early May, even in Virginia, might have been analogous to modern battle fatigue. See Eric T. Dean, Jr., *Shook over Hell: Post-Traumatic Stress, Vietnam, and the Civil War* (Cambridge, Mass.: Harvard University Press, 1997), 131.

21. After indeed surprising the Confederates, Butler wasted precious time by digging defensive positions. Once he felt secure, Butler advanced, sending the First and Second Brigade toward Chester Station along the route of the Richmond & Petersburg Railroad (*OR,* ser. 1, 36[pt. 2]:591).

22. With Pond absent on "detached service," acting General Officer of the Day Voris took temporary command of the First Brigade (ibid., ser. 1, 36[pt. 2]:44).

23. Voris reported that his command contained "539 enlisted men and 26 officers" from the 67th and "one section of the First Connecticut Battery" (ibid., ser. 1, 51[pt. 1]:1124).

24. The Confederate attack found Voris essentially isolated. The nearest Union brigade was a mile to his right, another three miles south. When Gillmore sent in the reinforcements Voris requested, he posted them in a crescent. The 67th Ohio took the center, the 13th Indiana the left, and the 169th New York the right. African American cavalry from the Eighteenth Corps guarded the flanks, and several smaller

units were in reserve (ibid.). "GLC" described the 67th Ohio's role in this battle and particularly praised Voris's combat leadership. He "was at all points on the line observing the progress of affairs, giving orders with the assurance of a veteran" (*Herald,* May 28, 1864). See William G. Robertson, *Back Door to Richmond: The Bermuda Hundred Campaign, April–June 1864* (Newark: University of Delaware Press, 1987), 123–27.

25. Voris miscounted enemy strength, largely because difficult terrain prevented accuracy. Confederates outnumbered his force only in the battle's initial stage (Robertson, *Back Door to Richmond,* 128).

26. Brig. Gen. Adelbert Ames, commanding the Third Division, Tenth Corps (*OR,* ser. 1, 36[pt. 2]:14).

27. This detachment came from the Eighteenth Army Corps, Third Division, First Brigade, under Brig. Gen. Edward A. Wild (ibid., 16).

28. Col. Joshua Blackwood Howell, 85th Pennsylvania, the First Brigade's senior officer, now took command. In his official report, Howell especially singled out Voris and the 67th Ohio. Their position "was gallantly held by the gallant colonel and his brave regiment" (ibid., 45).

29. Voris's official report appears in ibid., ser. 1, 51(pt. 1):1224–25. His overall role in the Battle of Chester Station appears in ibid., ser. 1, 36(pt. 2):36, 45–47, 109–10; *Blade,* May 18, 19, 1864; *Herald,* May 14, 20, 1864.

30. 1st Lt. Henry W. Wallick, Company C, and 1st Lt. George M. Ballard, Company C (*Roster,* 5:578; *OR,* ser. 1, 36[pt. 2]:19).

31. Voris's gripe missed a larger point. Newspaper coverage concentrated on the larger and more critical battles of the Wilderness and Spotsylvania, May 5–12, 1864.

32. Surgeon Forbes backed Voris's self-satisfaction. "Col. Voris . . . is highly complimented by the commanding General, and deserves some substantial acknowledgment of his services" (*Blade,* May 19, 1864).

33. The qualities Voris prized did gain the attention of Commager's superiors. He became colonel of the 184th Ohio Volunteer Infantry Regiment and was discharged as a brevet brigadier general of volunteers (*Roster,* 5:565).

34. Major Butler left the 67th Ohio on Oct. 10, 1864, to assume command of the 182d Ohio Volunteer Infantry Regiment. He ended the war with the rank of brevet brigadier general of volunteers (ibid.).

35. The Battle of the Wilderness, May 5–7, 1864.

36. Voris's periodic loss of vitality stemmed from the undiagnosed bullet fragment near his bladder.

CHAPTER 7:—*"Constantly under Fire"*

1. Clark, *Thirty-Ninth Regiment,* 75–186, covers the regiment's record prior to this campaign.

2. The 39th Illinois (First Division, First Brigade) had 173 total casualties from May 5–31, 1864 (*OR,* ser. 1, 36[pt. 2]:13, 85–86, 88–89, 91).

3. 6th Connecticut, First Division, Second Brigade; 13th Indiana, Second Division, Second Brigade (ibid., ser. 1, 36[pt. 2]:110–11).

4. The sounds Voris heard came from the Battle of Drewry's Bluff that began at 4:45 A.M. on May 16 with a Confederate attack on Brig. Gen. Charles A. Heckman's First Brigade, Second Division, Eighteenth Army Corps (*OR,* ser. 1, 36[pt. 2]:212, 236–37, 247–48, 253–54).

5. *New York Herald,* May 14, 1864. Such selective coverage reflected regional biases and readership preferences. As an example, the *Beacon* adopted a local slant

when reports about Chester Station reached Akron: "Our people have reason to feel proud of the mark which our fellow townsman—the gallant Colonel [Voris]—is making for himself and them in this present struggle" (May 19, 1864).

6. Confederates captured Heckman and some 600 of his men (*OR*, ser. 1, 36[pt. 2]:78–80). The Battle of Drewry's Bluff became the 39th's "first real battle." They lost 119 officers and men (Clark, *Thirty-Ninth Regiment*, 187).

7. These stragglers possibly came from the 9th New Jersey. See *OR*, ser. 1, 36[pt. 2]:78–80; J. Madison Drake, *The History of the Ninth New Jersey Veteran Vols . . .* (Elizabeth: Journal Printing House, 1889), 194–97, 202, 398–399.

8. Voris was not boasting. After Butler's defeat at Drewry's Bluff, he withdrew the Army of the James to a defensive perimeter at Bermuda Hundred, anchored by the James and Appomattox Rivers. With his forces checkmated, Butler fell short of achieving his prime objectives (*OR*, ser. 1, 46[pt. 1]:20; Robertson, *Back Door to Richmond*, 170–242).

9. At the Battle of Ware Bottom Church, May 20, 1864, Confederates captured rifle pits along Gillmore's front early in the morning and threatened to "overwhelm" the 85th Pennsylvania. Amid heavy fighting that afternoon, Howell's brigade regained the lost ground. The 67th Ohio marched "double quick" under Voris's incessant prodding, Howell reported, and was the key in blunting an enemy counterattack. "In about thirty minutes" of severe fighting, Howell continued, "I lost 149 men, killed and wounded" (*OR*, ser. 1, 36[pt. 2]:278–81, 51[pt. 1]:Supplement, 1237–38).

10. Capt. George Emmerson, Company F, died May 23, 1864. After recovering from this wound, 2d Lt. Charles E. Minor, Company B, mustered out of service, Dec. 7, 1865. 1st Lt. John C. Cochrane, Company K, developed gangrene and died, May 29, 1864. The 67th Ohio totaled 9 killed and 60 wounded (*Roster*, 5:573, 597, 611, 623; *OR*, ser. 3, 53:478; *Blade*, May 27, 1864; *Herald*, June 4, 1864).

11. For an extended survey of such conditions, consult [U.S. Surgeon General's Office], *The Medical and Surgical History of the War of the Rebellion (1861–1865)*, 3 vols. (Washington, D.C.: Government Printing Office, 1870–1888), pt. 1, vol. 1, appendix, 148–202, pt. 3, vol. 2. See also Frank R. Freemon, *Gangrene and Glory: Medical Care during the American Civil War* (Madison, N.J.: Fairleigh Dickinson University Press, 1998).

12. Brig. Gen. William S. Walker's capture by the 67th Ohio produced an unexpected dividend. Military maps in his possession gave Union forces an invaluable overview of troop disposition in his command and the location of Confederate forces from City Point to Richmond (*Herald*, June 4, 1864; *OR*, ser. 1, 36[pt. 2]:276, 36[pt. 3]:140; Robertson, *Back Door to Richmond*, 228).

13. *Blade*, May 28, 1864, listed the total casualties in these two battles. Surgeon Westfall combined pride with regret in explaining these unprecedented figures: the 67th Ohio's "good name here is operating to its disadvantage, as its sterling qualities are too frequently called into requisition in posts of danger where many regiments dare not to be trusted" (*Herald*, June 4, 1864). Voris found consolation for these sacrifices in his religious faith. He sponsored prayer meetings, conducted some of them, and authorized resolutions passed in the regiment's name to honor "fallen comrades" (ibid., July 9, 1864). See also Drew G. Faust, "The Civil War Soldier and the Art of Dying," *Journal of Southern History* 66 (February 2001): 3–38, for the connection between religious faith and death.

14. James Ballard, a prominent Toledoan, arrived at Bermuda Hundred to take his son's body home for burial.

15. An abatis, cut trees with pointed tops, interlaced by branches, set on the front of a entrenched line, faced the enemy.

16. Grant had an equally harsh appraisal of Butler and sought a face-saving way to remove him without forfeiting Butler's political support of Lincoln. See Ulysses S. Grant, *Personal Memoirs of U.S. Grant,* 2 vols. (New York: C. L. Webster, 1886), 2:74–76.

17. Recognizing that his promotion hinged on firm political support, Voris relied on two prominent local politicians, Rufus Spalding, his congressional representative, and William H. Upson, a former Summit County state senator, currently a delegate to the party's national convention.

18. Gary W. Gallagher, *The Confederate War: How Popular Will, Nationalism, and Military Strategy Could Not Stave Off Defeat* (Cambridge, Mass.: Harvard University Press, 1997), presents a scholarly assessment similar to Voris's contemporary judgment.

19. Ohioans shared Voris's pride. Reviewing the 67th Ohio's recent combat record, the *Blade* editorialized that "a braver regiment is not in the service. None have been more thoroughly tried and certainly none have come out of the trial more triumphantly" (June 3, 1864).

20. 4th New Jersey Light Battery, Second Division, Second Brigade, Tenth Corps (*OR,* ser. 1, 36[pt. 2]:14, 61).

21. 1st Lt. William H. Kief, Company F (*Roster,* 5:597).

22. Howell's report left more to the imagination than direct censure of the 6th Connecticut. He mentioned that the regiment "had been ordered out" of their "intrenchments" and that the brigade "passed them on my way out." But Howell did not specifically reproach the 6th Connecticut, and he concluded that his entire unit never behaved "better" (*OR,* ser. 1, 51[pt. 1]:Supplement, 1237–38).

23. Brigadier General Terry, Voris's division commander, held him in high esteem. In reporting about Chester Station, Terry wrote: "Colonel Voris, of the Sixty-seventh Ohio, not only deserves most honorable mention, but the higher reward of promotion" (ibid., ser. 1, 51[pt. 1]:Supplement, 1231). When Terry took command of the corps on June 11, 1864, he "requested" Voris to "assume command of the Brigade at once" (Capt. George H. Hopkins to Voris, June 11, 1864, Voris, "Service File," NA).

24. After again shifting the Army of the Potomac leftward to flank Lee, Grant was now less than ten miles northeast of Richmond, near the small settlement of Cold Harbor.

25. For the same qualities Voris admired in Grant, see John F. C. Fuller, *Grant and Lee: A Study in Personality and Generalship* (London: Eyre and Spottiswoode, 1933); and John Keegan, *The Mask of Command* (New York: Viking, 1987), 164–234.

26. Emory M. Thomas, *The Confederate Nation, 1861–1865* (New York: Harper & Row, 1979), 67–224, elaborates upon those traits that Voris believed sustained the Confederacy.

27. Richard F. Bensel, *Yankee Leviathan: The Origins of Central State Authority in America, 1859–1877* (New York: Cambridge University Press, 1990), elaborates on this wartime centralization. Neely's *Fate of Liberty* explores some of the policies Voris urged.

28. Voris's views about how wartime hatreds would complicate victory probably stemmed from his experience with Confederate civilians in western Virginia and Suffolk. For a verification of his beliefs, see Brooks D. Simpson, LeRoy P. Graf, and John Muldowny, eds., *Advice after Appomattox: Letters to Andrew Johnson, 1865–1866* (Knoxville: University Of Tennessee Press, 1987).

29. The 67th Ohio lost 147 officers and men from May 5–31, 1864 (*Herald,* June 11, 1864; *OR,* ser. 1, 36[pt. 2]:14).

30. Heavy but largely ineffective shelling fell on the 67th Ohio's picket line from June 1–3, 1864, causing five casualties (*OR,* ser. 3, 53:478).

31. On July 10, 1864, the regiment's manpower report listed 565 officers and men. Of these, 108 were on sick call (ibid., ser. 1, 40[pt. 3]:140).

32. Ohio supplied 35,982 "Hundred-Days Men," organized in forty-one regiments and one battalion. Although these men expected noncombatant duties, shortage of troops in the Union army forced four such regiments into the Army of the James. See Reid, *Ohio in the War*, 2:208–20; Jim Leeke, *A Hundred Days to Richmond: Ohio's "Hundred Days" Men in the Civil War* (Bloomington: Indiana University Press, 1999).

33. After the costly defeat at Cold Harbor, June 3, 1864, Grant moved the Army of the Potomac on another flanking maneuver, this one across the James River toward Petersburg and Butler's position at Bermuda Hundred (*OR*, ser. 1, 40[pt. 1]:12–14, 21–27).

34. Redans, field works usually constructed from earth and timber, shaped in an inverted V, protected artillery from enemy fire.

35. As General Officer of the Day, Voris anticipated an early morning assault on his picket line along the front at Bermuda Hundred. Acting on his own initiative, Voris counterattacked with units from the First Brigade, capturing Confederate breastworks, thirty stands of small arms, three officers, and twenty-six men (*OR*, ser. 1, 40[pt. 1]:683–86, 51[pt. 1]:Supplement, 1167–68). Sgt. Maj. Emil Rampano, Company A, received promotion to second lieutenant, May 25, 1864 (*Roster*, 5:566).

36. Albert B. Buttles, a Franklin County, Ohio, Republican, was a delegate to the national convention (*Leader*, June 7, 1864).

37. While Voris and his command were on picket duty, they heard "heavy and rapid firing in the direction of Petersburg," prompting one soldier in the 67th Ohio to exult that Grant "has caught the rebels napping south of Richmond" (*Blade*, June 25, 1864). This observation was too optimistic. Grant's orders to extend the siege lines around Petersburg largely failed.

38. Howell wrote that 133 men, "being new to fire broke and run, with the exception of two or three companies." These men, added Brig. Gen. Robert S. Foster, who briefly led the Tenth Corps's First Division, were "100-days" men (*OR*, ser. 1, 40[pt. 1]:683–86).

39. Capt. George L. Childs, Company C, regimental adjutant (*Herald*, Apr. 9, 1864; *Roster*, 5:578).

40. President Lincoln arrived at City Point on June 20, 1864, to confer with Grant. Afterward, the presidential party watched an informal review (*New York Times*, June 26, 1864; Horace Porter, *Campaigning with Grant* [New York: Century, 1897], 216–24).

CHAPTER 8: — *"A Desolated Country Cursed by Slavery and Slavery's War"*

1. A squabble between Chase and Secretary of State William H. Seward over New York City Custom House spoils precipitated Chase's immediate downfall. But Chase had sealed his fate months earlier with his abortive quest to replace Lincoln. After former Governor David Tod pleaded that ill health precluded taking over for Chase, Lincoln named Maine Senator William P. Fessenden the new secretary of the treasury. See Charles A. Jellison, *Fessenden of Maine: Civil War Senator* (Syracuse, N.Y.: Syracuse University Press, 1962), 180–82; Blue, *Salmon P. Chase*, 233–38.

2. Voris, like other Union officers, continued to overestimate enemy manpower, whom they outnumbered by better than two to one. See Emory M. Thomas, *Robert E. Lee: A Biography* (New York: W. W. Norton, 1995), 321.

3. Frustrated by silence about his promotion, Voris vented his feelings to Chamberlin. Ohio lacked influence in Washington with Chase gone, Voris fumed. Nor could he depend on Spalding or Upson. Worse, "Campaigning on the South side of the James is a poor place to electioneer" (Voris to Chamberlin, July 4, 1864, Johnson Collection).

4. Desertions plagued both armies. Lee advocated extreme measures only when the "interests and safety of the country" were at risk (*OR*, ser. 1, 42[pt. 2]:1169). Terry issued a similar notice. Fearing that fraternization would encourage desertions, Terry banned any future "intercourse" with the enemy. Only enlisted men, accompanied by an officer, could cross "our picket-line toward that of the enemy." In all other instances, "every sentry on the picket-line" must "fire at once, without further orders" (ibid., ser. 1, 40[pt. 2]:594). See Ella Lonn, *Desertion during the Civil War* (New York: Century, 1928).

5. Grant issued Special Order No. 82 to clarify this policy. He stipulated that the army would not force Confederate deserters into "military duty" that might lead to their capture. Deserters could if they desired, on taking an oath of allegiance to the United States, serve as noncombatants at the same pay scale as civilians. Deserters who took an oath not to continue fighting would receive food and transportation to their homes, provided they were within Union lines (*OR*, ser. 1, 42[pt. 2]:555–56, ser. 3, 4:90–91).

6. Lt. Gen. Jubal A. Early led his veteran force of around 14,000 men in an extended raid from June 24–Aug. 4, 1864. They invaded Maryland, reached the outskirts of Washington, collected tribute from residents of Hagerstown and Frederick, and eventually burned Chambersburg, Pa. Early had two aims, each unachieved. He sought to free Confederate prisoners held in Maryland and to force Grant to relax his pressure on Lee's Richmond-Petersburg front by transferring large numbers of troops northward. See B. Franklin Cooling, *Jubal Early's Raid on Washington, 1864* (Baltimore: Nautical & Aviation Pub. Co. of America, 1989).

7. *OR*, ser. 1, 37(pt. 1):181–91, 334, 363, 40(pt. 2):599, 619, covers much of Early's raid.

8. While illness was common in the Army of the James, sick call was often a way to avoid combat. On July 10, the 67th Ohio had 19.5 percent of its enlisted men on sick call (ibid., ser. 1, 40[pt. 3]:140).

9. At the Battle of Monocacy (July 9, 1864) east of Frederick, Md., Maj. Gen. Lew Wallace suffered a technical defeat against Early but managed to gain time for the arrival of some reinforcements Grant sent to defend Washington. See B. Franklin Cooling, *Monocacy: The Battle that Saved Washington* (Shippensburg, Pa.: White Mane, 1997).

10. Early chose not to assault Washington after deciding the city's defenses were too formidable (*Leader,* July 12, 13, 18, 1864; *Herald,* July 12, 14, 1864).

11. On July 18, 1864, President Jefferson Davis replaced defensive-minded Gen. Joseph E. Johnston as head of the Army of Tennessee with the more aggressive Gen. John B. Hood. The conflicting reports Voris described probably referred to Hood's ineffectual attack (July 20, 1864) on Maj. Gen. William T. Sherman at the Battle of Peachtree Creek, some three miles north of Atlanta. See Albert Castel, *Decision in the West: The Atlanta Campaign of 1864* (Lawrence: University Press of Kansas, 1992), 189–212.

12. Capt. Lewis Cass Hunt, Company A (*Roster*, 5:565). Brig. Gen. Henry J. Hunt served as chief of artillery, Army of the Potomac. Lewis Cass, a native of Exeter, N.H., and a one-time Marietta, Ohio, attorney, was a distinguished prewar Democratic

politician. See Willard C. Klunder, *Lewis Cass and the Politics of Moderation* (Kent, Ohio: Kent State University Press, 1996).

13. Col. Louis Bell, 4th New Hampshire, Third Brigade, Second Division, Tenth Army Corps (*OR*, ser. 1, 40[pt. 2]:325–26).

14. Voris relied on secondhand information for this criticism. African American troops did perform bravely at the Battle of the Crater (July 30, 1864). Yet Voris was correct in one way: incompetent officers often harmed the Army of the Potomac's efficiency (*Herald*, Aug. 3, 1864; *OR*, ser. 1, 40[pt. 1]:17–117; Cornish, *Sable Arm*, 273–77).

15. Allen C. Guelzo, *Abraham Lincoln: Redeemer President* (Grand Rapids, Mich.: William B. Eerdmans, 1999), lists Lincoln's motivation for such days of fasts and prayers.

16. An official court of inquiry about the Crater held Burnside, Brig. Gen. James H. Ledlie, and Brig. Gen. Edward Ferrero responsible for the slaughter of Union troops, African American and white alike. Ledlie resigned on Jan. 23, 1865. Burnside followed, Apr. 15, 1865. Ferrero stayed in service, and for unclear reasons received a brevet to major general, Dec. 2, 1864.

17. The discharge of veteran troops at the expiration of their terms, the integration of the remaining men in new regiments, and the introduction of untested recruits often lowered the efficiency of various units in the Army of the Potomac. *OR*, ser. 1, 40(pt. 2):588, notes a typical format.

18. Barton, a recent arrival at Bermuda Hundred, was supervising nurse in a Tenth Corps field hospital on the James River (Pryor, *Professional Angel*, 127).

19. Maj. Gen. James B. McPherson died July 22, 1864, at Atlanta. For a study of his career, see Elizabeth J. Whaley, *Forgotten Hero: General James B. McPherson* (New York: Exposition Press, 1995).

20. Barton was a few months short of her forty-third birthday when the thirty-seven-year-old Voris made this patronizing statement.

21. Voris wrote that he hoped Barton would renew their friendship, pledged to help her in her "good work," and admitted that he relied upon her if he was again wounded and needed "some kind angel of mercy to look after me" (Voris to Barton, Aug. 13, 1864, cited by Oates, *Woman of Valor*, 264).

CHAPTER 9:—
"I Would Not Feel It Any Degradation to Command Colored Troops"

1. *OR*, ser. 1, 42(pt. 1):99–100, ser. 3, 3:478, covers Voris's combat record during this period.

2. Voris took personal command of four companies, B, D, H, and I, and "led the battalion in the assault on the first line of rifle pits" (ibid., ser. 1, 42[pt. 1]:696).

3. The brigade lost "about one-third of its effective strength" with the 39th Illinois having the heaviest losses. The 67th Ohio had "light" casualties (*Blade*, Aug. 26, 1864; *Herald*, Sept. 10, 1864).

4. In the midst of the fighting on Aug. 16, 1864, Voris assumed command of the First Brigade when heat prostration forced Howell's "temporary absence." He returned two days later, and Voris reverted to his regimental duties (*OR*, ser. 1, 42[pt. 1]:119, 686–89, 696, 701).

5. Brig. Gen. John R. Chambliss, Jr., the commander of a Confederate cavalry brigade, died on Aug. 16, 1864. The regiment took "a very perfect map" from his body detailing the "complete fortifications" around Richmond "and the surrounding country on both sides of the [James] river" (ibid., ser. 1, 42[pt. 2]:204, 210, 249, 313, 316, 1189).

6. The 67th Ohio lost 42 officers and men. By contrast, the 39th Illinois suffered 103 casualties (*Blade*, Aug. 27, 1864; *OR*, ser. 1, 42[pt. 1]: 119).

7. The Tenth Corps, including the 67th Ohio, moved from Bermuda Hundred to the Petersburg front, a distance of some eight miles, on Aug. 25, 1864 (*Herald*, Sept. 1, 1864).

8. The 67th Ohio "now occupy the trenches," the *Blade* explained, "and every exposure of a head or part of a person is greeted by a shot from a rebel sharpshooter" (*Blade*, Sept. 2, 1864).

9. Fatalities were generally light in these exchanges (ibid., Sept. 8, 1864).

10. *OR*, ser. 1, 42(pt. 1):651, 713, covers these events.

11. Dorothea Lynn Dix, the head of the Department of Female Nurses, had established these guidelines. See Helen E. Marshall, *Dorothea Dix: Forgotten Samaritan* (Chapel Hill: University of North Carolina Press, 1937), 204–9.

12. The 320 kegs of gunpowder, weighing four tons, had left a visible cavity, about 30 feet deep and 170 by 65 feet in area. See Noah A. Trudeau, *The Last Citadel: Petersburg, Virginia, June 1864–April 1865* (Boston: Little, Brown, 1991), 102–27.

13. Dr. James Westfall had replaced Forbes, who resigned on Oct. 7, 1863, as regimental surgeon (*Roster*, 5:565).

14. General Hood evacuated Atlanta, Sept. 1, 1864. Maj. Gen. Henry W. Slocum's Twentieth Corps took possession the following day.

15. After sending Thomas to middle Tennessee to counter Hood, Sherman cut his army from its supply base and began his "March to the Sea" and then northward. See Joseph T. Glatthaar, *The March to the Sea and Beyond: Sherman's Troops in the Savannah and Carolinas Campaigns* (New York: New York University Press, 1985); Lee B. Kennett, *Marching through Georgia: The Story of Soldiers and Civilians during Sherman's Campaign* (New York: HarperCollins, 1993); and Charles Royster, *The Destructive War: William Tecumseh Sherman, Stonewall Jackson, and the Americans* (New York: Alfred A. Knopf, 1991), 3–33, 79–143, analyze this operation

16. The Battle of Olustee, about fifty miles southwest of Jacksonville, Fla., took place, Feb. 20, 1864.

17. Democrats nominated McClellan for president and George H. Pendleton as vice president. Under Vallandigham's leadership, Peace Democrats, or Copperheads as their opponents labeled them, dominated the platform committee. They considered the war a failure, assailed Lincoln's alleged erosions of civil liberties, and sought a negotiated peace. See William F. Zornow, *Lincoln and the Party Divided* (Norman: University of Oklahoma Press, 1954), 129–40.

18. Grant also worried about the military implications of McClellan's nomination. Grant wrote Secretary of War Stanton that, while Confederate deserters "are nearly universally tired of war," other potential deserters hesitated, because "they believe peace will be negotiated after the fall elections" (*OR*, ser. 1, 42[pt. 2]:804). See also Harriet C. Owsley, "Peace and the Presidential Election of 1864," *Tennessee Historical Quarterly* 17 (March 1959): 3–19.

19. Camp Holly was slightly north of Deep Bottom.

20. Voris reported to Terry that Confederate artillery shelling fell along the brigade's front, and sappers labored at night to extend enemy lines. In frustration, Voris complained that "musketry" in the dark was ineffective in "preventing their work." Acting on this intelligence, Terry ordered the brigade not to waste ammunition, "unless the enemy advanced" (*OR*, ser. 1, 42[pt. 2]:765, 792, 803, 850).

21. On July 18, 1864, President Lincoln issued a call for an additional 500,000 volunteers. If states did not meet their assigned quotas, a September draft would fill

such deficiencies. As Voris observed, these stipulations provoked a new round of partisan bitterness between prowar forces and Peace Democrats. *Beacon,* Aug. 4, 1864; *Herald,* Sept. 15, 1864; *Leader,* Sept. 17, 1864, touch on this situation.

22. Mollie was Voris's sister-in-law. Three of Voris's younger brothers served in Illinois regiments. Roswell Voris died at Andersonville Prison. 1st Lt. Henry Voris (1864) and Capt. Samuel P. Voris (1865) died from war-related causes. After the war, Voris dedicated three memorial windows in Buckley Chapel to honor his brothers's memory (Janet Hewett, ed., *The Roster of Union Soldiers, 1861–1865: Illinois,* 3 vols. [Wilmington, N.C.; Broadfoot, 1999], 3:326).

23. Howell was severely injured (Sept. 8, 1864) when his horse stumbled and rolled over his body. Interim command of the First Brigade passed to Francis Pond, the senior officer. Pond, however, fell sick with some undisclosed "illness." Four days later, Terry reassigned Pond to the Third Brigade and replaced him with Voris. Howell did not recover, dying Sept. 12, 1864 (*OR,* ser. 1, 42[pt. 2]:713, 755, 765, 792, 812, 1005). Both Howell and Voris were Freemasons.

24. Voris referred to a confused policy centering on a War Department directive covering whether a person who had received such a promotion automatically became liable for three years of further service. Grant and Meade protested that this policy, if implemented, would dissuade meritorious men from accepting promotions and would create animosity among those who had already received promotions. A wiser approach, they urged, lay in giving such men the option of reenlisting or serving out their remaining term (*OR,* ser. 1, 42[pt. 2]:757, 770).

25. For the week of Sept. 15–22, 1864, Voris reported no enemy movement along his front, beyond constant but harmless shelling (ibid., ser. 1, 42[pt. 2]:850, 872, 895–96, 906, 928, 962).

26. Voris's three-year enlistment ended Oct. 2, 1864.

27. Maj. Gen. Philip H. Sheridan scored a major victory in the Shenandoah Valley at the Battle of Fisher's Hill, Sept. 22, 1864. See Jeffry D. Wert, *From Winchester to Cedar Creek: The Shenandoah Campaign of 1864* (New York: Simon & Schuster, 1989), 47–116.

28. Rear Adm. David G. Farragut had sealed Mobile Bay as a port for blockade runners. See Chester G. Hearn, *Admiral David Glasgow Farragut: The Civil War Years* (Annapolis, Md.: Naval Institute Press, 1998), 235–303.

29. For an analysis of Sheridan's strategy and tactics, see Gary W. Gallagher, ed., *Struggle for the Shenandoah: Essays on the 1864 Valley Campaign* (Kent, Ohio: Kent State University Press, 1991).

30. Voris's front remained quiet during this period. The First Brigade suffered only three casualties, two from the 67th Ohio (*OR,* ser. 1, 42[pt. 1]:133).

31. On Oct. 15, 1864, Butler had forwarded the recommendation for Voris's promotion, but a bureaucratic bungle delayed the "communication" for ten days (Butler to Stanton, Oct. 25, 1864, in Benjamin F. Butler, *Private and Official Correspondence of Gen. Benjamin F. Butler, during the Period of the Civil War,* 5 vols. [Norwood, Mass.: Plimpton Press, 1917], 5:279; *OR,* ser. 1, 42[pt. 3]:351).

32. Maj. Gen. David B. Birney led the Tenth Corps from July 23–Oct. 10, 1864. He assigned Voris to temporary command of the First Brigade (7th U.S. Colored Troops [USCT], 9th USCT, and the 127th USCT), Third Division. Pond resumed command of Voris's former brigade. Birney also urged Voris's promotion for his "gallantry and efficient service" (*OR,* ser. 1, 42[pt. 3]:67, 90, 146, 42[pt. 3]:90). Terry concurred, believing that under Voris "there is no better Brigade in the Army" (*Herald,* Oct. 8, 1864).

33. The Tenth Corps now contained fifteen African American regiments (Cornish, *Sable Arm,* 266; Trudeau, *Last Citadel,* 228). The 67th Ohio skirmished once during the first week of October 1864, losing five men out of an aggregate thirty-two in the First Brigade (*Blade,* Oct. 15, 1864; *OR,* ser. 1, 42[pt. 3]:144).

34. Originally the only western brigade in the Army of the Potomac, the Iron Brigade had suffered high losses, especially at Gettysburg. By 1864 the reconstituted Iron Brigade had lost its earlier character. See Alan T. Nolan, *The Iron Brigade: A Military History* (New York: Macmillan, 1961).

35. Capt. Thomas Ward, Company E, and 1st Lt. Emil Rampano, Company G (*Roster,* 5:566, 578).

36. Voris's former brigade charged the Confederate position at the cost of 180 officers and men, the 67th Ohio alone accounting for 65. Voris's African American brigade engaged in the same action, with 15 casualties (*OR,* ser. 1, 42[pt. 1]:146–47; Cowan to Voris, Aug. 2, 1864, OAGC).

37. Voris likely knew that Terry, recently promoted to brevet major general of volunteers, had endorsed his promotion. "Colonel Voris," Terry wrote, "in every action in which he has engaged, has exhibited fine qualities as a soldier, and on several occasions has been conspicuous for capacity and courage" (Terry to Lt. Col. Edward W. Smith, assistant adjutant general, Oct. 20, 1864, Voris, "Service File," NA).

38. In ordering Pond to be reassigned back to the 62d Ohio, Lt. Col. Edward Smith informed Terry that Butler "directs that you detail a competent officer to command the First Brigade" (*OR,* ser. 1, 42[pt. 3]:279; *Roster,* 5:325). This rebuke did not harm Pond. After the war, Ohio voters twice elected him state attorney general.

39. At the Battle of Cedar Creek, Oct. 19, 1864, Sheridan's troops ended the last Confederate threat to Union control of the Shenandoah Valley (*OR,* ser. 1, 43[pt. 1]:30–31).

40. The Eighteenth Congressional District consisted of Summit, Cuyahoga, and Lake Counties. Such a district formed the administrative unit that implemented the draft. Frederick A. Nash, a former Akron mayor, was provost marshal in the Eighteenth District, headquartered in Cleveland. See Nash to Cowan, July 28, 1864, OAGC; *Beacon,* July 29, 1896; Lane, *Fifty Years,* 265; Murdock, *One Million Men,* 4, 95.

41. On Oct. 26, 1864, Voris was "reassigned" to command his previous brigade (Voris to Smith, Oct. 26, 1864, Voris, "Service File," NA; *OR,* ser. 1, 42[pt. 3]:370, 465).

42. Grant confirmed Voris's promotion on Oct. 21, 1864. But various administrative problems, mainly "the irregular manner in which the recommendations from the 10th Corps were received," kept Voris a colonel (Smith to Terry, Oct. 21, 1864, General Order No. 31, Voris, "Service File," NA; *Herald,* Mar. 4, 1865).

43. Glatthaar, *Forged in Battle,* 35–80, 146, 166, 200, 234, covers how the War Department raised USCT units, selected their officers, and their combat record at Petersburg.

44. Voris recommended against an assault after his brigade probed Confederate positions. Enemy lines, he reported, were "quite strong and with considerable force behind them" (*OR,* ser. 1, 42[pt. 2]:395).

45. On Oct. 27, 1864, the First Brigade went on a reconnaissance mission and collided with Confederates near Darbytown Road. In the ensuing battle, Voris lost 36 men. Although he professed satisfaction with his troop's performance, Voris admitted a problem existed. Because of recent deaths, promotions, or resignations, the heads of each regiment had "little experience" (ibid., ser. 1, 42[pt. 1]:691–92, 695, 697; *Blade,* Nov. 4, 1864; *Herald,* Nov. 6, 1864; *Leader,* Nov. 10, 1864).

46. Capt. Ward died, Oct. 26, 1864, at an army hospital in Hampton, Va. (*Leader,* Nov. 8, 1864).

47. The Union had turned back Maj. Gen Sterling Price's raid into Missouri at the Battle of Westport, Oct. 23, 1864. See Jay Monaghan, *Civil War on the Western Border, 1854–1865* (Boston: Little, Brown, 1955), 325–37.

48. In May 1863, Peace Democrats had held a rally at Indianapolis to protest Vallandigham's arrest.

49. Ames, who led the Tenth Corps's First Division, headed the corps from Nov. 4–18, 1864. During that period, Voris filled Ames's position as division commander (*OR,* ser. 1, 42[pt. 3]:514–15).

50. Jane A. Voris, Voris's sister-in-law, lived in Nashville, Tenn.

51. For more information on this and other USCT units, see *OR,* ser. 1, 42(pt. 3):50, 68, 90, 253, 465, 490–91, 515–16, 552; and Noah A. Trudeau, *Like Men of War: Black Troops in the Civil War, 1862–1865* (Boston: Little, Brown, 1998).

52. Jean H. Baker, *The Politics of Continuity: Maryland Political Parties from 1858 to 1870* (Baltimore: Johns Hopkins University Press, 1973), 113–37, covers the topic Voris raised.

53. In the presidential election, the Republican Party campaigned as the symbol of national unity by adopting the name, National Union Party, and selecting Andrew Johnson, a prowar Tennessee Democrat, for vice president. To appease antislavery groups, the party endorsed a proposed constitutional amendment to abolish slavery. See *New York Times,* June 6–8, 10–11, 1864; David E. Long, *The Jewel of Liberty: Abraham Lincoln's Re-election and the End of Slavery* (Mechanicsburg, Pa.: Stackpole, 1994); Michael F. Holt, *Political Parties and American Political Developments from the Age of Jackson to the Age of Lincoln,* (Baton Rouge: Louisiana State University Press, 1992), 321–353, elaborates on Lincoln's aims.

54. A *Leader* reporter made a similar observation about changing racial attitudes toward African American troops among Confederates. They had initially "made it a rule" to fire first at "colored soldiers," but "now they do not fire upon them more promptly than white soldiers. Deserters also are willing to accept food from colored soldiers, and will sit and chat with them" (*Leader,* Oct. 1, 1864).

55. President Davis touched on a number of topics in this address, notably his suggestion about the possible use of enslaved African Americans as troops (Dunbar Rowland, ed., *Jefferson Davis, Constitutionalist: His Letters, Papers, and Speeches,* 10 vols. [1923; rpt., New York: Arno Press, 1973], 6:384–98).

56. 1st Lt. Rodney J. Hathaway, Company D, regimental adjutant since May 1864, mustered out of service at the end of his enlistment, Nov. 10, 1864 (Voris to Hill, June 3, 1863, OAGC; *Roster,* 3:565, 584).

57. Blanche C. Williams, *Clara Barton: Daughter of Destiny* (Philadelphia: J. B. Lippincott, 1941), 139–40, notes Voris's aid in the construction of Barton's personal quarters.

58. Dr. Martin S. Kittinger (100th New York) was the Tenth Corps's chief surgeon at Petersburg. Dr. George H. Leach was the regimental surgeon for the 57th New York Voluntary Infantry Regiment. David Wardell wrote for the *New York Herald.*

59. Smarting from his inability to break out of Bermuda Hundred, Butler planned a new movement by first building a canal at Dutch Gap, an oddly shaped neck of land jutting into the James River. Using this waterway, naval gunboats would then shell Confederates at Drewry's Bluff, forcing them to evacuate, and opening the way to Richmond.

60. On Nov. 10, 1864, Ames ordered Voris's First Brigade and Dandy's Third Brigade to again secure the route along Deep Bottom (*OR,* ser. 1, 42[pt. 3]:654, 716).

61. Voris waited nearly two weeks before requesting a thirty-day leave of absence "to visit my family" and to raise "four hundred men" for the brigade. Voris justified his request by emphasizing that he had served "for 38 1/2 months, and only been off duty sixteen days, unless disabled by wounds or disease" (Voris to Capt. Adrian Terry, assistant adjutant general, Dec. 12, 1864, Voris, "Service File," NA).

62. Hood's frontal assaults at the Battle of Franklin (Nov. 30, 1864) resulted in a costly Confederate setback. See Jacob D. Cox, *The Battle of Franklin, Tennessee: November 30, 1864* (New York: Charles Scribner's Sons, 1897); Anne J. Bailey, *The Chessboard of War: Sherman and Hood in the Autumn Campaigns of 1864* (Lincoln: University of Nebraska Press, 2000).

63. War Department General Order No. 297, issued Dec. 3, 1864, combined "white troops in the Tenth and Eighteenth Army Corps" into the Twenty-Fourth Army Corps, under Maj. Gen. Edward O. Ord. Foster's First Division, Twenty-Fourth Corps, contained four brigades. When Voris received his leave on Dec. 14, 1864, Osborn took over Voris's First Brigade (39th Illinois, 62d Ohio, 67th Ohio, and 199th Pennsylvania). Before Voris left for Akron, Foster expressed "his high appreciation of the zeal and ability with which Colonel Voris has discharged his duties as brigade commander" (*OR,* ser. 1, 42[pt. 2]:111, 42[pt. 3]:791, 802, 888, 1123–25; Voris to Foster, Dec. 12, Foster to Voris, Dec. 13, 1864, Voris, "Service File," NA; *Blade,* Dec. 23, 1864).

CHAPTER 10: — *"Each Day Brings the War So Much Near a Close"*

1. Voris arrived home in "jaded" health on Christmas Day, 1864. Even so, he spoke for more than two hours a week later at the Akron Ladies Soldiers' Aid Society. He praised Northern women for their sacrifices, especially Lydia. Predicting victory, he cautioned that "the fall of Richmond may not end the war; the destruction of Lee's army will." For the sake of justice, he urged the adoption of the proposed amendment to end slavery, "the cause of the war." As for the future, he advocated peace without vengeance and sectional reconciliation (*Beacon,* Dec. 25, 29, 1864, Jan. 5, 1865; *Herald,* Apr. 8, 1865).

2. Congressman Spalding maybe had advance warning that Nash faced an indictment for misusing government funds. Fearing the scandal might hurt future recruitment, Spalding sought a sound Republican replacement with an impeccable war record and a public reputation for honesty. Voris had these credentials. See *Herald,* Mar. 11, Apr. 5, 1865; Eugene Murdock, *Ohio's Bounty System* (Columbus: Ohio State University Press, 1963), 44–45.

3. Little had changed during Voris's leave. Cold weather during the winter of 1864–1865 hampered active campaigning on the Petersburg-Richmond front. But one personnel change did affect the command structure. Bvt. Maj. Gen. Alfred Terry, Voris's chief supporter, led the detached Second Division in Butler's attack on Wilmington, N.C., a key Confederate port for blockade runners, guarded by Fort Fisher. When Butler again bungled, Grant replaced him with Terry (*Herald,* Jan. 14, 21, Feb. 25, 1865; Hiram Ketcham, "Diary of Hiram Ketcham," Feb. 6, 1865, CAC; *OR,* ser. 1, 47[pt. 2]:129–30, 577).

4. Fort Fisher fell to Terry's forces, Jan. 15, 1865. Butler held no field command

for the remainder of the war. By contrast, Terry received a "Thanks of Congress" and promotion to brigadier general of the regular army. See *OR*, ser. 1, 42(pt. 1):964–65, 974, 46(pt. 1):401–2, 47(pt. 2):74, 78, 83; Rod Gragg, *Confederate Goliath: The Battle of Fort Fisher* (New York: HarperCollins, 1991).

5. Total Union casualties came to 659 (*OR*, ser. 1, 46[pt. 1]:405).

6. The attempt by Confederate gunboats to disrupt the Union position along the James River was as ineffective as Voris claimed (ibid., ser. 1, 46[pt. 2]:218–69).

7. Francis P. Blair, Sr., with Lincoln's tacit approval, had visited Confederate authorities in Richmond to explore the possibility of a negotiated peace. See Ludwell H. Johnson, "Lincoln's Solution to the Problem of Peace Terms, 1861–1865," *Journal of Southern History* 34 (November 1968): 576–586.

8. Lee confirmed Voris's observation. Writing to Secretary of War James A. Seddon, Lee worried about "the alarming frequency of desertions from this army" (*OR*, ser. 1, 46[pt. 2]:1143, 1229–31, 1254).

9. President Davis named Alexander H. Stephens, John A. Campbell, and Robert M. T. Hunter as peace commissioners. They met on Feb. 3, 1865, with Lincoln and Seward at Hampton Roads (*Herald*, Feb. 5, 1865; Welles, *Diary*, 2:230–32, 235–36).

10. Confederates evacuated Charleston, Feb. 17, 1865.

11. Grant used City Point, Va., as his headquarters.

12. Negotiations broke down. Confederates rejected Lincoln's insistence on making peace and reunion contingent upon their acceptance of emancipation and the Thirteenth Amendment, which had recently passed Congress but still needed ratification by the states. See Alexander Stephens, *A Constitutional View of the Late War between the States: Its Causes, Character, Conduct, and Results*, 2 vols. (Philadelphia: National, 1870), 2:599–624; Rowland, ed., *Jefferson Davis*, 10:275–76; Richard N. Current, *The Lincoln Nobody Knows* (New York: McGraw-Hill, 1958), 243–47.

13. Brig. Gen. Newton M. Curtis, a Medal of Honor awardee, had been wounded in the attack on Fort Fisher (*OR*, ser. 1, 42[pt. 1]:400, 403).

14. Union troops captured Wilmington, Feb. 22, 1865. Terry's Tenth Corps then reinforced Maj. Gen. John M. Scofield's Army of the Ohio and joined Sherman's northward march through the state.

15. Maj. Gen. John Gibbon, head of the Twenty-Fourth Corps, believed deserters were confined to "bounty jumpers." For that reason, he authorized a $100 reward and a three-month leave to any Union soldier or officer who shot or captured a deserter "going to the enemy" (*OR*, ser. 1, 46[pt. 3]:65–66). Fred A. Shannon, *The Organization and Administration of the Union Army, 1861–1865*, 2 vols. (Cleveland: Arthur H. Clark, 1928), 2:49–99, surveys fraudulent enlistment practices.

16. In accordance with legislation Congress had passed in July 1864, a draft began on Feb. 15, 1865, in any subdistrict that had not filled its assigned quota (*Leader*, Dec. 22, 1864, Feb. 12, 1865; *Herald*, Feb. 4, 11, 16, 18, 1865).

17. Voris was premature. Although his promotion was backdated to Dec. 8, 1864, his brevet was not official until Mar. 11, 1865 (Voris, "Service File," NA; *OR*, ser. 1, 46[pt. 2]:789; *Blade*, Mar. 11, 1865; William Nixon to Elijah Whitmore, Apr. 18, 1864, Whitmore Papers, CAC). The derogatory label of bobtail general denoted a brevet brigadier general of volunteers, usually militarily deficient and nonprofessional, who owed his position to politics.

18. Terry took formal possession of Wilmington, Feb. 23, 1865 (*OR*, ser. 1, 47[pt. 2]:89, 559–60).

19. The 184th Ohio Volunteer Infantry Regiment served mainly in Tennessee and Alabama on garrison duty (*Union Army*, 2:442).

20. The First Brigade retained the 39th Illinois, 62d Ohio, 67th Ohio, and 199th Pennsylvania.

21. Many of Voris's fellow soldiers did not share his abolitionist beliefs. James M. McPherson, *For Causes and Comrades: Why Men Fought in the Civil War* (New York: Oxford University Press, 1997), 19, 110, 117–30, 146, expands on this subject and notes why some Union soldiers moderated their racism as the war continued.

22. Voris had just received $371.32 in salary and incidentals for the period, Dec. 31, 1864–Feb. 28, 1865 (Voris, "Service File," NA).

23. During its existence, the 67th Ohio suffered 529 casualties out of 1,726 officers and men who served in the regiment for varying terms, a 30.65 percent casualty rate. See William F. Fox, *Regimental Losses in the American Civil War, 1861–1865* (Albany, N.Y.: Albany Printing, 1889), 330.

24. On Feb. 24, 1865, the War Department approved Grant's endorsement that Voris would remain "in service, until the expiration of his last muster" (Voris, "Service File," NA).

25. On Mar. 27, 1865, the First Brigade, First Division, Twenty-Fourth Corps, broke camp and moved along New Market Road toward Hatcher's Run, southwest of Petersburg. Four days later, the First Division encountered entrenched Confederate pickets at Hatcher's Run, skirmished with them, and captured 325 prisoners (Ketcham, "Diary," Apr. 2, 5, 1865, CAC; *OR*, ser. 1, 46[pt. 1]:130).

26. Sheridan crushed the Confederates at Five Forks, a key highway intersection, on Apr. 1, 1865. Grant realized that this victory blocked the Army of Northern Virginia's gateway to the southwest and ordered a general assault on the entire Petersburg-Richmond line. For an overview of these movements, see Larry M. Logue, *To Appomattox and Beyond: The Civil War Soldier in War and Peace* (Chicago: I. R. Dee, 1996); Chris Calkins, *The Appomattox Campaign: March 29–April 9, 1865* (Conshohocken, Pa.: Combined Books, 1997); and Jay Winik, *April 1865: The Month that Saved America* (New York: HarperCollins, 2001).

27. Hunt was promoted on Mar. 18, 1865, following Commager's departure (*Roster*, 5:566). The 67th Ohio lost 62 troops in this action (Hamby, *Sixty-Seventh Ohio*, 19). Voris recorded 67th Ohio's role in the attack on Fort Gregg in his official report: "The regiment assaulted the angle next to the road, and passed round to the rear of the fort by its front on the road. Being too lightly supported, the men were compelled to take to the ditch, which to the rear was so deep with water that it was impossible to pass through it to the sally-port, which was attempted by my order, the water in that part of the ditch being so deep that the men could not wade through it" (*OR*, ser. 1, 46[pt. 1]:1189).

28. Voris heaped praise on his regiment in this report and also ensured that the high command appreciated his contribution to Fort Gregg's capture: "My officers and men behaved with great gallantry, and were among the very first to reach the work. This I know, for I was personally present with them" (*OR*, ser. 1, 46[pt. 1]:1189).

29. Trudeau, *Last Citadel*, 378–97, details the Twenty-Fourth Corps's role in this part of the Appomattox campaign.

30. On Apr. 6, 1865, the First Brigade fought at Rice's Station, at an angle southwest of Five Forks, where the Confederates "in heavy force" had thrown "up intrenchments." In the brief fray, the 67th Ohio, supporting the 39th Illinois, lost an additional seven men (*OR*, ser. 1, 46[pt. 1]:1186–87).

31. *Herald,* Apr. 7, 1865; and Philip Van Doren Stern, *An End to Valor: The Last Days of the Civil War* (Boston: Houghton Mifflin, 1958), 160–63, touch on the events Voris recounted.

32. Reports of this action at Farmville appear in *OR,* ser. 1, 46(pt. 1):1187.

33. These events are listed in ibid., ser. 1, 46(pt. 1):129, 1178–203; and Calkins, *Appomattox Campaign,* 162–63.

34. One of Voris's enlisted men wrote home that, while history would credit Sheridan's cavalry for trapping the Army of Virginia, those "men will say the 24th Corps won the day" (*Blade,* Apr. 26, 1865).

35. The 67th Ohio lost 73 officers and men from Mar. 27–Apr. 9, 1865 (*OR,* ser. 1, 46[pt. 1]:1188).

CHAPTER 11: — *"A Black Woman Had Rights"*

1. *Leader,* Apr. 12, 1865, lists the Twenty-Fourth Corps's itinerary in the days preceding Lee's surrender.

2. The First Brigade, First Division, Twenty-Fourth Corps, was stationed at Burkeville, Apr. 19–21, 1865 (*OR,* ser. 1, 46[pt. 1]:129).

3. Union troops occupied Mobile, Ala., Apr. 12, 1865. Johnston surrendered to Sherman on Apr. 26, 1865.

4. Hamby, *Sixty-Seventh Ohio,* 21, follows the regiment's movements during April 1865.

5. The *Herald,* Apr. 8, 1865, had reprinted and commended Voris's speech to the Ladies Soldiers' Aid Society.

6. Not all the 67th Ohio accompanied Voris to Richmond. Company H went on detached burial duty to the Cold Harbor battlefield (Hamby, *Sixty-Seventh Ohio,* 21).

7. Ernest B. Furgurson, *Ashes of Glory: Richmond at War* (New York: Alfred A. Knopf, 1996), 326–40, expands on this description of Richmond in ruin.

8. Special Order No. 120, May 3, 1865, Voris, "Service File," NA. This directive also made Voris the administrator and supervisor of "negro affairs" in the "Sub-District" (*OR,* ser. 1, 46[pt. 3]:1088–89, 1213).

9. Col. Edmund Fontaine. The Virginia Central Railroad had formed an important Confederate supply link between Richmond and the Shenandoah Valley (ibid., ser. 1, 14:502).

10. Four small companies remained at Richmond. Six other skeletal companies were stationed in Voris's subdistrict (ibid., ser. 3, 53:Supplement, 476–508; Ketcham, "Diary," Apr. 28, June 1, 1865, CAC).

11. Commodore Uriah P. Levy, after purchasing the run-down estate in 1831, recorded a complicated will that deeded Monticello to the United States. Confederate authorities confiscated the property and sold some parcels. By the time of Voris's visit, the estate lay in ruins. See *Blade,* Dec. 1, 1864; Marc Leepson, *Saving Monticello: The Levy Family's Epic Quest to Rescue the House that Jefferson Built* (New York: Free Press, 2001).

12. Gen. Edmund Kirby Smith, commander of Confederate forces in the Trans-Mississippi West, surrendered May 26, 1865.

13. Much of Voris's uncertainty about amnesty mirrored the conflict between President Johnson and congressional Republicans over which branch of government, executive or legislative, would determine the process. Eric Foner, *Reconstruction: America's Unfinished Revolution, 1865–1877* (New York: Harper & Row, 1988), deals with the entire nature of Reconstruction.

14. In response to these labor problems in 1865, many former Confederate states passed restrictive "Black Codes." Voris sought to prevent such economic exploitation of free African Americans in his jurisdiction. Holding meetings with "all classes of people at various country seats," he warned whites against any attempt to re-create slavery in a fresh "guise" and established a "uniform price for labor" (Ketcham, "Diary," June 1, 1866, CAC; "West in the War," 511–12).

15. Demobilization left many regiments in the Twenty-Fourth Corps understaffed. By September 1865, the 62d Ohio and the 67th Ohio were consolidated (Hamby, *Sixty-Seventh Ohio*, 21–22).

16. On July 27, 1865, Terry sent Voris a copy of a telegram to "Suspend the mustering out of Bvt. Brig. Gen. Voris until further orders" (Voris, "Service File," NA).

17. General Order No. 65, War Department, Adjutant General's Office, June 27, 1867, officially approved Voris's promotion to brevet major general "in the Volunteer forces, Army of the United States," for "distinguished service in the field." This promotion was again backdated, this time to March 15, 1865. See Voris, "Service File," NA; William Frayne Amann, *Personnel of the Civil War,* vol. 2, *The Union Armies* (New York: Thomas Yoseloff, 1961), 17–18.

18. No correspondence exists from Aug. 5–Oct. 30, 1865. Lydia visited her husband in Virginia the last two weeks of August, and he took a leave in Akron for most of September and parts of October and November (Voris, "Service File," NA).

19. On Dec. 3, 1865, Voris received a ten-day furlough before *"mustering out"* at Columbus (ibid.; *Blade,* Dec. 15, 1865; *Leader,* Dec. 18, 1865).

20. The *Charlottesville Daily Courier* editorialized that "General Voris has conducted himself in command here in the kindest and most considerate manner and has shown himself a faithful and just officer. He leaves with the best wishes of our people" (cited in *Beacon,* Feb. 9, 1964).

Index